STAGES OF TRANSLATION

STAGES OF TRANSLATION

INTRODUCED AND EDITED BY DAVID JOHNSTON

absolute classics

First published by Absolute Classics in March 1996, an imprint of Absolute Press, Scarborough House, 29 James Street West, Bath, BA1 2BT, England.

Assistant Editor: María José Sánchez Blanco

Cover and text design: 6/26 Graphic Design, 26 Noel Street, London.

Printed by The Longdunn Press Ltd, Bristol.

ISBN 0 748230 75 4

CONTENTS

INTRODUCTION

Some hold translations not unlike to be
the wrong side of a Turkish tapestry
JAMES HOWELL

This book was conceived out of absolute madness.

It was the Spanish philosopher Ortega y Gasset who talked pityingly of the 'misery and grandeur' of translating, and this particular translator was constantly renewing his promise to himself not to take on any more translations. As an academic, I told myself I would no longer jeopardise my reputation as a serious scholar by undertaking what even many linguists consider to be mere jobbing, provoking the derision of those most traditional sectors of academe which still persist in viewing translating as a sort of collaboration with linguistic cads and cultural bounders (it still surprises me that many colleagues working in literary disciplines remain blind to the omnipresence of translation in their field); and I would never again oblige myself to wrestle with impossible verbal and dramatic equivalences for long hours on end – terrifyingly long hours when set against the short time available for getting the translation done (why is it that even when plays have been around for three hundred years, theatre companies invariably commission a new translation just a couple of months before rehearsals are due to start?) I would be absolutely mad to consider doing even one more translation, I told myself. . . and yet here I was agreeing to edit a collection of essays and interviews dealing with precisely that, the writing of translations for the stage.

Absolute madness, however, lay behind the genesis of this volume in a more literal sense, in that this was the name given to the event held to celebrate the collaborative links between Absolute Press and London's Gate Theatre, which at that moment was staging my adaptation of Lope de Vega's *Madness In Valencia*. While other publishers (I make this observation from the standpoint of an independent academic) were flooding the market with translated playscripts that were barely readable never mind speakable, Absolute had always sought to publish translations that had been proved on stage. The staged work of people like Adrian Mitchell, John Clifford, Nick Dear and Laurence Boswell had already done much to kindle public and critical interest in the fascinating riches of the Spanish Golden Age, and the timely publication in Absolute Classics of versions of the great triumvirate of Lope, Tirso and Calderón confirmed the status of these writers as acknowledged giants of the European stage. As a professional Hispanist, I felt more than a passing debt of gratitude to Absolute Press, and so it seemed to me entirely appropriate that it should be Absolute who published a book of essays in which translators for the stage were given the opportunity to discuss their work both in terms of the process of translating itself and as part of the collective enterprise of making theatre. This resultant collection of voices from the field is the first of its kind to be published, and the questions it raises and the issues it explores will, I am sure, prove invaluable in furthering the growing debate as to the status of translation in contemporary English-speaking theatre, as well as giving illuminating insights into the ways in which translators work. For the purposes of ease of consultation, all of the essays and interviews in the book have been classified in subgroups in the index. These classifications can only be broadly accurate, however; what characterises all of the contributions in this book is the restless questioning of the art of translation, and as such many of them range over a number of related issues.

When the idea for the book was first discussed on that evening in December 1993 I had been translating (and subsequently adapting) for the stage for seven years. As a translator I had developed, as translators for the stage invariably do, a growing awareness of the difficulty of avoiding an interaction between my own voice as translator and the voice of the original author, of the impossibility of producing a seamless second garment through some process of invisible stitching. And as an academic I had begun to reflect increasingly on the meaning of what I was doing, on my sense that I was translating to a pattern, one that perhaps could be developed into a viable theory of translation practice. This process of reflection was further stimulated – to put it mildly – by a radio programme I had heard in which the Gate's production of *Madness In Valencia* was being discussed. In particular, a pair of critics were mulling over the role of the Doctor, a character who in Lope's original serves primarily as a mouthpiece for the (then) advanced world of Valencian mental health-care. It was clearly not possible to recreate this functional role (even if it had been, the character would have been deadly dull), so I decided to highlight the Doctor's more comic elements, enlivening his interaction with other characters in the asylum by turning his long disquisitions on the nature and tell-tale signs of sanity and madness into hopelessly inadequate, essentially comic, personality-tests based on the association of ideas. My consternation grew as I listened to the two critics discussing Lope, in all seriousness, as a hitherto unsuspected precursor of Freud. Not that I felt guilty about this (at least not in the way Freud understood guilt), because I remained convinced that those scenes of the play involving the Doctor could not have worked without such a change. And the change itself was hardly radical after all, because what I had done was to hook this character onto one of the main thematic axes of the work – the relativity of madness and sanity. But the incident did prompt several very basic questions. Why, for example, had the producers of the programme not thought it important, or simply worthwhile, to consult the translator as to the exact status of the piece they were talking about? Were they not aware of the dangers implicit in such a discussion? The play was clearly labelled a 'version' (although to my mind it was no less faithful to the original for that). Did they assume that the translator was an invisible presence, like a pane of glass, to use the conventional metaphor, through which the original work could be scrutinised with every detail accurately in place?

The incident gave me no pleasure. In a British theatre which, for a whole variety of reasons, is turning increasingly to translations of new plays and new versions of old plays, it seemed to me that it was high time that the very specific business of writing translations for the stage was considered in terms of the multiplicity of approaches that practitioners themselves bring to it. That is not to say that this book entirely eschews issues of theory, but the theory of translation, like literary theory, must by definition derive from an analysis which is *a posteriori*. A conviction common to all those who reflect upon their work in the pages that follow is that there can be no hard and fast rules concerning translation for the stage, that there can no more be a prescriptive theory for translation than there can be for the writing of a play or a poem. Rather than centred upon the theory of translation, therefore, or on translation seen from the perspective of the science of language and linguistics, the essays and interviews contained within this book tend to consider translation as an extension of stage-craft, another activity to be understood as an integral strand of that multilayered process of making a play work on stage.

That is not to say that there is a common view held of translating by translators themselves. As the following pages make clear, translators do not share a common methodology or even hold to a similar viewpoint on the perceived status of translation in the theatre. In particular, there is some considerable divergence among practitioners not only on the principal issues of the scope for personal creativity, or voice, in translation, whether translators should play feudal servant to their master, or if they are a second author in their own right, a Cervantes to Cide Hamete Benengeli, but also on the question of the translator's linguistic competence in the target language. This latter point provides one of the major bones of contention between academic, or literary, approaches to playmaking, and a more purely theatrical view; the first one is legitimately concerned with the play at the level of its constituent semantic units, the level of detail, while the other, although not abandoning word-based analysis, is much more concerned with the play in terms of dramatic impact. It is, of course, a basic difference, and like all differences at base it contains within itself the possibility of a whole variety of eclectic approaches; but in the universe of play translating that does not make it any less the *prima mobile* that sets the spheres spinning, either in defence of the original author's words as fixed on a page, or of the reconstruction of his or her desire to create a memorable night in the theatre.

The metaphor of the *prima mobile*, which, in a neo-platonic scheme of things, causes the spheres to spin out of love of God, strikes me as being particularly appropriate in this discussion of the forces which are prime movers in translators' approaches to their work. Even the most casual of glances at the essays contained within this book will reveal that translators of drama are impelled by a passion that is partly unconditional love for a work distant through time or place, but – crucially – whose vision connects most intimately with their own experience of the world, and partly a sense of the grandeur (to use Ortega's word) of their role as mediators, if not between God and Man, at least between Racine or Pirandello and their public today. Small wonder then that translators, whilst recognising the need for caution and relativity of judgment when it comes to discussing the practical outcomes of their work, are often also ready to couch their working codes of practice in the morally absolutist terms of principle, fidelity, love and integrity. For me, one of the most fascinating aspects of this book is the way in which translators negotiate between the moral absolutism of their love for the original author or work, and the pragmatism that comes driving out of the knowledge that the creature created from that love is not just a private thing; it has to function under public scrutiny.

Under the scrutiny of public *and* critics. This raises another question which sparks off a variety of opinions. Do translators wish to be given public recognition as progenitor of their love-child, or do they think it only right and proper that they should remain behind the scenes, invisible if invaluable handservants? The question, as I have already indicated in the case of Lope's Valencian doctor, is also of relevance to critics who have to discuss, for example, Marivaux or Euripides in terms not just of a particular performance but also of a particular linguistic re-clothing, and to an audience which may or may not choose to go to see a Brecht simply on the basis of whether it is an apparently straightforward translation by A N Other or a 'new version/adaptation' by David Hare. 'Straightforward' translation and adaptation/new version come to represent opposite poles of fidelity; rightful inheritor, upright and true, and bastard child, wickedly lively and devil-may-care.

Of course, this is another basic difference equally subject to constant and careful negotiation. Translators *are* extremely conscious of the label given to their finished product, designed to serve both as an indicator to audience and critics of the nature of the beast, and, naturally enough, to give due recognition to their own level of contribution. But in practice there are numerous examples, both lovingly and frustratedly detailed in the contributions below, where translators swing between both positions in the same play, even in the same scene. Decisions have to be taken at every individual stage of the process, and the translator's sense of the dialectical relationship between the formal expressive qualities of the original and the impact of the putative version leads to a pragmatism which combines the rigour of literary criticism with the flair of dramatic re-creation. All translations, in whatever field or for whatever purpose, are ultimately judged by purely functional results. A Hispanist, let's say, spends several years translating *La Regenta*, the greatest Spanish novel of the nineteenth century, a reader somewhere pronounces it 'a good read', and the functional success of the translation has been achieved; conversely, we have all been victims of the electrodomestic confusion that arises in the wake of instruction manuals poorly translated from the original Japanese or Korean.

It is surely a basic truth that all language acts are essentially acts of communication, even if what they are choosing to communicate is that there are whole areas of human experience which are ultimately incommunicable. We don't need to delve too deeply into reception aesthetics or information theory before realising that, if that is the case, the receiver is as central to the act of communication as the sender. In the case of literature, which is clearly an extended, more highly self-conscious, language act, the receiver is no less central because, as proponents of reception aesthetics would argue, the word-based work of art exists not on the page but in its active re-creation or, as Roman Ingarden has termed it, in its 'concretisation'. These issues are central not just to our practical study of literature in general, but also to our particular understanding of the dynamics of stage/audience complicity. On one hand, therefore, the immediacy of reception in theatre gives translating plays virtually a paradigmatic status within the study of translation while, on the other hand, a consideration of the theoretical issues thrown up by translating for the stage gives us a series of illuminating perspectives on the constituent elements which come together in the making of a play in performance – 'concretisation' in its most vividly elaborated form.

All of the contributors to this volume have considerable experience in writing for the stage, often in terms of writing their own plays, and in the case of translation, of working always with a *mise en scène* in view. Emerging clearly from their reflections on their work is the inseparability of play and performance, of text and representation. Scholarly translation, meaning by that a translation that is linguistically and formally faithful to the maximum degree, is not discussed here because it is fundamentally page-oriented. That is not to say that such translations serve no purpose; indeed, as Eric Bentley has noted, any major foreign play should be published in both strict and freer form (as he himself has done with Brecht's *The Good Person Of Setzuan*). The problem arises when scholarly translations seek to pass themselves off as 'acting versions'; at that point they can obscure the real dramatic qualities of the playwright they profess to be serving. An overly 'faithful' translation, in this sense, like a loving dog gambolling round our feet at the most inopportune moments, can often make a foreign play awkward, torpid, colourless, like a Turkish tapestry viewed back to front, as James Howell observed in the eighteenth century. The mind may be capable of reconstructing the original tapestry from its reverse side, just as one can perhaps tease out the dramatic qualities of a play from a scholarly translation; but translation and adaptation for the stage (or screen) are activities concerned crucially with the impact of immediate reception.

As a result of this, many of the essays and interviews contained in this book reflect upon the sort of choices the translator is involved in as being similar to those confronting a genuinely creative writer. There is a clear consensus that there are myriad solutions in the target language for every single form in the source text. Otherwise translation would be more a branch of philology than a creative process. Where contributors tend to disagree most acutely is in how they delimit that creativity. Clearly, once one recognises the inevitability of making choices, which will either ensure or preclude the character, expressiveness and voice of the target-language text, one is also recognising that the translator will inevitably impose his or her own reading on that text. It is at this point that translating for the stage connects with drama criticism, and several of the pieces in this book are extended literary analyses of plays, upon which the decisions inherent in the translation process are based.

However, in the imposing of a reading upon a play, translators move into a more radical area of re-creation. Aristotle wrote, or at least his translator claims that he wrote, that 'a good metaphor implies the intuitive perception of the similarity in dissimilars', and in many ways this is what translators do when they write a version of a foreign play. In other words, they recast its external form so as to protect its range of meanings. There are some who see this procedure as positing the possibility of an infinite enrichment of our repertory, because, after all, setting, for example, Calderón's *The Surgeon Of His Honour* in Samurai Japan in order to enhance the impact of the honour code, leaves the original *El médico de su honra* wholly unscathed, still open to the most lavishly faithless or slavishly faithful productions imaginable. Other commentators, however, are much less happy about this type of procedure, seeing it as poetic licence in its most facile form. In that respect, this book has no editorial axe to grind. Every single translator in this book is more than capable of justifying the linguistic, cultural and – especially in the case of Scottish, Irish and Canadian contributors – the political implications of his or her readings, as well as the working decisions taken as a logical consequence of those readings.

Another issue which is given a variety of treatments in this book is that of the impact of performance specifics on translating plays. Different degrees and levels of translation, transformation, version-writing, transpositional metaphors etc. are ensured not just by linguistic and literary differences. Translators are often also acutely aware of the particular space for which they are preparing their work, and accordingly incorporate into their new version specific complicities with specifically envisaged audiences as well as actors. In that sense, the oft-asserted *vita brevis* of theatre, in contrast with the *ars longa* of dramatic literature, is not simply a way of distinguishing between production and publication values; it can frequently be the very epitome of the translator's consciousness, just as it frequently is of the director's. The ephemerality of a stage production, the result of an ongoing process of interpretation and angling/redirecting of the codes for specific performance written into a playtext, becomes virtually a *sine qua non* of the art of theatre translation. Because even in those cases where a translator is not working towards a particular space or group of actors, he or she will still, in all likelihood, be angling the new version so that it penetrates into a particular consciousness, culturally and linguistically defined by the English (or any other) language in current usage. No wonder then that so many translators themselves insist on the essentially short-lived nature of the work they produce.

Of course, in practice, specifically-angled translations are very often successful in places remote from the informing culture and linguistic fabric for which they were prepared (I had such an experience, which I still fail to fully understand, when the *Blood Wedding* which I had done for Scotland's Communicado was performed with equal success in Tennessee). In the same way that those plays whose first line of engagement is with local issues expressed through local language can subsequently speak to audiences of all sorts of provenance, so translations and adaptations geared towards the specific can also transcend what is only an apparent limitation.

There are a range of other specifics which translation, if it is to be functionally successful, must sometimes take into account. Translation can involve moving from one medium to another (theatre play to radio script, stage to screen) or between genres (novel to play). In many ways, such transfers throw a sharper light onto the process of adaptation as a dialectical process; a constant movement in the translator's mind between two competing consciousnesses, the awareness of how one set of conventions works in the target area, and the agonising sense of the very different functioning of the source text. In that way, the essays in this book which deal with transfers between media and genres can be read, in their turn, almost as heightened accounts of the process of stage translation itself, paradigms for theatre adaptation in their own right.

As editor I owe debts to many people who worked on this project at various stages and who helped define its contours. First and foremost, to the talented writers and translators, the leading practitioners of the art of stage-translation at work today, who contributed essays and interviews, and whose pausing to reflect on their craft has opened up this range of illuminating perspectives on the making of theatre; secondly, to those who word-processed and transcribed the fruit of those reflections – especially Bronagh, Heather and Jennifer; thirdly, I gladly acknowledge the invaluable friends with whom I have tended to mull over these things, under a whole variety of circumstances, especially Joe Farrell, Gerry Mulgrew, John Clifford, Laurence Boswell, and, recently, David Farr; fourthly, to another friend, John Macklin, with whom I organised a pioneering one-day conference on the translation of Spanish plays a short five years ago; fifthly, to Gaynor MacFarlane, for organising and recording the Gate Theatre translation session; sixthly, to my own university, Queen's in Belfast, for the generous financial support which made the publication of this book possible. Finally, I would like to dedicate this book to the poet Carlos Alvarez, whose poetry I have had the privilege both of translating and reading in public with him, and who once put translation and adaptation into this illuminating (if extreme) perspective:

'Perfect translations do exist. I know of one, for example, of the *Poem Of The Cid*'.
'What is it?'
'*The Song of Roland*'.

FATAL ATTRACTION

Steve Gooch

Steve Gooch studied French and German at Trinity College, Cambridge and Birmingham. His early plays and translations helped establish the pioneering Half Moon Theatre in the early seventies, when his first Brecht translation – *Man Is Man* – was produced by the Royal Court and subsequently by the RSC. Since then his work has been widely produced in a variety of media. Further Brecht translations include *St Joan Of The Stockyards*, for the Derby Playhouse, and *The Mother*, for the National (published in Methuen). Among the modern playwrights he has translated are Fassbinder, Kroetz and Mueller. His association with Mueller goes back to the 1972 Royal Court production of *Big Wolf*, and he has also translated Mueller's radio plays *Rosie* and *Delinquent* for the BBC. Steve Gooch has also worked on adaptations of *Great Expectations*, *Candide*, *Fuenteovejuna* and Terence's *The Brothers*. More recently he has been commissioned to produce versions of Wedekind's *Lulu* and *Marquis Of Keith*, for Red Shift and the Gate respectively (to be published by Absolute), and of Tankred Dorst's post-reunification play *Mr Paul*, for the National. He is currently working on a film version of his play *The Women Pirates*, for Roger Corman's Transpacific Corporation.

The very act of speaking is a kind of translation. From a baby's first words to a dying man's groan, people's urges and needs attempt to cross the divide of understanding between transmitter and receiver. Even within intellectual discourse the desire to persuade other people has to find its appropriate expression within a given tradition. In this sense the distinctive 'voice' of an individual is formed by the three-way traffic of communication between people and their surroundings.

In a world of satellite communications – not to mention a two-year cycle of world-cinema repeats on television – those 'surroundings' can become pretty extensive. And while the voice of the individual is squeezed into ever narrower channels, the media barons are creating a multi-lane highway in the other direction. Into this world steps the translator, someone who probably has a natural receptivity, a propensity for listening, understanding, and interpreting rather than imposing his or her views upon the world. For this is not, in the first instance, an egocentric activity. Its commonest motive is to build bridges and promote the exchange of ideas and experience.

Exchange, in the sense of dialogue as it expresses the clash of characters' discrete aspirations, is of course central to drama. This is also the literary form most dependent on speech as a physical, rather than intellectual, activity. As such it plugs directly into the emotions of its characters, its practitioners and ultimately its audience. It also demands a healthy egocentricity – the author is displayed through the play, the actors in their roles. Thus, translators of plays often find themselves 'translating' twice: first, into the foreign language; then, into the primal motion of the characters.

In addition, translators can often find themselves filling in (if not falling down) the gap between the practitioners' demands. On the one hand the original author, on the other hand the receiving culture; on the one hand the actors, on the other hand the audience. It is the translator's business to be aware of both sides of the argument, while their collaborators are primarily only interested in – let alone aware of – one.

When this more individualistic side of the theatre is compounded by a predominantly competitive economic system, the tentative desire to build bridges finds little comfort and even less reward among the jostling claims and counter-claims of the other participants. A translator could be forgiven for believing that the only common path to the truth of the play lies through the translation. But actors can't act what they can't perceive, and if a translation doesn't communicate directly, directors rarely have enough time to provide a compensating explication (always assuming they've seen the difficulty themselves). More common is the resort to some dramatic precedent within the home tradition. When you consider that translators also have egos, may also have faulty perception, and are also on display, the chances of the original play being squarely represented are slim indeed.

In this context translating plays can only be an act of love. For me it invariably has to do with discovering in the original play some new and slightly exotic quality quite outside the more familiar ground of home-grown plays, which I feel the home audience should know about: like a love affair with a fascinating foreigner whom you feel compelled to introduce to your family. I was once asked to translate some journalism and, although I liked the pieces concerned, I found the work quite different. It didn't draw me in the way a good play does. There seemed to be nothing else beyond the sheer literalism of the words. With a play, you are drawn in behind the dialogue to the imagined world of the characters' lives and ideas. Drawn in, fascinated, and wanting to tell the family.

The first plays I translated were done as a student, looking for something to direct. This was almost exclusively about the joy of discovery. First being introduced to the 'alien' world of the original text, then finding out how it worked on the rehearsal floor in English. As a student of languages who also did a lot of theatre, the difference, in both texts and production, between our culture and the rest of Europe was striking – most notably in the engagement with ideas. Even the socially conscious playwrights of late fifties and early sixties England seemed stuck in the literal-minded depiction of an everyday class-conscious reality which made metaphor impossible. Whenever 'ideas' surfaced in a British play, they appeared whimsical or clodhopping or grafted on like some overpowering Ibsenesque symbol. The more I looked at this, the more it seemed this limitation was in the dialogue. Writers seemed so hell-bent on getting their characters' language and milieu 'right' that what was actually expressed was often mundane and trivial.

It's still the case today that the language of most commercially successful English plays relies on tickling the nerve-ends of our national class-consciousness. A whole range of social responses is invoked by verbal mannerisms, which in turn imply a particular milieu, which in turn enable the audience to 'place' the characters within well-worn social definitions. Even in the large subsidised theatres, the audiences are there, primarily, it seems, to have their sense of social superiority massaged. Not just in new plays, but even in the acting style of classics, nothing tickles an English audience better than showing up some social gaffe which they, of course, would never commit. If you can get a laugh playing *Macbeth* like Noel Coward, why struggle to find the unique style in something strange and new?

I resolved to try and 'elasticate' the language of my own plays so as to remain true to the actual experience drawn on for the play, but also to enable the play to carry a broader significance. Leaving university, I was awarded a creative writing and travel scholarship on the strength of some scenes for a play I'd sketched in this mode. Initially the stretch I'd set myself proved more than I could cope with. But for the travel part of the scholarship I'd gone to Berlin and witnessed rehearsals of Brecht's *Man Is Man* at the Berliner Ensemble, so I turned in a translation of that play, just to prove I hadn't been idle. Apart from the play itself, my greatest discovery of that visit was that, even with so many months of rehearsal that a whole morning could be spent on a mere half-dozen lines of text, the Ensemble itself could end up keeping in the production a moment that was pure accident. The second great discovery was that Pinter and Stoppard played better in German.

I had already grown weary of the mannered, stagey ambiguity with which Pinter was delivered here, so it was a delight to see a West Berlin production of *The Homecoming* where the subtext was played with greater explicitness. I imagine that both the translator and actors may have had difficulty either understanding or transposing the social nuances of the English original, and had been forced to dig out as much hard evidence of the plot as they could. The play was much harder, much more tense, and far less stagey than any English production I've seen before or since. Similarly with *Rosenscrantz And Guildenstern*, a play I saw first in German. Stoppard's familiar philosophical concerns were brought out with a great physical and colourful theatricality which dwarfed the fudged productions I saw in England later.

Back home from the scholarship I submitted my script of *Man Is Man* to the Royal Court, where I'd been a member of the Writers' Group in my last months at school. Thanks to the Brecht estate's preference for another translation (which neither the Court nor Stoke-on Trent, who were also interested, wanted to do), it was two years before my translation finally got on. For a few years it was very popular, enjoying amongst others an excellent production by Howard Davies at the RSC but as soon as John Willett's 'official' version was published, it was no longer performed.

During the mid-seventies I was also discovering the new German playwrights of the period and felt an almost missionary zeal about introducing the then unknown Fassbinder, Kroetz and Harald Mueller to a still largely insular and culturally xenophobic British public. Both in subject matter and style these writers were pushing beyond boundaries known to the theatre world in Britain. Given my disaffection with the class-ridden, contemporary English tradition, it was perhaps no surprise that these plays represented a context that I felt I could engage with more readily. Needless to say, they met with the cool reception reserved by viewers for all truly challenging innovation – in their case (as with Brecht) this was aggravated by the common booword 'teutonic'. It was only when Fassbinder's films became known, and Kroetz's work was picked up by so many small theatres, that attitudes began to change. Mueller – to my mind the psychologically most interesting of the three – is still not well-known.

Cultural xenophobia can express itself in a number of ways. Because my own plays were produced in the East End and I translated from German, many people I met in the theatre at that time assumed I must be Jewish. At the Greenwich Theatre I was even asked if English was my first language (also, if I was a member of the Communist Party). A fellow playwright used jokingly to recommend my mother's chicken soup. I had hoped that translating would keep me going financially while I worked on my own plays. This hope backfired in two ways. First I earned less from translation than playwriting; second, I became identified in people's minds as a translator first and an original playwright second.

One of the difficulties I observed in rehearsing these plays is that actors can sense when the method of playing them is different from what they're used to, but they have no first-hand experience of what that method is. If you play Shakespeare or Restoration Comedy or Pinter, you'll have, for better or worse, models to work from. But what actor can afford to spend time off touring the Continent, watching avant-garde plays in a foreign language in order to stimulate their style back home (even if direct simulation were desirable)? Directors may be able to explain a play's intention in words, but enabling actors to feel a style for themselves is another matter. I remember, on the inaugural production at the Half Moon of *Jungle Of The Cities* – which I hadn't translated but was called in to help with – the actor playing Schlink was having great difficulties with the American-translated text, till I realised the character seemed to read like Charlie Chan. Once the actor knew how to read it, he could then build a performance.

This is a good example of the way text works for an actor. It's not so much a question of the literal meaning of the words as being able to plug into the condition of which the words are a symptom. There is an act of translation in this for the actor, too. Each word on stage operates like a signpost guiding the actor (and, indeed, audience) from moment to moment along a cognitive journey. And, ultimately, the journey is more important than the signposts. Unfortunately, the stylistic range of English text-based theatre remains pitifully small (things are perhaps changing in the more visual dimensions); so the temptation to 'translate' into this diluted range rather than extend into unknown territory is enormous.

For this reason, as with a new play, there is a strong argument for the first production of a foreign play to be as true to the text and production intentions of the original as possible. At least then you have a better idea of what you're departing from. For years I kept a cutting of a Michael Ratcliffe review of Corneille's *Le Cid* in which he confessed that, never having seen the play before, he felt scarcely qualified to comment on it. If only the same humility were displayed before new indigenous plays.

Brecht in particular has suffered enormously in this country from early 'versions' (actually, an awful word to describe what should be a precise art). Mainly due to the paucity of our language-learning tradition before Wilson's Labour government of the sixties, early Brecht translations were either academically hidebound (some still are) or arbitrarily slangy. Consequently it seemed terribly important in the seventies to represent the work as faithfully as one's own limitations would allow.

That was the intention behind my translation of *The Mother* in its original production at the Half Moon. But when Belt & Braces did it on tour a couple of years later, the selfsame text was given the company's broad popular treatment (much to the chagrin of some traditionalists) while still remaining true to the points of the original. Indeed, many people felt the politics communicated more directly. This taught me that acting style is not a matter of text. While the adoption of a particular acting style can unlock a play for an actor, (as in the production of *Jungle Of The Cities* mentioned above) this doesn't necessarily mean that that style reflects the original, nor that a production style should be imposed on the text. In fact, the imposition of a particular style upon the text probably creates obstructions for subsequent productions.

This is not a matter of 'purity' but of being true to one's perception of what is integral to the original. Reaching wholesale for a generalised production 'fix' often neglects, or sits uncomfortably on, specific moments in the play, creating confusion for actors and audience alike. The real point is that actors must be able to wear the language of the play like clothes. They must be able to put the text on and feel they can breathe in it, move around freely and find its physical expression from within themselves. The language must be 'natural', by which I mean current, intelligible and meaningful at more than just a literal or conceptual level. This is not the same as 'naturalistic', a badly-defined word that always causes so much trouble in discussion of theatre style – particularly with anti-naturalist writers like Brecht. The twin crimes of translation are academicism, where obscure literary or social references (which sometimes only the translator can perceive) are pursued to the detriment of idiomatic English; and the opposite ill where, in order to make an irritating foreigner 'accessible', an off-the-peg style is reached for, so that a Marlene Dietrich of a play can end up looking like a Peter Lorre. This latter option usually involves bringing in a playwright whose style touches all those class-conscious nerve-ends the English love to have tickled, or trying to graft on an artificial style, botched together from a few fashionable playwriting techniques which offer no integral emotional consistency to the actors.

When I see either of these approaches adopted I feel a sense of betrayal, like watching a friend in court who has been fitted up by the police. My beautiful, strange exotic lover has been scandalously misrepresented as a tart of commercialism, or a yuppie fraud. All playwrights run the risk of becoming the victims of directors' upward mobility, but foreign playwrights (especially the dead) have even less chance of defending their honour. The innate difficulty is that the qualities one is hoping to make known have to be worked at, dug out. They aren't given on a plate for the director to take for granted, so that he or she can soar off into some wonderful interpretation which shows off his or her originality; the fatal attraction needs to be discovered all over again, this time through the flesh and blood of the performers.

This is not to say that a translator can't be wrong. Sometimes it takes work on the rehearsal floor to reveal what is really going on in a scene. This is often the case with Brecht, where the text frequently represents the tip of a rehearsal iceberg. What often appears mysterious on a page can seem transformed once the spatial relationships between characters on stage are realised. At the same time, language itself can carry an energy which, if not conveyed adequately, can undermine rehearsal before you start. A good case of this is Brecht's treatment of the *Measure For Measure* story. In English translation the play can seem wordy and tedious. In German it crackles with an electric irony. You have to tap into the energy behind the words in order to offer actors something to work with.

This is why the term 'purism' is so inadequate to describe the wish to dig out what is unique in the original. Time after time English companies give up before they've properly started on foreign work. If they can't 'eat the pudding' immediately (to borrow from Brecht), anxiety can lead to ditching the whole attempt. This is why the phrase 'it works on stage' is so inadequate to judge the performance and reception of foreign writing into the English stage tradition of

Wilde, Coward, Orton and Bennett. Neurosis may be an interesting subject for drama itself, but it's absolute death on the rehearsal floor.

That's why I've found the straightforwardness of translators working on my own plays so refreshing. There is a simple concern to get down to what's going on in the play, uncluttered by the self-conscious *angst* which is almost a badge of honour amongst the luvvies. Not that they've always got it right. Germany is the only major country in which *Female Transport* hasn't been seen because I rejected an absolutely accurate but to my mind totally wooden translation. In other countries I couldn't be so self-destructively scrupulous because I didn't know the language. Against that experience, however, Erich Fried's precise and fluent translation of *Women Pirates* was superb, but absolutely gutted by a gimmicky production which managed to cram riot police, mud wrestling, the Ku Klux Klan and the Spanish Inquisition into its eighteenth-century story. Against that again, the French translation of *Mister Fun* was loose but executed by a playwright director with a flair which fulfilled all the intentions of my original.

Does this go some way to explaining the notion of 'fidelity' in translation? If you love a person, after all, you hate to see your view of them misrepresented or misunderstood — even if you yourself are blind to their worst qualities. 'Faithful' certainly can mean 'objective' in this context because the translator's subjectivity necessarily stands behind his or her efforts. This is not simply a matter of how you *view* the foreign work, but also of the geographic, cultural and social limits through which your unconscious use of your home language has been formed. You have to acknowledge that translation is a matter of subjective and relative strengths and weaknesses. If on top of this you then try to impose the further subjectivity of 'interpretation' in production, you depart progressively further from the original engine of the work, by which I mean the complex system of internal references that gives each play its unique dynamic.

Recently, for a new edition of my book *Writing A Play*, I attempted to define what distinguishes style in a writer's text from the style of its production. The only satisfactory identification I could come up with was the unspoken connections from line to line in the dialogue, originating in the author's mind, which as spectators we're then drawn into and follow. What happens in this process is that an audience plugs in, as it were, to that original engine, and there then takes place an instinctive and intimate sharing of the subjective world of the author. That kind of recognition is also a necessary first stage if an actor's interpretation of a part is to be successful. If you can't share those synaptic leaps, no amount of thesaurus bashing, reading of critical works, acting training or 'experience in the field' will compensate. In the end, a translator's love for a play, like that of a director, actor or member of the public, can only be requited by a wider public enjoyment of the dynamic of those synaptic connections.

Once that dynamic is reasonably well understood, perhaps through a number of slightly different translations and interpretations in production, there is no reason why a play shouldn't be 'adapted'. One should be strict about using this word. It implies the notion of being adapted to some secondary purpose; and whether this is in order to say something slightly different from the original, or to apply the play to some particular new context, it is essentially different from translation. That's not to say there is anything wrong with adaptation *per se*, provided it is acknowledged as such. Too often translation and adaptation are thought of synonymously, and this can lead to false expectations. Indeed, unless it's a first production (for reasons described above) there's no reason why there shouldn't be an infinite number of 'versions' of a play. But there is always the danger (as with setting a classic in a period different from that conceived, dressing up a new play) that you wrench it so far away from its 'engine' that is internal dynamic is lost.

This danger is commonest when a translation doesn't come up to a director's or producer's expectations − whether because the dialogue isn't fluent enough, or because it reveals aspects of the play which don't accord with the director's production intentions. This all comes down to the view of the play in the translator's or director's head, and whether the two coincide. If they don't, no amount of fiddling with the text will write the play the director sees in his mind's eye. And no amount of ingenuity in the production will satisfactorily rewrite the translation to allow actors to intuit the original. Sometimes these differences can be as basic as a matter of people's different social backgrounds.

Social conditioning can reflect itself in any number of translators' foibles. A translator may admire an original playwright for the earthiness of his language, his humour, or his grandeur. Consequently, these are the qualities he tries to bring out in his translation. The director may feel that earthiness is just token slanginess, that the humour is over-rated, and that the grandeur is pure melodrama. Both these views of the work will threaten to get between the actors and their personal digesting of the text, unless all parties are aware of the intrusion their very involvement can precipitate. Just as actors receive confirmation of their performances through the audience, so translators need the feedback of actors' work to test whether their linguistic instinct makes sense to anyone else. For this reason it does no harm to test-read a translation with actors before it's finally chosen for production. The very act of speaking a script aloud can often reveal whether it will offer the kind of dramatic currency which will lead to a free but exact exchange between the actors.

Once you see that a script broadly works in this way, you should be wary of changes for change's sake. All the connections and connotations which go to make up the final weave of the play won't become apparent till quite late in rehearsal. To pull at threads early on can destroy the gradual build-up of a collective feeling for where the heart of the work, and its innate style, lie.

For, just as translators are restricted by their conditioning, so are theatre managers and directors. Bad enough that a director wrongly assumes a fashionable quality in a play and attempts to fit a quart into a pint pot. Even worse when pressure comes from a theatre manager (closer to the media barons' six-lane highway) for a play to make a publicity splash because of a false perception about its potential public impact. The scream behind the original author's work will be difficult enough to transmit without trying to second guess its public reception.

TRANSLATING FOR THE LOVE OF IT

NOEL CLARK

Noel Clark has worked and travelled extensively as a foreign correspondent for the BBC's World Service, and was Head of the BBC Central European Service between 1977 and 1985. Since then he has been a freelance writer and broadcaster, and literary translator from French, German, Dutch and Polish. With Absolute Classics he has published Joost van den Vondel's *Lucifer, Three Plays*, by Corneille and *Three Comedies*, by Aleksander Fredro (staged variously at the Bloomsbury Theatre, the Gate, and broadcast by World Service Drama). His translations of the work of the Dutch writer Roel Adam (*The Day After Tomorrow*) and of Molière (*School For Husbands* and *School For Wives*) have been performed at the National Theatre and broadcast by the World Service respectively.

Translating plays is for me the most fascinating, challenging and addictive of word-games. Sometimes it can also be tantalising and frustrating. Never quite knowing in advance, however, whether a play that excites one in the original, can be made to work in translation for stage or radio, is all part of the fun. This may sound an unprofessional approach to a craft (if not an art) which has only in recent years begun to be taken seriously in this country. Not being a literary translator by profession, I should perhaps explain that I am also neither an academic nor a playwright. My experience has been in journalism, broadcasting and language study.

The impulse to translate for pleasure, I suspect, sprang from the same source as my one-time reporter's urge to share the excitement of news with the largest possible audience. A lingering, childish wish to impress may also have played a part, at least when, as a sixth-former, I first became aware of the charm and possible utility of literary translation.

Finding myself with time to spare at the end of an 'A' Level German paper, but too diffident to tempt the gods by walking out early, I decided to kill time by trying my hand at a rhyming version of one of the pieces set for prose translation – an extract from *Faust*, Part One. Greatly daring, I appended my effort to the prose rendering requested. I like to think it may have helped in the days when every trick seemed worth performing, if you wanted to get to a university and hadn't the cash.

For years after that, translation – mostly of verse – was an agreeable hobby. Attempting poetry translation from Polish, for example, proved a relatively painless way of getting to grips with the grammar and idiom of a complex and highly inflected language. In recent years, I've had time to indulge a preference for translating verse drama, but there's still an element of serendipity in my choice of what to translate. My views on how the job should be tackled are, however, a good deal less rigid than when I began.

My aim, at first, was to try in some small way to widen the limited range of European 'classics' available to the theatre-going public in English. I felt that a few at least of the plays which had stood the test of time in their countries of origin – plays in lesser known languages, by authors unheard of by most of us – must surely be worthy of our attention. Neither publishers nor theatre directors, I suspected, would be prepared to pay for the translation of such works – sight unseen, authors unknown. The plays would first have to be made accessible in English. Translating them, therefore, might prove in the end a labour of love. It was a risk I decided to take, rather than accept that good plays could only be written in major languages.

My plan was to translate only from languages I knew well enough to read with pleasure and to choose only plays which made an immediate personal appeal. I wanted my translations to be actable and speakable as well as attractive to the general reader. If they could interest scholars, too, so much the better.

Early in the eighteenth century, Alexander Pope, translator of *The Iliad*, wrote this: 'It is the first great duty of an interpreter to give his author entire and unmaimed; for the rest, the diction and versification only are his proper province, since these must be his own...' Pope argued that it was not the function of the translator to improve on the original, even when tempted to do so. At the same time, he felt that more men had been misled in the past by 'servile, dull adherence to the letter' than had been deluded in his own day by what he called the 'chimerical, insolent hope of raising or improving' their author in translation. He went on to warn translators not to be deterred from fidelity to the original for fear of 'incurring the censure of a mere English critic.'

Pope was of course, referring to the enormous challenge of translating Homer. But his principles seemed to me still relevant to the problem of presenting any foreign classic *for the first time* in English translation. After all, how would we feel about Shakespeare, Marlowe, or Shaw being introduced to foreigners in an 'updated' or 'relocated' version, for fear the audience might otherwise fail to 'get the message' or perceive the qualities of timelessness and universality essential to a 'classic'.

I took and still take the extremely controversial view that a would-be translator of plays should have, at least, a considerable reading knowledge of the language from which he proposes to translate. Fluency in speaking the language, though clearly desirable, is by no means essential. It does seem to me, however, that the translator's ear ought to be attuned to the speech rhythms of the foreign tongue. Failing that, as he sits in his study, reading the original text, how can he hope to hear the characters speak and see them move clearly enough for him to develop an empathy with the author, to catch his tone and understand his purpose? Equally, any translator who aspires to write for the stage must have a keen ear for the speech rhythms of his own tongue.

Recently it has become fashionable to commission 'translations' by established playwrights, more or less well known to the public, but who sometimes lack the linguistic desiderata for the job. In such cases, the playwright may re-work an unvarnished text prepared for him by a specially commissioned, though not always credited, linguist. To my mind, however, this is not 'translation' in the commonly accepted sense of the term. The playwright is, in fact, 'adapting' someone else's translation. He may even be doing no more than updating and re-jigging some earlier, unstageable and out-of-copyright translation of an already well-known foreign classic, deemed worthy of an airing.

There may be compelling box-office reasons, as well as artistic and aesthetic arguments, in favour of hiring adaptors. It seems to me, however, that the play-goer with no access to the original will be misled, if what he has paid to see is described as 'a new translation by A.' rather than, say, 'A version by A, based on a translation by B'. In countries where, thanks to a less-known language, literary translation and the function of the translator have long been better understood and more highly valued than has often been the case in Britain, specialists would blanch at the mere thought of their national classics being recycled by monolingual 'translators'.

I now have serious doubts whether – at least, in the theatre – it is ever possible to give an original author in translation 'entire and unmaimed'. Nevertheless, I feel the public should always be told by theatre managements precisely what is on offer – much as the purveyors of cake-mixtures and patent medicines are required to alert us to the presence of additives in their product. In the case of an established 'home-grown' classic – say, Shakespeare's *Othello* – it may be in order to transport the action to Orpington or Stockton-on-Tees, provided the characters speak the words of the Bard. If, however, the original were to be presented through the modernising prism of a contemporary playwright's vision and voice, then I, for one, would sooner have an entirely new play on the theme of jealousy or whatever. To take comparable liberties with an unfamiliar foreign classic, would seem to me a grave discourtesy to the author – dead or alive – to his national culture and, not least, to the audience, assuming that at least some of its members would wish to know what the author wrote as well as what he had in mind.

With so many fine classic plays of our own, why – in any case – should one pay to see a foreign classic in translation? If I didn't know French and had never heard of Molière, curiosity might impel me to see *The Miser* in English for what the play could tell me about the French and their sense of humour, as well as the period in which it was written. I would hope not only to enjoy the play, but also to get an impression of the author's style and to gain an insight into the means by which he constructed a comedy capable of entertaining and stimulating French audiences for nearly three centuries. It follows that I would want the play presented, as nearly as possible in the original form, by a translator and director with the humility to let Molière do the talking. By all means, devote their wit, ingenuity and imagination to the task of making his voice heard across the culture chasm, always bearing in mind, however, that it is the author's voice I want to hear, not theirs.

With these thoughts – prejudices, if you like – and resolutions, I embarked on my first play translation: *Zemsta* (*Revenge*), a Polish classic comedy of the early nineteenth century, in rhyming verse, by Aleksander Count Fredro. The author – a one-time staff-officer to Napoleon – later became known to his compatriots as 'The Father of Polish Comedy'. To us in Britain, it seemed, neither he nor his works were known at all.

I chose *Revenge* for several reasons. For one thing, the play made me laugh the first time I read it. For another, I was excited by the paradox of a Polish author who had delighted his contemporaries with comedies written during some of the darkest days of Poland's tragic history – plays familiar to most Poles from schooldays onwards and which figure still in the repertory of theatres up and down the country. It seemed astonishing that we should somehow have overlooked an author of such repute, writing in the second most widely-spoken Slavonic language, with a literary tradition six centuries old. But, if *Revenge* could appeal to one English reader, it seemed reasonable to assume that others, too, might enjoy it, given the chance. I didn't try to find out if *Revenge* had ever previously been translated. I still can't imagine myself being moved to re-translate a foreign play by reading it for the first time in English. That would be as dreary a task as re-writing yesterday's news.

There seems to me no harm, however, in a translator looking at previous translations, if they exist – *after* completing his own version. He may, indeed, have a duty to do so. Only the most arrogant translator would rule out the possibility of having misread or misunderstood a word, line or passage of the original. Often his own sixth sense will alert the translator to a possible misapprehension. In which case, study of an earlier version can help to clear up a doubt or suggest a fresh approach. When 'stumped' by some archaic word or phrase in a foreign classic, I always try, if possible, to seek enlightenment from a 'school' edition of the play with text-notes in the original language.

Rarely – especially in dealing with verse – need a translator fear being tempted to adopt a predecessor's rendering in any detail. There are too many different ways of conveying the sense of a word or phrase. However, since translation implies a personal response to the author's text, to read someone else's version first would be to risk preconditioning or, at least, colouring one's own response to the original.

For me, the excitement of 'discovering' a memorable foreign play – even if it later turns out that others have been there before me – is an essential stimulant to translation 'on spec'.

In tackling *Revenge*, it never occurred to me that anything other than a rhyming verse translation would do. As far as possible, I set out to follow both Fredro's short, brisk lines and his complicated rhyme-scheme. He himself had been reacting against the tyranny of alexandrines and rhyming couplets. For the audience of his day, indeed, this break with tradition was part of Fredro's charm. Even before I had finished reading *Revenge*, the mental ferment of translation – rhymes and all – had already begun to simmer. When I eventually came to look at earlier American prose versions of Fredro's verse-plays, I couldn't help agreeing with the distinguished Polish poet and critic, the late Antoni Slonimski, who once wrote that Fredro in prose would be much like Renoir in monochrome.

There were, of course, problems. Some of the characters in *Revenge* were referred to by already obsolete hereditary court titles, e.g. Czesnik (Cup-bearer), once responsible for serving the King at the table; Rejent (Notary), originally a leading Court official at the Bar. The special associations of such titles for a Polish audience would in any case be lost on foreigners. So, for ease of comprehension as well as scansion, I decided to suggest the pre-eminence of the Cup-bearer among the local landed gentry by calling him Squire. Similarly, I somewhat downgraded the Rejent by calling him simply a Notary. These and other characters also have surnames indicative of personality. Dyndalski might have been rendered as Dither and Milczek as Tacit. I deliberately left these names in Polish, however, partly because what they say and do tells us all we need to know about the characters and partly as a reminder that they are Poles and the creatures of Fredro – not Sheridan.

These seemed to me necessary and justifiable liberties. A Pole, however, might argue that the transformation of Czesnik to Squire already diminishes the play's satirical impact by failing to convey the aura of old-world nobility that clings to this impetuous, irascible, gallant, outrageous and sometimes ridiculous character. But what else could one call him in English? Cup-bearer? Black Rod? Gentleman of the Bedchamber? All hopeless.

Here was a Polish comedy of character and manners. Something, no doubt, would be lost in translation. But perhaps not all that much, if one tried to ensure that the anglophone Squire and the rest of them approximated in speech and action to Fredro's originals. Oddly enough, the Cup-bearer's eccentricities, which the Poles consider so very Polish, could well be those of an English country gentleman – an ageing and peppery Squire of noble ancestry and military background – in the early nineteenth century.

Some Polish critics have maintained that Fredro's plays, especially *Revenge*, are so Polish in essence that they can neither be translated nor appreciated by foreigners.

They may be right, but I must disagree. What the critics say of Fredro may be true of others among Poland's most revered nineteenth-century writers, whose inspiration was perhaps too deeply rooted in the national psyche to survive a transplant. Fredro, on the contrary, with his gentle humour, compassionate satire and sense of fun, strikes me as potentially among the most accessible of Poland's literary 'greats' of the past.

Indeed, leaving aside the problem of rhyming verse, the difficulties facing the translator of Fredro are those which the literary translator of any European classic may encounter. These include the occasional use of regionalisms, outdated slang, unfamiliar proverbs, and − perhaps most troublesome of all − puns. How one handles these problems seems to me a matter of taste. Ideally, one looks for a suitable equivalent in the host language − not necessarily to be found in any dictionary. There are no hard and fast rules and few perfect solutions.

My feeling is that a translator does best to rely on style, vocabulary and grammar to represent geographical, educational or class differences among the characters. If and when it comes to a stage production, a director, knowing the abilities and limitations of his cast, will be able to judge whether, in the context of his production, an identifiable regional English accent will 'work' if used, say, by a servant in a play set in South-Eastern Poland.

Slang, with its brief life-span, is probably best avoided in translation, if there is any danger of the authentic 'period' equivalent in English sounding strained or incongruous to a modern audience. Ephemeral slang, more than anything, is apt to shorten the shelf-life of a translation. Proverbs, on the other hand, can often be aptly matched in the host language. But a translator is either very lucky or highly ingenious if he manages to transplant a pun. Foreign similes can sometimes sound attractively quaint if translated literally, though they may, in fact, be mere clichés in the original.

A Pole 'drinks like a tailor' whereas an Englishman 'drinks like a fish'. But a servant in one of Fredro's plays, describing his master's over-indulgence at a party, says 'He drank like the dragon'. Feeling that 'dragon' (Fredro's reference is to a specifically Polish legend) just wouldn't do in English − though powerfully evocative of a fire-breather's thirst and vast capacity − I opted for 'whale' as, at least, more arresting than 'fish'. As I write, it occurs to me that I could perhaps have got away with turning the Polish dragon into a fireman. But no, I couldn't. Metre and rhyme in the context decreed a one-syllable word. In another Fredro play, a girl says scornfully of her lachrymose lover: 'He wept like a beaver' − a common enough simile in the literature of the day − derived, according to an old-fashioned Polish lexicon, from huntsmen's tales of beavers bursting into tears when cornered. I found the image so appealing that I adopted it forthwith. In my version she says: 'He blubbered like a beaver!' Well... why not? After all, the play is a comedy.

How did I fare with these Fredro translations? Two of the plays were broadcast – five years apart – by BBC World Service Drama, which offers its listeners a weekly sample in English of the best British and foreign plays. A Fredro volume containing three of his comedies has been published by Absolute Classics with Arts Council support. At the time of writing, however, it still remains for the 'Father of Polish Comedy' to make his first British stage début. The spontaneous enthusiasm of Fredro's first professional British director, Gordon House, and of the actors who took part in the BBC broadcasts of *Revenge* and *Virgins' Vows*, encourages me to believe that sooner or later Fredro will be staged in English.

Meanwhile, I had turned my attention to another great 'unknown' – Holland's 'Prince of Poets', Joost van den Vondel, whose seventeenth-century drama *Lucifer* – the tragedy of a reluctant rebel – predated Milton's *Paradise Lost* by thirteen years. Though Vondel was the undisputed literary master of the Dutch Golden Age, and *Lucifer* generally held to be his greatest work, the play had never been staged in Britain. Having chanced upon a copy in Dutch in an Oxford bookshop, I read it with a mounting excitement and an irresistible urge to see it performed in English.

This would clearly not be easy, despite the fact that *Lucifer* – undeniably a great play – had been banned after only two performances at Amsterdam City Theatre in February 1654. Its denunciation by Calvinist zealots as 'impious, lewd, godless and full of the most false and arrogant notions ever to spring from the mind of man' sounded like a first-class recommendation for revival in our own less reverent age. However, for all its majestic language, wit, imagination and occasional sly, raunchy humour, *Lucifer* was a play of its period, written in rhyming alexandrine couplets, its tempo that of a majestic river, rather than a turbulent stream. The characters, all angels and as such, supposedly sexless, would in practice need to be male. No parts for women, alas! Moreover, some of the speeches, though magnificent, were also impossibly lengthy by present-day standards. Finally, each of the five acts ended with a chorus, designed to be sung by choirs of loyal or rebellious angels.

I was determined to translate *Lucifer* in its entirety for the page, before adapting for the stage. This I did, keeping the rhymes but substituting pentameters for the alexandrines. The resultant compression helped to speed up the action. Diction was a more serious problem. Vondel's characters speak the Dutch of three and a half centuries ago. To attempt some kind of neo-Miltonic English, I felt, would yield at best an unsatisfactory pastiche, at worst a parody. With the need for clarity and ease of comprehension uppermost in my mind, I decided to aim for a style of English, somewhat more elevated than our modern colloquial forms, yet rarely archaic – rather as Schlegel and Tieck did in German, with their celebrated nineteenth-century translation of Shakespeare. However, given that mine, in deference to Vondel, was a rhyming translation, I could not obviously hope to rival the often near-literary fidelity of the Schlegel-Tieck translation of Shakespeare's blank verse.

Encouraged by the positive reaction of Dutch and English scholars who read my version in typescript, I set about abridging and adapting for the stage. Out went the choruses, though not without regret. The choruses, in irregular metre with a complex rhyme-scheme, had been by far the most difficult part of the text to translate. Pruning the speeches was less painful. What really hurt, partly because I suspected that Pope might not have approved, was limited but radical surgery on one or two scenes. Notwithstanding, the end product was all Vondel; nothing invented but, here and there, drastic cuts and several couplets transposed or allocated to other speakers, to heighten the drama or clarify the argument for a modern audience.

In the end, the emergence of *Lucifer* from study to stage was due to a happy conjunction of circumstances: a British director who happened to be searching for a Dutch play available in English; the then impending Anglo-Dutch tercentenary celebration of William and Mary's ascension to the British throne; vigorous support from the Dutch Embassy in London; a vote of confidence in the translation by eminent academics in both countries and the indispensable financial backing of Dutch and British sponsors, public and private. *Lucifer* was presented in my abridged version at London's Bloomsbury Theatre in June 1988, the complete text later being published by Absolute Classics.

The *Lucifer* experience made me think seriously about the relationship between the translator and director. Fortunately, the director, Peter Benedict, shared my view that we owed it to Vondel and a major Dutch classic to respect the author's intention and his text. He accepted that I had gone as far as I judged expedient in the matter of diction and versification in order to make the poetry of the drama, as well as the author's seventeenth-century wit, humour and philosophy accessible to a modern audience.

The problem of presentation, however, raised formidable issues. *Lucifer* had been conceived by its author as an epic on the grand scale, set in Heaven, with a large cast of extras, music, choirs and elaborate stage machinery which had involved a huge outlay by the Amsterdam Theatre. Though Vondel gave no stage directions, his militant angels – loyalist and rebel alike – would doubtless have appeared in military uniforms of the period, for Vondel's audience was meant to understand the great conflict in the heavens (described but not seen) as reflecting the then contemporary struggle for Europe between the forces of Christianity and Islam. I had retained, however, only the eight principal characters of the original. Our limited financial means, moreover, dictated extreme economy in the matter of set and costumes. Clearly, the onus to achieve credibility for Vondel's text would rest on the skill of our actors and the imagination of director and designer.

As things turned out, the heavenly action took place in a kind of celestial, white-walled boardroom, with a very tall window looking out on the blue crystalline void of infinite space. The angel Beelzebub – a managing director figure with portable telephone – sat behind an immense desk on which the angel Apollion, fresh back from a reconnaissance mission to the planet Earth, emptied his plastic bag of fruit and flower samples from the Garden of Eden. It was the angel Apollion's report of the enviable conditions and conjugal delights enjoyed by God's latest creatures – Adam and Eve – which sowed the first seeds of jealousy among the sexless angels, leading eventually to the great revolt against God, headed by Lucifer, for reasons both complex and tragic. The angels wore neither nightshirts nor uniforms but more or less modern business-suits with patterned silk waistcoats to indicate rank.

None of this resembled at all the images I had in mind while translating the text. Yet for me – and I believe for most of those who saw the play – it 'worked'. At any rate, I like to think that one or two of the Dutch visitors who told me they had appreciated the full import of their neglected classic far better in English than they'd ever done in Dutch were not just being polite. Yet this was unmistakably Vondel's play – not mine. It was, I suppose, my response to Vondel's words, reflections and humour, interpreted by the director and his cast. On balance, I felt between us we had done our best to deliver our author if not 'entire', relatively 'unmaimed'. As for Heaven and the angels, after all, their appearance is still anybody's guess. Dutch and British reviewers were generous in their appraisal and any lingering qualms on my part were put to rest on learning that one modern Dutch production of *Lucifer* had the angels in bowler-hats and city-suits, sitting on swings as they debated.

As a translator, I have always greatly enjoyed attending rehearsals, either for a stage or for a broadcast production. In the case of a foreign play, the translator – *in loco parentis* for the author, living or dead – may on occasion need to 'fight his corner' but must also 'know his place'. I do not believe the original script should ever be treated as an infinitely negotiable commodity which director and cast can tinker with at will, (if it's that bad, it should have been rejected earlier). However, certain defects may come to light only when actors speak the lines in earnest and the play begins to take shape as the director conceives it. The translator is there to protect the original, but also to help when required – if he can.

The sense of a line may be quite obvious to the translator, who has had the benefit of reading the original but less so to the actor or, indeed, to the director. This may emerge during the initial read-through. If the actor is getting the emphasis wrong, the cause may be a misplaced comma, a fullstop omitted in the script, or an unfamiliar word being mispronounced. It may, however, also be a less than happy rendering by the translator. If the director offers the actor no spontaneous guidance, it's perhaps best for the translator to comment privately to the director, rather than publicly to the actor. It doesn't help if the translator gives the impression, in front of the cast, of behaving like a director *manqué*.

By the same token, translators are probably well advised to resist unilateral requests from actors to re-cast certain lines they may feel could be improved. Such suggestions are best filtered through the director who may, in any case, not agree that change is needed. Obviously the translator should be ready to consider any such request from the director and, if convinced, re-write. Equally, if he doesn't agree, he should be prepared to explain why not.

Though much opposed in principle to translators inserting extra matter into a classic text, I did once yield to temptation in the case of a rhyming verse play adapted for broadcast. Quite rightly, the director had pointed out that radio listeners to an abridged version of the play, with no sight of the actors to aid comprehension, might be baffled when one character, who had imagined himself at death's door, was suddenly restored to rude health by the most perfunctory assurance that he had not been poisoned after all. Could I supply one character with an extra quatrain or so to clarify? Feeling like a forger, I obliged. It seemed to work well enough but the insertion was spotted by one acute, English-speaking listener in the long-dead author's country of origin. 'I don't think I should admit to having done that if I were you,' he told me, when we met a year or two later. I took care to expunge my intrusive quatrain before the complete translation was published.

Apart from trying to introduce little-known plays, in so-called 'minority' languages, I have also ventured to question the conventional British assumption that the neo-classical tragedies of Racine and Corneille must be rendered in blank verse, if not prose, because – if rhymed in English as they are in French – audiences might laugh. Why should they? Is it because we associate the use of rhyme with pantomime? Because English rhymes have been so over-worked, they are all too often predictable and an audience is apt to be bored, if not annoyed, by the inevitable repercussion of line-endings? Or is it because the triumph of the Shakespearean tradition in these islands proves that rhyme, as Dryden and others came to believe, is not appropriate for the expression of lofty or tragic sentiments?

There is doubtless some truth in all of this. It seems to me, however, that if the great tragedies of Racine and Corneille have so often failed to satisfy in English blank verse translation, the real reason may be that Shakespeare and Milton have taught us to expect from blank verse, poetry of a peculiarly rich and vivid texture, far removed from the elegant but passionate simplicity of the French neo-classical masters. The latter, by contrast, worked within strict confines, being obliged, by order of the Académie Française, to ring the changes on an approved vocabulary of only about 2,000 words, arranged in twelve-syllable alexandrines whose couplets had to alternate 'strong' rhymes with 'weak'.

If a translator attempts to 'raise' Racine or Corneille in blank verse to the level of our expectations, he will find it hard not to enliven the bleak text of the original with gratuitous images, bombast or the odd purple patch. If he doesn't, the audience or reader may wonder why he didn't just settle for prose, instead of labouring to hammer these seemingly endless ritual incantations into verse, albeit blank.

As long ago as 1713, in his spoken prologue to a production of Corneille's *Cinna*, in blank verse, at the Theatre Royal, Drury Lane, the playwright Colley Cibber, who is credited with the translation, had this to say:

> This author, to delight a barbarous Age,
> Strews not with gasping heroines the Stage.
> We bellow forth no highflown gingling traps
> To bite transported Witlings of their Claps;
> No ghost is raised; no incantation sung –
> Nor a stuffed Oedipus from window flung.
> We, of the French, their stage decorum prize
> And justly such absurdities despise,
> Approve their unity of Place and Time
> And shun their trivial points and gaudy rhyme...

Far from shunning 'gaudy rhyme', I favour embracing it in an attempt to come to terms with the apparent forbidding austerity of the neo-classical tradition. By imposing our own blank verse pentameters on Racine and Corneille or, for that matter, on Vondel – the Dutch author of *Lucifer* – we may simply be widening still further the cultural gap between their age and our own in which, after all, many poets of distinction, most notably Tony Harrison, have demonstrated in and out of the theatre, that rhyme can, in fact, still delight the ear, while heightening our emotional and intellectual responses.

In translating tragedies by Corneille, Racine and Vondel, I hoped, by retaining metre and rhyme and adopting a moderately elevated style of English, to make the plays easier to digest while nevertheless preserving the conventional distance between the audience and the characters – most of whom are larger and grander than life. However much we may be moved by their dilemmas, we are not expected to identify with the protagonists of these plays. They inhabit another dimension – as they always have done – a region where it is natural for them to express their thoughts and passions in rhyming verse.

In our own day, no less than three centuries ago, it remains for the actors to persuade us that this is an acceptable means of communication, at least for a couple of hours at a time. The last thing the actors should do, to my mind, is try to deliver their rhyming speeches as though they were prose, or sound unduly solemn because 'this is a tragedy'. There are lines in all of these plays which allow for momentary relaxation of tension. If the audience laughs, so much the better. We have no way of knowing whether the Amsterdam audience in the mid-seventeenth century laughed out loud when Beelzebub asked his emissary, the angel Apollion, for further details of how Adam and Eve were making out in Eden: '*Wat dunkt u van zijn ribbe en lieve gemalin?*' But the Bloomsbury Theatre audience certainly did when they heard him inquire, with a faint leer: 'Yes, what about that rib? How's married life?'

On the face of it, there may not seem much to laugh about in Corneille's moving drama *Polyeuct* – the tale of a Christian martyrdom in third-century Armenia. But when Polyeuct, with the enthusiasm of a neophyte, urges his Christian mentor, Nearchus, to join him in what promises to be a suicide raid on a pagan temple, the audience at the Gate managed a chuckle for Nearchus's timid rejoinder: 'Frankly, I'm loath to follow you...' ('*Je ne puis déguiser que j'ai peine à vous suivre...*') That, I feel almost sure, is what Corneille would have wanted.

From these excursions into unfamiliar territory I have derived great pleasure and a few gratifying commissions. More significantly, perhaps, I have convinced myself that there can be no such thing as a perfect or final translation. Possibly the most a translator of plays can hope to achieve is what seems to him or her, at the time, a fair balance between fidelity to the original and the primary need of the audience to be entertained.

THE STAGES OF A TRANSLATION

ANTHONY VIVIS

Although maintaining close links with the academic world, Anthony Vivis is a freelance translator who has been translating drama since 1966. He has been extraordinarily productive especially in his translations and adaptations from German, and has had nearly thirty different plays performed on stage, by dramatists as diverse as Goethe, Brecht, Fassbinder and Kroetz. Anthony Vivis has played a crucial role in introducing the variety of German-language theatre onto the British stage (and abroad), a role which, since 1971, he has enhanced through his extensive work on radio drama. He is a firm believer in the collaborative nature of theatre-making, and has often worked with co-translators and co-adaptors. Some of his work has also been seen on television: two plays by Karge, *Conquest Of The South Pole* (co-translated with T Minter) and *Man To Man* were performed on Channel 4 and BBC 2, in 1989 and 1992 respectively. His translation of Wedekind's *The Empress* was adapted as an opera for Channel 4, in 1994.

Happy are those who hear the word
unspoken by all the tongues of the world;
underlying the language that wishes dictate
it lends to our life a greater weight.

[Rilke wrote this dedication in Muzot, February 1924, inscribing the lines in the *'Duineser Elegien'*, to Witold Hulewicz. Hulewicz, whom Rilke describes as a 'faithful and energetic mediator' was Rilke's Polish translator. He lived from 1895 to 1941, when he was shot.

In an English translation by Jean Boase-Beier, I have placed four lines at the start and the remaining four at the end of this article. The thoughts and feelings which Rilke expresses in these lines accord with those principles to fidelity to the word and scepticism about its ultimate veracity which I see as an essential basis for a translator's attempt to recreate a text originally written in another language].

In *After Babel*, which George Steiner published first in 1975, then republished in 1992, he shows that 'understanding is translation'. An implication of this provocative insight is that understanding translation is of the utmost importance. In

35

his specially written lecture for the BCLT (British Centre for Literary Translation), given at the University of East Anglia, in April 1994, Steiner quoted St Jerome, the patron saint of translators: 'The translator brings home meaning and sense as captives and slaves ... are brought home by their Roman conquerors'.

In revising for this article a lecture I had given at UEA in February 1992, while Translator in Residence with the BCLT, I often thought of Martin Luther in his spartan study at the Wartburg. Can we translators, I wondered, continue recreating the language of another culture and time, while hearing, in Steiner's telling phrase, the 'doors of our mother tongue slam shut behind us'?

I was also conscious of what Steiner went on to lament as the lack of reliable information about translators' 'process experience'. Whilst acknowledging the importance of 'working notes and drafts' on the art of translation left by Holderlin, Walter Benjamin and Buber, among others, Steiner described translation as a 'fiercely singular, solitary, almost autistic act'.

Perhaps this explains why, in Steiner's view, there are very few great translators, 'far fewer than great writers'. Such figures as Florio, Urquart, Luther and Schlegel and Tieck work, Steiner argued, in 'obsessed isolation, often against the grain of their own sensibility, often under material circumstances of deprivation and neglect'.

Here, as elsewhere in his lecture, Steiner was reminding us that the exact art of translation is also exacting. Not simply because most serious translators will forego such trappings of material success as security and solvency. Though perhaps this is preferable to what Steiner called the 'controlled suicide' of writer-translators devoting their lives to translating potboilers instead of more serious, more enduring work – given, of course, that serious publishers can find, or create, an enduring market for them.

In a country as insular as Britain tends to be, it helps a translator to have a stoical disregard for the usual manifestations of material prosperity. Perhaps they distract and divert the mind from the exactitude of an art whose real reward may be to hear between the lines of a translation what Walter Benjamin called 'the lost universal, Adamic tongue'.

This article will set out my experience of being a professional translator, mainly of German drama, from the late sixties onward. Then I shall present two case studies. They are translations I was recently commissioned to make for radio and the theatre. The radio play *The Pond* (*Der Polenweiher*) by Thomas Strittmatter had its first broadcast in Jeremy Mortimer's production, on BBC Radio 3 on March 17th 1992. This was also the date on which the Haymarket Theatre, Leicester premiered Julia Bardsley's promenade production of *Dead Soil*, my translation of Franz Xaver Kroetz's play *Bauern Sterben*.

If language is awry, we cannot say what we mean. If we do not say what we mean, we cannot produce any works of literature. If we do not produce any works of literature, morality and art cannot thrive. If morality and art do not thrive, there can be no justice in the world. If there is no justice in the world, no nation on earth can know how to live. Make sure, then, that you always give language due attention, for that is where all the problems start.

Confucius believed, with Brecht, that where language is concerned the truth is concrete. Karl Kraus believed the same, though in ironical vein he once wondered why anybody bothered to translate anything: 'It's like swatting a fly twice'.

Steering a course between Confucius the sage and Kraus the satirist, we move from the shallows of why we translate into the deeper water of how we translate. My own guiding principle has been the attempt to recreate – rather than reproduce or reinterpret – a text written in a language other than English. This is not simply because the history, traditions and grammatical mechanics of German, say, are vastly different from those of English, despite many common factors and overlaps. Translations are written to be read, heard or seen. The reader, viewer or listener cannot take in the original, even if he or she is familiar with it, whilst receiving the translation. The translation stands for the original, conveying its essential qualities but independent of it whilst interdependent with it. This means that the translation must stand on its own as a work of art, as well as being an accurate and convincing rendition of the original.

A literal rendition can be valuable in an informative way, especially in nuts and bolts technical translation where there is a right and wrong way of explaining the ins and outs of gaskets, say. Some theatres, especially those in this country which receive state subsidy, believe that a literal translation of a classic European play can be handed over to a writer to be made speakable. The implication is that translators marginalise themselves to a kind of library life by being linguists or academics. They can, it is conceded, chart a course through a dictionary but are all at sea with actors. This approach leaves the original text broken-backed.

In the process of translation, essential decisions are made during the immediate, in this case the so-called literal, translation. Often direct literal renditions are – or later turn out to be – the best. Sometimes there is an exact equivalent between source and target languages. At other times a harsh, abrupt translation of a word or phrase jolts us into a new awareness because the translation is unexpected.

Interpretation also has its place in translation. If a writer has deliberately subverted the grammatical rules – as, for instance, the poet Sarah Kirsch does – the translator must first work out what rules are being broken and why. Only then can he or she create an equivalent effect, or at least attempt to, in English.

Perhaps the best proof of translation's role as recreation rather than reproduction is provided by the work of gifted self-translators, such as Oscar Wilde or Samuel Beckett. A play like *Salome* or *Godot* has two independent lives in French and in

English because the authors have creatively expressed, or re-expressed, the play in two different languages. What is vital to the moment of translation is the spark it ignites in the mind, the imagination of the recipient. Embers centuries-old can be re-kindled by an inspired translator.

Translating a play is an act of Hubris, with Nemesis waiting in the wings. After nearly thirty years, I still open no dictionary before I have not only read but lived with a text, perhaps for months or even years. Reading is a painfully acquired skill, as important to a translator as working drawings are to an architect. I first try to get an overall impression of the style, idiom, themes and attitude – in Brecht's word, the 'Gestus' of the play as a whole. I get to know the characters. Who are they, how do they relate to each other and us, the audience, who are strangers to them? How important is each character to the action – when on the stage or off? How important is the subtext? Is what the characters say or do always to be taken at face value?

Reference books are essential tools for translators, who are expected to be multi-informed. Despite having access to the excellent library at UEA, I try to keep a good stock of reference books at home. Good dictionaries – American ones as well as German-English, German-German and Dudens – are vital. I often use a thesaurus, after worrying at a word or phrase without one. I regularly consult the Penguin Dictionary of Proverbs, sometimes Brewer's Phrase and Fable, quite often the Bible in the Authorised King James's Version.

I try to let the source text speak as directly as possible. I usually write my first translation draft by hand on a writing block which I can take with me. If the original text is manageable enough, I will take it and the notebook around with me, and if possible work at the draft wherever I happen to be, even on a train or the Underground.

The first draft I try to get done as quickly as possible. It is a chore which has to be done but can then be left to one side. To allow breathing space for future drafts, I usually write alternatives – a different adjective, noun or tense, say – over and below the real line. Far from confusing me, I find this three-way choice trebly helpful. For later drafts, I work on a laptop wordprocessor in more or less monastic concentration. I find the cursor as immediate as a moving finger. But having writ, thanks to the editing function, I can cancel out a line – or, if necessary, a whole page – of it.

From the second draft onwards, I find it important not to be too draconian. Sometimes, lucky strikes in the first draft, when I am less inhibited, turn out to be best, and I keep them or come back to them.

By the third or fourth draft, which I have probably printed out in rough, to live with and work on, I hope to be near a reading draft – i.e. a draft plausible enough to show someone else for their comments. Ideally, after the reading draft has gone out, a face-to-face meeting follows with the person commissioning to discuss in detail where the work goes next. If there has been a reasonable gap, I will then go back to the text and rework where necessary, being careful not to assume that only new ideas, only changes, are good. If the author or his or her agent has asked to see the text, one is sent when I have finished the main work.

Throughout rehearsals I keep a hotline open to a director or producer. As often as possible, without disturbing the separate creative process of production, I attend rehearsals – more seen than heard.

The translator has to write the dialogue the actors act, the director directs, and the critics criticise. It must therefore be approached in the same way that a writer would tackle it. With two differences. Basic dramaturgical decisions have already been made by the original dramatist. This is a freedom. Yet the translator is limited to a mode of expression he or she can at most recreate, not originate. This is a responsibility.

Both the responsibility and freedom are greater if, as I generally like to do, you translate work by playwrights new to this country, new to the English language perhaps. In these cases, there is no groundwork of reception to build on. There again, you are not restricted by expectations of style, fashion or reputation. The writer is your translation. For good or ill.

In piecing together a mosaic of method, some basic questions are helpful. What period is the play set in? In what location? Is the dialogue a localised idiom or specific dialect? Do you need to consult special dictionaries, a local native speaker or send queries to the author or agent? Is the cast size realistic for a production in Great Britain? If too large, can roles be doubled or trebled without damaging the play's integrity? Is the theme potentially interesting to a British audience? Are references in the text best left specific to their context or do they need transposing? What are the author's instructions or recommendations on this? Whilst you cannot answer questions like this all at once, they can serve as threads to guide the translator through the labyrinth.

Crucial to a successful translation of drama – if not to all literary forms – is the attempt to recreate an appropriate rhythm. The rhythm of dramatic dialogue, of which most but not all plays mostly consist, is a complex and living organism. Rhythm is the energy, the heartbeat, the metabolism of language. Variations in rhythm alter emphasis, pace and through them, at times, meaning.

The relatively simple element of word order can change a rhythm, and with it the whole accent of a sentence. When Brecht was explaining 'Gestus', by which I believe he means the attitude a character has, and by extension the dramatic vigour or control a character has, he quoted a sentence from the Bible to bring the point home. If you say 'The pure in heart are blessed for they shall inherit the earth' you are making a clear if somewhat bland statement. If you use the same words but change the order of the two: 'Blessed – or, with greater emphasis – Blessèd are the pure in heart for they shall inherit the earth' your words, your statement, are much more arresting. In time, by repetition and association, they accumulate the power of proverb – a form in which English, like German, is immensely rich.

Not only must the rhythm place the words in the most effective sequence and balance, but it must also operate between speeches within scenes and between one scene and another. My analogy for effective rhythm is that the line should spring back when heard, as if a foot were stepping on a camomile lawn, and, if possible, release an equivalent pungency. I can understand why Gerard Manley Hopkins developed sprung rhythm.

A good reader of poetry will make a line resilient when heard. Just as an actor in the theatre will pace and pitch dialogue. Both must seek out and express the surface as well as the underlying rhythm. These may contrast or conflict.

Overall, I try to imagine the translation of an entire play as one sentence. A long and complex sentence, in which the clauses are scenes, the punctuation marks pauses or blackouts, the main verb the plotline. If the rhythm ever sags, the line, the speech, the scene will lose its springiness, and as a result the audience's attention will wander.

In trying to combine dialogue and rhythm I have often thought of a phrase I learnt from Elias Canetti while working with him on an English translation of his play *Hochzeit* (*The Wedding*). To distinguish between different characters' speech patterns Canetti would speak of their 'acoustic mask'. He argued, and certainly demonstrated in his texts, that each character's choice of words, especially the recurring patterns, the rhythm and the idiom or dialect each character uses, marks out that particular character as vividly as any visible features. Unless a translation can recreate such acoustic masks, the language is likely to remain at worst cardboard, at best wooden.

In working as a full-time professional translator mainly for the stage I divide my time roughly into three: a third to get the work, a third to do the work, a third to market it. In the first and third stages I have invaluable help from Joanna Marston, my representative. I am also fortunate in having built up several relationships with editors, directors, producers, theatre managements and publishers. Basing myself on the proposition that a translator is a writer who translates, I try to interrelate these aspects.

The BBC, especially Radio Drama, is the greatest patron of the arts in the United Kingdom, including the art of translation. Whilst there is understandably strong competition for broadcasting space from original writers, both living and dead, it is sometimes possible to interest a Radio Drama producer or editor in new work from abroad, as I shall explain in more detail in the case study of the Strittmatter play *The Pond*, which I translated and adapted for Radio 3.

The Arts Council, London, devotes a sizable proportion of its grant aid for literature to work in translation – not least, most of the funding for the BCLT. In addition, in April 1991 the Drama Department at the Arts Council for England established a separate scheme within its New Theatre Writing programme expressly for theatre translation. Awards of bursaries for translators and funding for theatres willing to commission a translation from the original language are now available – by competition as funds allow. More significant than the amounts of cash involved – which are likely to stay stable if not increase – is the recognition by our leading arts organisation that in the terms of grants awarded translation is comparable to original writing.

The market for translated plays in television or film is very limited, especially where contemporary works are concerned. This is hard to understand. Whilst it is next to impossible to predict whether a new German play, say, will be popular with audiences and/or critics, the reaction can be surprisingly positive. In 1987 Pierre Audi at the Almeida Theatre commissioned Tinch Minter and myself to translate Botho Strauss's play *The Tourist Guide*. It did not break box office records. However, especially in the light of a less than ecstatic reception for Strauss's play *Great And Small* in the West End some years previously, the production and text were favourably received. So much so that in a recent article on Strauss in the *Independent* Pierre Audi said that the production which meant most to him during his years at the Almeida was *The Tourist Guide*.

Translations of two plays by Manfred Karge: *Man To Man* and *The Conquest Of The South Pole*, the second of which I co-translated with Tinch Minter, both of them originally directed by Stephen Unwin, have transferred from theatre to screen. Performed at the Traverse Theatre, Edinburgh, and the Royal Court, London, in 1989, *The Conquest Of The South Pole* was filmed first, directed by Giles Mackinnon. With the backing from Channel 4 as well as the BFI, the film was also shown on television.

In 1992, Screenplay on BBC 2 transmitted a film, directed by John Maybury, of *Man To Man*, jointly produced by Basilisk Films and the BBC, with Tilda Swinton repeating the role she created in 1988 at the Traverse and the Royal Court, London. The film is now being distributed abroad as a television film by the BFI.

Whilst it is impossible to predict what material is likely to appeal to television or cinema, my feeling is that there is a more immediate link between theatre work – especially that produced in small fringe art theatres – and BBC Radio. Part of its now threatened public service role is, in my view, to support and produce more challenging work of a non-populist nature. Which does not mean that Radio 4 and The World Service do not broadcast new drama in translation. They do.

In the case of both Karge plays, the translations of the original stage play were published – by Methuen. This has greatly helped to circulate the texts and undoubtedly contributed to further productions in the UK and in English-speaking territories abroad.

They were also used as the basis of the screenplays. In the case of *The Conquest Of The South Pole* crucial differences soon became apparent. Perhaps the most obvious was that film action moves more slowly, and more literally than stage action. Although you are likely to earn more, at least in the short term, for film or television translations, very little critical attention is paid to the works, least of all as dramatic texts. Nor is it likely that a text will be rescreened in the way that a stage text may well be given fresh productions by other theatres. The further up the slippery slope of commercial exploitation a text goes, the more likely it is to be compromised as a text, and the less likely to retain the original author's and translator's artistic imprints. Whilst there is generally more money and attention paid to new translations or adaptations of classic works, they generally have a short shelf life. Translations of contemporary plays, whilst more difficult to place and less well funded, often have more staying power in the long run.

Case study 1: *Der Polenweiher (The Pond)* by Thomas Strittmatter

Der Polenweiher is Thomas Strittmatter's third play, and it was premiered in Konstanz in 1984 when he was 22. It is the first of his plays to be translated into English. Having been sent the German text in May 1990, I read and re-read it during that autumn, decided I wanted to translate it, cleared the rights with my agent's help, and set up a modest seed-corn subsidy – small grants from the BCLT and from Strittmatter's publisher and agent in Germany.

I then wrote a treatment. This consisted of a two-page synopsis detailing the action, themes, characters, approach, and set design, followed by about 10 pages of dialogue to give a realistic feel of the finished translation.

In a country where few theatres read a foreign text in the original language, it is essential to make a submission dramaturg-friendly. You must allow your sample dialogue to develop, change, strengthen in the course of time, as a result of the translator's deepening experience of the text and of comments from outside.

In the case of the Strittmatter, I decided that the text might be suitable for radio, and I submitted the treatment to a German-speaking producer at the BBC, Jeremy Mortimer, with whom I had worked on four other German plays over the years. After two or three meetings with him and the slot editor for Radio 3, Jeremy Howe, in August 1991, I was commissioned to translate and adapt the play for radio.

With the producer's agreement, that October, I submitted my translation of the whole text of the stage play, complete with stage directions. A longish personal meeting confirmed my choice of a neutral rural idiom which avoided harsh modernisms – the play is set in the Black Forest between 1943 and 1946. Characters' names, place names and phrases like '*Heil Hitler*' were left as they stood. Otherwise, I found ways to avoid specifically German forms of address, such as 'Herr So-and-So', '*Gnädige Frau*', etc, which to my ear in this context would have sounded false.

Other dramaturgical changes were needed. We decided to incorporate the atmospheric stage directions into the role of a narrator-protagonist built up out of one of the main characters, and use this narrator to shape the action more transparently for radio. Other purely visual moments were restructured into self-explanatory dialogue which avoided over-explicit signposting. I also translated into rhyming-verse extracts from Goethe's *Faust* quoted in the text, sometimes substituting passages from *Macbeth* where the *Faust* references were less clear. The final radio text was delivered in November 1991, the text recorded in January 1992, and first broadcast on Radio 3 on March 17th.

The recording itself took place in Bristol, in Christchurch Studio, a well-equipped studio ideally suited for recording drama, with editing facilities on the spot – which the BBC has since closed. The producer had decided to use West-country voices for the rural idiom though I made no attempt to write West Country – whatever that is.

The translation of *Der Polenweiher* was recorded as written. At only one point that I recall was there a query from an actor. A character says that the boy's father is away, 'in the field. Russia'. The actor felt that this could be misinterpreted – in a farming community – to mean the father was near the house, working in a field. He wanted to change the line to 'at the Front. Russia'. First, this did not make sense because in the latter stages of the play, getting towards 1994/45, there was no German front in Russia. And checking the German, I confirmed that Strittmatter's dialogue '*im Feld. Russland*' conveyed literally the same ambiguity as the English. I am now trying to place the play in the stage translation. Some theatres have shown interest in the initial treatment, which I have since revised. I was also able to check some remaining queries with the author's agent in Germany, enabling me to make a final theatre text.

Case study 2: *Dead Soil (Bauern Sterben)* by Franz Xaver Kroetz

Franz Xaver Kroetz is one of the most widely translated of contemporary German authors. Productions of plays such as *Geisterbahn* and *The Nest* at the Bush Theatre, as well as *Through The Leaves* and *Request Programme* in Edinburgh have helped establish Kroetz in Britain. Over the past two or three years, however, his work has been less in evidence here. When looking through several new plays from the mid-eighties onwards, I was therefore faced with a new dilemma.

The play which struck me most forcibly was called *Bauern Sterben*, literally 'Peasants [or Farmers] Are Dying'. One of the play's main images is earth in which nothing will grow, and the themes of death and destruction are strongly present. I decided to translate the title as *Dead Soil*.

I then needed to decide which of the three texts by Kroetz I should translate. Two texts were written in Bavarian, and one of these was an 'experiment', a dramatic sketch Kroetz had written after early rehearsals in Munich. Following a visit to Calcutta in 1985, Kroetz wrote a *hochdeutsch* version, in collaboration with Alexandra Weinert-Purucker.

In the course of directing the Munich 'experiment' over several months, Kroetz wrote a full dramatic scenario mostly in Bavarian, with sequences of standard German. These, Kroetz specifies, are to alternate abruptly with the Bavarian dialogue to open up more stylised, lyrical veins in the text at appropriate points. This mainly Bavarian performance text is the one he wished to have translated.

One of Kroetz's gifts as a dramatist is his skill in giving dramatic expression to characters who are inarticulate or can express emotion only primitively. Paradoxically, characters need subtle language to express their inarticulacy. If characters speak in a non-standard way, their language must reflect this too.

Kroetz asks for a 'broad, rough style of presentation, even on the primitive side'. I felt I had to invent, as Kroetz did, a language rooted in a recognisably rural English idiom but not specific to one region.

My approach was to subvert normal grammar according to patterns which repeat but which also vary from character to character. Thus, the language the characters speak is neither a dialect nor standard English. It is a broken-down colloquial speech – what Elias Canetti might have called a series of cracked acoustic masks.

However we build, with whatever art,
beyond all bridges lies a world apart
from the hectic thrill of the daily round;
a serene exchange on common ground.

SERVANT OF MANY MASTERS

JOSEPH FARRELL

Joseph Farrell is a journalist, broadcaster and Senior Lecturer in Italian at the University of Strathclyde, in Glasgow. He is well-known as a theatre and arts critic, both in the press and on radio, and in recent years he has become both a regular contributor to, and presenter of, programmes like Kaleidoscope and Night Moves. He brings together his love of Italian and of theatre in his translation work, and has done much to further the cause of Italian drama in Scotland and England. His personal links with Dario Fo and his collaborative work with Borderline culminated in the critically acclaimed production of *Mistero Buffo*, with Robbie Coltrane. The production was subsequently televised by the BBC. He has also worked on De Filippo and Goldoni, and his translation of *His Lordship's Fancy* was recently staged at the Gate, in London. Among his published translations are Dario Fo's *The Tricks Of The Trade* and Vincenzo Consolo's *The Smile Of The Unknown Mariner*.

'A translator', in the words of the German philosopher Franz Rosenzweig, 'is the servant of two masters'. The description is in itself perspicacious but it has, for those with a knowledge of theatre history, tantalising associations which deepen and enrich it. No doubt Rosenzweig's two masters were intended to be author and public, or source culture and target culture but, whatever his intentions, it is tempting to link his *mot* with the title of Carlo Goldoni's play *Harlequin, Servant Of Two Masters*.

In the play, Arlecchino intrigues and tricks his way into the service of two lords. Gluttonous and avaricious by nature, his ambition is no higher than to receive salary and victuals from both, but the world of comedy is harsh and he ends up being roundly beaten by each in turn. He himself is unsure of his allegiance to either, they are unaware of each other's existence, and all Harlequin's wiles are directed towards keeping them in this state of mutual ignorance. On the other hand, he alone is fully aware of the foibles, the quirks, the eccentricities as well as the talents and abilities of the one and the other, and uses all his legendary cunning to serve the two, in his own way. Paradoxically, he represents the only link between them until, in a flash of recognition, they come to acknowledge their previous acquaintanceship. At this point, Harlequin is redundant.

Few translators in any genre risk the physical abuse that Arlecchino suffered, but it might be helpful for a moment to see the translator not merely as servant of two masters but as Goldoni's Harlequin. At his best, he acts as messenger between two sides with limited knowledge of each other. His trade is slightly underhand and he finds himself handling goods which are not his own. Guileful and resourceful, out to entertain and serve, the translator, again like Harlequin, takes his rank among the below stairs classes. This allocation of a servant role is valuable not only in checking any incipient tendency towards individual egomania, but in establishing a hierarchy of importance. Francis Steegmuller, the skilled translator of Flaubert, wrote that when he had completed his *Madame Bovary*, he felt inclined to insert his name as author. It is undoubtedly an eery, disorienting sensation to have written every word uttered by the characters, to have solved the various problems of idiom and tone that inevitably arise, to have devised arresting phrases and witty repartee, and yet to realise that the play is not yours and that the primal inspiration cannot be attributed to you. (It may, of course, happen that what seemed hilariously funny or dazzlingly brilliant when set down on the page will seem to an editor or director boringly banal or expendably crass, but that is a different kind of dilemma – and experience).

No good will come, as Harlequin found, from aspiring to a place alongside the Grandees, since the result is likely to be pastiche. An author like Dario Fo has on several occasions thundered against the invariable tendency of translators, always and everywhere, to consider themselves more perceptive, witty, and more theatrically adept than the mere playwright. This trait is expressed, Fo has written, in the zeal to splash colour where the writer has chosen greyness, to use a broad brush where he painted in fine strokes, to abandon all carefully achieved moderation and restraint in favour of excess, and to caricature where the benighted writer has opted for the delicate touch. The Harlequin translator knows that such misguided presumption leads to misfortune. Translating is the invisible art, in the sense that the good translator, like the trusty butler, must accept being ignored as proof of a job well done. He is expected to be heard, but not seen.

To change image, the translator operates near frontier posts, like a smuggler, creeping across the border with contraband goods which will inevitably be damaged in the crossing. Difficulties with the customs men are a small matter when compared to the level of damage unavoidably done to the goods. The theoretical problems of translation can be reduced to determining the level of damage which is inevitable, and how much can be avoided. Pushkin defined the translator as a 'courier of the human spirit', while Gogol, less flatteringly, suggested that the ideal translator should be like a window pane: the reader should not be aware he is there. In any discussion of translation, someone will produce firstly the Italian pun – *traduttore, traditore* – and secondly Robert Frost's celebrated line to the effect that 'poetry is what is lost in the translation'. This view will generally be distorted to make it imply that all that is included under the heading 'aesthetics' will inevitably defy the efforts of even the most skilled of translators. There have been proponents of the 'translation is impossible' school at least since Dante, but if translation is impossible, it is also indispensable, inevitable and, at its best, enriching.

There have been translators since the unfortunate construction, and destruction, of the Tower of Babel, and there have been theorists of translation for at least as long. Until recently, the two went together, for it is not possible for a human being to indulge in a complex activity such as transferring emotion and thought from one language to another without pondering what he is engaged upon. Probably there are no dilemmas relating to translation which were not adequately expressed by St Jerome, the translator of the Bible from Greek, or by Leonardo Bruni, the Florentine humanist who rendered Plato into Latin. It is odd that there is no store of thought specifically relating to the theatre, when we consider how theatre has lived on theatre from the earliest days. Perhaps theatre translation, as distinct from adaptation, is a very recent phenomenon. In other ages, it was taken for granted that a foreign work would be remoulded for local taste and consumption.

Perhaps that is again becoming the mode. At this stage, it is essential to distinguish the different forms of practice in the field of translation. John Dryden, himself a translator of Virgil, believed there were three distinct headings under which translation could be grouped – the 'metaphrase, the paraphrase and the imitation'. By metaphrase, he meant 'turning an author word by word, line by line into another language'; by paraphrase, 'translation with latitude, whereby the author is kept in view by the translator, but his words are not so strictly followed as his sense'; and by imitation, he indicated a style of work 'where the translator (if he has not lost that name) assumes the liberty not only to vary from the words and sense, but to forsake them both as he sees occasion'.

With the addition of nothing more elaborate than a series of footnotes, Dryden's table should suffice to cover the entire field of translation activity, but contemporary practice in theatre is more complex. In theatre in Britain, current usage allows the term 'translation' to stand for three distinct approaches: the literal translation, the performance version prepared by someone who may not have any knowledge of the original language, and finally the adaptation, or what in music would be called a 'variation on a theme'. Even if – or precisely because – there is a move underway back towards the primacy of the remoulded work, it is worth insisting on the distinction between the translation and the adaptation, and on the desirability of making clear to an audience, and to an author, what service is being offered.

Christopher Hampton (in a National Theatre *Platform Paper*) spoke of his outrage when he discovered that his French translator had altered his play substantially, even substituting an alternative ending. The translator refused Hampton's request to reinstate at least the ending, leaving the unfortunate author with no choice but to withdraw his work. He had ordered a translation but was served an adaptation, and sent it back. Dario Fo had a similar experience in this country. His first work to be performed here was *Accidental Death Of An Anarchist*, in a 1979 production mounted by Belt and Braces which used a script prepared by Gavin Richards, who also starred. Fo came to see it at the beginning of its West End run, and his outraged reaction during the interval has become the stuff of theatrical legend. Fo does not speak English, but was aware that the pace, the momentum, the slapstick style did not represent the play he had written. In addition, he heard his name mentioned in the play as an object of ridicule for his supposed refusal to introduce women characters into any of the central roles. He was also aware that the plot itself had been more substantially modified than Christopher Hampton's. With this particular play, Fo had done many rewrites, sometimes evening by evening, in accordance with emerging information of the subjects he was featuring, but none of his versions had featured either of the two alternative endings which Richards had incorporated into the play. Finally, he was aware that Richards had cut some of the characters, especially the bishop who appeared as one of the disguises which the madman investigator dons in the latter part of the work. For Fo, this character was indispensable to his conception of the play, since his presence indicated the complicity of the church in the cover-up which Fo was exposing.

In the dressing room, anxious friends explained that Richards had transformed the play in accordance with British theatrical traditions, employing music hall devices and approaches where Fo had used a spirit more in keeping with Italian *commedia dell'arte*. Fo was not mollified, although he did not take his dissent to the extremes of Hampton. The Gavin Richards version has enjoyed enormous success in this country, but Fo's play has never been seen in Britain in a shape which faithfully reproduces the original. Even the 1990 version by Alan Cumming and Tim Supple, described by the publishers (Methuen) as 'faithful to the clear sighted insanity of the original', was another free adaptation which updated the play's attack on the abuse of political power. *Accidental Death...* has become the all-purpose radical protest play, employed in Britain to support the most varied causes and decry the most diverse wrongs – to satirise Anthony Blunt, to protest at the treatment of the Birmingham Six, to attack Establishment figures like judges, Tories and policemen. Fo himself, it may be added, has come to see this flexibility as a sign of the play's strength and as a proof that the theatrical situation he had created was not merely durable but pliable.

The paradox is that Gavin Richards's *Accidental Death...* set an unfortunate precedent, but remains the most successful transposition of Fo into English. The precedent lay in the freedom to present a free adaptation as Fo's work, while the success lay in Richards's ability to maintain that most elusive of qualities – the spirit of the original – and to identify a means of uniting Fo's farce with political commitment. Virtually all subsequent transformations of Fo's plays have opted for one or the other, usually for the slapstick, with the result that there has emerged a

British Fo who has an imprecise, tenuous and shifting relationship with the Italian Fo. The Fo familiar to the British stage has none of the subtle modulations of his Italian original, and none of his ability to merge farce with anger, let alone with tragedy. In addition, British Fo displays and exemplifies the worst failing of the whole adaptation ethos; he assumes that the audience can only cope with what is already familiar, and is incapable of facing the challenge of the foreign. (Hampton's French translator is there to prove that this failing is not exclusively British).

This cosy provincialism underwrote the version of *The Pope And The Witch*, translated by Ed Emery and reworked by Andy de la Tour. The English version is a technicolour imitation of *Il papa e la strega*. The demand for transformation, rather than translation, indicates that the original did not conform to the expectations of the commissioning body. To raise the joke count to a level expected of British Fo, Mr de la Tour used an array of four-letter words and gave the cardinals in the Vatican the names of the Italian World Cup-winning team. Predictably, this enraged Fo, so the printed version carries an erratum slip as hilarious as anything Fo could have invented himself: 'The characters' names shown on the cast list and referred to in the adaptor's note were subsequently changed, at Dario Fo's request, as follows: Cardinal Vialli is now Cardinal Pialli, Cardinal Schillaci is now Cardinal Stillaci...'. More serious was the switch in emphasis away from a discussion of drug problems towards the supposed conspiracy to murder John Paul I. The murder conspiracy theory had been made popular by the film *Godfather III*, which had been released about the time of the first production of the English-language version of the play in the West Yorkshire Playhouse. Homicidal skullduggery in the Vatican was by then a familiar theme, lending itself to clichéd expression. It was easy to portray cardinals, or any Italians, as having mafia features, but difficult to devise a style which would combine farce and the pressing problem of drug abuse. The English version, as is often the case in the adaptation process, ducked the hard challenge in favour of a soft option.

This is not, however, a plea for the production of literal versions of Dario Fo. His plays are simply not effective onstage in that form, and indeed much of their Italian success is down to the fact that the work of Fo the writer is adapted onstage by Fo the actor of genius. Foreign translators/adaptors must devise some equivalent. When Morag Fullerton and I prepared the version of *Mistero Buffo* which was performed by Robbie Coltrane in various theatres in Scotland, and subsequently broadcast on television, we discovered that what was regarded in Italy as Fo's most successful and representative piece of work was, in a faithful translation, flat and dull. The work consists of individual scenes culled from medieval sources, depicting such incidents as the raising of Lazarus or the legend of the blind man and the lame man. These sketches contain two separate sections – the medieval material itself and Fo's explanatory prologue which, in his supposedly humorous style, pointed to parallels in contemporary life. The humour did not carry and the parallels made little sense to a British audience. At this point, it was clear that rigorous accuracy would have been self-defeating, and would have done nothing for the greater glory of Dario Fo. The author wanted them to laugh, wanted them to think, wanted them to get angry over popes and politicians who abused power. If the British audience ended up with some scanty information over why Pope Boniface VIII in the twelfth century, or Giulio Andreotti in the twentieth, were scoundrels, they might be mildly edified, but, more probably, they would be roundly bored, and the emotional/intellectual appeal Fo sought to make in the here and now would have been lost.

The main task is to locate the mainspring of the work, to identify with the author's intentions or, as the saying goes, 'get under his skin'. In that spirit, the introductions were totally rewritten so as to turn the satire against Thatcherism and Health Service reforms; the politicians pilloried were no longer Bettino Craxi or Ciriaco de Mita but Sir Geoffrey Howe and Teddy Taylor. There were also difficulties with the sketches themselves. The language of the published version required attention so as to brighten and enliven it. The first requirement of the theatrical translator is that he display what Eric Bentley terms 'histrionic sensibility'; in other words, an ability to write dialogue which is speakable and has stage quality. One of the key words for *Mistero Buffo* is '*giullare*', the minstrel figure, the singer/dancer/musician who lived by his takings, and whose nearest modern–day equivalent is probably the busker. Fo performed *Mistero Buffo* in the guise of a modern day '*giullare*', performing all the parts in turn. It was not helpful to have this vitally important word translated into English as 'jongleur', even if we were told as justification that the word can be found in the Shorter Oxford English Dictionary. To ask the audience to bring along a French rather than an Italian lexicon is not to provide them with a translation, especially since the French in question has misleading connections with the English 'juggler'.

Any rules in theatre translation must be weakly drawn and subordinate to changing needs, but there can be little dissent over the requirement that the language of translation, or adaptation, be intelligible and natural, be vivid and colourful, and be written with a rhythm which allows it to be spoken with ease and grace by an actor. There ought to be equally little dissent over the need to maintain the distinction between translation and adaptation, and to publicise it as clearly as health warnings on cigarette packets. The distinction is under threat from various quarters. I have no sympathy with the modish term 'subvert'. The translator, in this view, will win praise for his willingness to 'subvert' the original text, be it poem or play. There is a seeming democratic force to this argument; it gives scope to the frustrated creativity of those who are not themselves capable of inventive writing but who can batten onto the works of others, switching, distorting, or 'subverting' them. The disadvantage of this view is that it allows an audience to be duped. If I go to the theatre to see an English version of *Tartuffe*, I expect to see a play which is as close to Molière as may be, just as when I go to a restaurant I expect to receive my *veal alla marsala* as it was prepared by the chef; I have no interest in the frustrated sensibilities of a waiter who aims to improve the chef's work by splashing tomato ketchup over it, any more than in the intellectual or domestic circumstances which may lead a translator to subversion.

A play is, of course, more than language, and the essential distinction between translation and adaptation lies in the respect not for the language but for the non-linguistic elements of the drama. As a rule of thumb, a translation becomes an adaptation when the transformation involved is more than linguistic. Dario Fo is a very particular case of a writer who *requires* adaptation rather than translation in the sense I have suggested. He is a political radical and a theatrical conservative, and his theatre is founded on a union of these two elements. He takes his plots from the headlines of the moment, but many of his most representative characters are modern versions of familiar figures from the Italian theatrical tradition. The madman with the talent for impersonation who conducts the investigation into police corruption in *Accidental Death Of An Anarchist* is an updated version of the Harlequin figure from *commedia dell'arte*, and while the play may seem like a piece of wildly inventive madcap farce, it is in fact based on the death in custody of the anarchist Giuseppe Pinelli, who had been arrested by the Milan police for alleged complicity in causing an explosion at a bank in 1969. To make an impact, Fo has to be set in a different political and theatrical landscape, or transported into another culture.

But his is a rare case. The shamanistic associations of the word 'culture' are now taken as indisputable justification of the notion that each translation is *ipso facto* an adaptation. The references, the thought processes, the associations aroused by words are believed to be in conflict from one culture to another. The notion of 'culture' is in danger of losing its humanistic, cosmopolitan overtones to acquire the unyielding dogmatism of an apartheid system. 'Cultures' are now widely assumed to be wholly self-contained, exclusive, mutually incompatible entities which reject the intrusion of codes and experiences from any neighbouring system with the zeal of the body's immune system. The Indian critic and writer Rustom Bharuchu wrote a book, *Theatre And The World*, which argued that theatre was not of the world but was specific to a number of non-communicating, tightly enclosed capsules called 'cultures'. Peter Brook, on this view, was guilty of cultural piracy when he produced in the West *The Mahabharata* from Hindu texts. As an instance of the only acceptable way of producing plays from other cultures, Mr Bharuchu offered his own experience of taking *Request Concert*, a (wordless) one-woman play by German author Franz Xavir Kroetz, to Calcutta, Madras and Bombay. In keeping with his belief that the play was 'intrinsically western', he did extensive workshops with the chosen actress and other interested parties so as to strip it of those elements considered alien, and to fully immerse it in the cultures of the countries where it would be seen. The conditioning creed was that there is no overriding corpus of experience, and certainly no common humanity, which transcends culture.

It may be that the gulf between East and West is so deep as to render this process desirable or at least useful, but some such defence is now routinely adduced for every removal of a work from its native surroundings, even inside European cultures, and its relocation nearer the audience's home. The differences between, for example, Spain and Britain are not so extreme as to put discussion about experience in one country or culture beyond the grasp of people in another. Translation, not merely the uprooting which is adaptation, is possible since a translation ought to be an arena for an encounter between cultures. Where the adaptor, or director, believe such efforts are futile, or where they have simply low expectations of what an audience can cope with, their efforts are channelled towards lessening the impact of that encounter. There is a loss in this process, and in the refusal of the challenge of the new and unfamiliar which it implies. Audiences are never to be allowed to come to grips with the Germanness of a German theatre work, or with the Spanishness of, say, Lorca. If a decision is made to set Ibsen's *An Enemy Of The People* in the Highlands of Scotland, because of presumed parallels between the religious gloom and the oppressive culture of both nineteenth-century Norway and contemporary Argyll, the changes involved are not substantial, but for that very reason it is not clear why the switch was thought helpful. Disappointingly often, such switches are made in accordance with facile preconceived notions. It has become standard to set *Tartuffe* in the nineteenth century, because for the modern mind 'hypocritical' and 'Victorian' are taken as interchangeable.

When the transformation is less complete than it was in the case of Mr Bharuchu's production, the results are at best incongruous, at worst grotesque. The Dublin Gate produced a version of Lorca's *The House Of Bernarda Alba*, which planned to use Irish rhythms of speech and turns of phrase. The idea is unexceptionable in concept, and was employed to great effect by Frank McGuinness in the version of *The Three Sisters* which he wrote for the Cusack sisters. It requires that the translator have as fine an ear as a piano tuner; in the case of the Lorca, the whole impact of the play was ruined by the opening words spoken to the servant by Bernarda as she returned from the funeral of her husband. 'More elbow grease', she said with the solemnity of an Antigone addressing Creon; but the words in that context jarred with the audience, and the play never recovered. Even more unfortunate was a production of the same play by the talented Charabanc company of Belfast. Programme notes indicated that the action was to occur 'somewhere in contemporary Ireland', but while some of the characters underwent a name change, others, confusingly, retained their Spanish names. The characters complained incessantly of the torpor induced by the stifling heat and beating sun – of Central Ireland. The 'greenhouse effect' may be a menace, but has not yet reached the stage where inhabitants of the Counties Cavan and Monaghan daily wilt under the effects of the sun's midday rays as do the people of Andalusia. All coherence was lost.

Adaptation and translation are not two sides of the one coin; they are in conflict with one another, particularly when the adaptor is the wholly new figure of the surrogate, or pseudo-, translator. The justification for this figure arises from the undoubted fact that for a translator the more important language is not the language he is translating from, but the language he is translating into. There are learned studies of the number of mistakes D H Lawrence made in his translation of the Sicilian writer Giovanni Verga, but who will care? No one will wish to sift through a translated work which is pedestrian, pedantic or dull, no matter how accurate. The ideal in translation is fidelity plus flair, and it is not impossible to attain. The translator is only the Harlequin; he does not create structure, plot, character or momentum. If it is difficult to find translators with the flair, it is impossible to find surrogates with the commitment to fidelity.

There is the risk that this harping on about fidelity will sound merely po-faced, or take on the ring of spluttering conversation among permanently indignant, aging gaffers on a park bench. There can be no sane objection to adaptation, provided that it has the courage to speak its name. The genuine adaptor is a co-creator who forges his own work in the light of the sun. For some theatre-goers, the prime concern in an evening's theatre is the quality of the work staged before them, not with whether it corresponds to some unknown original written in a far-off land for which they care little. For writers too, considerations of respect for some original may seem otiose. Theatre has always lived on theatre, writers have always plundered each others' work. Molière borrowed from Plautus for *The Miser*, only to see his work cheerfully plagiarised by Fielding, who disingenuously claimed that his work was a mere translation of Molière's original. The *Menaechmi*, whose comic situation derives from the identity problems twins create and experience, provided Shakespeare with inspiration for *The Comedy Of Errors* and Dario Fo for *Trumpets And Raspberries*. Bertolt Brecht pickpocketed John Gay to make *The Beggars' Opera* into *The Threepenny Opera*, and Dario Fo tried to do the same, only to be stopped in his tracks by the Brecht estate. There's the rub. Those who do the adapting are more happy about the process than those whose work is adapted. As with all acts of larceny, however civilly executed, the victim rarely regards the deed with the same light-hearted nonchalance as the perpetrator. Brecht's heirs wished to safeguard Brecht from the operation he had done on Gay, and Fo, however willing he was to freely remould Brecht, was unhappy with the Gavin Richards job on his work.

These works could be categorised, using terms more common in musical parlance, as 'variations on a theme', similar to Rachmaninov's variations on a theme by Paganini. Rachmaninov's is a new composition which proclaims its indebtedness to an admired model, and which can thus either compete with the original, or illuminate and enrich it. Similarly, a Picasso painting might cast a new light on the Velázquez which inspired it, or a Manet illuminate further a Poussin, without pretending either to be the original or a mere copy. The same approach has been employed in theatre, without the dignity of a name.

The surrogate 'translator' is a new figure. The fact that he blurs the distinction between adaptation and translation is a small thing, but the fact that he has, in general, no more knowledge of the culture he is handling than has a dilettante with a metal detector of the Roman treasure trove his machine has uncovered, is a more serious matter. Normally a well-established writer, he will justify his activity with a claim for sharper intuition and deeper empathy. Some unfortunate drudge will be commissioned to provide that most mysterious thing – a literal translation – to which a star name will add the glitter of lilied phrases and wittily turned dialogue. If the translator accepts a role as servant of two masters, the surrogate owes real allegiance to only one – his own language and culture. The debt to the absent author will be met with an appeal to instinct, which is a patrician synonym for guesswork. Dusty Hughes converted Gorky's *Philistines* and Bulgakov's *Molière* from the Russian using a translation prepared for him by someone with a knowledge of the language. He later wrote: 'I am convinced that the best person to stand in for a playwright is another playwright: you have a feeling for the work that gives you a head start on an academic . . . It's the texture of the language that is important, and you can't achieve a consistent tone in anything unless you know how to do that as a writer yourself. To me, having one's own individual voice is worth any amount of nit-picking over the exact meaning of words'. The use of the term 'academic' is underhand; in Britain, the word is roughly synonymous with tedious, tiresome, fatuous, humourless and drab. The debate, however, is not between the robotic 'academic' and the intuitive writerly approach, but about the level of knowledge of the original play which is indispensable to the production of a work which merits the title 'translation'. How can it be attained by someone not familiar with the tricks of speech of the original characters?

No sane individual will dispute that on many occasions the adaptation process has produced that magical brew which is the very essence of theatre. C P Taylor's *Schippel* was accepted by all as a vast improvement on Sternheim's *Burger Schippel*, on which it was based, but even with the deftly fashioned works a great deal is of necessity sacrificed. This procedure would not be tolerated in any other literary genre. A supposed translator who published a version of Dostoevsky in which several characters were omitted, others remoulded in accordance with the received wisdom of the translator's age, where various episodes were re-directed and the tedious philosophical matter between the dramatic action was curtailed, would be derided. However estimable the final version in itself, it would never pass muster as a representation of Dostoevsky. On the other hand, Chris Hannan prepared for the RSC a version of Ibsen's *The Pretenders* which cut away large swathes of the original and presented the work in a colloquial, conversational idiom which was far removed from the tone of the original. It drew the comment from Michael Meyer that 'it bears only the most peripheral relation with what Ibsen wrote. Hannan has written his own play'.

The problem is more thorny when the foreign writer is unknown, for it is singularly difficult to fathom the logic which leads translators or directors to feel sufficient enthusiasm to wish to present, for instance, Hauptmann to a public who knows little about him, only to conceal his distinctive intellectual and dramatic qualities behind an adaptation that gives the audience no indication which sections represent the vision of Hauptmann and which the enthusiasm of his presenter. It would be considered eccentric to introduce an unknown tenor to Covent garden, only to arrange to have his voice drowned by chorus and orchestra.

Something comparable is tolerated, or even encouraged, in several theatres. First-rate writers from abroad are now more frequently heard than they were in the past, but are all too often asked to keep their voices down. My preference is for those companies – Glasgow Citizens, the Gate, Cheek By Jowl, to choose a few at random – who allow foreign writers to remain foreign and slightly strange, and do not attempt to squeeze all that is disturbingly familiar out of them. It is difficult and hazardous to attempt to offer the whole world of an unknown playwright, but the challenge is rewarding.

THEATRE PRAGMATICS

DAVID JOHNSTON

David Johnston teaches Spanish at Queen's University, Belfast. His first translation, *Blood Wedding*, was commissioned by Communicado, and won a Fringe First at the 1988 Edinburgh Festival, and since then he has published translations of other plays by Lorca. Since 1991 he has enjoyed a close working relationship with the Gate Theatre, working firstly with Laurence Boswell on the award-winning Golden Age Season (for which he wrote versions of *The Gentleman Of Olmedo*, *The Great Pretenders* and *Madness In Valencia*) and on *Bohemian Lights* (the recipient of the LWT Plays On Stage Award). In recent years he has worked with David Farr, writing both the acclaimed *Boat Plays* (a verse adaption from the Portuguese) and *The Barbarous Comedies* (in which Valle-Inclán's trilogy was adapted as two self-contained plays). He has developed a growing interest in the theoretical aspects of translation over the last few years, and this article is an expanded version of a piece published in *The Knowledges Of The Translator*. Most recently he co-translated (with Laurence Boswell) Calderón's *The Painter Of Dishonour* for the RSC.

The perspective of this essay is less that of the theoretical linguist than that of a translator who has written both for stage and page, in themselves quite different activities. It is founded, therefore, not on any traditional sense of equivalence in the theory and practice of the science of language, but on the rites of passage in preparing plays for a paying audience, rites of passage secured – and secure – in the belief that different types of translation, in the final analysis, as Neil Bartlett has wisely declared, simply make for different kinds of night out in the theatre. In itself, this proposes a kind of theatre pragmatics in that the view of translation upon which this article is based, like the approach of pragmatics to discourse analysis, derives from a sense of language in action, in this case, of language in stage-function.

Clearly, the distinction that we may make between the play text and the act of performance marks the line of demarcation between literature and drama. As Eric Bentley has observed in his seminal *The Life Of The Drama*, a play has a dual existence, as a written text and as a script for performance. This duality, however, does not presuppose a natural balance, or even a truce, and in particular a literary-based criticism imposes a deformation on the play by ignoring the patterns for performance which are encoded in its scripting. Our first approach to the play is of course through the text, and all too often in our universities it is the text we 'teach' almost by default, as a partial substitute for the play as an integrated whole. If we give *excessive* authority to the text (and in the case of historical plays in particular this has often been fixed by subsequent editors rather than the original author), we are creating the danger of enshrining 'sameness' both in the canon of performance virtues and as a criterion for judging the validity of drama translations. There is a not insubstantial strand of academic criticism which, consciously and unconsciously, compares what has been achieved on stage with an inherited view of the author's original intentions. I am not echoing here the modish refusal to allow authors to possess and articulate intentions, but given the various strands in theatre, requiring to be decoded by a whole series of different talents – actors, set-designers, directors, choreographers – even the author becomes simply another spectator of his or her own play. We are all fundamentally spectators, and any attempt to develop a criticism or to write a translation from an authorial perspective, as the distinguished theorist Hans-Robert Jauss has noted, draws upon an unmediated knowledge which we cannot in reality possess. A play text is a special form of scripting which, even from the pen of the most prescriptive of dramatists, cannot be taken as anything other than providing a springboard towards performance. What are the implications of this for the translator of plays?

In the most direct sense, it means that the translator's perspective on the play in hand is necessarily more akin to that of the spectator than of the author, and that any translation done with performance in mind must seek to create not a linguistic construct based on the interrogation of authorial intention but a living piece of theatre developed from a dramaturgical analysis of the original text. In other words, theatre translation, like that of poetry, cannot solely be considered a linguistic question which can be resolved through the application of pre-formulated principles or procedures. At the heart of the creation of the playable translation is a dramaturgical remoulding, because such a remoulding creates the vehicle which transports – the root meaning of the verb to translate – the audience into the experience of the play. In other words, rather than giving new form to an already known meaning, translation for the stage is about giving form to a potential for performance. It is about writing for actors.

If translators are to re-capture the poetry, the style, the flavour, the colour of the original stage language – the sort of things that Frost declared as being inevitably lost in the translation – they must be able to do more than understand the original; they must be able to ascribe to each element of the stage language (including its relationship to paralinguistic elements like colour, scenic image etc.) its exact weight, its exact function, its exact place – location *and* dislocation – in the 'horizon of expectations' (the phrase belongs to Jauss) of the original audience, and to recreate that weight, function and place in the target text. This involves an inter-rogation of language and of culture (seen not only as the informing context of the original text, the broad assumptions of both the everyday and the heightened life expressed there, but also as a way of making theatre characterised by elements specific to a certain time and place). Only by this very full interrogation can drama be re-created with something of its original impact, or its potentiality for new impact be unleashed. In the final analysis, it is an experiential rather than a linguistic loyalty which binds translator to the source text, and it is this loyalty which permits the creation in the target language of a product which functions as theatre and not solely as a piece of linear narrative.

This presupposes a particular form of contribution on the part of the translator; namely that the translator as dramaturge must provide, in the sense of making explicit, in the target-language text (and, in an ideal world, subsequently through active participation in rehearsal) an array of information which is encoded in the culture-specific frame of reference or the paraverbal elements of the original, so that the final process of reconstitution can take place on stage in as complete a way as possible. A fairly straightforward example of this need to investigate extra-textual circumstances occurs in Lope de Vega's *El caballero de Olmedo*, which I translated into English as *The Gentleman From Olmedo*. This is a work whose initially playful mood is underpinned by a sombre sense of imminent sacrifice and inevitable loss. Lope's contemporary Spanish audience would have known the popular snatch of song that inspired the dramatist to flesh out the tale of the murder which took place on the road between Olmedo and Medina, thereby permitting him to exploit that prescience in order to create a kind of complicity between stage and audience in which the light and dark of human existence are experienced in simultaneous co-existence. If the translator is to re-create that complicity, so central to the theatrical experience of the play, he or she must provide this information to the audience from the outset. From the variety of possible solutions open to me, ranging from paralinguistic transmission through set design or Christological symbolism to the contriving of scenic image or dream sequence, I chose the most simple one by providing a pre-echo of the song (sung in the original in act three) at the beginning of the play. I found this solution to be the most effective and coherent (in terms of the dramatic logic of the work) in bathing the subsequent action in the light of that tragic expectation which Lope's original rests upon for much of its theatrical impact.

This type of dramaturgical analysis as the step immediately prior to the surrender of script to director is perhaps all the more necessary when one is dealing with a classical play. Translation is always, to some extent at least, an act of clarification, and therefore in the case of a playwright distant in time like Lope de Vega (or one like Lorca, distant by virtue of the unique intensity of his dramatic poetry) the translation may well be more accessible in English for a contemporary English-speaking audience than it will be in the original language for a contemporary Spanish-speaking audience. In itself, this sentiment reflects both the opportunity open to, and the responsibility assumed by, the translator of plays. On one hand, translators for the stage can definitively enrich the repertory of plays and authors in performance (in this respect, the opportunity for translators from Spanish, for example, to function as cultural enablers has never been greater than at the moment), but, on the other hand, they must ensure that the play actually works on stage, that it lives and breathes in the mouths of its actors.

Jeremy Sams, in the National Theatre's *Platform Papers* on translation for the stage, talks of having been excited by the sense of newness he felt when he saw Peter Brook's *La tempête*, in Paris. I was fortunate enough to see the same production in Glasgow's Tramway Theatre, and I felt that it exemplified another issue which is central to the discussion of the strategies open to those whose central concern is the translation of the experience of theatre in one language and culture into another. Crucial to Brook's production was his weaving of the fact that the play was a translation into his re-constitution of *The Tempest*. By gathering together a multi-cultural cast, including several Mali and Senegalese, to speak Jean-Claude Carrière's materially rich lines, thereby permitting his actors to give voice to the sort of accents Parisians would normally associate with the dispossessed, and frequently despised, tones of the immigrant, the director entered into collusion with the translator to extend the range of Shakespeare's most mature reflection on the use and abuse of power, and the healing hand of tolerance, into the present moment. In other words, the confidently self-aware translation, which aspires to being something other than the transparent pane of glass can feed off its condition as translation to contribute to the theatrical complexity of the performance. The fact that a play is performed in translation affords – imposes – a new level of interrogation in the multi-layered process of transforming written text into stage language. In particular, the play's status as play in translation allows translator and director to continue the process of the subversion of language, of appearances and of theatre itself which conditions the primary complicity between many great plays and their potential audience.

I came across this situation when I was translating and adapting Lope de Vega's baroque masterpiece *Lo fingido verdadero*, commissioned by and performed in the Gate Theatre, London, and subsequently published as *The Great Pretenders*. The English title, covering for the original which means 'The Feigned Which Is True', in itself gives an indication of a work which moves through various levels of deception to question the bases of our relationships with ourselves, with others, and with God. Of all the Spanish playwrights Lope is perhaps the most complete man of the theatre. In his *Arte Nuevo*, he had defended, not without a certain characteristic irony it must be said, the concept of contemporary taste against what he considered to be the excessive, indeed anti-theatrical, restrictions of classicism, a defence based on the eminently practical recognition that theatre is an ephemeral art, that the determinants of any production are forged by what is possible under certain specific conditions and for a specific *mise en scène* which is directed towards a specific audience. *Lo fingido verdadero* is above all the apotheosis of the Roman actor Genesius, canonised after his crucifixion by the Emperor Diocletian in the third century, at the same time as the theatres of Rome were plunged into enforced darkness. But, written at a moment when Lope was also having problems with the temporal and spiritual authorities of his own times, the play is as much the apotheosis of Genesius the actor as of St Genesius Martyr. Even at the end of the play, Genesius himself is not able to say with any degree of certainty whether or not his provocative, ultimately fateful, conversion to Christianity in the full throes of performance before the Emperor might not have been the result of his own empathy with his emotional portrayal of a Christian martyr. In that sense, the work centres not only on its own theatricality, but also exploits the metatheatrical to question the bases of human motivation and, interestingly, to delve into the links between entertainment and power. This is further complicated by the fact that in the first act alone we witness the death of three emperors, all of whom are playing their parts in the theatre of power; from there we move to the Voices Off situation in which Genesius's troupe performs in front of Diocletian, the ultimately surviving emperor, a series of performances in which the emotions and desires of the actors become hopelessly entangled with the lives of the characters they are representing.

So, by playing with the multiple mirrors of theatricality, this remarkable play subverts the bases of all appearances, especially the appearances of theatre itself. If the translation were not to subvert itself as well, specifically through the refusal to be seamless, invisible, it would be failing the play as play, minimising the totality of its impact on its audience in London in 1991. This subversion was achieved through a variety of linguistic and paralinguistic strategies – a series of self-regarding intertextual references to Shakespeare, anachronistic confusions on the part of characters between Spanish and Latin which reminded the audience that they were watching an originally Spanish play about Vulgar Latin-speaking characters (and therefore should not take the present English version at face value), sweeping changes of register, and actors (playing actors) beating out syllable counts on their hands.

Now, of course, this forces us to confront the central issue of where the translator stands in relation to the source text *qua* original work of theatre. Borrowing from Valle-Inclán's celebrated localisation of the literary character as either kneeling before, standing eye to eye with or rising above the author, we can say that the traditional view held of the translator is as subordinate to the original intentions of the author, no matter how these may be elicited or quantified, and that the quality of the translator's achievement is measured through self-effacement. Not that I'm suggesting here that the translator should feel him/herself to be somehow superior to the original author – the 'I'm doing them a favour, so anything goes' attitude. However, in the same way that a guide must assume control in enabling even an emperor to cross unknown terrain, so the translator must be primarily responsible for ensuring that the source work functions in the context of the conventions, expectations and possibilities of the target theatre.

This brings us back to the apparently simple idea of writing for actors, to the question of stage language. What is it? How are we to recognise it? Quite clearly, even in the theatre of realism, it is not ordinary language. Words spoken on stage, like a chair sitting in the middle of a set, are imbued with the extraordinary significance of theatre. Gesture, rhythm, sometimes rhyme, enrich the reception of the words, so that it is not a question, therefore, of writing naturally, but of creating a new stage language in every new play, consequently in every new translation. Sean O'Casey puts it with characteristic forthrightness in *The Green Crow*, the deliberate mundaneness of his expression emphasising his point: 'Take people off the street or carry them out of a drawing room, plonk them on the stage and make them speak as they speak in real, real life, and you will have the dullest thing imaginable'. It's not a simple question of 'originality' of language, especially as we all know that the concept of 'originality' is anything but simple and that most writing is born in the shadow of what has gone before, deriving from as well as contributing to a tradition. Rather, then, in the act of translation, we are talking about the re-creation of a language that is, in the original, inherently creative, a system of echoes, repetitions, responses, dramatic mainsprings and correspondences which are all primed for the moment of performance and which contribute to that concordance and careful discordance of character voices which maintain the cohesion of the source text. That situation in itself places a creative onus on the translator to produce lines that are not solely speakable for actors, but which also re-create style, voice, by avoiding flattening out the original or producing the type of cryptic nonsense, the fruit of an excessively literal stamp of mind, which typifies most Lorca translations and which had led, by the mid-eighties, to the widespread belief in British theatre circles that Lorca was unplayable in English. In particular, the translator should be aware that he or she must search for the dramatic pattern of stage grammar which underlies narrative detail, otherwise the resultant lack of cohesion, the piecemeal writing, will confuse the audience's ability to respond to the immediacy of the information flow through which character and situation are communicated.

Guillermo Cabrera Infante, the Cuban novelist now resident in Britain, sums up this creative challenge posed by translation in characteristically lapidary fashion. His 'writers rush in where translators fear to tread' reminds us that the translator must replace the essentially 'abstract, static and unidimensional' search for equivalence (the adjectives belong, at least in this particular order and application, to Mary Snell-Hornby) by a willingness to resort to the same type of qualitative leaps of expression which characterise creative language. Jakobson's famous assertion that 'poetry is organised violence committed on everyday speech' is also applicable in great measure to drama, and the translator of plays, in terms of profile, must possess both the stylistic confidence and the sense of functional drama to communicate both organisation and violence, concordance and discordance, to the target audience. Sean O'Casey, for example, created his own inimitable style, his own voice, which like that of Lorca, drew upon a whole series of popular echoes preserved in song, in street rhymes, in heightened speech forms drawn from a recognisable community voice. The 'organized violence' committed by both of these writers on ordinary speech takes the form of the paring away of all of those elements which inhibit the play in terms of its emotional reception, an intensifying of language through images and echoes which are both new and remembered. This is the strategy of the dramatist, the violence that he chooses to commit on language in order to create a language that is qualitatively new, and it must be the strategy of the translator as dramaturge if that play is to enjoy the same impact in performance. Equivalence, in short, is based on theatrical re-enactment rather than simple linguistic accuracy.

It is this capacity that we find in writers like O'Casey (but perhaps not Shaw), Valle-Inclán and Lorca, to create a type of play in which the stage language and the dramatist's sense of life combine to create a complicity between stage and audience which is virtually unique to that author – hence we can refer to O'Casey's innovative tragifarcical vision, Valle-Inclán's '*esperpento*' (John Lyon translates this in his version of *Bohemian Lights* as a 'travesty', Maria Delgado, perhaps as an exercise in what Steiner called 'elucidative strangeness' leaves it in the original, while I called it a 'groteskery'), and Lorca's '*duende*', that moment, to use the phrase of dramatist and translator John Clifford, when 'Lorca's theatre hits the audience in the solar plexus of their emotions'. The language of these three playwrights marauds through and beyond the frontiers of conventional linguistic expression, allowing us to refer to plays like *Red Roses For Me*, *Bohemian Lights* and *Blood Wedding* as richly innovative, highly personalised pieces of work. In other words, ideotexts.

It is when one comes to deal with plays like these, among the most forceful in their respective languages, that the limitations of traditional views of the translator become most apparent – by traditional, I mean what Genista McIntosh, Executive Director of the National Theatre, refers to in the *Platform Papers* as a 'squeamishness . . . about messing about with the original, which seems to be characteristic of a late twentieth-century response to translation'. Admittedly, the phrase 'messing about with' does little either for her case or mine, but her more graphic 'squeamishness' clearly reflects an impatience with the type of translator whose formalistic respect for the original boils down to little more than an obsession with linguistic equivalence, with literal accuracy. Because this attitude *does* persist. There are still translators who produce versions made heavy with the quest for literal equivalence. Sometimes they result in a dull, perhaps even confusing night in the theatre; at other times they lead to a new foreign dramatist being blacklisted as artistically inferior and commercially unsound (a recent example of this happened with Loose Change's version of the Spanish playwright Antonio Buero Vallejo's *The Sleep Of Reason*, a life of Goya that both American translator and British director left top-heavy with a clutter of incidental historical detail that destroyed the powerful complicity between stage and audience upon which this play depends). And there still are critics who either compare versions on the basis of 'x is more accurate than y here' or 'this translation is better than that one', as though it had managed to approximate more completely to some notional perfect performance that the critic carries round in his or her imagination. There can no more be a perfect translation than there can a perfect performance; both *mise en scène* and translation are essentially concerned within the actualization of a series of potentialities within the source text in a way which respects both the internal dramatic coherence and external theatrical complicity of the play.

Fidelity to these principles will inevitably bring difficult decisions. These can sometimes involve actual cuts. For example, in my *The Gentleman From Olmedo* I chose to cut Alonso's opening speech from thirty lines to fifteen, although not because I did not know how to translate them or through intellectual laziness or dishonesty, as a traditional academic critic might have suggested on subjecting my version to comparative scrutiny. In great part it was because, in a hothouse theatre like that of Lope's Madrid where all the actors who specialised in doing young gallants were well known to the audience, this type of opening speech was originally intended to be a sort of cameo introduction, a *tour de force* for the gallery, rather like a sax solo in a jazz concert. With Lope still a fragile newcomer to the English boards (this was the first play in the eventually award-winning Spanish Golden Age Season, the first in British theatre history), it seemed to me as translator and to Laurence Boswell as director that at this time and in this place a prolonged discourse on neo-platonic correspondences would actually serve to break the complicity so exquisitely crafted by Lope, and which we had striven to maintain through the pre-echo of the mysterious song. We simply ungilded Lope's lily. Another production, under new circumstances, might very well reach a different conclusion, and there is a note in my published version of the play giving putative directors precisely that freedom.

At other times, of course, this process of adaptation may solely involve substituting one image or metaphor for another in the interests of maintaining the degree and angle of complicity of the original, working from within the recognised grammar of images of the original in order to maintain cohesion. By this, of course, I am referring not simply to the problems posed by figurative language, but additionally to the cultural resonance and dramatic weight attached to particular motifs, images and metaphors, their specificity of place in the horizon of expectations of the source-language audience. This is particularly important in translating the work of Lorca, in whose theatre symbols and motifs, drawn from or contrasted with the world of nature, depend on a complex system of specific cultural resonances for their dramatic impact. In *Yerma*, for example, the anguished protagonist laments her isolation from the flow of life, her sense of being excluded from the bounty of nature, with the powerful image '*el aire me ofrece dalias de luna dormida*', literally 'the breeze offers me dahlias of sleeping moon'. In terms of Spanish cultural resonance, dahlias are flowers with funereal overtones; in Britain they are faintly funny, with overtones of an Eastenders'-type allotment. My solution was to turn the menace of Lorca's dahlias into 'frozen flowers of the sleeping moon', additionally helped by the assonance. This simple example, I hope, gives an indication of how every physical detail has to be analysed in terms of its conceptual content and dramatic force, before an equivalent in English can be negotiated.

But the most widespread view of adaptation is that the translator has played something of a more active role (I hope I have now shown that this perception is by and large based on something of a false dichotomy) and has moved the action either through time or space in an effort to vivify the re-enactment. If we accept this view, then my *Bohemian Lights*, is an adaptation rather than a translation since I chose to set it in pre-Rising Dublin, rather than the Madrid of 1918/19. The reasons for doing this were carefully set out in the audience programme, and have much to do with the play's central experience of a national history as a nightmare of rage and impotence. Setting it in Ireland allowed me to retain for a specific audience much of the difficulty of the original text (using, for example, a specifically Dublin lexis), for Valle-Inclán's ideolect derives simultaneously from a vivid street slang (some of it now unfamiliar to a contemporary Spanish audience) and the language of culture, of poetry, in heated bar-room discussion. Furthermore, as B W Ife pointed out in his *TLS* review of the play, the comparison between Ireland and Spain is particularly apt, because 'Valle-Inclán worked hard at his text, publishing it first in 1920, and revising it twice before the definitive text of 1924. What becomes stronger in the successive versions was the overt political commentary ... The move away from the generalized post-Bolshevik disturbances of Madrid to Dublin before the Easter Rising gives extra force to Valle's final vision of the piece'. This states the essence of the dramatic interrogation to which Boswell, as director, and I subjected the work. For the audience to understand, indeed to feel, the raging frustration born from the inability to influence a history flaring out of control (from which the play's shaping aesthetic, the '*esperpento*', is born), the sociopolitical co-ordinates of that history must be located within the target audience's horizon of expectations. Otherwise, in this the play's first-ever outing in English, we would not only have seriously weakened its dramatic drive, but the audience would have experienced it as a myriad of disparate details and uncoordinated voices. Valle had only been performed once before in England on a professional basis, as far as I am aware (Loose Change's version of *Divine Words*). For this performance of *Bohemian Lights*, therefore, the translator's negotiation between original text and target audience must be based on the awareness that the audience has no established frame of reference from which to respond to this notoriously difficult play. In order to enable a clarity of focus on the dramatic and thematic patterns upon which the play is constructed, difficulties of Madrid surface detail – names of politicians and places, specific events etc. – were replaced by a more immediately accessible set of details. Michael Billington, writing in the *Guardian*, however, stated that he would have preferred to have seen the play in its original setting – the translation to which he referred in his review, however, is very much geared towards the page, and comes complete with over one hundred explanatory footnotes. Even so, I have to confess that I have some sympathy with Billington's view. But as a translator I felt myself very much on the horns of a dilemma; on one hand I knew this was the play's first ever outing on the English stage, while on the other I was convinced of its unperformability in an unadapted form. My sole intention at this point was to establish Valle-Inclán as a major force on the stage, where he belongs. The particular strategy (which I do not claim as being the only possible strategy) for providing a speakable and actable version of *Bohemian Lights* was geared wholly towards that end. In the case of *The Barbarous Comedies*, on the other hand, I had no difficulty in preserving the original Galician setting because its atmosphere is struck through a universal ruralism and not the heavily-textured specifics of the intrigues of Madrid's cultural and political world. It is with something between wry amusement and open bafflement that I record that while the *Guardian* described *Bohemian Lights* as too Irish, *Silverface* (the first of *The Barbarous Comedies*) was felt to be too foreign. It's not just a case of the translator who can't win; this is symptomatic of a British theatre that hasn't yet clarified its relationship either to translation or to the journey towards otherness that lies at the heart of our experience of non-English language theatre.

It would be in the interest of all of those who work in theatre and who sell their wares to the public to have a common definition of all these words – translation, adaptation, version – or at least to agree that one should always be open about the process used in bringing a particular play to the stage or even to the page. However, in the final analysis, every act of translation for the stage is an act of transformation. The distinction between translation and adaptation is one which is difficult to understand fully, unless it is to refer to translation as the first stage of linguistic and broadly literary interrogation of the source text, and adaptation as the process of dramaturgical analysis, the preparation for re-enactment. If translators from Spanish, my own area of professional interest and personal commitment, are to keep open the window of opportunity which has opened up comparatively recently on the English-speaking stage for Spanish language theatre, then they must prepare speakable and actable stage versions. They must write for actors.

NEIL BARTLETT: A DIFFERENT NIGHT OUT IN THE THEATRE

IN CONVERSATION WITH DAVID JOHNSTON

Neil Bartlett has translated Molière (*The Misanthrope* and *The School For Wives*), Racine (*Berenice*), Marivaux (*The Game Of Love And Chance*) and Genet (the first English-language version of *Splendids*). His translations have all been published and have been produced at the RNT, the Derby Playhouse, the Lyric Hammersmith, the Edinburgh Lyceum, the Arena Washington, the Goodman in Chicago, and at over fifty other theatres in Great Britain and America. In addition to his work as a translator, Neil Bartlett is a director, performer, designer, librettist and author. As part of the independent theatre company GLORIA he has created a sequence of ten original works of music theatre, including the acclaimed trilogy *A Vision Of Love Revealed In Sleep*, *Sarrasine* and *Night After Night*. He has written three films for television, and has published short fictions, the novels *Ready To Catch Him Should He Fall* and *Mr Clive And Mr Page*, and the history *Who Was That Man; A Present For Mr Oscar Wilde*. He is currently Artistic Director of the Lyric Hammersmith.

DJ: There's very often more than a whiff of high-minded suspicion in academic circles that theatre practitioners, like yourself, actually don't have any of the foreign language. Is that true in your case?

NB: When I'm in France, I speak tourist French, so I can bluff my way through most things in French. And when I work translating French I use a dictionary constantly. I translate in a very studious, meticulous way precisely because I am a theatre artist as well as a writer, and one of my primary concerns, to do with the particular writers I have translated, is that they are writers to whom the stress and patterns of syllables is of paramount importance. So translation for me is a very precise verbal game; I'm not translating on the level of 'what does this mean?', but rather in order to reproduce, as accurately as possible, the theatrical cadence of a precise sentence. That's the essence of my work as a translator.

I suppose what I'm trying to say is that I don't translate spontaneously. Once I translated a libretto, *The Magic Flute*, with the help of someone who is bilingual in German, and there I worked from a literal translation. But that's a completely different kettle of fish, translating words to be sung, because in that case it's much more relevant to be familiar with the conventions and possibilities of musical theatre than the actual language of the original, but I couldn't conceive of translating for theatre in a language of which I knew nothing. It's not so much access to vocabulary, but rather, for instance in a Genet text, being able to distinguish between where Genet is making his text sound like Racine and where one of his characters is speaking nineteen-forties gay slang. You have to be able to sense the theatrical difference between these two verbal frames of reference, otherwise you can't even begin to think about how the play works on stage. So I wouldn't, and couldn't, translate Brecht, much as I would like to; it just wouldn't make any sense to me.

DJ: Given your emphasis on rhythm and verbal music, how do you work in practice?

NB: I work by speaking the lines out loud – that's the way, for example, I've just finished working with the Genet text *Splendids*. The only thing the actors want to know is 'How do we say it?', and they're right. How *do* we say it, how *do* you get this thing into your mouth? I don't translate plays to get them onto the page. I translate plays to get them into the mouth. So cadence and stress and the theatrical use of punctuation is something I'm obsessive about.

DJ: Tell me a little bit more about this idea of theatrical punctuation.

NB: It's to do with the particular works I've translated. Marivaux always wrote in prose, whereas Genet writes something that we don't actually know how to describe – certainly 'prose' wouldn't do as a technical description. Racine is probably the best example, though. On paper a Racine text is profoundly undramatic. I don't mean simply the stereotypical view of Racine, i.e., that nothing happens, no-one goes anywhere, and there's no on-stage action. But what does happen in a Racine play is that people talk themselves to death, people just talk. He has a tiny vocabulary, hundreds of words, whereas Shakespeare's drew upon thousands of words. So what Racine can do with the placing of a comma can break your heart! Let's find an example in *Berenice* – what could be grander than the famous last line of *Berenice*, where the first ten syllables are given to one character, and the last two syllables of the line are given to someone else? From my own translation:

Berenice: ... I'm ready. They're waiting. Don't follow me, don't try.
(To Titus)
For the very last time, goodbye, my Lord.
Antiochus: Goodbye!

In my translation Antiochus says 'Goodbye' instead of 'Alas' not solely because nothing in English rhymes with 'Alas', but also because the rhythm of that – 3,3,4,2

— is perfect, it's unbreakable. It would certainly be wrong to change the pattern of the syllables thinking that it won't matter, because it does, absolutely.

DJ: It's rhythmical pacing, isn't it?

NB: It's rhythmical pacing and it's writing for actors; the construction of that last line recapitulates the whole construction of the play. In the play, Berenice's action in relation to Titus has three full stops; she tries three times and then the fourth time she releases. It's all to do with her breath. 'I'm ready'. She holds her breath and then, for the only time in the play, she speaks on an exhalation for the very last time. 'Goodbye, my Lord.' And that word 'Goodbye', which is the most terrible word in Racine's entire vocabulary, is uttered the last time she ever speaks. Of course, I'm saying things that an actor would never articulate. I never heard Lindsay Duncan say any of this at rehearsals, but she *knew* why Berenice's penultimate line was constructed within these strict syllabic confines.

DJ: Were you consciously modernising here as well?

NB: This is where you have to know your history. If in the twentieth century you go to the theatre and the word 'alas' appears on stage, something definite is happening; either one is witnessing the performance of an ancient text, or one is in a kind of period reproduction. The word 'alas' is meaningless, it doesn't have social value for us. On the other hand, the word 'goodbye' does have an immense and immediate significance for us. In the original Racine text Antiochus's word has a very precise quality that has to do with the construction of the narrative of the play. She is speaking to Titus in the presence of God, in the presence of her own death, and therefore Antiochus may not intrude. Which is why 'alas' is not a word in the French classical translation which is addressed to a concrete person; it's addressed to oneself or to oneself in the sight of God. One of the reasons why I've done it like that is that when Berenice says 'Goodbye' — goodbye to Titus, goodbye to life — she is saying farewell to the man she loves. And Antiochus is actually saying, on behalf of the audience, goodbye to her. He is releasing the breath — it's hard to put this into words, but you have to imagine how the actors would say the word — so that he is telling us we have been in the presence of royalty, been in the presence of Berenice herself, this evening, and that now that has come to an end, that that world has gone forever because she's just said goodbye to Titus. Technically the only thing that matters is that it's done on an out-breath. The translator has to find the word in English where the actor can project that.

DJ: Does this huge amount of technical interrogation mean that your translations have to be performed in a certain way, that you translate in a way which is so geared towards a particular view of performance that they couldn't be appropriated by different directors with radically different styles?

NB: You would think so, but my translations are very widely produced in America, and have been used by all sorts of people in lots of different ways. These texts are the mapping of modern language and modern theatre over the language and theatre of another time and place, and the ultimate goal – or my ultimate goal – as a translator is to make them sound both English *and* foreign. Racine's work, for example, is profoundly rhetorical, that is, his drama is the drama of breath, of listening, of silence – my use of twelve syllable couplets for *Berenice* echoes that in a formal way, while much of the actual language reflects the way we speak now. The important thing is that that sort of tension is there, that it's maintained – after all that's one of the prime reasons why we use historic texts to make theatre. But I don't think there are any hard and fast rules for assuring the maintenance of that tension. In the same way, I think it made enormous theatrical sense to translate Marivaux into something akin to the British theatrical conventions of the nineteen thirties and forties, where you have high speed, clipped, very resonant prose. If you take, for instance, *Brief Encounter*, where a phrase like 'This is my friend, he's a doctor' can convey a huge kind of narrative circular emotional resonance in exactly the same way as Marivaux creates the tense interplay between his characters. Now if anyone reacts to what I've done with Marivaux by saying 'Oh, he's being stupid, why has he done Marivaux in that way? I don't like it', then that person simply doesn't understand the reasons why I've been drawn to that text in the first instance and which have informed the act of translation at every moment. Again, if you think *The School For Wives* is a high-minded, esoteric, naturalistic essay on the psychological destruction of two people by each other, then that's how you should do it. I think it is that, but it's also written in the language of high-speed rhyming comedy, so that when Arnold finally exits from the stage saying '*Ouf*', it's simply a wonderfully effective gag – just as the maxim speech in the rules of marriage scene in *The School For Wives* is an amazing scene of physical comedy. If you don't like my taste on that, then in that case I think it would be very difficult to handle my translation. So you make your own.

DJ: What you are saying now recalls something you once said in the *Guardian*, namely that different types of translations simply create different kinds of night out in the theatre. I've always thought that was a very wise thing. You clearly still stand by it.

NB: Absolutely. If you're doing *The School For Wives* at the Almeida or the National, you're working with different artists and you're working with a different audience. I created the *The School For Wives* for the Derby Playhouse and made Arnold a Tory town councillor. Now people may well go 'Oh, how clever, how perverse, what an interesting take on things'. But it wasn't any of those things – it was because we were making that particular production for the Derby Playhouse.

Apparent oddities are rooted in the specifics of the production and of the original text. I'm obsessive to the point where I become unpleasant to know when I'm translating; I develop speech defects because my mind is so in tune to the rhythm of the text that I lose my command of English. At the same time, it's obsessively detailed. The Genet translation, which I've just completed, was written in prose, yet occasionally the characters, who are nineteen-forties gangsters, speak in rhymed alexandrines. Genet did that for a reason; therefore when he does a twelve-syllable sentence in the middle of a prose speech, I've translated a twelve-syllable sentence. Nobody in the world will know that except me. At the same time as being that correct, I cast this production before I made the translation. And I had a tape recorder on my desk with some voices of the actors who are going to be creating the English-language premiere of the play here in the Lyric. So I've got Genet's text and I'm listening to a tape of the voice of the actor, and for me as translator the quest is to marry that particular voice to the voice of the text. That's my night in the theatre; but it really does depend where you're doing it. Perhaps people don't think about that enough, but if you have to speak Racine in a studio theatre, it's a very different technique vocally from speaking it in a five-hundred seat theatre, in the same way as nobody would expect a lead singer in a club to project to the top of their range in the same way as the soprano in the opera hall; it's all to do with the scale of the rooms they play in.

DJ: I'm very struck by how your view of translation is informed by a whole range of specifics, the space, the particular actors, and so on. But you also came into translation out of a series of more personal reasons, meaning by that the way the play impacts not just on your artistic sensibility, but also on your private experience.

NB: I'm a very lucky artist – except, perhaps, that luck had nothing to do with it. Apart from a few rare exceptions, I generate – in other words, I'm in a position where I choose the work that I do. It may not be obvious, but most artists, like other people, don't choose what jobs they do. I've made it my business to be largely a self-employed artist. So I only do pieces that I care very much about, and more often than not it's a marriage of circumstances and motivation. It's no accident that the pieces I do are all about impossible love. What do *Berenice*, *The School For Wives*, and *Le Misanthrope* all have in common? There's a strand in a lot of my work concerning the notion of impossible love, a love where the impossibilities are simultaneously emotional and social. So for instance, because I was known at the time of *The School For Wives* as a gay performance artist, I would read Agnes's letter, which begins 'I want to write you a letter but don't know how' – a letter that I found so moving, because you have a sixteen-year old who has been locked up all her life and when she sees a young man, she falls for him, and in the reading of that letter I would answer the question of why I had translated that play – I *am* Agnes. It's as simple as that.

Then at the time of *Berenice*, other people were asking me, as I was myself, if I was going to do a piece of work about AIDS. And the answer was always no. I don't like pieces of work which are *about* something – issue-based work is anathema to me, it's not the art I make. At that time my bedtime reading was

Berenice, so when I met Tim Albery and he told me he'd always wanted to do a Racine play, we quickly decided to work together on it. *Berenice* is a play about what it feels like when you know you are going to have to say goodbye to someone; but it takes a very long time for you to reach the point where you can actually bring yourself to do it. The play isn't about AIDS, of course it isn't; and I never said it was going to be about that, although if asked, I could say that for me, that is exactly what it's about. It is a play which describes the grief of loss, but my experience of other people's death is primarily through the situation of AIDS. Of course, we could devise, write, translate a contemporary play *describing* contemporary grief over the losing of someone in a long drawn-out, protracted way, but there can never be a text which makes you *feel* grief in the way Racine's does. I think that the *Berenice* text is the greatest description of what it feels like to have your heart broken by loss ever written. So there are very private reasons why I translated this piece, and I am an artist who transforms private reasons into oblique public gestures.

DJ: Does this mean that there's a part of your artistry which can only be expressed through translation/adaptation?

NB: That's a very good question. So why do I do this? Why don't I create an original work about someone like me trying to express what they feel about AIDS? Actually the answer is that if there are some things of which we cannot speak, let us make a translation. For me, there are some things I don't want to talk about. I think colloquial speech, realistic speech is an inappropriate way of talking about love/death, therefore, I choose to borrow these pieces with their extraordinarily fine high language.The people whom I translate are the highest of stylists, Racine, Marivaux and Genet – the highest in the pantheon, inhabiting the very stratosphere of literature, especially when we consider them technically. They provide me with a direct arena of expression that is reflected in other ways throughout my work; I write operas and musical comedies and strange sort of semi-pornographic and semi-religious performance pieces and I direct extremely theatrical versions of extremely theatrical texts. That's my language. But I do find that the dead are a great alibi; that's why we do these plays. I wouldn't dare say what Berenice says, but Racine did, and that provides a great opportunity for me.

DJ: So you work very much from the sensibility of the gay translator. . . is that a fair statement?

NB: Oh, it's absolutely fair. I am an artist and I am gay, but not necessarily in that order. Everything I do is informed by my cultural position.

DJ: Including, of course, your choices of what you translate?

NB: Everything, absolutely everything. And people should think about that because although I've just done Genet, I don't know if anyone would read my translation of *Berenice* and say this is distinctively the product of a gay sensibility?

DJ: No, I don't think so. But you've already said that you come to that text in the guise of an alibi-maker, which has always struck me as one of the most interesting and intimate ways of understanding the work of any translator. Besides, I think that people generally have a very limited idea of what gay culture is.

NB: That sounds odd, but I'm sure it's true. Basically we say, if it is a gay translation of *Berenice*, then that means Berenice was some sort of drag queen, doesn't it? Or that there should be some sign of gay culture in the transference from one language to another, and that's not what I mean at all. All I would say is that my experience of a distinctive part of the gay life of the late eighties and nineties allowed me to feel that I was entitled to the miracle of that play. If you're not emotionally entitled to do it, then you shouldn't. It's not to be taken lightly.

DJ: You've actually talked about a whole battery of attributes a translator must have, the technical skills, the actors, the emotional commitment...

NB: Although I'd also like to say that I don't think this is how it always needs to be done. I'm an admirer of people who just do it. Where we're sitting here, in the Hammersmith Lyric, an Edwardian artist called Herbert did a very famous production of *La vie parisienne*, a wonderful piece of theatre although he never even read the original – he just listened to the music, and then wrote the story and the words to it. But it's still a great translation, a great contemporary version of that piece. I can't stress too strongly that I don't think mine is the right way to do it. This is the way that I do it, which people may or may not find useful for their own theatre practice. But there's another way of doing it, where you just say 'Darling we've got to get this show on in two weeks, so we'll just write something', and I admire that enormously. A translator for whom I have the highest admiration is Robert David Macdonald, who has the great ability to do both. With his left hand he's the most scrupulous of translators, and with his right he pulls off the most amazing kind of stunts. What he's saying is 'Let's not worry about what happened in the original show, let's make it our show', and he does that with the most rock-bottom fidelity to the inspiration of the original. He knows why he's making theatre and it shows in every line of his translations. He's translating every sentence as a theatre artist, and he's a gift to actors.

DJ: But is there not some kind of confusion for the ordinary person who wants to see the play as to whether it's by Lorca, say, or by Robert David Macdonald? I suppose I'm coming back to the rather more academic gripe which I voiced in my first question.

NB: Well in that particular case it was by Lorca because that was one of his most faithful versions. But what does fidelity mean? All the old points about whether we are being true to the spirit or to the letter are really important. The answer is, on the broad canvas, we will be true to both, thank you very much. But when there are occasions when it's impossible to be true to both, then go for the spirit. The theatre artists whom one really loves, the authors one really loves, I know if they could phone us up from Hades, which is where all artists end up, they'd say 'Good on you, what's the house? Are we selling many tickets?' I'm being funny, but I really believe that. I don't have any time for 'Oh, you translated that word wrong!'

DJ: In his article in this book, Joseph Farrell uses a metaphor which clearly alludes to the possible dangers – or irritation – inherent in intrusive translation. He talks about being in a restaurant and ordering some wonderful dish from some wonderful chef and on the way out the waiter, with his frustrated creative sensibilities, adds tomato sauce in a belief that this would improve the dish as a product to be consumed. How do you feel about it?

NB: It's a useful metaphor, a very precise one. It's not 'I dropped the tray and picked everything up in a different order'. It's 'I put ketchup on top of it'. You're putting something on top of something. What you're actually saying in the context of historic pieces is that, in order to make this work as a contemporary piece, we have to add another dimension, throw something on top of it. If you're doing that you should say so, and it's a dangerous game. A lot of people, notably some academics, had a problem with my *Misanthrope*. The first line of my translation is 'What's up Doc?' and people said 'For God's sake, we've come to see a Molière play! How dare you say that? That's a classic example of putting ketchup on top'. But I would say, in all good faith, that the first line of *Le Misanthrope* is '*Qu'est-ce donc?*' It is, in its own time, a radically informal, cheeky, transgressive opening line, and the relationship between the characters is of a man who makes bad jokes at a man with no sense of humour. Now can you think of a more exact replacement for '*Qu'est-ce donc?*' Some people have said of my own work, 'He's throwing ketchup on top of it'. My answer is I've got very substantial academic grounds to do with the study of theatre history, in addition to a knowledge of the plays, for doing what I've done. I've caught the spirit, I've translated the letter, I've made a night out in the theatre. A different night out in the theatre.

DECLAN DONNELLAN: THE TRANSLATABLE AND THE UNTRANSLATABLE

IN CONVERSATION WITH DAVID JOHNSTON

Together with Nick Ormerod, Declan Donnellan founded Cheek By Jowl in 1981, a company that was rapidly to become one of the most exciting and forceful in British theatre. Characterised by its commitment to classic theatre, the company's twenty-three productions to date have included *Andromache*, *The Cid*, *A Family Affair* and, in Donnellan's own version, *Don't Fool With Love*. Through this commitment, the company has played a vital role in turning British attention to the great classics of European theatre, sharpening audience appetite and paving the way for the current revival of interest in drama in translation. In addition to his directing work in the National Theatre – *Fuente Ovejuna*, *Peer Gynt* and *Sweeney Todd*, among others – Declan Donnellan has also directed *The Rise And Fall Of The City Of Mahagony* for the English National Opera, and has co-written and co-adapted a number of works, including *Lady Betty* (with Paddy Cunneen) and *Vanity Fair* (with Nick Ormerod). With a number of prestigious awards to his credit, he is without doubt one of the leading directors of the last fifteen years.

DJ: Can I start by asking you why you choose *Don't Fool With Love* as your sole piece of translation to date?

DD: For very practical reasons; it was in French and not in verse – so some of the insurmountable challenges were removed. I felt that I knew the language of the play in the sense of dramatics, style. I would like to go on to try some Racine and Corneille, but they are really very difficult. It's important to know the range of appropriate options open to you in English in order to keep within the horizons of the original writer. I can do that with De Musset.

DJ: One of the phrases that people use a lot nowadays is 'to get inside the skin' of the original writer. As a dramatist in your own right, did you find an immediate empathy?

DD: Yes, I felt that I knew what the play was about. Although I have to say that's not usually the case when I direct Shakespeare; we discover what the plays are about in rehearsal, but I don't feel I do anything as a dramatist on that scale. Of course there were many things we did discover in rehearsal. But I did find it quite easy to translate that particular French clarity. It's interesting that there's no real word in French for 'confusing' or 'misleading', although the French get very angry when you suggest that their language might have certain inadequacies. They say *'non, non, ambigu'* when actually 'ambiguous' is a completely different word from 'confusing'. I have had rows with very intelligent French people who cannot see the difference between ambiguity and confusion. French is all to do with being clear, neat and precise, and I felt that I could deal with that whereas I wouldn't particularly like to translate, for example, poetry by Baudelaire, because his work is much more dependent on romantic ambiguity. *Don't Fool With Love*, although looking forward to the Romantic period, has its roots very much in eighteenth-century reason.

DJ: But there's no shortage of the purple passages of high-flown romanticism.

DD: I coped with them as best I could. The translator needs to be aware of the possible dangers in any particular style; there comes a moment when you have read it and reread it, then you put it down and try to re-form it. But it comes from a totally different part of your brain, so there is no actual mechanism by which you can actually translate systematically. There is no such thing as a uniform approach to translation. In translation you are re-forming something. At times you have to confront that strange artistic creature of having to forget in order to remember. You learn the sentence or section you are doing, you learn it as completely as you can and then you put it down and somehow you have to forget it so that you can re-create it. Whereas in the next section, you find that you can re-form it virtually as it stands in the original.

DJ: The thing that strikes me as very interesting about your experience is that you must have been very much the servant to the master on one hand, while on the other you are your own director for your own company. You are loyal to De Musset in the first instance and subsequently you channel the play towards your expectations of actual performance.

DD: The way that Nick Ormerod and I work is that we don't really have a very clear view of what we are going to do at the outset. We select the play, we choose the actors and then assemble in a room to try and do it as well as we can. What is unusual about how Nick and I work together is that he does not design any of the costumes or set or come to any production conclusions until we are well into rehearsal. That's why it's very difficult for us to work at The National, because designs have to come beforehand, so we don't have the luxury of being able to respond to whatever happens to come up in rehearsal. It was quite simple being two masters because I translated the play as well as I could from De Musset's point of view, and then as director I went in separately and I cut the bits I would normally have cut anyway, treating it as I would any normal given text. The truth is though that I found very few pieces of the translation that I wanted to change in rehearsal, and very often the pieces that I did attempt to change drew quite cross reactions from the actors because they were very fond of the original translation. I found that quite funny.

DJ: So you actually approached the play in separate stages, one as translator and later on as director/adaptor?

DD: I translated the play because I knew I was going to direct it, but I found that they were from very different parts of my mind. In fact, in rehearsal I was always referring back to the French original. I took that as my text.

DJ: Had your work as translator finished by the time you started to direct?

DD: It had, but I did make some changes. I have to say that I have seen some terrible things happen in rehearsal when people don't commit to the text before rehearsal begins. That actually undercuts the whole experience of writing a new play. It's genuinely very undermining for the actor to feel that the ground rules are changing underneath him because when there are so many variables, the only constant is the text. If the text starts to change, it's not always wrong; it can be very exciting. But in an English rehearsal period we are very wary because we have only six weeks, which is really *just* long enough; long enough for the actors to tackle their parts, but if you start to change the text in the six week period, then I think you are asking for trouble.

DJ: When you were involved in the process of translation, did you introduce any structural changes? For example, to the chorus?

DD: The chorus is as was. It was very well received although one right-wing newspaper was very cross, saying that we had tried to change Shakespeare into a house dramatist and that we had invented the scene with the Duke of Arden's father dying. But it *is* in the original. We have to try and take that as a compliment because originals are often much more extraordinary than you would imagine. The trick is to recognise what will work. The abrupt ending, the way the chorus finishes, all of that is in the original.

DJ: You pre-empted my next question, about the abrupt ending.

DD: Very often, when you translate, it is important to be able to preserve the rhythms of the original, wherever they work. '*Adieu, elle est morte*'. '*Adieu Perdican*' just translated exactly as it is. Nick and I have done a lot of work abroad; we did *Macbeth*, for example, at the Finnish National Theatre in Helsinki. Finnish, as you know, is a non-IndoEuropean language, which means that, unlike languages like Rumanian, where you can identify verbs and nouns and can vaguely work out what people are saying, Finnish is completely different. I was working on the great temptation scene between Macbeth and Lady Macbeth, the 'Will you do it, will I do it?', which climaxes in the 'If we fail. . .'. The impact of the scene relies on the fact that it is the first time Shakespeare uses 'we' in the scene. I was trying to work on this word 'we', developing this idea that 'we' signalled the first time they had come together as a unit. I was very frustrated and couldn't work out why it was taking so long for the actors to grasp that, before realising that it had been translated as 'what will happen if it doesn't work'. I learnt a lot from that about the implications of translation. Another wonderful example is 'tomorrow and tomorrow and tomorrow', where the difference lies between good Finnish and bad English. Shakespeare sometimes doesn't write what we consider 'good' English. I have learnt quite a lot negatively, and one of the values which has emerged from that learning process is that of simplicity. I think it is quite useful being a director because you tend to get used to translators showing off. There is a line in Ibsen that says 'This house smells of death', translated recently as 'It has a posthumous air about it'. The general point is that translators can often try to make things more complicated than they need be.

DJ: Leaving your Shakespeare aside, Cheek By Jowl tends to specialise in translated plays. What do you look for in a translator in or a piece of translation?

DD: Well, I think I look for various things; first of all you have to know the original. . . I mean the spirit and energy of the original.

DJ: Do you need to know the language of the original?

DD: You don't need to understand the language to understand the sense of the original. It's very difficult to explain. I do read a lot of translations and I have done an enormous amount of work with translators, as you say, so I've built up a sense of something – the spirit of the play, I suppose you might call it – which needs to be contained within the translation for it to work on stage. So that is one very important thing – that the basic spirit of the play is translated. Of course when you come to a very great play like a Shakespeare, there are a great many plays in there. As I said, Nick and I work all over the world with actors who very often do plays in their own language. Last summer in Nantes, under the auspices of the European Theatre Union, we did a workshop on *Measure For Measure*, with two actors from each of the participating theatres. So we had two Russians, two Rumanians, Swedes, French, Hungarians, Catalans and so on, all doing *Measure...* in their own languages. One central point kept emerging in our discussions. It is a very great play but what you often find is that a translator, no matter how excellent, can only translate one part, so that you might get somebody who is very good at finding a voice for Macbeth, but who has no means of doing the heightened poetic pieces. And very often you will find that the same writer is unable to do what Shakespeare does and that is to bring you down smoothly into the domestic banality of some lines; to change gear the way Shakespeare does. That quality is almost impossible to find. I think the other thing to say is more subjective. If I read Lope de Vega, for example, there are certain spiritual weights that you need to feel that the translator has, and if that is something the translator doesn't have in their range, then their work will always be limited in that respect. They might be wonderful translators, but they shouldn't be working on Lope.

DJ: Does working with translators give you more freedom as a director than working with the original writer?

DD: I have very little experience of working with original writers. I have always had a very good time working with my translators, although where problems may arise is with poetry because we all have completely different attitudes towards poetry. I don't mean by that that a piece can be 'too' poetic or 'not sufficiently' poetic, because that's more open to an objective judgment. The question is *how* to tackle poetry and what sort of poetry to use. In Cheek By Jowl we were in this extraordinary position, in the middle of the eighties, of starting to premiere some of the world's great classics. The question to ask is why these plays hadn't been translated. One of the reasons, of course, is parochialism but another compelling reason is the terror of poetry from another culture and the terror of that culture itself. One of the reasons that so many of my generation of directors are going back to pillage the seventeenth century in order to unearth the great scripts, is because they are full of poetry, politics, sex, the super-natural – a whole range of ambitious themes that very often modern writers seem afraid to do. I think the nexus of it all is this business of poetry. Human beings need poetry; it's not something that gets turned on and off in a generation. I think we all share a permanent and deep need for poetry, and if we are deprived we will go mad; we have to turn to poetry from other cultures and from other times in order to satisfy our own need for poetry. I feel very strongly about this and if poetry isn't being written in a way that is somehow accessible to us, the result is that most people begin to feel self-conscious about opening a book of poetry. So theatre is a place where we can find access to poetry and opera, which is another form of poetry. I think that people love poetry in plays, and that it is an unwillingness to try to translate poetry, or a difficulty in understanding the translation of poetry, that has prevented British audiences from having access to these major plays for so many hundreds of years.

DJ: So it's more to it than just the functioning of a parish-pump mentality?

DD: It is partially that, and that's what I used to think. But working so closely with translations over the years has brought home to me very forcefully just how hungry for theatre poetry we've become. About fifteen years ago the man who took over the Poetry Society referred to himself as 'the undertaker of poetry in Britain', a remark that got him the sack. It's no coincidence that over that last fifteen years the translation of foreign plays, especially poetry-rich foreign plays, has been mushrooming.

DJ: So, as translator you must have the ability to create the poetry of the theatre, because obviously the poetry of the page and the poetry of the stage are different creatures.

DD: Racine and Corneille are written in alexandrines and one of the reasons why the British public have had Racine and Corneille censored from them for many years is that there are academics who say that the alexandrine cannot be translated. I think that's a rather precious statement. Of course you can't translate the alexandrine; you cannot translate anything at all, and if you do translate the alexandrine into English, and you are not careful, it can sound like a pantomime. On the whole it is difficult in English to make rhyme sound anything other than clever and slightly hollow in that clever way. English, however, does lend itself to blank verse although there are also other verse forms that you can use. In other words, you have to re-conceive the whole thing in an *English* way. Also the whole structure of thought that runs through and structures the alexandrine is very difficult for an English audience. There are very few concrete images in Racine and Corneille; it is form as a devil of the intellect. Very often you have ideas and dialect juxtaposed or an essence which, if not wholly abstract, is certainly intellectual and cerebral. That doesn't really work in English. You actually need much more concrete Anglo-Saxon images in order for people to understand speech – that's what Shakespeare understands. Having worked through Racine and Corneille, I don't think that this is just a question of Shakespearean style – it is his style but it is also the way we understand text in England; we need a poetic image. So in order to do Racine and Corneille well, you have to re-invent poetry as a system of imagery. You have to change the arguments and, essentially, make those cerebral comments poetic – by poetic I mean concrete – in order for the whole to work.

DJ: So poetry on stage is less a matter of form than it is of impact and reception?

DD: Yes, I think it is. You have to invent the whole poetic medium; you may use the iambic pentameter or, if you are fantastically brave, the alexandrine, but then you have to understand that the alexandrine in English means something different to the alexandrine in French. It's very difficult to generalise, and I would be very wary of someone who tells you what form should be used because I think each generation, each production, needs its own translation. People should be translating more rather than less, and we shouldn't get too pompous about the system of translation, because some people do get prissy and pompous and pretentious about these things. The consequences are clear. You'll have people like Racine and Lope unperformed in England for another three hundred years if translators allow themselves to be inhibited by getting it 'wrong'.

DJ: And 'getting it wrong' can be moving too far away from the original or sticking too grimly to it?

DD: Yes, all translation is an agreed negotiation. One must be careful of course, because basically one is balancing the vanities of the writer and what they want to do, with what the whole exercise is about. I think, that said, it depends where you draw the balance. When we have done plays we have never done adaptations, but translations that stick as closely as possible to the original. That's the paradox of translation, isn't it... it's the pursuit of an impossible ideal. One of the great virtues of a translator is to recognise whatever is in the original that will work almost literally, and what won't.

FIRST THOUGHTS TOWARDS A TRANSLATION. EURIPIDES'S 'PROBLEM PLAY': THE *HERAKLES*

DAVID RUDKIN

Since 1966 David Rudkin has written six film scripts, including *Therese*, an adaptation of *Thérèse Raquin*, and the beautifully lyrical *December Bride*. As well as extensive work for television, including *The Green Knight*, for Thames, and *White Lady*, which he also directed, for the BBC, his radio work includes three translations of classical plays – *Hippolytus*, *Hecuba* and *The Persians*. His ten principle stage credits range across an RSC version of *Peer Gynt*, *Hansel And Gretel* (also for the RSC) to *Moses And Aaron*, a singers' translation of the libretto of Schoenburg's opera, for the Royal Opera House.

Time was, I approached the act of 'translation' as a comparatively relaxing exercise: at least I did not have to *originate*. That was long ago. Increasingly, translation has become for me a miserable business. I hear, or delude myself I hear, exactly what note a particular word or phrase in the original is striking; and know, desolately, that there is no string in all the English instrument that I can tune to it. At least in my 'own' work, concept and language come as one. So I translate less and less now; and I intend the translation project I discuss below to be my last.

The *Herakles* has traditionally been considered a 'problem play' – by scholars, that is: for it has never won through into modern theatrical life. The 'problem' is that at the half-way mark the gods intervene with a destructive action seemingly so meaningless it appears to fracture the play into two morally anomalous halves. Gilbert Murray abjured the play as 'broken-backed'; Swinburne pronounced it a 'grotesque abortion'. As recently as 1952, one critic has argued even that in this *Herakles* we have in fact two shorter, discrete works, promiscuously yoked. Yet Robert Browning declared the *Herakles* the 'perfect piece'; it mattered to Browning enough for him to translate it. And that giant among nineteenth-century scholars, Wilamowitz, though (or because?) much troubled by the 'problem' of the play, yet chose this *Herakles* as the subject of the first of his great commentaries. Our own century soon saw arguments emerge, disputing that there was a 'problem' at all. In 1916 – dark mid-year, perhaps significantly, of the Great War – a Cambridge scholar published a paper whose title contentiously proposed the 'formal beauty' of the *Herakles*. The argument essentially was that, so far from rendering the play meaningless, the 'fracture' in the *Herakles* in fact is a manifestation of the play's moral meaning. This was a prophetic, and fruitful, insight. Perhaps our twentieth century was already proving a more Euripidean age; in this sense, I mean, that to understand Euripides, we need only look about us, at our world.

I start – where better? – at line one. An old man comes forward onstage, and addresses us:

> Who, of mortal kind, does not know of the co-husband with Zeus, the Argive Amphitryon whom Alcaeus once upon a time begat, the son of Perseus: I here, father of Herakles ...   .

This is fatal. 'Who doesn't know me?' he asks. Pretty well the whole modern audience doesn't know him. (Except for us few Classicists, sagely nodding as we slot in our mental footnotes). Our audience is worse than in the dark: already at line one they're feeling excluded from the discourse. A translation that goes up with lines like this is in auto-destruct from the start. Nor will this be a problem only of an extinct mythscape, strewn with fossils or defunct heroes and dead gods. We have alien *concepts*. What does 'co-husband with Zeus' *mean*? Euripides's audience had no problem with that: their supreme sky-god Zeus came to a mortal woman by night; disguised as her husband, he fathered on her a son, Herakles. The cuckolded human husband, meanwhile, was Amphitryon, now the old man before us onstage. Yet in this very opening sentence, he also calls *himself* the father of Herakles.

Our modern difficulty, however, is not with the motif of a god impregnating a human woman to beget a semi-divine son. Modern mythic cinema is arguably as close to Athenian theatre as we can come: no problem onscreen, with a Superman figure, miraculously engendered on earth by a flash of light from outer space. (To Superman himself, we shall return). Our – if I may apply the word – conceptual difficulty is with *dual* paternity: two fathers for this one same son, one father the Supreme god, one father a man. Unless, of course, old Amphitryon humbly regards himself as only a surrogate father, rather as we're officially supposed to think of Joseph to Jesus. Yet this Amphitryon doesn't see himself at all like that: '*My* son', he says proudly of Herakles three times in this Prologue; and climactically he describes him quite exclusively as 'high-born son of *my* begetting'. So, both Zeus the god and Amphitryon the man *are* this Herakles's father. We have here an idea so difficult, so alien to our audience, as translator we might be tempted to consider cutting it. The question is, will this paternity motif recur: will it prove *thematic*? For if so, so far from cutting it, we're going to have to grasp this alien concept and mediate it to our audience at the very outset.

I mentioned Joseph and Jesus. Is it so alien a concept, a son of God having also a man for a father? The First Gospel lays out a genealogy of Jesus to specific ideological purpose: to demonstrate that the Child of Bethlehem, on Joseph's side, is descended from the Royal House of David, and thus is by blood a King of the Jews. Yet this same genealogy culminates in a Jesus born of a virgin.

Already, within forty years of his dying an insurgent's death on the cross, a native Jewish Messiah-figure is taking on characteristics of a half-divine hero-figure of Eastern Mediterranean gentile mythology. We mustn't work this Christos-Herakles analogy too hard: but it is resonant — especially where their story-patterns coincide. Its value to a translator is that it shows this extinct Herakles, son of a god *and* son of a man, as not so alien a figure to us after all. I say the analogy with Christos: not Jesus, the Jew himself lost to us long ago, but the Christos he became (Christos is simply Greek for *Messiah*) — the cultic figure. And the Christos I see our Herakles particularly resembling is the Christ of the Mystery Play. And perhaps we feel here the first turning of a key, to unlock this alien Euripides piece, and set its native power free. For to Euripides's audience Herakles was *theirs*. A towering form, god-endowed, yet man, in their own past where myth's becoming history. He has driven filth and darkness from the earth; he has laid the foundations of what his audience deem the civilized world; he has even 'descended into Hell', and risen... So for our modern English-language audience, our opening lines must awaken like associations, native and immediate, of our own. A tentative rendering begins to shape itself of these first lines: not a translation yet, far too soon to venture that; but a note we might strike at the start. An old man comes forward on the stage. 'You all know my story. The man whose wife was visited by God: and she conceived, and bore a son, to be our saviour...' Not one word of the original Greek is lexically represented; but, present onstage, an equivalent *significance*.

Meanwhile, in this old man's same Prologue, we encounter a casual-looking reference to the Labours of Herakles and why he undertook them. If Herakles nowadays is associated with anything at all, it is with 'Herculean tasks'. We may vaguely remember his cleansing of some 'Augean stables'. And didn't he have, or become, a pair of rock pillars holding up the sky at the Straits of Gibraltar? He's away on those Labours now; and this information will have unsettled Euripides's audience, for traditionally Herakles undertook the Labours after his wife and children were dead. In fact, the Labours traditionally resulted from those deaths. Yet here on stage are those very wife and children, still alive, waiting for Herakles to come home. Why is Euripides so violating the traditional story? He must have some reason; and his audience will be alerted. Our modern audience don't carry the tradition within them, so their expectations cannot be 'dislocated' in this way. The translator will have to consider by what means some similarly unsettling effect may be achieved. Meanwhile we learn also that Herakles has undertaken these

Labours to appease a hostile King, and to buy safe-passage for his own father Amphitryon back from exile. Now as there were also other traditional causations for the Labours, the translator should be wondering, (as the Athenian audience might be), why has Euripides selected *this* one? We note that it's the father-motif in play; and the *human* father, and this time a reciprocal angle upon it, Herakles in filial aspect as a *human* son. It looks as though the issue of paternity is being emphasized. Is the difficult question of Herakles's father(s) becoming thematic after all? And now, to complicate the matter, Euripides adds two further causes for the Labours: and they're an excellent example of how Greek Tragedy is, in an absolute sense, quite untranslatable. Euripides, in the person of the old man Amphitryon, suggests also that Herakles has been compelled to the Labours 'by the goads of Hera'. Then he adds: 'or through necessity'. Hera is the Queen of Heaven, consort to Zeus, Supreme God: Euripides's audiences knew that; ours don't. And what are her 'goads'? And what is this alternative 'necessity'? The translator must add these to the growing list of conceptual difficulties. Also we must ponder the fact itself that for these Labours we are being offered three distinct causations:

1. A motivation in Herakles himself, a human purpose: son to help his father.
2. External to him, a divine compulsion: a sovereign goddess 'goading' Herakles.
3. An existential cause: Necessity.

This multiple causation we meet elsewhere in Attic Tragedy; scholars sometimes call it 'over-determination', a usage I find misleading, for it suggests that otiose causations are being heaped upon one act. Surely what we have here are three distinct *perspectives* through which to view these Labours. Without enlarging the spoken text, or intrusively explaining, the translator yet must have the spectator visualize the Labours in these three aspects:

1. Herakles, in function of his own consciousness, has *chosen* to undertake the Labours for human reasons of his own.
2. At the same time, the Queen of Heaven is compelling him to them, for reasons of *her* own.
3. Simultaneously, there is some Necessity at work.

That much existential insight is crucial to a modern audience's understanding of this Euripidean universe.

But the difficulties are not only philosophical. In the narrative foreground also, conceptual problems arise. During Herakles's absence, when he is about his Labouring, a foreign interloper, Lukos, has usurped the throne. He has dispossessed Herakles's royal wife and children and old father Amphitryon, and now needs to kill them to secure his position. The wife, three little sons and Amphitryon are clinging to the sanctuary of an altar, the altar of Zeus the Saviour: this is the opening stage-picture of the play. Only the return of Herakles can save them. But Herakles is away on his Twelfth Labour, deep in the kingdom of eternal night beneath the earth, sent there below to bring up captive into the light what Christians might call the Hound of Hell. Herakles has been away below so long now that there is despair of his ever returning. In Death he has, presumably, met his match. Now this usurper-tyrant Lukos is not found in the tradition. It seems Euripides has invented him to serve his unorthodox narrative scheme. The name 'Lukos' means wolf. Without being seduced into landscapes of lycanthropy, the translator should at least reflect upon the wolf as a peculiarly troubling presence out on the shadowy fringes of our civil consciousness. Look out in the dark, and we see the wolf looking in. But however we anglicize the name – Lukos, or Lycus – to modern non-Greek audiences the name does nothing. Our version will need somehow to keep that wolfish, pre-urban aspect of the character present in our audience's consciousness. For a man called Wolf suggests a fusion of man and beast: and Herakles will have taken on other man-beast adversaries already in the Labours. There is a suggestion, then, in this usurper's name that this WolfKing might be characteristic of that world which Herakles's Labours are cleansing.

WolfKing can be an elemental foe of the old man, the wife and the children – and literally elemental, as when he sends for tree-trunks to be felled from the slopes of Parnassus, and brought and packed around the suppliants at the altar to burn them alive, but of Herakles himself, he can assassinate only the myth. Thus, playing on two similar but unrelated Greek word-roots, he sneers that Herakles never throttled the Nemean Lion with '*brakh*' – his bare hands – only with '*brokh*' – a snare.

Should we try to render this word-play? The Athenians had a higher dialectical regard for paronomasia than we do; so any word-play in an English version should make a potentially respectable point. And some sort of jest is needed to energize the jibe. So our Lukos might sneer, for example, how the 'tale of the lion has grown in the telling'. That's a local textual matter, and simple. But now Lukos embarks on an argument that poses the translator a serious *cultural* difficulty. Herakles, he says, was not even brave: he used that 'cowardliest of weapons' the bow. This is treacherous territory for a modern translator. The bow and arrow, to us, are emblem of all that is proverbially antique. But to Euripides's audience they were state-of-the-art weaponry, and still controversial, as to us nuclear or chemical weaponry might be. Another problem, more of diplomacy than concept, is that WolfKing's thesis is not unsympathetic to us. The bow is a shoot-and-run weapon, long-distance; cowardly, therefore. Courage is to square up to your enemy, man to man. Herakles's old father Amphitryon defends the bow: the imperative in battle, he argues, is to deal your enemies maximum harm at least hazard to yourself and your own. Courage is better served, and effected, by sophisticated weaponry. This disputation, arrow *versus* sword, reflects an ongoing public debate in Euripides's own society; and many in his audience had experienced combat at first hand, so it will have been a living issue for them. Thus some commentators argue that the scene has no integral function in the play, particularly as the debate onstage is all about the *topical* weapon, the bow, and no mention at all is made of Herakles's other iconic armament, the club. What the translator faces here is a problem of dramaturgy. This debate, quite alien to us, occupies much of the opening scene, and as it stands, gives the play a crippled start. So perhaps we should pause to consider whether there is some *dramaturgical* reason why WolfKing's animus against Herakles is all against him in his *archer* aspect? Plainly, the audience is intended to be on the archer's side in this debate. And the bow is being characterized as an advance on earlier techniques of combat, and more beneficial to one's own society. Is therefore Heracles himself being characterized in some *progressive, civic* aspect? Are bow and arrows thematic too? In negotiating this debate scene with a modern audience, the translator is going to have to alert them, with suggestive wording, to larger, living issues lurking in the apparently arid dispute.

The Chorus – old men, angry at their age and impotence – mount a great funerary dirge to the memory of Herakles. 'We shall sing', they tell us, 'of him that is gone into the dark of the earth and her depths: Son of God, do I call him? or offspring of a man. . .' The dual-father theme again. They start to hymn the Labours that he did – and the translator must consider these with care, for different versions of the Herakles story list different Labours, so Euripides's choices may be orchestrating a chosen theme. First (and always first, in any list), his Herakles wrestles down the Nemean Lion, king of beasts, who has been terrorizing a grove sacred to God Zeus in Heaven – his divine father. Herakles's First Labour – and it's a resonance with Christos that our text might risk – is 'about his Father's business'. Then he casts the lion's flayed hide about his own neck and shoulders – rather like a Pawnee medicine garment; the power, the 'mana' of the Lion, he makes his own. Next, with his 'lethal arrows' – his *progressive* weapons – he lays low the Centaurs, half-horse, half-man; and, third, a feral feminine, the ravaging Hind of Ceryneia. These Second and Third Labours are against forces characterized as inimical to agriculture, the Centaurs storming mountain-farm communities ('*therap-nai*', the root found in English '*thorp*' and the Welsh '*tref*' to this day), the Hind trampling crops. From beasts and monsters, we come at Labours Fourth and Fifth to monsters of *men* with bestial ways. One feeds his mares on human flesh; the other beheads all travellers who come his road, and builds a temple of their skulls. A picture is emerging, of Herakles, the Civilizer: his mission '*exhemerōsai*', to pacify, make amenable, the earth. The next three Labours show Herakles annexing for humanity what we might consider divine powers. Sixth: from the far gardens on the Western edge of the earth, he plucks the golden apples of regeneration. To reach this Far West of the world, the Seventh: to still the sea, for human traffic; and, once here, he is called upon for the Eighth: for a while to take the firmament upon his shoulders. But there is no imputation of transgression. By his Labour at Gibraltar,

Herakles demonstrates that he can sustain the cosmic order by his own '*euānoría*', his 'noble powers as a man'.

Across now, for Labour Ninth, to the opposite North-Eastern ends of the known world, the Sea of Azov, and the conquest of the Amazons. We seem to have a trace-print here of the original assertion of patrocracy over the matriarchy. Offensive to the Politically Correct, maybe, Herakles's conquest of the Amazons is characterized as part of the Greek act of Civilization. The translator will have to grasp that meaning, and negotiate it. Else it's an aspect of this Amazon Labour to which a modern audience might well mis-react.

There is a further aspect to it, one that in bald translation will pass a modern audience by. To Euripides's audience, he who vanquished the Amazons was not Herakles at all, but their own legendary founder, Theseus. This Ninth Labour is thus set at odds with the audience's own proud inheritance. Why is Euripides doing this? No traditional canon constrains him to choose the Amazons for one of his Herakles's Labours, so he must have a thematic purpose. Note, however, that precisely by omitting him he succeeds in bringing Theseus into the discourse with his Athenian audience. The most, it seems, that a modern translator can try to achieve here is to insist in the suggestions that this Herakles figure will prove connected, in some significant way, with the modern audience's own civic order. And now Euripides could close his catalogue, at Tenth, with the great climactic labour, the Descent into Hell, as we would call it, from which Herakles is now expected never to return. Thus the great wake for Herakles could end in darkness, ferrying us back into the narrative landscape of the play itself. So why does Euripides choose to add an Eleventh Labour, and a Twelfth? He's not obliged to. The temple of Zeus at Olympia might have metopes depicting twelve Labours, but other contemporary architecture was showing ten, even nine; and Sophocles in *his* Herakles play had contented himself with six. To go the whole dozen, Euripides must have reason. Yet for Tenth and Eleventh, Labours he need not give us, Euripides reverts to monster and man-beast: rather in ring-composition mode, to Labours like the First. At Tenth we find the Hydra – one of the oldest Labours in the tradition, to judge by its narrow regional reference. (The many and self-multiplying heads befigure an unsalubrious marshy area – hence the watery name – just south of Argos). This Hydra, a memorable image and still proverbial, was ultimately to settle in the tradition as his Second labour, and it seems strange, after labours of Cosmos and Civilization, to find the next adversary so local and bizarre. But lurking in the mention of the Hydra is a phrase telling how Herakles 'coated her venom about his missile-heads'. Those arrows again. Already twice in this catalogue the lethal arrows have been narratively in use – against the Centaurs (Second) and against Kuknos (Fifth) of the temple of skulls – so perhaps there is *thematic* emphasis in this late placing of the salient act, the poisoning of their tips?

We can never know how this passage was danced or sung, nor what emphasis such orchestration brought to it. We can speak only of a *poetic* effect, on us: for this sequence of Labours seems less a chronological, more a thematic order. Envenoming the arrows, as it were, so 'anachronistically' late as Labour Ten, serves to bring the arrows themselves into focus. And as though to confirm this, these same arrows are next immediately dispatching Labour Eleven – the 'three-bodied cow-herd' Geryon. One might reasonably have expected Herakles to use his three iconic weapons here: bare hands to kill one of the bodies, his club on the other, and arrows on only the third. (So tradition had it). Euripides has his Herakles use his arrows on all three. The arrows begin to look thematic indeed.

(At this juncture, the translator should start to consider also how this Chorus of old men is to be *staged*. We must not strait-jacket a director into any one solution; but once we realize how thematically salient is the detail of this choral Ode, we have to start thinking how to conceive a text that can be properly communicated from the stage. With each play, this problem has to be resolved anew; perhaps even with each individual Ode within a given play. In this one instance, we might for example think in terms of the Japanese 'wake', where each mourner takes it in turn to speak of a good deed the dead has done).

Herakles of course is not dead. He does come home. That much of the unexpected we do expect. His return is in effect a Resurrection, and one verb used of it is a form of the verb still proclaimed in Greek churches on Easter morning: '*anesti*', 'He is risen!' But amid the rejoicing, an Athenian audience will be wondering: isn't Herakles supposed to bring up from the dead their Founder-King Theseus too? As with the Amazon Labour, here again the absence of Theseus would alert an Athenian audience. (But not us). And now Herakles explains: it was rescuing Theseus from Hades that has delayed him so long. What had brought the living Theseus there below need not concern us here: what is significant is that this unorthodox Herakles, and the audience's own founder Theseus, are now being in some way explicitly connected. The audience's own civic order is to prove thematic too. The translator's solutions will need to suggest this.

Herakles meanwhile has snatched his old father, his wife and three little sons from the very jaws of death. He is vowing to cut off WolfKing's head for 'dog-meat' – beast for beast. He enters the Palace, his children after him, '*epholkides*','little boats in tow'. (The Greek word should alert the translator: has Euripides chosen so striking a metaphor without good reason?) And soon, from within, the desolate howls of WolfKing himself are heard. Aha, the chorus cry, 'There starts a music to my ear. . .!' Rejuvenated, dancing, they break out in a hymn of exultation that sounds a note reminiscent of the Old Testament: 'Oh shining ways of the seven-gated city, lead the dance. . . Tree-clad crag of Parnassus, exalt my city with a joyful noise!' That same 'tree-clad Parnassus' had been about to furnish WolfKing with a pyre for cremating Herakles's family alive. Now that mountain is being reclaimed, as it were: restored, exultant, to celebration of her rightful Lord. (This is a manifestation of the play's organic process, an event in its *image-system*, and the translator's wording should illuminate an internal echo such as this). Then, at the climax of their jubilant Resurrection Ode, of Herakles the chorus cry 'Of God he is the son. . . Co-begotten, son of a man and of God'.

The dual-paternity motif again, and vehemently active here. 'Late, but at last, he has come; and God's slow ways to man are justified. If, that is. . .' they somewhat troublingly conclude, 'gods still have a taste for what is right'. And now we are at the 'fracture', the notorious *coup de théâtre* that for so long and for so many has made a moral monster of this play. Enter two feminine divinities new to us. They come at the behest of Queen Hera of Heaven: her emissary Iris – to all intents and purposes, functioning onstage as Hera herself – and a subservient figure, Lussa, whose name means simply 'Madness'. Her orders are to assail Herakles, curdle his mind, and cause him to run amok and kill his own children: in the beautiful, terrible words of the Greek, 'have him send out across the waters of the dead the lovely garland that are his own sons. . .' This so that Herakles shall 'come to know the order of rage it is that the Queen of Heaven feels for him'. Cruel stuff, and troubling to any morality. Harsher is to follow. 'Else gods come nowhere, men shall stand too tall', if Herakles does not '*díken doûnai*': 'pay the penalty'.

So. Herakles is to be made to 'pay the penalty' – the Greek formula means literally *render justice*. This is stated as Hera's intention, so she is not indulging in some purely vindictive caprice. The translator's wording must make this clear – especially as many of a modern audience misconceive of Greek Tragedy as an amoral predestinarian mechanism. Scholars too have been seduced into nonsense here. Seeing only an atrocious divine spite at work, arbitrary and immoral, many great minds have toiled to rationalize it away by uncovering signs of incipient madness in the Herakles of the scenes preceding. One major scholar found megalomania even in the Labours themselves. This makes the immorality worse. It subverts the character of Herakles from the start; and if the Labours are mad, that subverts his civilizing achievement. (In fact, Herakles has been characterized as an exemplary son, husband and father by the code of the time). Logical nonsense too: if this Herakles were already cracking up, why need Hera intervene at all? Euripides in fact has specifically closed off this clinical line of escape.

Lussa, Madness herself, is reluctant to do as Hera bids her. Herakles, she says, is not at all a man one should afflict with madness: 'I swear by the Light of the Sun, I'm doing this against my will'. Madness herself does not want Herakles mad. In existential terms, this madness is psychologically and morally *inappropriate* to Herakles the man. In rendering this fearsome and alien scene, we must make the existential issues visible. There's no escaping into existential cruelty. The issue is, where is its *rightness*? Why Hera's rage against this Herakles? And for what, this 'just penalty' that she would have him pay?

Hera, as Zeus's wife, is angry at her husband's infidelity, and hates the bastard son, half-human, half-divine, he has begotten. This anthropomorphic theology looks, at first sight, naive. But Hera is more than cosmic protectress of marriage and the family; her conservatism runs deeper. There is an instructive parallel in another poetically rationalized mythology, Wagner's *Ring* cycle. Here too the Father-God has sired a bastard son on a mortal woman. It's part of a cosmic scheme that Wotan has, to breed a hero, independent of himself. Wotan's wife is aggrieved and angry, as Hera is: and what Fricka sees is that her husband's experimental intervention in human genetics will ultimately lead to the undoing of the gods. She prevails on Wotan to destroy the halfgod son. She's acting to conserve not marriage so much as the *cosmic* order. What Fricka overlooks is that the bastard halfgod has already himself begotten a son: the hero Siegfried, who ultimately *shall* bring Valhalla down. Fricka should have exterminated the halfgod's offspring too. Perhaps this is a mistake that Hera is not making. The alien frenzies that she has Lussa inflict upon Herakles are precisely '*manías paidoktónous*', 'an insane compulsion to kill his own children'. And are the frenzies altogether so arbitrary? The translator must consider how the crazy killings are *characterized*. Euripides is horribly vivid here. He was notoriously interested (and clinically accurate) in the portrayal of abnormal states; but the translator must weigh whether Euripides's hideous imageries here are merely (as some have thought) baroque, or whether there is in them some dramaturgical process at work. For that will determine how the translator proceeds.

Earlier, we had been told how Herakles in happier days would play with his three sons a game of Kings. He would, in play, divide between them the three Kingdoms they would inherit, and invest each with one of his three iconic attributes: Lion Skin for the eldest, the Club for the next, Bow-and-arrows for the youngest. Now, in his madness, he mis-reads these sons of his as sons of the hostile king for whom the Labours were done. One by one, he proceeds to kill those sons he does not see for his own, and he does so *in a deathly perversion of the Game of Kings*. As once he had killed the Nemean Lion with his *bare hands*, so now his eldest son (whom he had once in play invested in the Lion-skin) he stalks in madness round and round a pillar, suddenly surprising the boy and felling him with his bare hands. The second son, to whom in the game he had 'handed down' the Club, now has that same Club 'brought down' (same Greek verb) upon his skull. The third son (mother too) he transfixes with an arrow from the Bow. Hands, clubs, arrows: his own Heraklean attributes, in murderous dysfunction. In mythic terms, Herakles has fallen in thrall to his own Shadow. We might note also a second aspect to the madness. The only member of his family he does not kill is old Amphitryon, his *mortal father*. A third aspect is what prevents him: the appearance of a third feminine divinity, Athena, who hurls a stone at Herakles's head (interesting image), and fells him unconscious to the ground. The translator needs to be pondering, what are the cultural, and social, and political, implications of all this? And how to tune our modern audience's perception into them?

Again, our own culture offers an instructive parallel. In the third *Superman* film, the hero – who can reverse the rotation of the earth – suddenly starts to misbehave. He smashes the glasses and bottles in a bar; he maliciously blows out the torch at the Los Angeles Olympic Games; he straightens up the Leaning Tower of Pisa... The audience laugh; but their laughter is uneasy: they know that something is wrong. And the children in the cinema know exactly what is wrong: they don't need scholars or footnotes – or a translator – to tell them. Superman is beginning to abuse his powers. Another suggestive parallel is with the *shtetl* figure of the Golem of Prague: a clay giant fashioned to protect the Jewish community from harassment, he evolves into a monster, destroying his own. Herakles, Superman, Golem: each is a creature of nature yet transcending nature, defying gravity and death, and working wonders. But by what taming are we to harness these godlike powers to safe service of a humane order? Perhaps now the motif that at the outset seemed so alien and extinct – Herakles as son of God *and* son of Man – might be about to make living sense to us after all. It must mean something that, socially perverse though it may seem, of all Herakles's family it is only his old mortal father who is preserved. It must mean something, too, that she who intervenes to preserve him should be Athena, protecting goddess of the audience's own civic order... The translator's wording must generate a sense that now at last some theme, working till now in the dark, is emerging towards the light.

And now Herakles wakes. He thinks he's still about his Twelfth Labour, still in Hell. But this around him, this is not the Hell he knows, the mythic Hell, as of devils and pitchforks and the damned. Where is King Pluto of this Underworld? Where is Persephone, the Virgin Queen of Night? Where is the doomed sinner Sisyphus? Scholars have found these an odd threesome for Herakles to look around for. If scholars have a problem, how much more of a problem will our audience have? The translator has to help them *visualize*. This King and Queen of the Underworld are infernal reflections, as it were, of the Sky-god father Zeus and Queen Hera of Heaven, who between them have brought Herakles to this extremity. As for Sisyphus, of all the damned, Sisyphus is the one figure with whom Herakles would most identify himself: mortal, doomed to toil for ever rolling a great rock uphill, and ever it comes back rolling down again... Some labour. But these mythic figures are nowhere here. This is no traditional Hell. To this new Hell he must awaken as a Hell that he himself has made, on earth, by abuse of his own God-given potency. And as his sight comes clear, and his consciousness emerges into the sunlight, and what actors beautifully call Shared

Reality, who is the first human person living that he does see and recognize? '*Páter*': Amphitryon, his 'father', whose function it now will be to rear his son, gently, line by line, into awareness of the carnage he has done. The problem at the core of the play is naked now: where is the *theodicy*, the divine justice, in what the Queen of Heaven has caused this Herakles to do? And as though to answer it, Euripides has one last shock in store, one consummating unorthodoxy. For what his audience would expect now would be the traditional *deus ex machina*, god exploding into epiphany, to impose a final disposition, and re-assert the cosmic order and our poor human place in it. But our audience do not have this expectation. It is up to the translator, therefore, to suggest by wording and staging how some equivalent expectation and surprise might be achieved. For last to enter is a man: *homo ex machina* – and none other than that very Theseus, whose role in this unorthodox mythic scheme has been so artfully prepared. To the murderous shadow that Herakles has become, the audience's own Theseus comes as the redemptive answer of a man. To persuade Herakles to live: shame-shattered, suicidal Herakles to live: to live with his past to live with himself, to live with others in a spirit of '*philía*' – not easy to translate: 'friendship' is an impoverished word now for this principle of kindly interaction among humanity. And Herakles will exit, 'epholkídes', 'in tow' as once his own children had been to him, the giant who has held up the sky, chastened now and led like a child, by Theseus, to begin a new life in that idealized landscape of institution and civic order, the audience's own city, Athens.

As in the *Oresteia* – which in its argument and triptych pattern this Herakles play so echoes – here too we end, though quietly, privately, intimately, with a great step taken in the social advance of humankind. Impressed by the civic humane argumentation of Theseus, Herakles recognizes in himself a creature of magnificent inheritance and appalling capabilities. Yet, unlike many cultures we could mention, Herakles will put his great mythic inheritance behind him. He puts aside even God his father: 'You, sir', he says to old Amphitryon, '*patéra antí Zenós hegoûmai*', 'not God but *you* I deem my father now'. Yet again, unlike ourselves, Herakles will not revise his history: he won't write off the horrors he has done, as something in some bad old past to be forgiven and forgotten. Those are the darker side of his magnificence, and he shall live with them. 'I shall', he says, 'endure...' 'Endure' what? There's a deep corruption in the Greek here. After the succession of ancient, then Byzantine, then Renaissance transcriptions through which a text such as the *Herakles* has passed, the translator will often, amid larger conceptual concerns, need actually to resolve or even conjecture what Euripides originally wrote. But the thrust of the contextual argument is surely that Herakles is resolving to repudiate shame-suicide, and *live*. Hera has caused this atrocity, yet he himself has *done* it. There came, in the end, a price to be paid for in the miracle-working halfgod that he has been. Perhaps this is the 'penalty' that Hera required of him. And he'll keep his arrows with him.

His arrows, note: not the club and lion-skin of his heroic, semi-barbarous past, but these arrows, sophisticated weapons of the modern age, that have been in thematic action all along. He considers abandoning these too: he imagines them clutching at him and pleading, these arrows, like guilty children chastened and afraid: 'We're what you killed your wife and children with; we are your children's murderers you're holding in your hands. . .' Yes, just as Hera did this, to remind a miraculous man of his place in the cosmic order; and just as Herakles did it – for him there'll be no sanitizing that – so too the arrows have their share in the responsibility. They may have had no mechanical choice, but they served an aspect of him that was tragically awry. For all that, '*ou leiptéon tád, athliôs de sôstéon*', he must not leave himself naked to future enemies; 'miserably he must keep these weapons', these miraculous state-of-the-art missiles tipped in Nature's venom – but keep them in an intimate awareness now of the atrocity they have in them to do.

Euripides is a dramatist of appalling moral clarity. His 'gods' are horrifically exact in the lessons they teach; and their theodicy, their just disposing, here brings Herakles to an adult clear-sightedness, a mature recognition of his lonely human self-responsibility, that shows up our late twentieth-century fundamentalism as so much infantile and craven-whinging. And – beyond Classicist audiences – this play's existence is barely known-of. For this reason, as with two translations I had previously done – *Romersholm* and *When We Dead Awaken*, plays likewise ill-perceived in our tradition, and ill-served – I sense a particular obligation to the letter of the original. The letter will always be my starting point and my continuing reference; but where a play is already visible in our tradition – a *Peer Gynt*, say, or a *Bacchae* – a translator may legitimately 'adapt' more, for there exists a perception against which variation may be discerned. With Ibsen, of course, apart from one or two Norwegian particularities, there is not the cultural chasm that gapes between us and the Greeks. Yet, chasm and all, that absolute Greek universe, especially as illuminated by Euripides, is our universe too. Perceptual divide, but no existential difference. This leads me, as translator, to a paradox. My first slow journey through a Greek text is an act of scholarship, decoding the play as a classical object. My second journey, which may come years later, is a conceptual exploration, much as I outline above. If opportunity allows, and I journey through this *Herakles* play a third time, it will be to stop at each beat, each note it sounds, and search to hear – or evolve – an English for it. And this is the paradox. The farther one feels one has come away from the letter of a text, the closer back into the text one comes – if, that is, one is original. And this has been my experience in my recent film adaptation of the *Oresteia* too. In cinema, the narrative procedures perforce break radically with the formal method of the Greek stage. Yet, even here too, in one's recreation, if one is asking the right questions, the answers will always be found in the letter of the source.

A BARBARIAN ACTIVITY:
THE PROCESS OF TRANSLATION OF EURIPIDES'S *THE IPHIGENIA IN AULIS*

COLIN TEEVAN

An accomplished linguist, Dublin-born Colin Teevan is a co-founder and former Artistic Director of the Galloglass Theatre Company (based in Ireland). In addition to *Iph*, a translation and adaptation of Euripides's *Iphigeneia In Aulis* scheduled for production in Dublin's Abbey Theatre in autumn 1996, he has also translated Giuseppe Manfridi's *Zozos*. He began writing plays as a student at Edinburgh University, and since graduating in 1990 has completed six original plays, the first of which – *The Big Sea* – has been revived several times as well as being translated into Italian, Portuguese and French – premiering at the Théâtre de L'Odéon in Paris before appearing at the 1992 Avignon Theatre Festival. Among his other plays are *Tear Up The Black Sail* (Project Arts Centre, Dublin, 1993), *Buffalo Bill Has Gone To Alaska* (Pigsback Theatre Company, Dublin Theatre Festival, 1993) and *Vinegar And Brown Paper* (Dublin's Peacock Theatre, 1995; subsequently revived). He is currently on a year's residency at the Tyrone Guthrie Centre in Co Monaghan.

Luckily for translators, Aristotle's book on translation was either lost or never written. The latter was most probably the case. We know the ancient Greeks cared little for foreign tongues; to their refined ears all other languages were a senseless gabble of bar-bar-bar. Hence, they called non-Greek speakers Barbarians. And doubtless, translation was seen as solely a barbarian activity; for to a fifth and fourth century Greek nothing could compare with the magnificent literary treasures written in his own language. And it was to these same literary treasures, most notably the genre of drama, that Aristotle, the world's first critic, turned his attention. While I am loath to agree with any critic, Aristotle does leave some helpful pointers for those barbarians intent on translating his native drama.

In the first three chapters of the *Poetics*, for example, he argues that though everything written in metre is poetry, all poetry is not the same:

> For it is possible, using the same medium, to represent the same subjects in a variety of ways. It may be done partly by narration and partly

by the assumption of a character other than one's own, which is Homer's way; or by speaking in one's own person without any such change; or by representing the characters as performing all the actions dramatically (Trans: TS Dorsch).

Having made the distinction between epic, lyric and dramatic poetry, Aristotle then goes on to characterise the epic and the tragic, illustrating that they are clearly different genres though they use the same medium: metrical language.

These distinctions might appear obvious to us today. More so, perhaps, since the lyric, epic and dramatic are no longer performed on the same public stage, and, in the case of the epic and the drama, rarely even written in verse. Yet however obvious these distinctions, the view seems to persist that the three Greek tragedians whose work has come down to us are poets rather than verse dramatists. The effect of this perception is that it is most often poets – and in this day and age that tends to mean lyric poets – who are approached to translate Greek tragedies for the stage.

In recent years, the Irish stage has hosted a multitude of such translations of Greek tragedies. Although many of these were successful, containing moments of great poetry and, perhaps, pathos, they also produced many more moments where the voice of the lyric poet 'speaking in his/her own person' submerged that of the character. Their relative success, I believe, was due to the quality of the poetry rather than the vitality of the theatre. In Greek tragedy, and most especially Euripidean tragedy, this is located most wholly in the individual at odds with the community and/or the gods, and in the original Greek these characters have distinctive voices. It is not the voice of the author.

The second problem with poetic translations as theatre is that they tend to rely too much on the word to the detriment, or indeed exclusion, of other aspects of the theatre. The Ancient Greeks did like to be able to hear all the words spoken during a performance (indeed, there is evidence that an audience would complain officially if it could not). However, there were other elements to Greek tragedy: Aristotle lists the six crucial ones as plot, character, diction, thought, spectacle and song. To these I would add mask (Aristotle does not mention mask since it would have been inconceivable to him to perform tragedy without masks). Of course, one is free to do whatever one wishes with Greek tragedies – they are, after all, now out of copyright. However, we should bear in mind that they were written for this spectacular theatre of music, masks and words. To strip them of these elements is to vastly reduce them.

Finally, there is a tendency in most contemporary translations and productions of Greek tragedies to adapt them to suit contemporary situations and issues. Once again, of course, there is no rule that says one cannot do this. but we should be aware that this serves to reduce the breadth of the originals.

In recent years, for example, Troy has been redrawn as an embattled Northern

Irish town. While this has served to lend a mythological dimension to an all too real struggle, our awareness of the details of that struggle conflict with the imaginary mythical world of Greek tragedy in a way that, I feel, hinders the suspension of disbelief necessary for the viewing of these dramas. Greek tragedy is consciously metaphorical rather than literal. Athens was embroiled in a thirty-years war with Sparta when Euripides wrote *The Trojan Women*, *Hecuba*, *Andromache* and *The Iphigeneia In Aulis*. Yet, while all these plays are concerned with war and its effect on humans and human relationships, Euripides did not choose to set them in his contemporary world of war-torn Athens, but in the mythical past of Troy. (If the battle of Troy actually happened at all, it took place four or five hundred years before the time of Euripides, a war whose details are found in the mythical rather than historical works of Homer). Presumably, Euripides located his works here because his interest and the interest of Greek tragedy was not the explication of the petty-politicking of contemporary Athens, but the much more general examination of the suffering of the individual in adversity. These plays are about all wars and, by avoiding the details of a historically real conflict, part of their assumption is that all wars have the same effects on their participants. Hence *The Trojan Women* et al are already about Northern Ireland, Bosnia, the Pelopenesian War, as well as Troy.

The one exception to this temporal distancing amongst surviving Greek tragedies is Aeschylus's *Persians*, but this is the exception that proves the rule. Although the Persian Wars were very real to the Athenians of his day, Aeschylus chose to set his tragedy on the subject in the mythical Palace of Xerxes at Susa – mythical to his contemporary Athenians at least. Like Shakespeare, who chose to set many of his tragedies in sixteenth-century Italy, the time was contemporary but the location existed in the popular imagination as an evil place of mythical proportions.

The Greek tragedians seemed to trust their audiences to make these metaphorical links, in a way that theatre practitioners today no longer seem to do – as the Director in Beckett's *Catastrophe* complains, 'For God's sake. This craze for explication. Every i dotted to death!' (Interestingly enough, a catastrophe is not only a disaster, but also the 'down-turning', or denouement, in a Greek tragedy).

It was perhaps for these reasons that Patrick Mason, soon after being appointed Artistic Director of the Abbey Theatre in late 1993, suggested that since I was that rare breed of playwright – one with a little Greek and no Latin – I undertake to translate one of the tragedies of Ancient Greece. The thinking behind the project was to have one playwright translate the work of another from the original with the goal of writing a piece of theatre – not a poetic text – that functioned in a correlative way to the original. By correlative, I mean that it should function in the same manner as the original, in a way that is meaningful for a contemporary audience without rewriting the original to fit contemporary circumstances. The piece we settled on was *The Iphigeneia In Aulis*, by Euripides.

At first glance the choice might seem a strange one. There were, of course, personal reasons; this was the first Greek tragedy I had had to translate at school, and the sheer passion and drama of its examination of human frailty has touched me in a way that subsequent texts, even the mighty *Oedipus Tyranos*, had not. Furthermore, the uneasy and sometimes bizarre mix of the painfully tragic and the incongruously comic, and the atypical inconsistency of its characters, which has led to its dismissal by many critics and scholars, including the peripatetic proscriber himself, had always intrigued me. I had felt that this was a play more sinned against than sinning; it needed exoneration.

There were, however, other influences in the decision. *The Oresteia*, the Oedipus plays, *The Bacchae*, *Medea* and a handful of other Greek tragedies are the staple of contemporary theatre's Greek repertoire. The fact that so many versions exist, so many famous productions have been mounted and that these plays have, to a greater or lesser extent, become part of the theatre-going public's consciousness means that new translations for the stage are required not to present a new translation of the original text but, rather, to put a new spin on an existing story. Putting a new spin on an existing story is, I admit, what the Greeks themselves did, but they were not translators, nor did they relocate Agamemnon, Odysseus etc. in the Athens of their day. *The Oresteia* suggested itself as perfect for a fragile post-ceasefire Ireland, but, as has already been argued, this would have been needlessly reductive. *The Oresteia* is already about post-ceasefire Ireland as it is about every state that has recently emerged from warring tribalism. To take a lesser-known play meant that the primary onus was to present the play.

The Iphigeneia In Aulis presents a heroic world in decay. The Greek army, which has assembled for the campaign against Troy, are stuck in the port of Aulis. The winds have died. They cannot sail. Agamemnon has been told by the priest Kalchas that he must sacrifice his daughter Iphigeneia in order for the army to set sail. Urged on by Menelaus, he summons Iphigeneia from Argos on the pretext that she is to marry Achilles. Though he changes his mind, it is now too late. Iphigeneia and her mother Klytaimnestra have arrived, and the army are aware of this. Iphigeneia at first pleads for her life, then accepts the inevitable and chooses to die willingly and heroically rather than ignominiously. When the sacrifice has been completed off stage, a messenger comes in to inform Klytaimnestra that at the last minute Artemis spirited Iphigeneia away, leaving a deer in her place. The play paints all the Greek heroes of Troy as petty politicians continually vacillating as they attempt to hang on to their positions and reputations. One is left wondering whether it is the Greeks rather than the Trojans who are the real Barbarians.

Disgusted by the political wrangling in Athens and the disastrous pursuance of the Pelopenesian War, Euripides spent his last two years in voluntary exile in the then semi-barbaric court of Macedonia. It was here he wrote *The Iphigeneia In*

Aulis. Or so it was thought for many years. This was to be my first surprise. It seems quite certain that Euripides did not write all of the play as we know it since he died, also in exile, before the work was finished. The work of many scholars has revealed that it is, in fact, one of the most heavily interpolated plays passed down to us from Ancient Greece. The play we take to be *The Iphigeneia In Aulis* is vastly different from the fragments of the work that Euripides actually bequeathed us. When the later additions are stripped away, we are left with a play with no real beginning, no bizarre comedy, no strange telling of Iphigeneia's improbable rescue, and many narrative holes. The rest appears to have been added by, in the first instance, Euripides's own nephew (also called Euripides), then actors, imitators of the comedies, and scholars. Professor Denys L Page, in his book *Actors' Interpolations In Greek Tragedy*, suggests that the play underwent a plethora of additions and amendments right down to the second century A.D.

This textual uncertainty has been considered by previous translators, some of whom have tackled the subject squarely, arguing that the job of the theatrical translator is to translate an effective piece of theatre, which the standard text is (if extraordinarily melodramatic as Greek tragedy goes). I am wholly in agreement with this. However, part of my project was also to translate the theatre of Euripides to the modern stage, so I decided to translate only the agreed Euripidean elements to see if a play could be constructed from them. After all, Euripides wrote this play at a time when his life, his society and, arguably, the theatre were in decay (in connection with this final point it is important to remember that Sophocles's *Oedipus At Colonus* is the only subsequent surviving tragedy). Why then should he not write a 'decayed' and fragmented tragedy? For this would also provide a suitable aesthetic structure for his examination of a heroic world fallen into a new barbarism of political expediency. With this in mind, I set about translating the fragments that scholars generally agree are by Euripides.

I have taken a long time to come round to a discussion of the actual translating of the verse of *The Iphigeneia In Aulis*. Yet it seems to me that this is quite natural, for in translating for the theatre, especially a play that comes from such a different society and which was written for a theatre so different from our own, translators must clarify in their own mind firstly what type of theatre they are translating a play from and for, and secondly how they are going to find a correlative setting and background for the work. These factors determine the style and type of language used.

So taking into account both the nature of contemporary translations and study of the text, I decided that my *Iphigeneia* should retain as much of the theatricality of ancient Greek theatre as possible: music, song, dance and mask. This is not just a stylistic choice taken independently of the material. If we take, for example, the question of masks, we can observe in this play continual references to the faces/expressions ('*omma*' in Greek) that people are wearing on particular occasions. Running through the play there is also the theme of the public mask and private face, and, in a more general way, Agamemnon's duplicit promise to Iphigeneia of marriage to Achilles is unmasked. Using these ideas, I have identified moments where the protagonists wear their public masks, but when alone or when their suffering becomes too great, they reveal their private selves. My translation of the play culminates with Iphigeneia, who as a young girl I saw without a mask until that point, putting one on as she accepts her public role. Masks are also larger than life and so this affects the type of language I had to write once the mask had been donned.

I also believed I should retain a mythical scope; but this had also to be accessible. How might I achieve that? The present is all too real and rational, no place for willing virgin sacrifice. We also are unremittingly historical and rational about our past. The mythological world of Mycenaean Greece is not contemporary Ireland's mythological and ethical touchstone, and to transfer a Greek myth onto the more proximate Ossianic heroes would probably spark a rebellion amongst the Fianna. So, I decided on the future.

Our future is to us what the past was to the Greeks. The future is the temporal location of many of our myths; the works of Philip K Dick, William Gibson and JG Ballard offer not only dystopian views of the future, but mythical interpretations of the present. The future seems the one place we can dream of a heightened reality; there we can build Mycenaes inhabited by superheroes and android slaves, and shattered Troys, reeling from nuclear holocaust. Yet, unlike relocating *Iphigeneia* at the commencement of some actual war, where many details would have to be preferred in order to make the world of the play believable, the barbaric tribal world of *The Iphigeneia In Aulis* is wholly credible in its location in some post-civilization barbaric future without changing a single detail.

The future also gave me the key to the type of language that was needed; not the techno-jargon of Gibson, but a language based on the Germanic elements of English. A post-civilized English. A language that has reverted to its tribal Saxon origins, just as Euripides's Greek heroes have reverted to the barbarism they have set out to defeat. For example, Greek uses the verb '*sphazo*' and its derivatives to denote 'slaying by slitting the throat in sacrifice'. Search as one might, there is no one word in contemporary English that conveys the meaning of such a precise ritualistic way of death. Yet in the neologism I compounded, 'to throatcut', there is some sense of the essence of the Greek word and, in its strangeness, some ritual sense.

There still remained, however, the thorniest problem: the metre. One cannot hope to imitate the metre of the Greek in English. Ancient Greek measures its metre in syllables, English by its stresses. That is to say, Ancient Greek verse is characterised by the regular alternation of long and short syllables; English verse, much as the school system likes to tell us otherwise, is characterised by a regular amount of stressed syllables in each line. Furthermore, since Greek is an inflected language, word order is relatively free, so that a regular metre can be maintained by changing the order of the words; English syntax is much more rigid, and it is rare that a completely regular metre can be achieved.

Euripides uses a whole variety of metres in *The Iphigeneia In Aulis*, as he does in most of his plays. To get a sense of what he was trying to achieve aurally, I read several passages of the play out loud. It seemed to me that the reason why Greek tragedies were written in verse was not only to express a heightened reality, but also to beat a thumping processional rhythm through the play. This rhythm changes depending on the character who is speaking, on the situation in which characters find themselves or whom they are addressing, and on whether or not the verse is sung. Since the language I was using was as Saxon in origin as I could contrive, the metre or variations in metre that suggested themselves were the stressed-based rhythms of alliterative and non-alliterative Old and Middle English verse. These rhythms I altered depending on character and situation.

At the best of times, Agamemnon is a complicated character in a complicated situation. Military leader and politician, he speaks a rhetorical and aristocratic Greek. The more complicated the situation, the more complicatedly alliterative and rhythmical his language becomes. When he learns of Iphigeneia's arrival, he reaches knotty zenith:

How cleartell this heartache?
How begin to break the binds
Of these webthreads in which I am entwined?
Some God gameplays me and my plans,
His cunning far outwits my wiles.
The rabble lives with lighter loads,
Unencumbered they can cry
When the fates fuck them around.
Not us people of position,
We must appearances preserve.
We are the slaves of our supporters.
I am shamefaced to show my grief.
Yet it is shameful not to shed a tear,
Such misfortunes now enmesh me.
With what words will I greet my wife?
With what face can I look at her?
Are things not badnews enough
Without Klytaimnestra coming too?
A mother must tend to her daughter
On her daughter's wedding day.
Though this father grieves at how

He must give his child away.
My fatewrecked child. My sad-starred, fate-wrecked child
Who will now honeymoon in Hades.
On her knees she'll beg me;
Don't marry me to martyrdom, Papa,
For you, then, will marry murder.

Iphigeneia, on the other hand, is an adolescent girl, unversed (if you'll pardon the pun) in the ways of the world. Hence her language is far more simple, clausally, alliteratively and rhythmically. Even when pleading for her life, she retains this simplicity:

If I could sing like Orpheus,
Who touched the hearts of stones,
I'd sing so every rock and stone
Would beg you not to kill me.
I would sing, but can't.
I have only tears
And these white arms
Which I now wrap round your knees,
An olive branch, I beg you
Do not kill me.
I am young, too young
And light is sweet to look upon,
In death I would be blind.

Every character in my translation has a distinctive diction and rhythm which alter as the situation alters and the characters change their positions. On hearing his daughter's plea for mercy, Agamemnon sheds the mask of deceit he has been wearing throughout the play. We see the real man speaking from the heart, and so the simplicity of language, relative lack of alliteration and the total disappearance of neologisms in Iphigeneia's speech is echoed in his:

I am not an animal,
I have not a heart of stone.
I dearly love my children,
I would be mad if I did not.
This thing, this sacrifice I dare
To do is dread beyond belief.
But not to do would be doom
Absolute. And so I must.

Iphigeneia, however, is moving in the opposite direction. She embraces the political cause of the Greeks and so her language, both alliteratively and rhythmically, comes to resemble that of her father at the outset:

As I've been standing here I've thought,
Thought of that which is being asked of me –
And have decided I must die.
Die for Greece. Die for her hero men.
Die famously and freely.
Die by my own consent
With no shallow thoughts of self.
See now how well I speak?
To me all Greece now looks in hope,
To me it lies to launch
Our shining ships on Troy.
To me it now falls to fend off
Barbarians from our land.
And by my blood I'll help to pay
Back Paris for his rape.
I must serve Greece
And so win my own fameglory.
It is not right for one like me
To love this life too much.
Our lives should not be lived
For just ourselves alone.
I was born for Greece not just for me.
Myriad men stand ready armed
Myriad more sit at their oars.
Greece has been sore wronged
And these Greeks would gladly die
For their beloved homeland.

The language and rhythms used by a character in a Greek tragedy tell us about that character and their state of mind. They must be in some way unique to that character. For these plays to work dramatically, the language and metre must be dramatic. This is an essential element of the type of poetry which is 'represented by the characters performing all the actions dramatically'.

The last aspect I wish to talk about is a translator's problem that is unique to the translation of Greek theatre: the Chorus. The tendency in contemporary productions, whether by decision of the translator or director, is to have choruses, often greatly reduced in numbers from their traditional twelve or fifteen, speaking or chanting the choric odes in unison. Some productions do brave sharing out the lines amongst the members of the chorus, but usually it has the same effect on the audience: deathly boredom. Why is it that this element of Greek theatre, which has the potential to be so spectacular, is usually the most tedious and lacking in character?

The first reason I would identify is that the choric odes were just that. Odes. Written to be sung. They were also written to be danced to in a large arena where their numbers and choreographical formations could be seen. Secondly, the chorus in Greek theatre had characters. In *Iphigeneia* the chorus are the callow young women of Chalkis, come to ogle the Greek heroes. They are an important counterpoint to Iphigeneia, the callow young woman who must grow up very fast. Their language, while sung, must have character. The character of flighty young girls. In translating their odes I worked from the notion of Irish folk songs which would possibly be set to a raucous punky folk music. When they enter, the girls of the chorus have one thing on their mind:

Chorus: Our fathers restrain us,
They're always trying to train us
To be their dutiful daughters.
But we've escaped our homes,
Beside the barren foam
Of Arethusa's virgin waters.
We've hiked our way
Around the bay,
From Chalkis on the straits
To catch a view
Of the stallion crew
Who'll Troy annihilate.

Troy they will sack
And bring Helen back
From Paris the thug
Who thieved her.
Revenge is the food
To put our heroes in the mood
And us Greeks will overcome.

As we neared our quest
We stopped for a rest
In the grove of Artemis's shrine.

A stone was stained red
With the blood of the dead,
The huntress's heavy fine.
A flicker of shame
In our hearts did inflame
At our flighty desires:
To ogle the fellas
The heroes of Hellas
And their ships
   And their swords
      And their spears
         And their skills
            And their skin
               And their strength
                  And their...And their...And their

(Paroxysms of adolescent girls)

Troy they will sack
And bring Helen back
From Paris the thug
Who thieved her.
Revenge is the food
To put our heroes in the mood
And us Greeks will overcome.

By the end of the play, they must sing and dance with the doomed Iphigeneia.
They too are characters who have gone on a journey and learned from the transpi-
rations of the action; their mood is very different:

*(Iphigeneia puts on her mask and dances with the Chorus. The Chorus at the outset are
too sad/stunned to dance)*
Iphigeneia *(singing)*: Give me garlands for my head,
Plait my hair with flowers,
Death must be my marriage bed
But by my death revenge is ours.

Dance around the Danaan ships,
Dance in sacrificial bliss.
With my lifeblood wet your lips.
Join great mother Artemis.

Chorus: The tears we have we shed them now,
For Artemis does not allow
A sacrifice to spoil with tears
And sentimental human fears.

All: Dance around the Danaan ships,
Dance in sacrificial bliss.
With my lifeblood wet your lips.
Join great mother Artemis.

Iphigeneia: O Mycenae, O my happy home,
To your halls I'll no more come.
Young girls who cry now for my fate,
You must support me, celebrate.

All: Dance around the Danaan ships,
Dance in sacrificial bliss.
With my lifeblood wet your lips.
Join great mother Artemis.

Chorus: Death from her this life must take,
Her resolution does not break.
The light of Hellas is her flame
Immortal, everlasting is her fame.

All: Dance around the Danaan ships,
Dance in sacrificial bliss.
With my lifeblood wet your lips.
Join great mother Artemis.

(The Chorus continue singing the chorus faster and faster as they dance off, leaving Iphigeneia dancing alone on stage)

Iphigeneia *(singing)*: O splendid sun, torch of our days,
Beacon of Zeus, I must now make my way
To darkness and eternal night.
Fare thee well beloved light.

All this said, whether my translation actually works on stage remains to be seen. As I write, workshops on the translated Euripidean fragments are only being scheduled.

Whatever the outcome, however, the process of translating a Greek tragedy for performance has proved intriguing in the questions it has raised in relation to character, metre, staging and how best to find contemporary correlations without destroying the essence of the piece. A barbarian activity. But a rewarding one.

TRANSLATING SCANDINAVIAN DRAMA

EIVOR MARTINUS

Eivor Martinus was born in Sweden but moved to England in her teens, giving her a degree of fluency in both source and target languages that is rare, even among translators. After publishing five novels and several short stories in her native country, she has concentrated on introducing Swedish authors into the British market. Even so, she has also had four original plays performed, *You* (Cockpit Theatre, London, 1974), *The Misogynist* (Echo Stage Co, New York, 1984), *Kvinnohataren* (Strindbergsmuseet, 1985) and *Behind A Dream* (Riverside Studios, London, 1989). Eivor Martinus has translated extensively from Swedish and Norwegian into English, and from English into Swedish. Among the plays she has translated into English are Guillou's *The Wolf*, Strindberg's *Motherly Love*, *The First Warning* and *Pariah*, all performed at the Gate Theatre and subsequently published by Amber Lane Press. Her translations of Strindberg's *The Great Highway* and *Chamber Plays* are published in two volumes by Absolute Classics. In addition to other plays by Strindberg (fourteen in all), she has also translated pieces by Ingmar Bergman, Thomas Dekker, Ibsen and Pär Lagerkvist. Her translations into Swedish include plays by Jonson, Stephen Lowe and Caryl Churchill. In 1994 she won First Prize in the Swedish section of the biennial BCLA competition in Oxford and the quality and importance of her translations into English have been recognised by the Swedish Society of Authors.

According to the Oxford dictionary to 'translate' is to 'express the sense of the word, sentence, speech etc. in or *into* another language'. Express the sense of the word... but what exactly do we mean by 'sense of the word'? The meaning of words changes, depending on period, region or social class. A word may have a literal meaning which would not translate accurately or happily at all into another language. We deliberately use words with a double meaning sometimes because we like to hide behind words. But the double meaning in one language is not likely to have the same degree of ambiguity in the target language.

On other occasions we use understatements or hyperboles which may be difficult to put across in another language, not merely because the word does not carry the same weight but because the whole practice of using understatements is something which is peculiar to certain cultures, notably English.

We use expletives which, by tradition, vary from country to country, depending on deep-rooted superstitions or religion. Words connected with the devil are much more shocking and effective in Swedish, for instance, than those associated, for example, with our reproductive organs. The Swedish for 'dick' is even used as a pet name for little boys. It is perfectly natural for a mother to address her little son affectionately with: 'How is my little dick today then?' Curiously enough, the female equivalent is not used in the same way. Similarly, words which were shocking a hundred years ago have naturally lost their edge by now, so we have to push the boundaries and try to find the modern equivalent, which is always a question of personal judgment.

The first prerequisite for a translator must then, surely, be a thorough knowledge of both the source language and the target language. Without that knowledge, no sensible decisions can be made as regards choice of words and an overall style, of whether regional and social accents are to be employed. This may seem obvious but it is far from the general rule. In fact, most 'new' translations of plays by Strindberg and Ibsen are simply a rehash of old translations backed up by a 'literal translation' which acts as a cover. It shows a blatant disregard for the translator and for the copyright laws of this country, but above all for the foreign playwright.

On the whole, I am very sceptical about the use of literal translations, except on those occasions when a literal translation is all one can possibly hope for, i.e. when doing conference interpretation. Then there is no time for reflection, no time for browsing through dictionaries, no time for choosing *le mot propre*. One is bombarded by the source language through one's headphones and at the flick of a button one is called upon to transfer that stream of words into the target language. It requires a wealth of knowledge, a rich vocabulary and a mind which can switch instantly from one language to the other. It is a skill similar to that of the translator except that speed is not of the essence, or should not be at least when translating fiction.

Unfortunately, there are an increasing number of 'translators' around these days who could not 'translate' on the spot, or any other way, for the simple reason that they do not know the source language *at all*, or have a very elementary knowledge of it.

How can this be? It is thanks to 'the literal translator' who is asked to provide a 'literal' translation for a writer or director who then pummels or interprets the text as he/she sees fit, and quite frequently that includes taking such liberties with the original text that it might even make nonsense of it. The name of 'the literal translator' does not usually feature largely and it is never clear how many alternatives were offered and how much of the context and general social and cultural background was explained to the official 'translator', whom I would choose to call the adaptor, but who inevitably gets the biggest billing.

One such instance is the version of *Miss Julie*, published by Methuen, in Helen Cooper's 'translation'. Ms Cooper acknowledges Peter Hogg as the 'literal translator' but even though Ms Cooper has no knowledge of Swedish she ventures into a confident introduction about the use of third person singular to denote 'a specially intimate relationship'. To the unsuspecting reader Ms Cooper's statement appears to have a ring of truth about it, and students of Strindberg will no doubt be happy to learn that the use of the third person singular as found in *Miss Julie* is a very intimate form of address. But, in fact, the opposite is true.

I recall all those years when I addressed my teachers, my aunties and uncles, even my parents in the third person. If I had used 'du' (the second person) I would have got a funny look or a raised eyebrow, especially before the age of eighteen which used to be the landmark as far as adulthood was concerned. In some cases it might even stretch to 'matriculation' (university entrance exam), which took place a couple of years later in Sweden. That was the time when you were formally asked to say 'du' to your superiors and elders and the transition was often marked by a toast known as 'du-skål'. That was how rigid social customs were during Strindberg's time, and right up to the fifties and early sixties when I grew up there. When a 'translator' gets the social and linguistic pattern so totally wrong as to suggest that addressing someone in the third person is 'very intimate', then surely it is time we discussed some basic rules of translation.

I mention this particular error because it highlights the extraordinary situation of Scandinavian drama in this country. There are very few translators from the Scandinavian languages in England and even fewer engaged in translating drama. The result is that errors go unnoticed, misrepresentation likewise, and there appears to be a kind of 'free for all' which certainly has not benefited Strindberg over the years.

Several of Strindberg's plays were first translated into English from German around 1914. These translations may have been pedantic and convoluted, but at least they showed an attention to detail which has often been lacking since. For instance, when first translated into English and American *Fröken Julie* became *Lady Julie*, *Lady Julia*, *Countess Julia* and *Countess Julie*, all of which are much closer to the original than the subsequent title of *Miss Julie*. The character Julie is the daughter of a '*Greve*', the equivalent of an Earl. It is quite obvious that Strindberg intended to stress this aristocratic background and to underline the class difference between Julie and Jean, her father's manservant. The reason why subsequent translations were called *Miss Julie* derived from a misunderstanding of and a lack of knowledge about Swedish forms of address.

Until the latter part of the nineteenth century there were three ways of addressing an unmarried woman in Sweden. 'Fröken' was reserved for the aristocracy. During the democratisation reforms at the end of the century the other two forms of address were abolished and 'Fröken' was increasingly used for all unmarried women. But when Strindberg was writing this play in 1888 'Fröken' would most certainly have been confined to the upper-class girl. Kristin, the cook, is never referred to as 'Fröken', for instance. More importantly, if we are to translate the title accurately and put it in an English context, the daughter of an Earl is most certainly a Lady, in name at least.

When working on Strindberg's *Lady Julie*, as I called it in my translation performed at the Duke of Cambridge Theatre Club in 1993, I was confronted with several problems to do with the value and weight of certain words. There is a great deal of violent sexual imagery in the play, and when it was first produced a hundred years ago people fainted with shock and had to be carried bodily from the auditorium. This effect obviously has to be recreated in a new translation, but the question is how to interpret the text in such a way that we stay true to the original both in word and spirit.

After Jean has killed the greenfinch, Julie explodes in hatred and says that she would like to see Jean's whole '*kön*' swim in a sea of blood. '*Kön*' has a double meaning in Swedish. It can refer to sex/gender in general but it can also refer to the sexual organ in particular. I preferred the latter but rather than having her say 'I would like to see your cock swimming in a sea of blood...' I chose 'balls' instead. The alliteration with 'blood' added an extra dimension and the result was a shocking outburst even in today's jaded society:

> Julie: Do you think I'm so weak... oh, I would like to see your blood, your brains on the block... I would like to see your balls swimming in a sea like that... I think I could drink from your skull, I'd like to wash my feet in your rib-cage and I'd like to eat your heart fried. You think I'm weak, you think I love you because my womb lusted after your sperm; you think I want to carry your brood under my heart and nourish it with my blood, bear your child and take your name... eh, what's your name? I've never heard your surname, I suppose you haven't got one. I was to be Mrs Mop or Madam Pighouse... you... dog who's wearing my collar, you boy who's got my family crest on your buttons...

Another powerful speech is the one when Jean responds to her aristocratic condescension. He compares her sexuality to that of an animal, which in Victorian times, when women were shrouded in mystery and coyness, must have been an outrageous remark, especially coming from a servant. It was obviously important to try and convey some of this initial sense of scandal that the play gave rise to.

> Julie: Stand up when I speak! Boy!
> Jean: Slut, slag, shut up and get out of here. Are you telling me that I'm coarse? I've never seen a girl of my class behave like you did this evening. Do you think a kitchenmaid would molest a man the way you do?

Have you seen a girl of my class offer herself like that? No, that's something you only see in animals and prostitutes.

When it comes to drama the creative input required from the translator often leads to a greater search for freedom than is necessarily good for the original work. Finding that delicate balance between a comprehensible interpretation and a faithful rendering of the author's words is crucial if the text is going to live in the target language. And yet the temptation to 'improve' is always there. The question is where to draw the line. I admit to quite a lot of editing in my work, especially when working with Ibsen, Ben Jonson and Thomas Dekker. Their verbosity often cries out for a bit of pruning. But I always acknowledge the cuts in the programme or introduction.

I shall concentrate on a couple of authors who have created a new tone or accent which, in the original language, forms an important part of the greatness of that particular author. Form and content are inseparable and yet, a translator, especially a 'literal translator', is required to serve up the contents in a new tongue, often stripped of all the distinguishing features found in the original. Sometimes I think it is fear of the unfamiliar, fear of foreignness, that prompts English translators/adaptors to recreate foreign drama to the point of adding whole scenes and changing the name and nature of characters, in other words fleshing out a new English play from the skeleton of a foreign drama. It may work, it will most probably be flashy, flamboyant and smooth, and the critic is more likely to notice that kind of 'translation', but does it actually present the original author in a true light? In other words, how far should we as translators go? When does a translation cease to be a translation, when does it become an adaptation?

In some cases it may be preferable to present a 'version' of a foreign play, i.e. to rewrite it in English in order to give a neglected work a chance in this country, provided the translator calls it a 'version' or an 'adaptation'. However, there must be certain guidelines for the translation of drama if we are to be serious about our task.

Crucially, how do we put across the idiosyncrasies of a foreign author in English? Should we try and give the text a foreign flavour or should we set it firmly in this country with regional and social accents and English – or British – metaphors? I have used both methods, and I suppose I follow my instinct when deciding how to interpret and present a particular text.

Strindberg, for instance, is often characterised by his short, discordant and yet rhythmic sentences. His metaphors take huge leaps and are frequently shocking and original. It is tempting to tone them down, to 'translate' them into something more digestible, and in some cases this may be the only way, but I always try as far as possible to stick to Strindberg's quirky imagery or to substitute it for something equally unusual.

As an example I could mention his little known one-act play *Pariah*. The opening scene of the play posed a problem. *Literally* the lines were:

X: The bells ring so drily, the flies are stinging and the hens are clucking. I was going out fishing, but I could not find any worm. Don't you feel nervous?

At first glance it looks completely mad, and there is no way one could translate that into English without padding the sentences gently. The laconic style, inherited from the Icelandic sagas and the Poetic Edda is very alien to the English idiom.

But, of course, this is a psychological drama and the character X is highly strung, presumably covering up his nervousness with a torrent of words which barely hang together. He changes tack at break-neck speed and leaves the spectator gasping for air. Added to that, there are some bizarre images. 'Dry bells' for instance. Was he trying to depict a hot summer's afternoon when not even the church bells give any kind of solace? And who has ever heard of *stinging* flies? Well, I can recall many a Swedish summer's evening when they do appear to sting as a matter of fact. If you are hypersensitive, even flies can take on a sinister form and presumably that is what Strindberg is trying to convey here. The word for 'cluck' ('clucking hens') in Swedish is *'skrock'* and if used as a noun that word could also mean 'superstition', which obviously helps to create the atmosphere of menace in this first passage. That double meaning is hard to put across, especially in a sparse dialogue like this. X's sudden and direct question to the other character: 'Don't you feel nervous?' could equally well reveal his own feelings. But none of this is much help when you are faced with the text and trying to give it some meaning in the new language.

This dense speech has to be loosened up in English, and as the play had only been translated once before in 1914 (from the German) I also had to convince people that is was worth doing. In my slightly freer version it read:

X: Yes, there are flies everywhere. And listen to the hens... Even the church bells sound thirsty, don't you think? I wanted to go fishing but I couldn't find any worms. It really gets you down this weather. Doesn't it bother you?

His question: 'Don't you feel nervous?' was moved down a few lines. It is remarkable how often Strindberg's characters refer to either themselves or their protagonists as being nervous. In the first act of *The Father* the Pastor is concerned about his brother-in-law's health:

Pastor: You must look after yourself, Adolf. You look nervous.
Captain: Do I look nervous?'
Pastor: Yes, are you sure you're feeling quite well?

Another common attribute is 'ridiculous', or 'cutting a comical figure', obviously something which greatly preoccupied Strindberg. The Gentleman in *Thunder in the Air* (*Oväder*) refers to it, as does the Captain in *The Father* (*Fadren*) and the husband in *The First Warning* (*Första Varningen*). It is important to capture the emotional tone of the original as accurately as possible. For example, in the one-act comedy *The First Warning* (1892), which is set in Germany, the husband upbraids his wife the morning after a party. His wife has received flowers from another man, which fuels the husband's jealousy.

Husband: Nice German custom to send flowers to other men's wives.

Wife: I think you should have left the party a little earlier, dear.

Husband: I'm sure the Captain is of the same opinion. But as I had the choice between staying behind and looking ridiculous or leaving the party and making an utter fool of myself, I decided to stay.

Wife: And make a fool of yourself anyway.

Husband: Why do you want to be married to a fool? I would never choose a silly woman for my wife.

Wife: Poor you.

Husband: Yes, I feel rather sorry for myself too. But do you know why I cut such a comical figure?

Wife: No, do enlighten me. Your answer is bound to be wittier than mine.

Husband: Because I'm still in love with my wife. . . even after fifteen years of marriage.

Wife: Is it really fifteen? Do you keep a record of every move?

Husband: No, I'm too erratic a player. But you who always treat life like a game would be well advised to count your moves.

The last reference to 'moves' and 'game' was an 'interpretation', as the original metaphor would have lost its meaning or taken on a totally different and undesirable meaning in English. After the wife says 'Is it really fifteen?' she adds *literally*: 'Do you walk around with a pedometer?' The husband then adds *literally*: 'On my thorny path? No! But you who *dance along on roses* should perhaps count your steps soon...'

The Swedish expression '*en dans på rosor*' ('dancing on roses') means life is easy, the English equivalent being 'a bed of roses'. In this particular context 'a bed of roses' would give rise to associations which are a bit too advanced for this little flirtation. Besides, you don't have to count any *steps* when you *lie* on a bed of roses. I decided that treating it like a game would give greater scope to play around with metaphors. And a game usually consists of certain moves, moves lead somewhere and you can count moves. It also has the advantage of making the wife seem a little calculating, but not blatantly so.

'You see the husband who is in love with his wife is in a terrible predicament', cries the jealous husband.

As you work with Strindberg you soon realise that he is very fond of 'settling his accounts'; he never seems to 'get rid of his creditors'; they turn up in his naturalistic period and stay with him right through to his last play. In *Thunder In The Air*, the first chamber play, the Man utters: 'I am just in the process of settling my accounts with the people now and I have already started to pack, so to speak, for the ultimate journey'.

Here I resort to a slight over-simplification. In the Swedish he says: 'I am settling my accounts with life and people and I have already started to pack for the journey'. I cut out 'life' and added 'so to speak' and 'ultimate' instead. The phrase would have jarred too much in English and yet I wanted to retain the meaning of a final reckoning. But over-simplification can also have its pitfalls.

In Strindberg's last play *The Great Highway* (*Stora Landsvägen*) the main character, the Hunter, says in scene seven: 'I want to be alone when I settle my accounts'. The Tempter answers: 'Ha! Ha! Is it time to pay the outstanding bills? In that case, I shall present you with invoices, bills and suits. . .' In Swedish the Tempter says *literally*: 'Has the day of payment arrived?' ('*betalningsdagen*'). It may look ambiguous to an English eye at first, because of the close resemblance to 'pay day' but they are two completely different words in Swedish. The day you get your wages or your salary is called '*avlöningsdag*'. An easy mistake to make if you are not too familiar with the language, but it can change the whole meaning of a scene. In one version of the play that I saw a few years ago the translator had chosen the word 'payday', which of course changed the meaning of this particular scene. By implying that it was 'pay day' we are confused about the Tempter's reference to bills etc.

Apart from problems with imagery and symbolism, there are other less tangible difficulties when it comes to translating Strindberg. Miss Lind-Af-Hageby, who wrote *Strindberg, A Study* in 1927, defined his style as follows:

> Strindberg introduces an idiomatic Swedish which, in a sense, is not reproducible in another language. His sentences, whether in the dialogue of a drama, or in the story of a novel, are wrought with a nervous force which is untranslatable. His phrases seem to be innervated, warm-blooded entities, and support the theory that the sentence preceded the word in the evolution of speech. He is often ungrammatical; each sentence is a living whole which cannot be divided. Analyse him with syntax and dictionary and you will find 'mistakes' and startling neology. The meaning will sometimes be obscure. But read him as you would listen to a piece of music with your ear to the harmonics, and you will find a consummate artist in words.

Strindberg also has a perfect ear for social accents, choice of register and words in his different characters. His text is a tightly woven tapestry, to use one of his own metaphors, with every character weaving his own particular thread. Finding an equivalent to this in the English language can be quite a challenge. Besides, Strindberg quite happily mixes a heightened prose with clichés when it seems right for the occasion, like in *The Great Highway*. The satirical passages are rendered in a staccato form which highlights the absurd elements, and the lyrical speeches are written in unrhymed, unnumbered iambic verse.

Translating Strindberg is a bit like following an expert partner in a tango. You've got to make sure you know the steps, then feel the music, adopt the correct stance, trust in your partner and let the dance carry you along. There are, of course, a few basic rules without which we could not venture out onto the dance floor. The tango is not an easy dance, nor is Strindberg an easy writer to translate.

He was steeped in a classical tradition which more or less ceased at the end of the sixties, he knows his Bible and frequently alludes to it, he knew about half a dozen languages, he was a practising artist and was no stranger to chemistry, physics or astronomy. All this knowledge is somehow absorbed in his writing and he often sends his translator on a detective hunt for flowers and fruit which are no longer known by the same name. It took me a while, for instance, before I realised that 'melon' was a special variety of apple at the turn of the century. I was also bemused by a reference to a tobacco plantation in *The Pelican* but apparently they did grow a certain kind of tobacco in Sweden a hundred years ago. When confronted with a number of mouth-watering varieties of apples in Swedish I realised that many of them had unfamiliar names and it would not do to use well-known English names, so I contacted a 'plant doctor' who runs a large gardening centre in Hampshire, and he managed to find half a dozen varieties which were cultivated at the turn of the century.

While translating Strindberg's plays I have often had to draw on my group of friends for advice: a lawyer who can explain the legal parlance, a clergyman who can place an allusion to the Bible immediately if I am in a hurry, although I have a very useful encyclopedia of Bible quotations both in English and Swedish. I also have two sets of Bibles in both languages: the modern version and the King James (and Swedish equivalent) version. Other essential reference books for translating Strindberg are works on Eastern Mysticism, Botany, Swedish and European History, craftsmen's terminology, Greek and Nordic mythology and technological terms which were extremely modern when Strindberg used them, but which are now out of date. There will undoubtedly come a time, very soon, when audiences need an explanation for a classical or biblical inclusion. For instance, when Lady Julie refers to Jean as Joseph (after he has rejected her advances) she is expressing the fact that she is hurt:

> Lady Julie: . . . how incredibly conceited you are. A Don Juan perhaps.
> Or a chaste Joseph who will not be tempted? Yes, I believe you're a Joseph.

The original Swedish read, literally translated: '. . . how incredibly conceited you are. A Don Juan perhaps. Or a Joseph? I do believe you're a Joseph!' The reason for including 'chaste' and 'who will not be tempted' was simply that I don't think that many people today would understand the allusion to Potiphar's wife and her seduction of Joseph in Egypt. An explanation was necessary here. It is no good having a footnote in performance.

Key-terms like 'guilt', 'blame', 'innocence' also abound in Strindberg's plays. Their emotional weight requires careful negotiation at every moment.

In the first scene of *The Father* when the Captain and the Pastor are talking to Nöjd about his relationship with the kitchen maid, the Captain plays around with the words '*skuld*', '*skyldig*', and '*oskyldig*' ('guilt', 'guilty' and 'innocent'):

> The boy is probably not entirely blameless. . . you can't tell of course,
> but the only thing we can be absolutely sure of is that the girl is not innocent.

The Swedish was funnier because Strindberg could use the same words, only adding a prefix and the meaning became ambiguous. The boy is probably not entirely '*oskyldig*' meaning two things: blameless and a virgin. Whereas the girl is definitely not a virgin, not innocent, i.e. '*skyldig*'.

One passage in act one of *The Father* which almost brought me to a standstill was Bertha's affectionate speech addressed to her father. *Literally* she says:

> Oh it is always so gloomy in there, so horrible, as if it were a winter's night, but when you come, father, it is like when you take out the inner windows on a spring morning.

In Sweden, they used to employ a system of secondary glazing which was fixed to the windows on the inside and left there throughout the winter. The fresh air would come in through the front or back door, but in the spring the inner windows were taken down and stored in the shed or the attic. A very dramatic event and a metaphor for spring, of course. Well, one thing is certain, we can't use the simile about the windows, I decided. Any 'double glazing' or 'secondary glazing' or American 'storm windows' would sound completely alien to an English audience in this context.

So we had to abandon that beautiful period image, but obviously it is important to retain the idea that the father represents all that is fresh, green and healthy whereas the rest of the household has a more suffocating effect on the young girl.

This view is given more poignancy as the play progresses, when the father is brought to despair and declared insane. In my translation, therefore, Bertha says:

Oh it is always so gloomy in there, so horribly dark. . . like a winter's night, but when you come home daddy, it's like spring's arrived.

Another difficult line was Laura's reference to their sexual relationship:

Although I enjoyed your embraces they were followed by a guilty conscience as if we were committing an incestuous act. The mother became her son's lover!

The Swedish word for incest is '*blodskam*' ('blood shame'). Laura actually says: 'as if the blood felt shame', a play on words which unfortunately I had to abandon in English.

In act three, scene seven, Strindberg offers a web of complicated opinions on the institution of marriage based on the image '*bolag*' meaning 'company' or 'partnership'. I had to find a metaphor which I could use all the way through the long speech. I could have used 'partnership', but it wouldn't have been quite so effective, so I opted for 'company', which in this instance lent itself to all the extended imagery quite successfully. But that was a rare coincidence.

Maybe the fault lies with the institution of marriage itself. In the past one married a wife, today one sets up a company with a woman who goes out to work, or one lives with a friend. And then — one either goes to bed with one's working partner or desecrates one's friend. What happened to love — healthy sensual love? It died in the process. And what issue comes from this limited company of love shares? Who is the main shareholder when the crash comes? Who is the biological father of the spiritual child?

In the third chamber play *After The Fire*, the bricklayer's wife breezes in with a surplus of energy which works as a paradigm both for Miss Hageby's point above and what I consider to be the central difficulty in translating Strindberg.

Wife: Now, let's have something to eat, dear. You must be hungry after all this to-do. . . I wonder if Gustavsson will scrape through. . . he'd already made a start in the greenhouses and he was just about to dig up the flower beds. . . go on, eat up. . . look, Sjöblom is at it already with his putty knife. . . it's a miracle that Mrs Vesterlund escaped like she did. Good morning, Sjöblom, you're not short of work now, are you? *(Mrs Vesterlund enters from the inn)* And good morning to you, Mrs Vesterlund, that was a narrow escape what with one thing and another...

    Mrs Vesterlund: I wonder who is going to reimburse me for my loss of earnings.

Strindberg's language is wild and surprising. The sentences form a whole which is very difficult to change once established and the rhythm creates a kind of poetry – actors have often told me that it is hard to cut a word or add a new one to the text. The sentences may be odd and incomplete, but they spring from the soul of the character, and that soul may only be translated accurately with due regard to the weight of the key-terms in the original.

Another Swedish writer, Pär Lagerkvist, who was in the vanguard of the expressionistic movement and whose metaphysical novels and plays on biblical themes earned him the Nobel Prize for Literature in 1951, presented me with a totally different set of problems. His finely wrought, sparse language, heavily influenced by the Icelandic sagas, looked almost too bare when translated into English. The text lay there like a tree stripped of all its leaves and somehow the English language demanded more than was necessary to make it evocative in Swedish. When I translated and dramatised Lagerkvist's *Barabbas* for BBC Radio in 1993 the producer, Ned Chaillet, suggested I use a Yorkshire dialect. The writer's simplicity and laconic expressions would lend themselves more happily to a Northern accent. After all, the Vikings settled there and some of their language lives on today.

The task seemed impossible at first but after immersing myself in plays and poetry by Yorkshire writers and after reading and re-reading the New Testament in the King James version, I compiled a notebook of favourite words and expressions culled from all these various sources. After a painstaking process and nine versions I was finally satisfied with the result and the robber who was released instead of Christ grew into a character of flesh and blood:

    Barabbas: I know not why I betook meself to Golgotha. It's a dirty, doleful place. Skulls and bones scattered far and wide and full of rotting crosses which are no use to nobody any more.

Lagerkvist often writes about simple, uneducated people and he uses a language which traces the original meaning of the word, even in the most banal expressions. It is not always easy to find an English equivalent to this. The English language is not hewn in granite, it flows freely and gently in a climate more temperate than the Swedish one. When Barabbas is musing on the fate of the crucified man he unwittingly uses some ambiguous words:

Barabbas: Straightaway I thought. . . when I left the dungeon and saw him there in the prison yard. . . summat odd about that fellow, I thought. Can't tell what exactly. . . it gleamed so bright around him. . . but most like I were dazed corse I'd come straight from yon dark cell.

Anyroad, it were plain to me that *there were no harm in him*. But it's nowt to do with me. They could 'a took whosoever they pleased. But it were him they nailed on t'cross. It were no fault of mine.

And when the robber reminds Barabbas how lucky he is to be alive: '*Damned lucky they released thee instead of yon teacher or whatever he were*' (in fact, Barrabas is damned from the moment he is released, as it turns out).

In other words, with Lagerkvist the problem is the reverse to the one I encountered with Strindberg. Strindberg's words are like seeds blowing about in the wind while Lagerkvist's are solid, polished stones, stationary and rounded. The challenge is always the same, though. How to translate that special quality into English in a way which makes it live in the new language? How to present foreign authors faithfully and at the same time convey something of their greatness in English?

The answer, simply, perhaps is that one should confine oneself to authors with a kindred spirit whose background and education is not too wildly out of step with one's own. Which brings me back to the subject of the tango. . .

'A MAN WITH CONNECTIONS'. ADAPTING GELMAN'S *NAEDINE SO VSEMI* FOR RADIO

STEPHEN MULRINE

Stephen Mulrine is currently Senior Lecturer in Historical and Critical Studies at the Glasgow School of Art. He is also a freelance writer, broadcaster and translator whose literary output includes poetry, short stories and criticism, although since the late nineteen-sixties he has mainly written plays for radio and television. In addition to fourteen original plays and over twenty adaptations for radio, he has written six plays for television, including *The Silly Season*, produced as a BBC2 'Play For Today' in 1980, and *The House On Kirov Street*, shown on BBC2 in 1984. Over a dozen translations and adaptations for the stage include his version of Gelman's *A Man With Connections*, the winner of a Fringe First award at the 1988 Edinburgh Festival, *The Bench* (also by Gelman, for the Traverse in 1990), Petrushevskaya's *Three Girls In Blue*, for the West Yorkshire Playhouse in 1992, and by the same author a double-bill of *Cinzano* and *Smirnova's Birthday*, performed by the Arts Threshold in Paddington. His adaptation of Yerofeev's novel *Moscow To Petushki* was performed as *Moscow Stations* at the Traverse Theatre as part of the 1994 Edinburgh Festival, subsequently moving to Broadway. Both his translation of the original novel and his stage adaptation are published, by Faber & Faber and Oberon Books respectively. He has also published Gelman's *A Man With Connections* and *Three Sisters* (both Nick Hern Books), and two anthologies of plays by Ovsrovsky and Turgenev are about to be published by Absolute Classics.

BBC Radio 3's November 1986 Russian Season of music and drama was planned many months ahead, and my contribution to it began with a general invitation, sent out from London to regional producers, calling for new translations of Russian and Soviet drama. Marilyn Imrie, who had worked as script editor on my television play *The House On Kirov Street*, and directed my play *Blokada* for BBC Radio Scotland, passed on this information, and after some abortive suggestions, Radio 3 eventually sent us a copy of Alexander Gelman's *Naedine so vsemi* (1982), one of a group of new Soviet plays, the rights to which they had negotiated with VAAP.

If we were to collaborate on it, Gelman's play had to appeal to us both, and this it did, as a well constructed two-hander, with a strong plot, tending to melodrama, but controlled by a vein of black comedy throughout. Like earlier Gelman plays, e.g., *Protokol odnogo zasedaniy* (*Minutes Of A Meeting*; 1976), and *My, nizhepodpisavshiesya* (*We, The Undersigned*; 1979), it is concerned with the ethics of the Soviet managerial class, which Gelman sees as under pressure from, on the one hand, the impossible demands of the Plan, and, on the other, Western-style consumerism. To a Soviet theatre audience, the rewards of Andrei Golubev's striving would be obvious enough in the appointments of his flat, with its shower, fitted wardrobes, modern telephone, etc., not forgetting his chauffeur-driven car; equally familiar would be the means by which that success was achieved:

Andrei: The fact is, in twenty years I haven't once – in any single year, quarter, month – not once have I even completed the Plan straight. There's always some sort of fiddle going on, even it is only petty. But if I play by the book, and report a shortfall, I'll be out the door. If they take a notion. Somebody's just got to want a new face and I'll be finished. That's all it needs, Natasha. That's why I've got to keep at it the whole time, diving about all over the shop – so nobody'll get any ideas. . .

The tragic background to the play, the injury to their son which causes him to lose both hands, as a result of Andrei's attempt to cut corners at work, is a part of a general pattern of moral collapse. Andrei recognizes this:

You want to know how I see myself? Eh? I mean, you tell me often enough – I've no conscience, feelings, the whole kit. But that's exactly what it is, a kit of parts. I can be clever when I want to, I can be dumb. I can be deaf and blind as well if that's what they want. Whatever's required, I'll dredge it up from somewhere. Mister Versatile, that's me. . .

Furthermore, he also sees Natasha not as a victim, but as an accomplice:

You know, whatever I do out there, you're involved here, Natasha, right up to the hilt You're just sticking your head in the sand. Face facts, sweetheart, you're in it for profit, worldly goods, same as me. My God, I'm your Five Year Plan, Natasha – it's a business arrangement we have, not a family!

Later, we learn that not only was Andrei responsible for his son's accident, he even used it as a means of emotional blackmail on his superior, appealing for an advance to make good a shortfall in the quarterly plan. Natasha's contempt for the man she has been married to for twenty years appears thoroughly justified, and indeed much of the business of the play is concerned with her attempts to leave, physically prevented by Andrei. However, Gelman makes it clear that Natasha is also compromised, as Andrei has suggested. Through her job at the library, where her superior Olga happens to be the wife of Andrei's incompetent foreman, Natasha is caught up in the same exchange of favours and petty bribery as her husband. It is merely a difference of degree, as Andrei emphasizes:

I've told you – I was twenty thousand short, and Nikitin wouldn't give me an advance without that road. I had to ask him, so he asked me. It's standard practice, Natasha. If you remember, you couldn't get the books you wanted in the library last year, you and Olga. You were wanting some stuff by Trofimov, and some other —
Natasha: Trifonov.
Andrei: Anyway, you were getting the brush-off from the department. And you came running to me – the book-buyer had burst a pipe, could I do something about it? So I gave him a couple of plumbers and *you* got your favourite author. And you were delighted. The plain fact is, there's a shortage of paper, and that's why there's no books. And I'm short of cement, that's why I'm out on twenty thousand. I needed that, the same as you pair needed your books. That's why I sent those men sent them to your book-buyer, *and* out to that road!

Again, when Andrei finally accedes to her demand that he quit his job at CDC, and suggests taking up an offer of a lectureship at the local building college, Natasha is alarmed at the prospect of having to get by on a hundred and twenty roubles a month – especially now they have a crippled son to support.

Ironically, Andrei has returned home with a major promotion to celebrate, just as Natasha has discovered the full extent of his criminal responsibility for Alyosha's accident. However, when he manages to convince her that resignation, at this juncture in his career, is not the answer, it is at the expense of a blank cheque, which Natasha promptly tries to cash:

Andrei, I want to get out of the library. I want to leave the library, so you can take me on at your place. I want to work alongside you, Andrei, to be *involved*, so I'll understand... If I'm going to live with you, then we have to share everything. I couldn't stand that Slutsky, but if there's going to be other people now, then I would have them here, put on a bit of a show for them — you could all get together here, discuss things... and I'd know everything that was happening. Please, Andrei, I want you to find me a job with the company. If you do that, then I definitely do think we could make a go of it. Will you do that? Andrei?...

Over Andrei's dead body, is the predictable response, but not until he has exhausted his repertoire of excuses. Gelman derives a good deal of comedy from this, but it is part of a larger structure of tactical manoeuvring, in which the need to dominate often appears to outweigh the actual issues. Indeed, it might be argued that the true subject of the play is 'choreography' – the way in which charge is met by counter-charge, logic is answered by rhetoric, posture deflated by riposte.

Characteristically, throughout, the harder Andrei works at confining the debate to cut-and-dried questions of responsibility, the deeper Natasha digs into their past, exposing him to a general moral censure, the basis of which is emotional, rather than rational. The fundamental question, for Natasha, is whether Andrei has ever really loved her; for Andrei, the question itself is irrelevant.

It was this structural aspect of *Naedine so vsemi* which also suggested an English title for the piece. BBC had bought the rights to the play as *Alone In The Crowd*. Apart from the heavy paradox, I disliked its overtones of advertising copy, and based my own version, *A Man With Connections*, partly on Andrei's persistent attempts to argue that one moral lapse has no connections with another, thereby to escape blame for the consequences of his actions. The scene following Andrei's first admission of guilt is typical, both in its modes of argument, and its grim humour:

Andrei (*sighs, then absurdly*): Natasha, you haven't got something I could take for a headache, have you?
Natasha: No!
Andrei: I've got a really splitting headache, you know?
Natasha: Go to hell. If you were to die this very second, I'd phone for a hearse and that would be it. I'd pack you off to the morgue, along with your suitcase. They could lay it on top of your coffin – all your worldly goods!
Andrei: Natasha, I'll need to lie down for a couple of minutes, my head's bursting.
Natasha: Stay where you are! You didn't have a headache then, did you. The day after – the *morning* after your own son lost his hands, when you had to run back to your work! Straight from the hospital, you just couldn't forget your twenty thousand, could you!
Andrei: Natasha, you're confusing the issue...
Natasha: Oh yes, you could still manage a few words of comfort for Alyosha's benefit – smiling through tears, like a human being. The consoling pat. United we stand. Only it turns out you were just play-acting,

your mind was on something else.

Andrei: I don't know what you're talking about. Stick to the point, Natasha.

Natasha: Of course it had to be in on time, hadn't it. You'd already sent word to Nikitin personally – in a desperate rush. So you'd be able to include that money in the quarterly figures. Creative bookkeeping! You knew Nikitin would sign – he could hardly refuse, could he, after what happened. You made a use of your own misery, Andrei, so you could close your bloody quarter!

Andrei: Natasha, there's no connection, you can't do this. Alyosha's one thing, and the plans another. I don't get paid for being a husband and father, you know. . .

In the course of the play's long arguments, Natasha's strategy is to prove causal connection between events, and thus, intention; Andrei's generally unconvincing defence is to plead coincidence, sheer bad luck.

In another sense of the word, both Andrei and Natasha owe their positions at work to the typically Soviet system of nepotism or patronage. Indeed, taken together, the unseen personnel of both Andrei's construction company and Natasha's library make up a flourishing family tree. Natasha's jibe at Andrei: '*Tebya snyat' ne tak prosto – ty zavyazan so vsemi, kak pauk!*' ('But they wouldn't sack you, they couldn't get rid of you *that* easily, you're too well connected, you're like a spider') might apply with equal force to herself.

Gelman's title of course emphasizes Andrei' solitude, and while translation is always a compromise, the implicit distinction between 'connections' and relationships, in which Andrei has signally failed, seems to me to embrace the original meaning.

An interesting feature of the standard BBC contract translation and adaptation is that the activities are separately costed, and the work of adaptation is better rewarded. I doubt if my experience is unique, but the adaptation of *Naedine so vsemi* was a comparatively straightforward process.

Two and a half hours of stage play needed to be cut, in the first instance, to ninety minutes for radio. This allowed the suppression of a good deal of exposition, long speeches in which Andrei and Natasha rehearse earlier marital crises, and effectively tell each other what they already know too well. Acceptable on stage, on radio this sounds contrived, not so much authentic dialogue as background notes for the listener.

Another technical problem concerned particularly Natasha's presence. *Naedine so vsemi* opens with an empty stage, and it is not until Andrei has entered, made several phone-calls and gone to take a shower, that Natasha staggers out of the bedroom wardrobe, in which she has been hiding. As a general rule, characters who don't speak in radio drama can be presumed dead, and I was therefore obliged to invent a brief establishing scene, a telephone conversation for Natasha, before Andrei's entry.

Natasha is also mute during much of Andrei's self-justifying rant, especially in the first act, and while it was important to retain that quality of silent recrimination, the occasional interjection from Natasha was essential, if only to make clear that the entire action was not taking place inside Andrei's head. In the second act, where the weight is more evenly distributed, Gelman's characteristic manner is to counter Andrei's operatic arias with equally long and shapely speeches from Natasha, and again, changes were made in order to keep both characters in the mind's eye.

It must be admitted that adaptation would have been far more difficult had the play been taken out of its Soviet setting. The speech conventions for radio adaptations of foreign-language drama is normally standard English, with only rural, or lower class characters in English regional dialects. For *Naedine so vsemi*, however, Radio 3 specifically requested Scottish voices, without a change of setting, and while that became the basis of a few critical reservations about the production, both Marilyn Imrie and I welcomed the decision.

In the first place Gelman's play is so rootedly Soviet in its concerns, that finding English, let alone Scottish, equivalents for a radical relocation would have been almost impossible. The shortcomings of the Soviet system, the *'blat'* ('petty corruption', 'bribery') and 'veshchemaniya' ('ruthless acquisitiveness') which have distorted the couple's relationship and occasioned their son's tragedy, are as much Gelman's target as is organization-man Andrei. Thus a root-and-branch English version, lacking the Soviet ideological context, would sound like a period piece. Gelman is not, I believe, being wholly ironic when Andrei offers in his defence:

> Natasha, I've got to work to the Plan, I have a responsibility, managing CDC's like a sacred trust... You surely understand that, you're supposed to have brains, with all your bloody library books!

And indeed the Plan is criticized as a tyrannical false god in Gelman's earlier work. Placing Andrei and Natasha in a Western mixed economy would accordingly have entailed structural changes of a sort to defeat the purpose of Radio 3's Russian Season.

However, my version employs a specific variety of Scottish-English, and while there appears no reason why Glaswegian should not be used as a translation medium, the force of convention greatly outweighs both reason and sentiment in these matters, and unless there were some advantage to be gained, my own instinct would have been to use standard English. *Naedine so vsemi* did seem to present certain agreeably Glaswegian features though, not least the quality of life enjoyed by Andrei and Natasha. A city with a *per capita* ownership of VCRs and micro-computers among the world's highest, conjoined to, and partly explained by, chronic deprivation, suggests a more appropriate linguistic environment for Andrei than the Oxbridge-Home Counties base of RP.

In that context, his middle management opposite number would read off his success in share prices; Andrei's status symbols are of a lower evolutionary order:

> Andrei: Of course, there's no lovers these days. Ever since I 'arrived', as you put it, you've been the faithful wife. . . now I'm earning three times the salary, now we've a three-room-apartment, a phone, a car – now it's *your* turn to be jealous, not *me*!. . .

Even Andrei's solution to the problem of his son's disability is framed in terms of low-level perquisites and contacts:

> Andrei: Also I got our mechanic to make notes on various gadgets they had. Like a foot operated switch for the TV – so you can change channels. You just press it, like so – are you watching? Natasha? One of these chaps had a push-button phone, he was saying, they're really neat. You pick up a pencil in your teeth – beep-beep-beep-beep – and you've dialled your number, no problem. The receiver's mounted on a sort of vertical bracket – you just put your ear against it, and. . .
> Natasha: You bastard! Shut up! Shut up!

Despite its bleak subject matter, there is comedy at every turn of Gelman's text, and in a Glaswegian version that aspect of the play came to assume a remarkably familiar cast. The creatures of Natasha's nightmare, for example, might have been Clyde-built:

> Natasha: I dreamt Alyosha was married, and his wife was throwing him out of the house. You were there, and we were trying to talk her round. She was a dreadful person – a big fat woman, hard as nails, and she was shouting, 'I've been running after this cripple of yours for three years, the flat's mine, I've paid for it!' You said something to her, and she shouted into the other room, 'Volodya, come and throw these people out!' And then this Volodya appeared – with huge hands, enormous, and a big moon face. This is my new husband, she says, I've been living with him for three months now. And then she turns to Alyosha. Go on Alyosha, tell them, she says.
> Andrei: That's awful!

Natasha: And then this Volodya comes up to you, and starts shoving you out, punching you in the face.
Andrei: Natasha, that's hellish!

It will be obvious from the extracts quoted that the dialect character of my translation is not strongly marked; it is Glaswegian mainly in its syntax and rhythms, the speech is that of well-educated citizens, and it was important accordingly that Andrei and Natasha should be played without condescension. And having determined on Bill Paterson and Phyllis Logan as ideal voices, producer Marilyn Imrie in fact delayed the studio recording until almost the last possible date, in order to ensure their availability. My only regret, from the entire experience, is that the vehicle for two quite outstanding performances was Alexander Gelman's play, not mine!

Translation is in a sense an attempt to agree irreconcilables, and while I have too much respect for Gelman to knowingly betray his intention, there are other masters to be served, equally demanding. In dramatic writing the characters exercise their own prerogative, and any playwright will recognise the phenomenon of dialogue writing as 'listening' for the authentic voice of an intimate, with its known rhythms and cadences. T S Eliot's comment on the subject of *vers libre* might equally apply to translation. No translation is free, to the man who wishes to do a good job. The necessity to re-invent Gelman's characters nonetheless, so that I might hear their voices, demanded a different sort of accuracy, as the term is commonly used of translations. Other people must be the judges of its success or failure, but the following extracts for comparison, finally are representative of my approach to the text throughout. Characters' names, incidentally, have been changed for ease of delivery in a rapid speech:

Natasha: And what'll you do with the people you've got now?
Andrei: Get shot of them! We're needing to turf half of them out anyway, and I'm just the man to do it.
Natasha: Oh yes? And how are you going to do that? They're all Slutsky's people. The first sniff of trouble, they'll be on the phone to Slutsky, and he'll tell you to lay off. And you won't go against Slutsky. He set you up in the job, after all. He doesn't know you're lying awake nights, getting big ideas. The only Goltsman he knows is his faithful wee dog that does whatever he tells it. He doesn't know the night-time Goltsman, only the day-time dog...

THOUGHTS ON TRANSLATING
FRENCH PLAYS

PETER MEYER

Peter Meyer's published translations include Seven Plays by Alfred de Musset (two of which were republished by Absolute Press in 1993), three farces by Feydeau, and *Professor Taranne* by Adamov. He has also translated many other plays by various authors for stage, television and radio. In 1985, he was commissioned by BBC Radio to do a new version of Anouilh's *Eurydice* to celebrate the author's seventy-fifth birthday, and this was staged at Chichester in 1990. His translation of Thirteen Monologues by Cocteau and Feydeau is due to be published in 1996.

The art of translation (and translators consider it an art, whatever their authors may think) does not lend itself to the formulation of principles. The rules one follows seem so obvious that they appear to be little more than platitudes and these jottings owe their existence solely to the enthusiasm and promptings of the editor of this particular book.

It is always exciting to receive a new French play, though this is all too often tempered by the agent proudly announcing that it has recently been hugely successful in Paris. Just as a musical is the surest road to success in London, so in Paris there is a seemingly limitless market for the boulevard play. This differs from the old English matinée play in providing wish-fulfillment therapy for middle-aged women. The leading lady is no longer in her first youth, but dazzles everyone she meets. A much younger man falls in love with her, or she effortlessly copes with difficult children or the trials of widowhood. Above all, she is wealthy, so she can be dressed by one of the great couturiers, with, if possible, several changes of costume. One wonders what deals have been done, when the programme announces that he dresses her offstage as well. Sometimes she has a mother, played by a former star. She too is upholstered, rather than dressed, by a great couturier and makes her entrance centre-stage, milking it for applause in a way that has not been seen in London since Marie Tempest. A recent play had no fewer than four leading ladies, three of whom had the expected change of costume, but the author made it up to the fourth by giving her a fit of hysterics to bring down the first act curtain.

It may not be realised that one of the most difficult decisions facing a translator is whether or not to undertake the task in the first place. Obviously, one must like the play, but one must also be in sympathy with the author's intentions. This frequently means an ability to distinguish between the sense and the sound, the meaning and the music, and then convincing him that a literal translation of his words would falsify something which he had written instinctively. With an author who speaks English, this is not always easy.

Having overcome these obstacles, one must then be confident one has the necessary background knowledge. I have in the past turned down a stage adaptation of Malraux's *La condition humaine*, as I knew little about Communism, and Adamov's *Paolo Paoli* because French politics between the beginning of the century and the outbreak of the First World War were a closed book to me. Other translators are not always so particular: a recent French translation, which I vetted for the Coward estate, showed an ignorance of English social conventions of the nineteen twenties which made nonsense of certain lines.

One must be sure that it is possible to make the play work in English in a way that will carry out what the author is trying to convey. I once had to refuse a powerful play that largely depended for its effectiveness on the contrast between the Biblical quotations of a peasant farmer, the provincial language of his family and the standard French of a daughter who had escaped to Paris. All my attempts foundered in mid-Channel and I could only suggest that it might work if transposed to Ireland. As I heard nothing more of the play, I can only assume it didn't.

Contemporary translations tend to date after about twenty years and if one is asked to translate a play that has been previously translated, one has to be particularly careful. This has happened to me with *Va donc chez Torpe* by Billetdoux and Anouilh's *Eurydice*, and in both cases I deliberately avoided looking at the earlier version. Some translators are less scrupulous. The Actors' Company once agreed to stage my translation of Feydeau's *Le dindon*, but a reluctance to return the script, after deciding that the director would make a translation of his own, aroused suspicions and it became apparent that use had been made of parts of my version. After intervention by solicitors, the Company agreed to pay a royalty and include an acknowledgement in the programme, but on the first night, at Wimbledon, they inadvertently omitted the acknowledgement from the programme and printed it on a separate slip, which they then inadvertently omitted to give to the critics. This resulted in an apology in *The Times*. I am sure Sir Peter Hall would never be guilty of such behaviour, but his recent translation of the same play was made after he had read my translation and indeed announced, apparently by mistake, that he was going to produce it. It would be surprising if some lines had not remained in his subconscious, which may well be why the *Observer* noted that his translation was not all that different from mine.

It is all too easy to be lazy and to use an English word or phrase that resembles the French. Thus '*Mon Dieu*' is the equivalent of 'Good Heavens', not 'My God',which one must then remember was never used in polite society before 1914. Colloquial language in a period play is always a problem. Aggressively modern words must be avoided and so must the archaic. One has to tread a delicate path between these two extremes, while at the same time avoiding a neutral flatness.

It is equally easy to transcribe an apparently insignificant French expression without understanding it. I once fortunately queried *Le bal de la montagne*, which turned out to be a lesbian ball in Paris in the 1940's (the play was about the French Resistance), and was intended to indicate the sexuality of the leading lady, an actress. An explanatory line had then to be added. I suggested that retaining the Christian name of Arlette might lead to a slander action from Arletty, but was told not to worry as the character was based on another actress whose second name was an anagram of the one the author had used in the play. So both names had to be changed.

It is not sufficient to understand the meaning of an apparently insignificant phrase, but one must also try to infer why the author has inserted it. Michael Gough once asked why he had to say 'yes', and I was luckily able to answer that it was reflective and used to introduce a change of pace.

Once one has decided on an English style that faithfully reflects the author's, the dialogue will usually flow naturally. Sometimes however, particularly with a long part, the character refuses to come to life. In that case the solution may be to write it for a well-known English actor, though this is very much a last resort, as the result may be disastrous, if the actor is not available. I have twice had to resort to this in radio plays by different authors, in each case using as a model someone I knew through having worked with him. The first was Ernest Milton, then in his late seventies, who had been a famous Hamlet forty years earlier. He had a very mannered delivery with a voice that would swoop through an enormous range and then light on a single syllable that could be drawn out for what seemed an eternity. He played the part to perfection. A charming thing about him was his reminiscences. One of his earliest appearances had been as Bassanio to Ellen Terry's Portia on the pier at Brighton. At the first rehearsal she said 'I'm used to playing opposite men who are young enough to be my son, but you could be my grandson'. Then 'You must wear a moustache!'

The other actor I took as a model was Richard Briers, but it turned out to be a low budget production and only the BBC Drama Repertory Company could be used. The first read-through did not work at all and I explained to the director what I had done. Then the play sprang to life and I asked the director how he had achieved this. He had simply told the actor to think of Richard Briers.

French is a richer language than English and tends to be more verbose, so it is a mistake to think that every word must be translated. Sentences frequently start with 'And' or 'But', which in English is apt to turn dialogue into chatter. They must nearly always be omitted. A favourite device is the use of three similar words to provide emphasis at the end of a sentence and one must not hesitate to cut one or two of them to avoid seeming over-literary. Even Feydeau, whose dialogue was exceptionally colloquial for the nineteenth century, occasionally used this embellishment. There is a recent tradition in the English theatre that Feydeau can never be cut. This is reputed to stem from the 1956 dress rehearsal of *Hotel Paradiso*, when Binkie Beaumont of H M Tennent, who were presenting the play, protested that a scene did not make sense. It was then discovered to be due to a seemingly innocuous cut. Like many traditions, it is only a half truth. Feydeau can be cut, indeed has to be for a radio adaptation with a time limit, but such cuts must be made with the greatest of care.

Noel Coward once complained to me that Feydeau never wrote a witty line. At that time I did not know that Feydeau himself had told one of his collaborators that wit must never be used unless required by the play or it would interrupt the action. In view of the wit for which Coward is justly famous, it makes one wonder why he agreed to translate *Occupe toi d'Amélie*, and a clash of temperaments may explain its less than warm reception in 1959, in spite of his brilliant title (*Look After Lulu*) and the presence of Vivien Leigh in the leading part.

Another cut that is nearly always necessary is the use of all those Monsieurs and Madames which are an essential feature of French conversation, but do not fit easily into English speech patterns. Indeed French words of any sort should be retained with reluctance. They are a trap for the actors, whose accents will invariably vary from the perfect to the Churchillian.

Names can sometimes be a problem. They may be difficult to pronounce or carry connotations in one language which would mean nothing in the other. In that case new names must be chosen that would be valid in both languages and if necessary make a similar point. In Feydeau's one-act play *Mais n'te promène donc pas toute nue* there is a joke, surprisingly vulgar for the period, based on a misunderstanding of a syllable of a character's name. In the translation he had to be given a new name in French in order to convey the same joke in English.

Like all rules, these must sometimes be broken. If one is an author's accepted translator, one has a duty to him which overrides one's views of a particular play. If his recent work has been regularly accepted by BBC Radio, the disagreeable task of refusing can safely be passed to them. Otherwise one has to choose between supporting or losing a friend.

Once the play is in the hands of a director, the translator's position is the same as an author's. If the play is unusual, some directors (Patrick Garland, Michael Rudman) invite you to give an explanatory talk at the first read-through. Some, especially in BBC radio drama with a limited time available, like you to be present at all rehearsals, others definitely not. It is desirable, if possible, to attend the first and some of the later ones, in order to deal with any difficulties as they arise.

One of the problems of attending rehearsals is the actor who habitually wants to re-write every line. Ralph Truman, who had been a powerful Mountjoy in Olivier's film of *Henry V*, was a well-known example. This is in marked contrast to most other actors, including John Osborne who played the lead in four Feydeau one-act plays on radio (each part being a self-portrait of Feydeau himself) and, following the practice he said to insist on with his own plays, never altered a word. Another difficulty is caused by actors' jokes, as will be realised by anyone who has listened to award-winners' speeches at presentation ceremonies on television. In both cases the best answer is a prepared avoidance technique.

It is important that notes should be given to the director, never to the actors. Judy Campbell once asked if she could transpose two adjectives, and who could refuse anything to Judy Campbell? But we forgot to tell the director and were punished by having to revert to the original script. It is equally important to indicate any changes without speaking the line. Actors like to find their own way and in any event do it much better. It was once explained to Judy Dench that 'Etc' was intended to be used as a catchphrase and she created a new word out of it.

It is also preferable to accept alterations unless they are vital. A young actor in his first big part once spoiled the balance of a line by using a different preposition with an extra syllable. I hesitated to point this out, for fear of destroying his confidence, until he eventually admitted he found the line difficult and asked for help.

Directors' requests for alterations can vary from the easy, such as extra lines to cover a moment, to the almost impossible. In the last category fell Stuart Burge's not unreasonable requirement of additional characters to people the stage in the last act of a Feydeau farce. I eventually solved this by introducing two actors from an earlier scene who could logically hand round glasses of champagne.

These reflections have inevitably been highly subjective and it would be arrogant to suggest otherwise. Every translator will approach the situation in his own way. In the final analysis the only essential, which must be continually borne in mind, is to please the author, the actors and the audience.

DAVID HARE: PIRANDELLO AND BRECHT

IN CONVERSATION WITH DAVID JOHNSTON

David Hare is one of the leading writers of his generation, a playwright and director who has brought an enriching flow of ideas to bear on the political and moral life of Britain. Since 1970 he has written fifteen plays, two of them (*Brassneck* and *Pravda*) with Howard Brenton, seven screenplays and five films for television. In addition to a single opera (*The Knife*, 1988), he has published two books of essays, *Writing Left-Handed* and *Asking Around* (1991 and 1993 respectively), in which he reflects with characteristic lucidity both on theatre-making and on the theatre's relationship with the world around it. Since 1992 he has also undertaken three adaptations: a second bite at an earlier version of Pirandello's *The Rules Of The Game*, and Brecht's *The Life Of Galileo* and *Mother Courage And Her Children* (1994 and 1995).

DJ: Did you choose the plays that you translated?

DH: No, what happened was that I was asked, when I first became a writer, to adapt a Pirandello play – *The Rules Of The Game* – for The National Theatre, which was then under Olivier, for Paul Scofield and Joan Plowright. I did it because it was just about the first job that I was ever offered. It was an unsatisfactory production. The play really did not work, for all sorts of reasons. And twenty years passed. . . I hadn't returned to adaptation on the grounds that I didn't regard it as real work. I regarded writing plays as my real business and I was very snotty about it and said 'It's just a way of making royalties, money off the back of another writer'. So, then, the Almeida announced they wanted to do my version of *The Rules Of The Game* and, having not looked at it for twenty years, when I cast my eye back over it, I felt such professional horror at the inadequacy of my version that I said 'Well, I'll do you a new version'. Of course, they were delighted, because they were getting a new version unasked, unbidden. . . And, so, that's what I did and I found it very stimulating. I suppose, I found it actually a great relief, for once, writing on somebody else's writing.

DJ: Unashamedly hijacking your own phrase, did you translate 'with your left hand'?

DH: No, no, I think that I'd wanted to. But I do think that a translation, a version, or whatever you call it, is inevitably a critique of a play, it's a tilt on a play, there is no way that it can't be. It's a matter of whether you want consciously or unconsciously to accept the fact that you are pointing up certain parts of that play and putting others in the shadow. It seems to me that an intelligent translator is a kind of substitute director, or like the conductor of an orchestra, bringing out certain themes, inevitably emphasizing. For me there was a sort of romantic criticism in Pirandello's writing about love. Underneath the apparent cynicism and the comedy, there seemed to me a real, almost cryptic, romanticism that I thought was very, very beautiful. I'm not sure I necessarily associate it with Pirandello but I thought I could bring that out and emphasize that in the English language, and that that would do the play a good service. And, sure, the play worked. It worked at the Almeida better than it has ever worked, precisely because it was a very romantic production and interpretation.

DJ: You use the word 'critique'. The translator, in a sense, is always making decisions which are based on an analysis of the text as a whole. And yet, in one place, you talk about the creative and the critical as being almost extreme ends, almost incompatible attitudes. Do they come together, in some way, in the translator?

DH: Let me try and answer that by going on to *Galileo*, which is a classically difficult piece to translate, for the following reasons. There's a version that Brecht wrote in Scandinavia, where he was in exile; it was performed in Switzerland, in Zurich, during the war in 1943, in his absence, and he never saw it. Then after the war Charles Laughton comes to him and says 'I'd love to do Galileo'. There is, then, an English version to which at least ten or eleven different people contributed individual lines or passages. Then, there's a third version, which was performed just before his death, and another version he was working on as Director of The Berliner Ensemble, in 1956. So, already, as someone who's going to try and do a play called *Galileo*, you've got so many versions, including one in bad English by Laughton and Brecht, who didn't speak very good English and who took advice, and maybe not very good advice, from people, about what he should do with his play... So you've got that classic translator's problem, 'Which version am I going to use?'

But, also, you've got an almost impossible richness of theme. You've got a play, first of all, that's identified with a production style, namely the German epic style of the fifties, as well as the music of that period, and which is always performed in that style. The play itself is so impossibly rich; it's been worked over so many times by Brecht that you do have to say this 'I think this is the line through the play that will hold it together'. So as a translator you reject certain passages as not finally being essential to what the play is about. On the other hand you develop certain passages that you do feel the play is about.

DJ: Can I ask why you chose that particular Brecht play?

DH: Simply because we wanted to continue with Richard Griffiths, who was the actor who played Leone in Pirandello, very brilliantly. So Jonathan Kent and I were discussing what play we would do with him next. We then said *Galileo* and I, again as a kind of distant director, thought it would be a fascinating experiment to try and get rid of all the detritus in German expressionism, of German epic, and see what you are left with at the centre of this play. It would be impossible to stage *Galileo* in that way at the Almeida, which is an intimate theatre. You can't do scene changes, there are no wings, there is no fly tower. It's not technically possible to do *Galileo* in the style in which it is always done. The Almeida is much more like a planetarium, a theatre which is ideally suited to plays the size of chamber pieces. *Galileo* adapted triumphantly to this treatment. It's such a brilliant play that I could take a line through it and produce a riveting version, but someone else could take a completely different line through it and produce a version which is equally valid.

DJ: You are describing the translator in a directorial, rather than authorial, sense.

DH: I think that's right. I think what I'm doing is essentially 'fitting up'. I knew Richard Griffiths's voice and I was fitting up certain passages for Richard Griffiths because he is so intellectually lucid as an actor; he's very unusual as an actor, in that he is able to play an intellectual in this very large body, but nevertheless has this very sweet romanticism, so that I knew that I was fitting it up, like the bespoke-tailoring for this actor. But I was also doing it knowing the theatre, knowing the kind of production Jonathan had in mind. For example, it was me as translator who reduced the cast from the normal forty to sixteen. I would have liked to have produced a *Galileo* – I first called it a 'pocket' *Galileo* – a *Galileo* that could be performed by any theatre in the world, with only eight characters. But that proved impossible. You can't do it with less than sixteen.

DJ: In spite of the way Brecht pillaged for his own plays – John Gay springs to mind immediately – the Brecht estate is notorious for being difficult to deal with for anyone who wants to make any change in the fabric of the plays. Did you have any problems?

DH: No, and I think there are two reasons for this. One of the reasons is that the Brecht estate fully understands that the fall of the Berlin Wall means that there has been a tremendous attack on Brecht's work, a sort of ideological attempt to ditch Brecht. There has been a great deal of thinking that now that we've apparently finished with Communism, we can finish with Brecht as well. They're not fools, they know that. A new generation must find a new way of doing these plays. In itself that's a powerful impetus for the constant production of new translations. Letting me do this was, if you like, a bit of a fall of the Berlin Wall in itself, a fall of the theatrical Berlin Wall. The other reason was that, because I am a playwright, they trusted me not to be riding a hobby horse; they knew that I didn't *need* to do this, that I was doing it because I genuinely loved the play, and that I was, I hope, a trustworthy person to do it. In the final analysis, they loved the version.

DJ: Leaving aside your theatrical motivation for doing the Brecht, did you choose the play at that particular time for extra-theatrical reasons, for example, not to look any further, the fall of the Berlin Wall itself?

DH: Yes. I wanted to prove that this was a great, timeless masterpiece, one of the great plays of the twentieth century, an inexhaustible piece. But I was also concerned with the writing itself, in the most direct way possible. The play is so long and so extended by songs that, although there are brilliant passages, you don't get the arc of the whole story. Neither do you get, though this is a word that is not associated with these late great plays of Brecht, you don't get that incredible deftness and economy of his writing. You only have to take a little bit of the accumulation out and people start saying 'God, I never knew Brecht was so fast'. That's when you see that every scene and every speech is adding something new. Howard Brenton worked on a version that was done here, a very faithful version. He told me that he couldn't quite fathom how easily Brecht conveyed information; for example you're only ten minutes into the play and you know everything about the arsenal of Venice, and you think 'How have I learned all that?' And yet, Brecht has got it all in.

DJ: What right does the translator have to foist changes upon the work of the original author, to say that he or she knows what the original author would have wanted today?

DH: I think that's the central question. I've been asked, although I don't think I will do it, to do Ibsen's *An Enemy Of The People*. I looked at Arthur Miller's version, and great as my respect is for Miller, I felt that this was a travesty, an example of a really bad translation. The theme of *An Enemy Of The People* is that man must stand alone against the crowd. Miller in the late forties, early fifties, the time of McCarthyism etc., can't really believe this. He's shocked that Ibsen doesn't really trust democracy. Miller said he was sure that there were certain passages which weren't what Ibsen would write now and he took them out because he felt them to be offensive to a modern audience. I think that is deeply wrong, because then you are betraying the writer through a form of political correctness, in the worst sense. What you're saying is 'I think if only he were around now, he'd be enlightened enough to remove that bit'. I think that Miller actually misses the whole glory of that play which is, as in *Coriolanus*, that Ibsen defines individualism for better and for worse. The character is heroic, but he is also totally insane, and a good actor will convey the fact that the man is mad and doesn't necessarily carry the author's wholehearted approval. Yet Miller was so frightened that it would appear that what Ibsen was saying was 'the man who stands alone is always right', that he wanted to censor the play; I think that is really bad translation, and in fact, in that sense, we can probably use the same yardstick for bad translation as we can for bad writing.

Saying that, Miller's play isn't a bad play; it's just not Ibsen's play, whereas I would claim that *Galileo* is Brecht's play. I know these things are impossible to define, you can't take weights and measures and so on, and judge the number of lines changed and passages altered, but if you don't allow the character his full horror as well as his appeal, then you are diluting Ibsen's play. And perhaps dilution is the most serious charge you can level at a translator of plays.

DJ: It's clear that your view of translation isn't based on a linguistic fidelity, but rather has more to do with getting inside the skin of the author or inside the fabric of the play.

DH: Yes, but I am vulnerable to the charge of arrogance precisely on that count, because I think Brecht got lost on *Galileo*. He worked for seventeen years, so long that he put so many qualifiers into the play that in the end he himself almost became confused about what he was trying to do. Then I came along and said 'Right, I am going to try and clean out the gutters here'.

DJ: When you approach the play and you are reading it, your prime questions therefore revolve around the intentions of the author. Many translators or critics will tell you today that the author can't be credited with such things

DH: That's just a fad. We have lived through that... isn't it over? Structuralism? What a cul-de-sac! I don't like the phrase 'author's intentions', anyway, because I remember Lindsay Anderson saying a wonderful thing about the film *If*. When he was asked 'In this film are you trying to say...?' he interrupted and said 'I am not trying to say anything. I *am* saying'. In the same way it's impertinent to talk about one's sense of Brecht's intentions because those intentions are wholly realised on stage. All I am saying is that sometimes it is covered in a bit of a clutter, i.e. overwriting, over-complication.

DJ: Ideological clutter?

DH: No. I think that the subject matter itself is so complicated that as soon as you say one thing, you can see the truth of the opposite and that therefore as a writer he tends to overwrite slightly in places. I wanted to 'strip a lot of that out' so that the play always moved forward.

DJ: Keeping with the phrase to 'strip out', one of the things that struck me about *The Rules Of The Game* was its clarity of line, its clarity of writing. That isn't true of the original, neither is it really true of anything that Pirandello wrote. I always find him, I'm afraid, a very wordy dramatist. Were you consciously aware that you were stripping down the language, was it something that you set out to do? Was it that you were more interested in the storyline?

DH: No, it wasn't simply the storyline. I think it is just a terribly funny play, and it plays wonderfully as a comedy. I was basically trying to make the wit as accessible as possible – by and large, the more economically you arrive at a point, the funnier it is. To me, as a writer, all dramatic dialogue is plainly about rhythm – take any great writer, who has rhythm, and then think about what the actor is trying to find. Usually the actor thinks he is looking at psychology, and he may well indeed be looking at psychology, but if he doesn't have the rhythm of the writer then he is wasting his time worrying about psychology. We've all seen actors who can't play Shakespeare, who can't technically manage Shakespeare. For them it doesn't matter what the hell they are worrying about. To me this is as true of prose drama as it is of poetic drama. I spend more time thinking about rhythm than I do about meaning. What I try to do is give whoever's personality I am working on a rhythm; it's not my rhythm, although it may be. When Richard Eyre read my version of *Galileo*, he told me he found it a little disturbing because he could half hear my rhythm and half hear Brecht's. The reason I believe that the Pirandello worked is that I gave it a strong, distinctive rhythm. Or your Irish version of *Bohemian Lights* was very strongly rhythmic.

DJ: That again, as you say, is a goal at the top of your mind. It seems to me that writers like Shaw, or Pirandello or Valle-Inclán are almost condemned to function better in translation now because their original writing is so heavily textured to a time that it no longer seems to work quite so well in the original. I find Shaw very prissy now – I think he sounds so much more alive in Spanish. When you moved from your first version to your second version of the Pirandello did you keep on stripping down to secure this rhythm?

DH: No, I virtually rewrote. I was shocked by my 1971 version, not just at how little I knew then about writing dramatic dialogue, but also that it was full of howlers. It was full of things that just weren't what Pirandello wrote, many misunderstandings of the text. It was quite plain I had simply misunderstood certain passages.

You cannot change the meaning of the line; that is invariable. You can cut, you can strengthen. I did certain things though, for instance in the famous scene where Galileo argues in reply to the little monk. The monk makes a great speech about how taking God away from people is terribly cruel; if you are a peasant what meaning does your life have, because at least God gives order. He also says you believe your suffering to have some point, but what do you say to the peasant who has had God taken away from him, that his suffering is now meaningless? It's Brecht who gives one of the greatest statements in defence of religion, and I felt that he did not give Galileo strong enough arguments in return. So I beefed those arguments up; I said this would be a better scene if Galileo came back stronger. I couldn't tell if this was a linguistic or a dramaturgical problem, I couldn't tell if in the German he does seem to come back equally as strong, but in the literal it didn't seem to me to have as much power. So I beefed it up to make it a more valid scene.

DJ: You're coming back again to this idea of the translator as dramaturg, rather than as someone who is concerned with linguistic accuracy. How did you do the Brecht? Do you speak any German?

DH: I did it from a literal. There's a wonderful book, a Methuen book, which isn't an attempt at an acting version. Someone has just written the literal meanings of every line and then put three versions of the play down side by side, all in one volume. It's excellent policy. To look at it from my point of view, terrible things have been done to my plays in German, things I regard as terrible. Scenes have been reset, jokes have been made about things that I don't make jokes about – for example, in a play like *Pravda* they'll put in references to Mrs. Thatcher. To me, that seems to be a kind of distortion; I would never do anything like that. Sure, the ethics of this are hard to define, but that does seem a travesty to me.

DJ: But there are legitimate places to recreate...

DH: There is a wonderful one about *The Secret Rapture* in Japan, where there is a joke about a character belonging to 'Christians in Business'. It's a very good joke in the English theatre, and there's always lots of laughter about Tom, the Chairman of 'Christians in Business'. I was asked by a Japanese translator to explain the joke about 'Christians in Business'. I started saying 'It's funny in England because of the idea of business being conducted in any way which is. . .' and the explanation dried in my mouth. That's the legitimate place to recreate.

DJ: If I'm reading you right, then you have very little means of distinguishing between translation, adaptation and version. I noticed in your Pirandello that you have 'translated and adapted by' on the cover, and on the inside 'version by'. You've used all three phrases that are in common currency.

DH: I didn't use those descriptions. They stuck them on. It really made me quite queasy when they said 'translation' because I said 'I don't speak Italian, how can you say I translated it?' I asked them if they could credit the person who did the literal translation but they told me I was better known. I know there's some commercial pressure, but I don't think that's right. But if you believe that theatre basically is created out of rhythm, then why not get a rhythm expert in to make a version of the play?

DJ: In your book *Writing Left-Handed* you keep coming back to this idea of the playwright as being someone sitting naked in front of the audience every night. Were you that involved with the Brecht?

DH: No, though it is very interesting that you are one step back. I very happily sat through six or seven previews, and I was very reassured to feel that it was Brecht on the line, not me. I thought that if I felt nervous it would be because I had in some way interposed myself too much. But because I quite happily sat through the previews watching people watch Brecht's play, I didn't feel implicated.

DJ: That's an interesting word.

DH: Well, I often think of a play as evidence against you. When a play comes off, I always think 'Oh, great! The evidence against me isn't available.'

LAURENCE BOSWELL: THE DIRECTOR AS TRANSLATOR

IN CONVERSATION WITH DAVID JOHNSTON

Laurence Boswell is well-known as a director whose work is characterised by its theatrical energy and breadth of dramatic vision. He trained at Manchester University and during the eighties worked both as an Assistant Director at the RSC and as a freelance. In 1990 he joined the Gate Theatre in London as an Associate Artistic Director, and became immediately involved with the award-winning Spanish Golden Age season, one of whose most acclaimed productions – Tirso de Molina's *Damned For Despair* – he adapted and subsequently published in Absolute Classics. Between 1993 and 1995 he was the Gate's Artistic Director, being responsible during that time both for the refurbishment and extension of the Gate and for productions of the scale of *Agamemnon's Children* and *Bohemian Lights*. He recently co-translated with David Johnston and directed Calderón's *The Painter Of Dishonour* for the RSC, and will shortly begin work on Ben Elton's new play *Popcorn*.

DJ: What brings a director to translate?

LB: As always, it's a question of the story. As a director, once you discover a good story, with a rich theme, interesting characters, sometimes you discover that the translator did not do the final bit of his job – the dialogue – so you have to find a form of words that releases the energy in the themes and in the characters in the play, so... that's why I do them.

DJ: What kind of translations have you done?

LB: The first one I did was *Punishment Without Revenge*, which is one of Lope de Vega's most sophisticated tragedies, then *Fuenteovejuna, Don Gil Of The Green Breeches* and *Damned For Despair*, these latter two by Tirso de Molina.

DJ: What difference is there between a director working from his or her own translation, and a director working from a translation which is either commissioned or stumbled upon?

LB: It's both a very useful and a slightly dangerous process because, once you plough into the world of rehearsals, one of the most important things, as you carve or as you dive deeper and deeper into each moment and therefore each metaphor and syllable of the text, is that you realise that you can sometimes not be your own best counterpoint. I think that, actually, one of the most creative ways of doing anything in the theatre – whether it's composing, writing or acting – is through a kind of mutuality, so that if a composer, say, attends rehearsals, then that composer can go off on a mad journey and the director can play the counterpoint, or the other way round. I think that things often work best in rehearsals... and one of the problems that I experience as a director working with my own translation is that you can lose that essential counterpoint. That's the difficult side. The good side is that, as a director, at every second you are present, managing, so that the shoe of the language can be fitted much more tightly to the situation.

DJ: How do you ensure that you are not moving too far away from the original text in terms of the range of meanings it contains?

LB: I think, as a reader and director of plays, and writer of scripts, that it is impossible to say that you know a play until you have gone through the dynamics of testing it in rehearsals. The rehearsal process inevitably takes you closer to the meaning of the play. You can sometimes indulge in what turns out to be a cul-de-sac, where you can get lost on a particular theme or idea, or overemphasize it. But then, as you stand it up and test it against all the different minds that are engaging with the play, the power of that group of people, all of whom are trying to understand and are living through the play from many different perspectives, you inevitably come back to the central energy of the play – perhaps that's a better word than 'meaning', especially for the translator. So, there's a multi-critical, multi-focused unit of people. On this project [Calderón's *The Painter Of Dishonour*] there have been about twenty-four minds obsessed with this play for the last eight weeks, sixteen of whom are actors, composers, lighting and costume designers... and everyone, coming from their different perspectives, combines to recreate the totality of the play. If you can create an atmosphere – which I always try to do – whereby everybody's perspective can find a voice, so that everything is negotiated through the rich focus of all those different minds, whether it be costumes, set, music, or the translation, so that everything can go through that sieve, it usually comes out richer. The translation is a voice among voices.

DJ: Looking over your productions of plays in translation, whether by you or not, how successful do you think you've been in recreating that original energy?

LB: When I read these plays – whether it was Tirso or Lope, or indeed Valle-Inclán – it was clear that here was a set of values, a range of emotional responses and a quality of emotional power, all very different from the Anglo-Saxon English ones. Therefore, even to begin to think of staging a play where you have to lean towards finding a different rhythm or a different emotional intensity in performance, you have to be fully aware of this otherness. It would be silly, not to say impossible, to pretend to be Spanish, but there's somewhere in between that English actors can locate themselves, as they respond to the Spanish energies which are locked into the text. So, a kind of hybrid is created which is a sort of exciting mongrel in the middle.

DJ: And yet, in *Bohemian Lights* you tried to create an Irish pedigree!

LB: Well. . . I know an Irish actress who came to see the last performance of *Bohemian Lights* and she said, 'That was so multi-cultural!' She said she could feel the Spanishness of the original, but that she also loved the frame, the lens of the Dublin world, which we put visually and linguistically in front of the text. And then she went on to say that a lot of the visual style and visual images reminded her of the Polish tradition. So, here was a Spanish play seen in London by an Irish woman, filtered through a Dublin lens with a Polish performance style. . . and that, I think, is a very exciting notion. What I mean is, if the translator is aware of the foreign rhythms of what he's translating, then no matter how that play is staged or adapted, its otherness will be communicated.

DJ: But how did you react to people who would along and say, 'But I wanted to see Valle-Inclán and that wasn't Valle-Inclán. . .' At whose door do we lay that one, translator or director?

LB: Well, I would like to keep the idea of fault or blame right out of the agenda. You know, I think I can recognise where that kind of response is coming from. There are those who regard theatre from the perspective of the 'connoisseur', as a 'library', a sophisticated kind of 'bourgeois delicatessen' where sophisticated middle-aged chaps pop round and say, 'Oh, I'll have my Valle-Inclán' or 'my El Greco', or 'my original recording of "The Rites of Spring" ', or 'my original manuscripts of a Dickens novel'. I think there's another way of looking at theatre, which is as a kind of living popular engagement between an audience and a company which wants to deal with the world as it is now. Valle-Inclán's play attacks some of the contemporary politicians of his world dangerously and libelously, and we would have just taken the sting out of all that engagement by leaving the play in its original context. I know that this is one of your favourite paradoxes – but by betraying him, we were most loyal to him. And, actually, to be fair, one of the critics said that it was a master stroke touching on the central kind of living political wound that exists between England and Ireland, which is still open.

DJ: I've heard you say that when you're preparing to direct a translation, you like to look at all the translations that exist of that play, good, indifferent and positively bad. Does that not lead to a danger of creating a sort of 'pastiche' version of the play?

LB: No. Strangely enough, in terms of the process of coming to terms with the play and its meanings, what I find incredibly useful is the most dreadful translation, which I consciously search out, the most archaic, academic, unactable, gobbledy-gook translation, which you can't even imagine presenting to a group of actors. Even a translation like that can lead you to a quantum leap of perception that would, otherwise, be very difficult to make. Let's take the text of any popular

Shakespeare play, say, *Macbeth*, as a particularly well-gilded example. Imagine the great production that Trevor Nunn did of the play in the seventies, or the wonderful production that the Rumanian director brought to the National five or six years ago, or the remarkable productions that have taken place in Russia, or the incredible version by Kurosawa. You look at those four different responses to a text and you find that they are radically different works of art, at every level. They've all responded to that text; their starting point was the language, but it has led them all somewhere else. And that's the important thing, I think, that people perceive that language is vital, but it is only one element at play: there is no definitive version, no sort of 'original manuscript' still available. That's another idea sitting behind some of the more inane literary and undramatic thought about translations – that there is a kind of ideal text somewhere, a kind of perfect translucent Calderón that can still be performed in the perfectly translucent seventeenth-century style – all we will have in that case is the perfectly dead piece of Greek pottery.

DJ: Do you sense a major divide between the academic world and the world of theatre in this sense? Almost an incompatibility, in that both are striving towards different objectives?

LB: Yes, but not quite that neatly. There are certainly academics who have a real sense of theatre, but within the academic world there is a culture that also exists within the theatre world, which seems to me to be inherently 'literary', and, therefore, inherently undramatic. And that is a generalization. I have worked with and I have spoken to many academics who have a great love of the theatre, and a great insight into the workings of the theatre, so, as a generalization, I would agree that some of the values that are inherited in the academic literary tradition are not helpful for drama, but there are certainly lots of individuals I know who are very aware that plays work wholly only in performance and not as works of literature.

DJ: Leaving aside what still seems to me to be your rather eccentric use of bad translations, do you think that some academic translations could be considered as obstacles to the plays actually being performed?

LB: Oh, without a doubt that happens. There's nothing like a bad translation to keep these old plays in the museums. But if you work from a bad translation, then you won't be bamboozled by the language. The only thing you have left are the deeper meanings, the deeper themes and the drama, the relationship that exists between the characters, the most vital stuff, which is always use of character, relationship, theme interaction. . . So that's why I use a bad translation, which I suppose is a rather eccentric – your word, mine would be 'sophisticated' – use of text. A bad translation certainly isn't actable, but it does force you to concentrate your mind on the energy of the play.

DJ: As a director, what is the difference for you between working with the translator, and living and dead playwrights in English? Does working with the translator give you more freedom to 'mess around' with the language? I'm consciously using a very pejorative phrase.

LB: Any opportunity can be abused. Conceiving a play from another language is both a necessity and an opportunity, and at that moment you come down really to the sensitivity and the intelligence of the translator and the director, both of whom respect the original and try to treat the original with both great reverence and great irreverence, in order to create a living version four hundred years later in a different culture of what that dead author wanted. So we are the living custodians of Calderón, as it were, but in this particular instance, we can't not be living in 1995 and we can't not be speakers of English.

DJ: That sounds very noble, very altruistic, but in the pressure of the rehearsal itself, when you are a week away from the opening and something is not working, is that really something that's foremost in your mind, when you are trying to find something that will actually work on stage?

LB: No, although the altruism is impacted into the practicality. You think 'How does that work? It's not working, let's make it work'. But this takes us into another one of the great myths of text. You can bet your life that if Golden Age companies that were performing a particular text thought a speech was too long or a joke didn't work, they would have re-written it; but we've only got the record of where they came to, as though the clock had stopped. A text is essentially a dynamic thing. The 'sacrosanct text' is a complete fantasy. I mean, from Euripides through Shakespeare to Lope de Vega, right down to the latest play by David Edgar that was at The Other Place last season, the idea or the desire of the whole group of people who are putting on a play is to make the story work, and the text will be beaten and twisted and turned to make whatever it is that group of people want to articulate. At the end of that, there will be a form of words which is like the kind of residue of that experiment. Now, to take that residue, as some people tend to do, whether they be academics or critics or wherever the conservative literary end of the market is, and to deify it, and to criticise every other group who tries to release other energies contained within the text, is to impose stagnation on theatre.

DJ: Let me go back to my earlier question. From your perspective as a director, do you have a hierarchy of living and dead writers in English, and as translator, where you will see that text of something translated from a foreign language as being – if you like – more provisional than, say, a Shakespeare or a text written by David Edgar?

LB: That's a good way of looking at it. There are very few living writers whom I've ever worked with who would come into rehearsals and say 'that text is sacrosanct!' They enjoy the process of rehearsals and they write their plays up or down or with that group of people, so, in most cases, the contemporary play is incredibly provisional, in an exciting way.

The translation of a play also has a wonderful freedom and provisionality about it, so the joker in the middle is the greater tradition of Shakespeare and Jonson, which people are much less likely to fiddle around with – and for all the wrong reasons, I think, precisely because it is congealed in time, because it's set in stone. However, if you look back, say, at the last twenty years of this tradition, of our response to Shakespeare, we are going through quite a respectful or conservative period of performing the full text, of not tinkering about with it. John Barton, who did *The Wars Of The Roses*, wrote three hundred and fifty lines of Shakespeare himself, and hacked plays to pieces. That went on right through the sixties and the seventies; Peter Brook did it, Peter Hall did it, for all the reasons why translators of four-hundred year old Spanish plays would re-write them, that is, to make them live now. . . That doesn't mean to say that you're diluting those plays. If we go back to Calderón as an example; if you were to take his long, buoyant, baroque speeches and boil them down to a kind of *Daily Mirror* tabloid intensity, that to me would be as obscene as not cutting a scene that doesn't work from a text! One is just trying to re-invent, with great respect for the original author – trying to recreate, four-hundred years later, in a different country and time, often involves a re-writing. And that isn't to betray the author.

DJ: Of course, one of the great watersheds in the performance of Shakespeare in this country was the dictat from Peter Hall, that 'when we perform Shakespeare let it be seen that there is a point of contact with the present moment', or words to that effect. When you come to choose a foreign text to be performed in English, do you look for points of contact of that nature, or do you consider the text as an end in itself?

LB: No. I find the 'otherness' of the play exciting. For example, in this play, *The Painter Of Dishonour*, the way that Calderón examines the conflict between the instinctual and passionate irrational side of the human nature, in conflict with its desire to create order and patterns and structures. . . that debate seems to me to be the relentless debate of Spanish drama, not to say all Spanish art. And it's lived in Calderón, or Lope, or Lorca with such an intensity and clarity and passion that it's presented in a new light, one that isn't shared by English authors. So, it is actually the 'otherness' rather than the 'sameness' that attracts me.

DJ: So what sort of difficulties are encountered by our directors and actors when they come to perform these sort of plays?

LB: The first difficulty is that the poor old director has to try and develop a vision attuned to the philosophical, psychological, emotional realities that the plays posit, and that then you have to move the actors towards that. The rhythms of Spanish speech are a good deal faster than English ones. English drama is generally used to the great multitude of words, and sits back on them and lets the language flow for language's sake. In a way, language is often used in English, I think, to avoid the moment and to control it. Because, what is it that England is good at but controlling the world through language? The great diplomatic tradition is one of the things that England is still good at. But the Spanish language is more nakedly emotional, more honed to the cutting edge of emotion. One of the things I'm always trying the actors to get at is actually to get the characters to meet the emotional situation head on through the language. So, you don't sit back, think and then speak. Speech, thought and emotion, all happen in this heightened intense moment, so you are actually trying to find a performance style which is incredibly intelligent and fast-thinking and emotionally powerful. And none of those things are particularly present in the English tradition. It takes a great deal of work to assimilate that.

The other thing is that there is a problem which we've inherited from the realistic tradition of the last hundred years, from Ibsen to Chekhov – both of whom are great writers, there's no doubt – but there has been a consistent and ongoing experiment in the naturalistic adventure, an experiment that started at the end of the nineteenth century/beginning of the twentieth, that has left us a legacy which, on one hand, is fruitful in that it demands an emotional truthfulness of character at every moment, but which is also a curse, because naturalism leads to the notion that what we are about on stage is the creation of a consistent world. Now, there isn't anything quite like life in that sense in Calderón. Calderón is the most beautifully and outrageously manipulative and provocative of writers. He uses drama in a kind of kaleidoscope of ideas that spins and whirls towards passion and insights, and he will quite naturally mix the naturalistic, satirical, philosophical and lyrical, creating even what we would call Brechtian moments in his work. So finding a style for the actors to have enough confidence to understand these plays to the extent that they are able to move through the register of farce, tragedy and so on, is extremely difficult, because this doesn't really exist as a living tradition in our theatre (there are only isolated outbreaks of it). So, that's tricky. Particularly with Calderón, because by the mid-seventeenth century hundreds of versions of the *comedia* had been written. It's as if all the Spanish Golden Age playwrights, it seems to me anyway, wrote just one play with similar characters, with exactly the same structure and dramatic rhythm. So, after forty-five years and probably certainly over two hundred goes at it, I think these playwrights were actually playing really sophisticated tricks and games with the form, and, as a result, in the acting tradition which had grown up around Lope, Tirso and Calderón you would have had the highest level of skill and dexterity in performing this type of play. Remember also they would have been performing to an audience which would be remarkably attuned to every twist and turn, nuances in register and meaning. So it is actually quite a daunting task to take a Calderón play out of its context, out of its tradition of acting skills, and try and to put it together in an eight-week appearance. This is the day after the first night, which is a kind of a little mourning day, when you look back over the life of the play in rehearsal... because something dies when the play opens, even though you know that something has been born as well, because the play is up in front of an audience now, but something dies in that process, and looking back, as you do over a life when a person dies, you kind of think: 'I now would have a wholly different and a wholly more skilled and sophisticated approach if and when I ever take on another Calderón'. Not regret, but the learning process which is involved in every creative process. It's true of the director, and I think it's no less true of the translator.

TRANSLATING COMEDY

KENNETH McLEISH

Kenneth McLeish is an extraordinarily accomplished linguist and translator. As well as having written and co-written with Frederic Raphael many original stage, radio and television plays, he has translated Aeschylus, Sophocles, Euripides, Aristophanes, Terence, Labiche, Ibsen, Strindberg, Feydeau and Ionesco. In the last two years he has also translated work by Holberg (*Jeppe Of The Hill*) and Molière (*The School For Wives*), and there have been acclaimed productions of, among others, *A Doll's House* and *Hedda Gabler* (English Touring Theatre), *Lysistrata* (at Manchester's Contact Theatre), Euripides's *Ion* (which opened in Greece before transferring to Britain) and the acclaimed *Agamemnon's Children* (the Euripides trilogy of *Elektra*, *Orestes* and *Iphigeneia*, which played in the Gate). In 1994 his new play *Omma*, a retelling of the Theban myths from his own translations of Sophocles, was produced at the Young Vic.

The comic moment

The theatrical experience consists of a series of moments of complicity between performer and spectator. At each of these moments, the performer reveals something to the spectator, or reminds the spectator of something already known – an emotion, an aspect of character, a relationship, a circumstance (such as a climate of political belief or religious thought) outside the specific content of the dramatic action but contingent on it.

These moments can be single, or multiple. They can involve one performer and one spectator, or many. Communication can be direct or ironical, overt or subtle, even intentional or accidental. But in all cases the essence of the experience is sharing. The spectator's participation is as crucial as the performer's; they work together to make the show, and without their complicity there is no show. Even when we read dramatic material alone to ourselves at home, we 'perform' it in our minds, we give it emotional (and sometimes physical) blocking in ways quite different from when we read poetry, say, or novels.

Of all kinds of theatre, none depends so much as comedy on the moment of complicity. Each laugh is like a spark, kindled in an instant (and often as quickly extinguished). It is as if the performer is making a series of propositions to the spectator – 'This is funny. So is this. So is this' – and the spectator is agreeing or disagreeing, each and every time. Even a sustained crescendo of hilarity depends on continuous ignition. Feydeau once calculated that there were 230 individual laugh points in *The Girl From Maxim's*, exactly placed, and that if as little as a minute went by without a laugh in any particular performance, that performance was doomed. When I translated Feydeau's *Pig In A Poke* I made sure there was a joke in the second line spoken: it was crucial to let the audience know that the fun was starting, so to speak, that they were licensed to laugh. In previews, the actor changed this line minutely and failed to get a laugh, leaving the play and cast struggling for several minutes; as soon as we restored the correct text, with its precise rhythm and timing, the problem was solved.

Performer and audience

In this contract of laughter, the performer is the main partner. All good performers lead their audiences, but comic performers do it more overtly and more consistently than any others – and many also allow themselves an extra irony, overlaying the entire show: shared knowledge with the spectators that what is happening *is* a show, that we are all there to laugh and that the comedy is contrived specifically to make us do so. Aristophanes, and to a lesser extent Molière, used the leading actor as a kind of hinge between the 'reality' of the people in the theatre and the 'illusion' of the characters within the show. An Athenian farmer or a French miser could step in and out of character, talking directly to the audience (in a manner of a modern stand-up comedian, to whose humour-mill anything and everything is grist) and then returning to his assigned role – and milking the humour of the switch each time.

In such a performance, an appearance of spontaneity is important. We hardly expect Edmund's soliloquies, in *King Lear*, to appear as if he were thinking them up even as he articulated them: our assent in their power is partly due to the artifice that we know this is pre-written (and pre-performed) material, not to mention fine poetry. But comedy, by its very nature, must seem fresh each time. The plays may be well-known and the routines familiar, but we look for a novel twist in every performance. If all Mrs. Malaprops drew on essentially the same repertoire of performing strategies, if the performer's personality were subordinate each time to a kind of tradition of playing the role, the play would die. The author's text, in comedy more than in any other kind of theatre, is a blueprint, a skeleton for what happens in performance, and without the performer, on the page, it can be about as exciting as a pricked balloon.

The translator of comedy

All this puts the translator of comedy in territory which is delightful to the ego, but full of professional beartraps. Literary translators, of every kind, are there because the authors aren't, because they're dead or otherwise incommunicado. This is all right for 'serious' work – the script of *Six Characters In Search Of An Author* or *A Doll's House* needs merely (merely!) to be rendered in accessible form in another language, to make an effect similar to that of the original on native speakers. There are choices and compromises to make, and the translator must bear his or her own audience in mind at least as much as the original readers or spectators. But, by and large, the strategies of communication are clear, and reasonably the same, from one language and set of circumstances to the other. The translator is a midwife, and the less obtrusive he or she is, the better.

In comedy, by contrast, the translator has often to play a far more aggressive role – creating not merely a text derived from a foreign-language original, but a mode of performance, a register, which will unlock the laughter latent in that text, and translate *that* into the terms of his or her own audience. In my experience, directors and performers of comedy often rely far more than their 'serious' counterparts on the physical presence and input of the translator during rehearsals. The texts have to be worked, mined for comic potential, and the translator is there both to assist in this and to pull the process back when it moves too far from (what seem to be) the original author's intentions. If rehearsing serious drama is like practising a symphony from the composer's fully-notated score, working comedy is like creating jazz.

To put the matter thus baldly is to risk being accused of creative arrogance. Why should a translator, that servant of the servant of the Muses, presume to intervene? A simultaneous interpreter, at the elbow of some great personage, is hardly expected to put a spin on the jokes his or her employer utters, much less replace them with new ones. The jokes should be rendered as they come, and take their chance. If this is the case with politicians and other VIP jokesters, why should it be different for professional writers? The answer is that most writers of comedy, unlike most VIP's, create precisely with interpretation in mind, and expect the collaboration of their interpreters. And with foreign-language comedy, translation is one part of that collaboration. I once saw a devastatingly funny parody of Edith Evans's version of Lady Bracknell by Louis de Funès of the Comédie-Française – was that 'arrogant'? And what of de Funès's translator, who turned Wilde's dialogue into cod-English grunts and whoops like something out of an Ionesco language class – was he or she arrogant? They did what they did and walked away, leaving Wilde's original (not to mention our memory of Edith Evans's performance) utterly unharmed.

Extent of intervention

Obviously, the amount and nature of a translator's interventions vary from play to play. A translator working on text-based, literary comedy might want to make very few changes, if any. *A Month In The Country* or *The Broken Jug* – not to mention such different but hardly less text-centred pieces as *Rhinoceros* or *The Eunuch* – create worlds of their own which depend in part on a dance of language and are self-consistent and entirely comprehensible. The translator's role is simply to find appropriate English utterance, and tampering in any way – for example relocating the action in a country or time different from the original – is overegging the pudding. (I once transposed *The Eunuch* from ancient Rome to pre-Revoutionary France, re-working it as what I fondly hoped would be a new *Marriage Of Figaro*; it died on me.)

With some authors the dramatic strategy, and hence the translator's approach, varies from play to play. Feydeau is a prime example. Outside France, he is chiefly known for half a dozen large-scale farces set firmly in the Belle Epoque, with big-moustached, ramrod-backed Lotharios, corseted matrons and frou-frou-skirted flirts out of any Toulouse Lautrec painting. If you work on *A Flea In Her Ear*, *The Girl From Maxim's*, *Sauce For The Goose* (*Le dindon*) or *The One That Got Away* (*Monsieur chasse!*), all you need do is translate what's there, taking care of the comic articulation and linguistic rhythms in English but otherwise letting Feydeau do all the work. (In *Sauce For The Goose* I did make the silly-ass Englishwoman Swiss-German, as her fractured English wasn't funny in a context where everyone else was speaking English instead of French; I changed the hunting expeditions of *Sauce For The Goose* to fishing, since hunting, in England, has different overtones from the innocent mass hobby it was in eighteen-nineties' France. But that was all.)

In other plays, however, Feydeau blends farce with social criticism of a quite different, subtler kind, using character and situation in a way less like his own 'big' farces than foreshadowing such later English writers as Travers or Lonsdale. *Pig In A Poke*, for example, set throughout in a single bourgeois household, depends on continuous but never-stated subversion of the nuances of polite social behaviour. The characters' emotions and obsessions keep making them forget the niceties of etiquette – and then they suddenly remember them, and fall back on them, in a way which shades farce into 'high' comedy and vice-versa. To see the point of this each time it happens, an audience needs a sense of period manners – and to English audiences, the manners and language of the French Belle Epoque are as remote as those of the Moon. When I translated the play, therefore, I reset it in Edwardian London, in the last moments of the late-Imperial glow which led to self-satisfaction, pomposity and rigid ideas of social hierarchy, duty and bourgeois manners – a close parallel to Feydeau's original period in France, and one which allowed, in English, the clash between etiquette and personal feelings to continue to control the whole action.

At the opposite end of the interventionist scale are comedies, such as those of the *commedia dell'arte*, which consistently use non-textual conventions. Lope de Vega, Goldoni, much of Molière are not so much complete texts as starting-points for performance. The words are a main strand of the entertainment, and need translating more or less as they stand. But there is also a second, equally important element, which is hidden or hinted at in such tantalising stage directions as 'He throws cushions' or 'He tries to dance but falls down three times'. In dealing with this kind of thing – or rather providing material for the performers to deal with it – the translator must briefly put on the shoes of the original author, must presume to interpret not statements but the assumptions and intentions which gave rise to them.

An excellent example of this kind of comedy is *Jeppe Of The Hill* by the 'Danish Molière' Ludwig Holberg: a piece about a drunken peasant taken, for a jape, into the local manor and persuaded that he's a lord, then arrested and subjected to a mock-trial and mock-hanging for impersonating his betters. In working on this play the translator needs to use three quite different strategies. The heart of it, a series of dazzling monologues for the peasant himself, needs no more than straight-forward translation: they are realistic, and character-based, as earthy as the man who speaks them. But this fails with the upper-class characters (a Baron and his Majordomo, a pair of bored, amoral aristos), and with the two *commedia dell'arte* clowns who play doctors, lawyers, courtiers and lackeys. The brittleness and vacuous viciousness of the aristocratic characters are apparent in what they say in Danish, but not in the way they say it. The prose is characterless, inert. To register the qualities I found in the dialogue – to 'stylise' the characters in a way Holberg's actors must have done by guying well-known social and performing conventions of the time, now lost – I decided to make the Baron and Majordomo speak a heightened English not available to the peasant characters, a fractured variety of the 'high style' favoured by Shakespeare's young bluebloods. The *commedia dell'arte* characters posed problems of a different kind again. They were clearly meant to perform a wealth of physical business, *lazzi*, but these were never described, merely indicated in the text. There were cues for music, and there were songs, again not spelled out but clearly intended. All this would have to be fleshed out in production – and therefore in the text on which the actors were to work. Eventually, after many drafts, I evolved a text which left Holberg's *commedia dell'arte* dialogue more or less as he wrote it (some of it, indeed, still in Latin), but filled out the songs and business in ways which gave the actors maximum scope, and rope. All this allowed the satirical, literary portions of the play and the *commedia dell'arte* sections each to work on their own plane, but also to move into and out of one another in a way which seemed faithful both to the production style of Holberg's own time and the (somewhat abbreviated) suggestions in his script.

Hidden style: Aristophanes as a case study
The process described above may seem more arbitrary, more self indulgent, to non-translators than it will to practitioners. What is it in a particular comedy that makes its translator choose to make a 'version' rather than a straight translation? The decision is not pure ego: if self-promotion were all that mattered, translators could

simply write plays of their own – and many do. It is not a simple lack of self-control, as when Nigel Kennedy (say) plays a jazz cadenza in the middle of Beethoven's Violin Concerto. (Well, not always. I swear I once heard the line 'they were forking each other under the table' in a Molière translation. It must have been an isolated lapse.) It is a question, rather, of faithfulness not to surface but to inner meaning, to the comic vision which gives the play its life.

The further back one goes in time, and the greater the writer, the more elusive this comic vision becomes. Aristophanes proves the point. Superficially, his plays seem to be huge holdalls of jokes, slapstick, satire, bawdy, lyric, parody and topical reference; a translator's nightmare. If you bog yourself down in detail, the Aristophanic spirit dies. In the past, some academic translators meticulously dotted every i and crossed every t, adding footnotes to help us see the point, and in the process destroying the humour. (I have seen 'authentic' stage productions along similar lines: equipped with masks, dance, patterns copied from Greek vases, male actors laboriously playing women – everything except Aristophanic funniness.) Some more modern versions have chucked out the original entirely, replacing it with today's topical references and attention-grabbing extensions and developments of Aristophanes's original ideas: effects plastered on the plays, and shifting them.

Both approaches – and Aristophanes is not the only victim, merely an egregious example of the kind of author people think they can treat as they like – begin from the same mistake, a wish to ignore or amputate the entire theatrical tradition between the original author's time and ours. One approach presents us with a piece which tries to set Aristophanes in his original context exclusively, as in a museum display; the other tries to make us think that he delivered his script just yesterday. In fact this tradition – and the modern audience's sophistication which goes with it – should help rather than hinder all present-day interpreters, and translators in particular. Aristophanes is bawdy – and since his time we have learned a thousand ways of articulating that, from in-your-face bluntness to double, treble and quadruple entendre. Aristophanes wrote dazzling comedy song-lyrics – and we have a tradition there too, of using particular kinds of rhyme, rhythm and verse-forms for particular effects. Aristophanes imagines wonderful slapstick sequences – and their progeny of pratfalls, double-takes, travesty acting and impersonation are familiar to us from countless shows on film, TV, stage and pier-end. Translators should neither high-handedly ignore all this material, nor use it to replace Aristophanes's original: they should simply be aware of it to help 'register' what is already there in the Greek.

When this is done – when one assumes, for example, that an Aristophanic scene of mutual insult or seduction may have things in common with such scenes in later comedy – what is revealed, paradoxically, is not a ragbag of effects but a single, controlling comic vision, a secure platform for all the absurdities, parodies and firework-dazzle showing-off which give the plays their superficial energy. It is this unstated vision, the fire and fuel of the whole experience, which bad translations ignore or distort and which a good translation should reveal. And what is true for Aristophanes applies to every other comic author whose plays we work on. More than in any other area of translation, except perhaps poetry, the comedy translator has to look for the impulse behind the words, and then try not to reproduce it but to realise it, in a way which will allow English-speaking performers and spectators to make the same kind of communication with each other as did the originals. This is the heart and soul of translating comedy – and if it requires 'attitude' in the translator, so be it.

'BUT THE SQUIRES ARE CRAMMED FULL WITH SORROWS'

KEITH DEWHURST

Keith Dewhurst is one of the most prolific and respected writers for British stage and television. As well as more than twenty plays for the small screen (including *Lloyd George* and *Last Bus*, winner of the Japan Prize for Educational Television), he was, among many other things, one of the original Z-Cars writing team. He has written fifteen plays, five of which – *Luggage, Lark Rise, The World Turned Upside Down, Candleford* and *Don Quixote* – were staged by the National Theatre between 1977 and 1982. *Pirates* and *Corunna!* were presented by the English Stage Company at the Royal Court. He has also published several novels, worked on and written a number of screenplays (including *The Empty Beach*), and in recent years wrote an adaptation of Bulgakov's novel *Black Snow*, perfomed to acclaim in the Royal National Theatre.

When David Johnston asked me to write about translating plays I said 'Can I write about adaptations as well, because in my head the two are mixed up?' He said 'Yes,' very generously, so that is what I will do. My credentials for the task are mixed: I speak passable traveller's French, and undaunted restaurant Italian; but if I am asked to do a version from another language I need literal translations. On the other hand, I have written for my living for more than thirty years, in many venues and situations, and bits of my own work have been translated into German, Italian and Japanese. Since I was not consulted, I have no idea how well.

Of course, we are asked to translate or adapt things because people like them, and my first thought is that it is difficult to know *absolutely* why. The reasons for the success of a play or book seem to be obvious in general, but prove elusive in particular. This is especially true when we sit in the theatre: the person in front has a big head, the air-conditioning may not be effective, and one of the actors mumbles. In the heat of such moments it can be hard to tell what specifically has worked the magic, and that's the trouble: writers do work in terms of the specific. It is down in the end to the choice of one word against another, or the rhythmic difference between one punctuation mark and another.

Who can say exactly what combination of words, scenes, characters and, subtly important, *omissions* is the secret of a writer's tone? Because if a writer's tone could be reproduced, someone would do it. We would all write like Tolstoy tomorrow. A writer's tone, by which I mean, I suppose, his apprehension of things as expressed in his own words, is crucial. Told one way, a story about a girl deciding whom to marry is Jane Austen. Told another, it is Mills & Boon. It is different, and works in a different way, which is why in most of the adaptations I have done for the theatre, film and TV, I have tried to alter as little as possible, and to preserve the tone.

I was convinced of the sense of this approach by a mish-mash adaptation of Stevenson's *Kidnapped* and *Catriona* that I did for the Royal Lyceum Theatre, Edinburgh, in 1972. Even twenty-odd years ago Stevenson's reputation was lighter than it is today, and the director Bill Bryden and I were determined to show the seriousness of his concerns. So we began with an invented scene of the Battle of Culloden, and then plunged into the murder of the Red Fox. This would have been fine had we not then gone back to the story of David and his Uncle. The moral is that if you are going to cut and re-shape, do it boldly. Remove entire narratives and never, in the theatre, go back in time. What saved our rickety construction was Stevenson's own dialogue, which sufficed for entire scenes and positively sparkled.

In a drama we must see the events happen. The story must be advanced by what the characters say and do. Editorial information can set up a novel but it cannot set up a play. It follows that the first task of someone adapting a novel is to identify the essential narrative. The second is to cast into scenes those parts of the essential narrative that are carried in editorial matter. Invariably this calls for the writing of dialogue that does not exist in the original.

People often say that novelists write stilted dialogue, but in my experience, the better the novelist the more speakable the dialogue. Novelists of a more civilised age wrote too much dialogue, perhaps, and in these cases filleting seems in order. Bill Bryden and I once had a project, never realised, to dramatise Fenimore Cooper. Had we come to grips with him I think that his descriptive passages would have seemed more tedious than his dialogue.

In scenes of high emotion Cooper's dialogue can be flowery, although who is to say that young people of the 1820s did not actually say some of these things? His soldiers and frontiersmen have many a pungent phrase, as do the characters of Cooper's ideal Sir Walter Scott. Scott was, after all, the first novelist to show social structures through individual representative types, and his books invariably dramatise well.

All in all, since the audience does not get to read the stage directions, and the only words they hear are those the actors speak, I do not see how we can convey a writer's tone without the use of his original dialogue. When there is no dialogue and some needs to be written, I am a great believer in the method employed by

David O Selznick when he produced *Gone With The Wind*. Use dialogue from scenes you don't need, or make dialogue out of the writer's editorial phrases.

This method worked very well for me when I adapted *Lark Rise* and *Candleford* from Flora Thompson, and Christopher Hill's history book, *The World Turned Upside Down*. This last is the classic account of the left-wing religious and social revolutionaries of the 1640s, and I was able to take much of the dialogue from writings or recorded utterances of the persons concerned.

Copyright permitting, one should also use where appropriate dialogue from other works by the same author. Anything for authenticity: although of course, sooner or later every adaptor must get inside the other writer's mind and come up with a pastiche. Reviewers of *Lark Rise* quoted more than once Flora Thompson gems that I had written while living at Palm Beach, New South Wales, but I never persuaded myself that I was doing anything more than paying Mrs Thompson homage. In fact, one of the reasons for the success of this show was that everyone who worked on it was persuaded that they should serve Flora Thompson and not themselves, a psychological trick that did not work on later occasions.

Lark Rise is a memoir, of course, and does not have a narrative, so it was necessary to invent one: in this case a day in the life of the hamlet. Its sequel *Candleford* required the same process. *The World Turned Upside Down* is a straight history book, and does not resemble a drama at all. But it does tell a strong story, and if one can come up with a scene for each key event, the job of dramatisation is not as difficult as it seems: witness the smoothness of David Hare's version of the memoir *Fanshen*.

I encountered much more intractable technical problems when I adapted Peter Corris's Sydney private-eye novel *The Empty Beach* for an Australian feature film in 1984. I think that the basic problem is one which crops up a great deal when entertainment fiction is adapted for the screen, and it is: what should one do when the incidental plots and red herrings take up far more time than the main story? In a book such confusions are acceptable. In a drama, all they are is confusing.

In Sydney, alas, we were not as bold as Robert Altman when he adapted *The Long Goodbye*. Our Executive Producer came late to the project after another script had failed to find finance, and brought in the director and me. Pre-production systems were already set up. My first task was a detailed scene-by-scene breakdown with no dialogue, to help people to budget and find locations. This put me off such treatments for life, if I was ever on them, because as soon as dialogue goes in so too does *character*, and inevitably things change.

But the co-operation was fun and the Executive Producer, on his way to some film market or other, would phone me from the International Transit lounge with suggested lines of dialogue. 'What we've got here is so big it'll blow this town apart' is one I vividly remember. Between us we managed to trim the sub-plots and to build the main story into a tale that linked politicians to organised crime. This is the great issue in modern New South Wales, and it is extraordinary that the Australian cinema has paid it so little attention.

Ironically, what doomed the film was neither the pre-production rush, nor our editing room cuts and post-synch dialogue. What doomed it was an antipathy between the star and the director. So we never rehearsed properly, a lot of parts were weakly cast, and many scenes played at cross-purposes. One can't really say how the adaptation worked because it never had a full chance: but certainly the problem was there and it was an interesting one. The only reason to see the film would be its photography of Sydney: it was by Johnny Seale, who later shot *Witness* and other Hollywood movies.

What even mucked-up films do with ease is to cope with numerous locations. In the theatre this can be difficult, and a constant problem that crops up in adaptations is the relationship between the material on the one hand, and theatre space and theatre mechanics on the other. How many of us remember old, and not so old, repertory adaptations of the Brontës and Jane Austen that struggled to cram the action into one set, or at best two, with a full scene-change at the interval? Most theatres were built in the nineteenth century with proscenium stages, and the convention of the proscenium is 'realism', which works best, as in Ibsen and Chekhov, when the stage represents one location at a time.

Shakespeare's Globe, for example, had a stage and balconies that did not change from one play to the next, and it was the dramatic convention of the day that the audience would *believe* that the scene had changed when told so by notice boards, the dialogue, or one whole lot of characters going off and another coming on.

Today our dramatic conventions, like our world, some would say, are all in pieces, and one sees many ill-executed productions and much sloppy writing in consequence. Not least because it is still true that the only way in which the proscenium can maintain spatial integrity is by raising and lowering the curtain.

Some would say: 'What about a show like *The Phantom Of The Opera*?' I would reply that firstly, music changes the rules of the space and brings frontal energy into play; and secondly, that stage machinery that costs millions cannot possibly be applied in every theatre. And a true convention, of course, is universal. By frontal energy I mean the recognition that the audience is present, as in music-hall, cabaret and concerts. In a true proscenium performance the actors speak to each other and the audience are 'fourth-wall' voyeurs. These problems of what the theatre can and cannot convincingly encompass lie at the heart of the way in which Trevor Nunn chose to present *Nicholas Nickleby*, and to decisions by William Gaskill, in *The Speakers*, and Bill Bryden, in many shows at the National Theatre, to take the action outside the proscenium altogether.

Thus I knew that *Lark Rise* would be performed in the promenade, and *The World Turned Upside Down* on a traverse stage running through the audience. I was free from the start to deploy epic narratives and many locations. This means that when an adaptor is working with a director he knows, and for a particular space, he can and should create the work to suit. The problem for translators, it seems to me, is the other way round.

More often than not a classical play in a foreign language was written for a kind of theatre space and theatrical conventions that no longer exist.

How should this effect what the translator does?

We are bound up here as well, I guess, with the entire problem of idiom: of what words mean in another language and culture. Lots of people must know the joke about Harold Pinter writing that someone 'watered the wicket', and this being translated into German as 'urinated on the gate'. A silly story, but it is the nub, because what writers express is not verbal liveliness for its own sake, but social forms and activities.

Modern English is the language of a society in which a particular accent is the hallmark of education, breeding and power. Bernard Shaw wrote a play about it, and although I talk with a Northern accent myself, I have no doubt that successful Essex businessmen are out there even now taking elocution lessons.

In contrast, the Venetian dialect of Carlo Goldoni, like the Neapolitan of de Filippo, was shared by aristocrats, gondoliers, maiden aunts and street urchins, so that the comedies of the *bella figura* bespeak societies with a profound sense of what people have in common. English, for all its self-renewing richness, speaks constantly of financial, cultural, regional and educational divisions. It seems to me that it must be very difficult to translate Goldoni and other masters of the classical comedy into modern English. If the language has a Scots or Irish lilt things may be different, as I know from a version I did of Molière's *The Miser*.

This was directed by Bill Bryden at the Royal Lyceum, Edinburgh, in 1973. There have been several versions of Molière in Scots, and this was one of them. It starred Ricki Fulton as Harpagon and was a success, being revived and sent out on tour. I had a literal translation of the play done by a bilingual actor friend, and worked from that. My only alterations were to thin Molière's expositional scenes very slightly, and, of course, to write my pastiche Scots dialogue.

We set the play in 1970s Edinburgh, and I was emboldened to glean words from Scott, Burns and Stevenson by the fact that I knew the actors reasonably well: they had forgiven and even enjoyed my *Kidnapped* foibles. They laid claim to a powerful race-memory, but none of them actually spoke eighteenth-century lowland Scots, and generally speaking they knew more about modern football than ancient vocabularies. And in any case, Bill Bryden was always more or less convinced that he was running a football club rather than a theatre troupe, an illusion that I was happy to share. When at the intervals we asked one another how the play was going we always said 'What's the score?' I would still recommend it actually as a useful metaphor.

So, speaking of Molière as though he were our star signing from Paris Versailles, we reckoned that one of his great qualities was that as an actor-writer he had a profound knowledge of how the audience was likely to react. A classic example of this is the scene between Harpagon and Frosine the matchmaker.

There are two actors on stage (Molière himself originally one of them) in a conversation that is going nowhere until Harpagon says: 'But tell Frosine...' and changes the subject. Laughter soon follows, and what is crucial and mysterious is the actual time that has been taken. Twenty lines, say, are not funny at all, and do not seem to be about anything relevant, but they lead inexorably to other lines that are funny. In situations like this we stayed very close to the master, even trying to match sentence lengths to those of the original French. We did a sort of tracing of Molière's instinct without understanding *exactly* how it worked: but work it did, and in the Scots ambience there were no cultural barriers, as there might have been in an English one.

I wish that I could draw equally confident conclusions from my adaptation of *Don Quixote*, but in all scrupulousness I cannot quite. The play was directed by Bill Bryden at the National Theatre in 1982, and on the whole it was a massive event which came a fairly massive cropper, notwithstanding the presence of Paul Scofield as the Don.

The redoubtable James Fenton, at that time drama critic of the *Sunday Times*, argued that my use of Thomas Shelton's original 1612 translation of Cervantes seemed pointless. I disagreed with this at the time, and still do. I believe that using Shelton and his robust Jacobean language instantly placed this material in a familiar convention. It enabled me to write an open-stage, quick moving, Jacobean-style epic narrative of a kind well-known to both actors and audiences. Differences between Spanish and English cultures as expressed in language would be compensated for by the fact that Cervantes and Sheldon had more in common with each other than we have with either: that is, in terms of their knowledge of the world and assumptions. The great age of one nation's literature would be rendered in words written during the great age of the other.

'Master' said Thomas Shelton's Sancho, 'I understand that the knights may have honour, but the squires are crammed full with sorrows'.

My theory was victorious, more or less, in the very simple scenes between the Don and Sancho, but overall the production was blurred. If I say that Bill Bryden *did* realise that the team was two goals down at half-time, but that I utterly failed to convince him that the deficit could not be pulled back without serious changes, I guess that I have said enough: from love, as well as from discretion.

What I did agree with in James Fenton's scathing review was his observation that the director, adaptor and designer seemed to have talked once and then gone their separate ways. Too much music was inserted in rehearsal, and the design was very unhelpful. The fact is that if the set exists merely for itself, and not to assist the narrative, there will always be goals in the Against column.

For knights, in Sancho's phrase, another reading might be directors; and for squires the writers.

Looking back, of course, the best book I ever adapted was the Bible, when I was Franco Zeffirelli's rewrite man on his *Jesus Of Nazareth* mini-series. I still have a Douai version given to me by the producer, and the whole thing was a very vivid experience. I cherish a Sunday lunch at which I sat between Valentina Cortese and Anthony Quinn, and it was a privilege to know the camera crew, who had worked with Visconti, but the fact is that our rewrites were more to do with previous scripts, one of them in Italian, and Franco's story boards than with the actual Bible. Actually his story boards were sensational: if he had shot them, instead of doing smotherage, he really would have been a great director.

As the *panettone* crumbled, however, I believe that I am the only writer to have walked out on Franco, as opposed to being fired. *On Brother Sun, Sister Moon* he fired at least fifteen. This is educational, of course. It teaches one to laugh at what is farcical, to accept that one will be badmouthed, and never ever, ever to write what one does not believe.

To return to *Don Quixote* – it does seem to me, in the ridiculousness of its scenery, to have been in many ways a harbinger of the next decade's theatre problems, and in a peculiar way those of translators.

What is difficult to render, after all, is not the literal meanings of words, but the gap between our assumptions and those of long-dead authors. One of these assumptions is the notion of what constitutes a theatrical convention and what does not. The conventions of medieval street theatre was that different scenes moved around on carts and the people milled about or stayed where they were. That is why Tony Harrison's version of *The Mysteries* needed a promenade procession. The convention of Athenian theatre was a fixed open setting. The entire point of Aeschylus is that it is static, verbal and declamatory.

Today most of the *fin de siécle*'s directors and designers want to present the essential conflicts of classical plays in a non-verbal theatre of design concepts, shapes and raw energy: the smart designers all do sets and props that *repeat* in visual language the spoken story told by the narrative. They think that people pay twenty pounds to look at the set for three hours. They and the directors they have enthralled do truncated myths for the video age.

But when the myths were *intended* to be declamatory and subtly verbal, where does that leave the translator?

Most living writers, of course, are out of the window, because they are too inconveniently *present* for the design-concept operators to work with.

But the translators: should they persist with verbal subtleties, knowing that the director may ignore them, relying instead upon a designer to produce a set which cannot in the end be more than an expressionist illustration, and which depends for its effect upon how much money the theatre has to spend?

The National Theatre can afford miracles of engineering. Your local Women's Institute Amateur Dramatic Society cannot.

Yet a convention, to be true, must be universal.

The entire point about theatrical conventions is that they are about shared understanding and access. They don't cost money. Anyone can take part. All that the proscenium needs, after all, is a curtain. Molière acted on outdoor platforms at Versailles and Shakespeare and Lope de Vega were done in tavern yards.

When the greatest plays in the world were written – and these are the most crucial plays to be translated – there were theatre conventions but no such thing as theatrical design. Historians, of course, will see the design-concept theatre that is upon us today as the mannerist phase with which all great creative surges end. Our problem is: can the future be more plural?

Many famous and well-meaning actors have pleaded for the preservation of the South Bank's Rose Theatre. What is interesting is that none of them seem to have noticed the most crucial thing about the Rose. That is that the excavations *prove* that it did not have a proscenium. So why perform it in one? Why subject us to endless design nightmares, when the very wood and stones taken from the ground there show us that they are irrelevant?

A translator's heaven, it seems to me, would be a theatre in which the money was devoted not to vain decoration, but to changing the space so that the classical plays could be performed in the conditions for which they were written. And I don't mean a museum – I mean a variable space that would make the plays sit up and *live*.

'Where will it end?', said the Liverpudlian who heard that the Beatles had made a million pounds each. Well, this writer's grouse will end with an affirmation. For all its frustrations the theatre can give blessed satisfaction, and a lot of mine came from my version of Mikhail Bulgakov's *Black Snow* which was directed by William Gaskill at the National in 1991.

The project was Bill Gaskill's idea, and being a natty draughtsman he was able to help me with my little views of how he thought the space and the production should look. We were put on to Patrick Miles, of Gonville and Caius College, Cambridge, who did a literal translation of the book and was a fund of good humour and scholarly assistance, not least because he enlisted his colleague Dr Julie Curtis, who is the leading English expert on Bulgakov. This was the best back-up possible as regards the text and the surrounding information. I worked very closely with Bill Gaskill and the designer Annie Smart, and as well as finding ways to do the editorial narratives and interior monologues we seem to have been true to Bulgakov's tone and his very personal blend of realism and fantasy.

We cut much of the beginning, amalgamated characters, altered and re-shaped throughout rehearsal and made a virtue of the book's lack of an end. It was Bill Gaskill's project, ultimately, and we all served it as well as we could. It was reasonably short, visually arresting, and musically-assisted: a production for the video age. Friends, like the Russian poet Andrei Voznezenski said that we had been true to Bulgakov, and that was very pleasing.

I'm not sure what the moral is. Except that Bill Gaskill, who is wiser than me, once said to an interviewer: 'Policy? Policy is the people you work with'.

JEREMY SAMS: WORDS AND MUSIC

IN CONVERSATION WITH DAVID JOHNSTON

Jeremy Sams studied Music, French and German at Magdalene College, Cambridge, and Piano at the Guildhall School of Music. He began his career working as a freelance pianist, including a stint on the QE2, but has since become a prolific and highly regarded composer, writer, translator and director. In addition to the thirteen shows he has directed – including *Mozart In Milan* (Barbican), *Le roi malgré lui* (Opera North), for which he co-wrote the libretto, and *Wild Oats* (RNT) – he has translated fourteen operas and eleven plays. Among the former are *The Magic Flute*, for a number of companies, *The Force Of Destiny* (ENO) and *Orpheus In The Underworld* (Opera North and D'Oyly Carte), and among the latter *The Miser* and Schiller's *Mary Stuart* (both RNT) and *The Orchestra*, soon to be published by Methuen Drama. He has composed widely for theatre and television, including a number of Shakespeare plays for the RSC, and he has written on many aspects of music, including narratives for a number of operas.

DJ: What sort of background brought you into the translation of opera?

JS: I started my career as a musician, a pianist in fact, but also as a linguist. I went to Cambridge to read French and German, then changed to music and became a pianist when I left University. So my speciality was really words and music, and how they fit together. I ended up in theatre as a composer. And then, gradually, I translated more and more plays, specifically operas. In terms of what you need to translate opera... things like being able to read music, understand voices, being able to understand, know, a few languages – although that's the least important of the gifts – the most important is to be able to versify, to spin verses. When you're translating a play you can do what you like, but imagine translating a play to a certain preordained rhythm – you can see how hamstrung you would be. Since then I've translated about twenty operas. My latest foray into opera translation was one where I analysed the particular very closely, then chucked out the text in every respect leaving the music and the characters, and wrote a new plot completely.

DJ: Why do you actually *translate* opera?

JS: Opera's about communication; opera is the broadest church of all. I know people who go to the opera and don't understand a word of what's being said, nor do they wish to. In that respect, the opera forum is unique, simply because people don't noticeably go and see foreign films without subtitles, just as they tend not to go and see plays without knowing what is going on. But people would gladly go to an opera under such conditions. The reason is because the opera covers such a broad church, all the art forms, that you can have a perfectly good time with your eyes shut, a perfectly good time not speaking the language.

Of course, it also depends upon what you mean by opera. There are those who go to the opera just to see an extravagant entertainment with a lot of money being chucked around the stage so that they feel better themselves about having more than enough money, so that they feel part of an exclusive club. One can't argue with them because what they are doing is perpetuating the reason behind why opera exists in the first place. When it was invented around the beginning of the seventeenth century by rich Florentine noblemen, they were really saying 'this is our club, and if you are rich enough you can watch a lot of conspicuous consumption in the name of Art'. That's how it started.

But I think opera is essentially about people in predicaments, who sing those predicaments, and we, the audience, hear what those problems are and empathise, and we weep or we laugh, or whatever. The essence of the experience for me is a dramatic one. Now, this is exactly what most composers felt too, which is why they make it quite clear that the opera should be in the language of the audience. So, when Wagner went to Paris he insisted all his work be done in French, as did Verdi. Similarly Rossini composed a great number of operas in French for the French public, and when Mozart wrote his operas in Prague and Vienna (operas in those days were for Italian-understanding audiences), he chose to go downmarket a bit, and wrote some in German for his German-understanding audiences. Composers have no overly precious scruples about this; they want people to understand what is going on. In Italy, the home of opera, that isn't a problem, because so much opera is written in Italian, which is why opera became an art form there. The problem faced by opera in England, however, is probably sociological as much as aesthetic.

DJ: Sociological?

JS: It's got something to do with the way we perceive emotion in this country, probably in Protestant countries generally...

DJ: It's true of Ireland as well.

JS: Yes, although I don't know how it managed to pass over there. Probably one of the reasons why we don't have an opera school in this country is not for the lack of good composers. Elgar is as 'good' a composer as Puccini, if you like, but we are talking about a different phenomenon. There is a view that you can't sing in English because of its difficult range of vowel sounds. That's nonsense. If you listen to the radio in any country in the world, at any moment, there are people singing in English. If you go to any church in the world you'll hear people singing very

172

frequently in English, through the great tradition of English oratorio, and then there's a developing strand of music sung in English through the Music Hall, the American Musical which informs American Jazz, which informs pop-music, and so on. They all show how easy it is to sing in English. On the other hand Czech and Russian *are* difficult languages to sing – in Russian everything is at the back of the throat, I don't see how people can sing in the language at all. And yet, there is a thriving opera school both in the Czech Republic and in Russia.

I'm going out on a limb here. I think it has to do with the function of opera in this county, and the way that emotion is somehow hermeticised, something that somehow belongs to foreign people. And so we can empathise with people who are in love, in pain, who want to die, who want to have sex – as long as they're foreigners. Things like '*je t'aime*' still provokes a reaction in English opera that is faintly ludicrous, that someone should be playing that bold card and saying 'I love you', or 'I'm dying', 'I'm in pain'. It's not what English people do. If you listen to English love songs, they're more to do with circumlocution.

The reason for this is, I think, linguistic, as well as sociological, although the two things are somewhat indistinguishable. Firstly because we have two languages in English, basically, the Anglo-Saxon and the Romance, and there are two or three words for everything. As you know, the Thesaurus is an English invention, necessary because we have two languages which are not superimposed but multiplied, so that the labyrinths of the English language are extreme. To cope with that we have imbued all these words, many, many words, with colours, with registers of meaning, with flavours that don't really happen in other languages.

English is therefore a very subtle machine to play on. To say 'I love you' is really too direct. What our language is good at is irony, because on top of the many labyrinths of words which mean things, there is also a whole number of opposites which have the same meaning, because they're heavily ironical.

DJ: It's the problem of writing in a language that's debased, whose long-established marketing ethos has devalued language's ability to voice the elemental qualities of our emotional world.

JS: I think that's right. So what we have instead is the minefield of language, all this endless, endless colour range of language, these different shades of meaning, all of which people recognise immediately. And, in that respect, English is as complicated as Japanese.

DJ: So one of the central problems facing a translator into English is, on one hand, its multiple layers of meaning, while on the other there is an ingrained cynicism in the language which means that it's not a good vehicle for expressing emotion in the raw.

JS: Yes. Although, of course, English *is* perfectly capable of the expression of emotion in its pure state – just people find it hard to perceive it. If one could change the views of the audience, that would be fine. But translation is always about working towards language as it will be perceived by an actual audience. If one uses an emotional word in English, one is making a choice which is not to beat about the bush, which in itself is tantamount to saying 'listen to me'. It is an emotional choice. That's why when I am translating opera and someone says 'I'm dying', people on stage find that uncomfortable, where the French *'je meur'* wouldn't be, even if they knew what it means. This isn't really about opera at all; it's to do with the sociological requirements of art, and there is still an ongoing sense, inherited from the nineteenth century when opera developed as an entertainment, that the people who champion our emotions, who go out there and show us on stage what love, death, sex, pain are about, should do so under the guise of a foreign language.

What I'm proselytising for is an English opera-language which is muscular and emotional, and made up of solid words, not of conversions, not of turning things backwards, not of poetry. The ideal of translating is to come up with a taut, muscular language, straightforward, emotional and yet not limply poetic, as straight and muscular as the music, which drives directly from A to B. If you listen to Verdi or Puccini, it's all about feeling, and yet it's strong and unabashed so that grown men weep, as they say. The odds are stacked against the opera translator from the outset in a way that doesn't happen in plays because people don't want to hear language in its unadulterated form. English *can* function like that, as can all other languages, but each level of choice in language distances the hearer farther from the root of the experience, its naked reality. So someone who says 'I love you' becomes as inopportune as the guest at a dinner party announcing 'I want to go to the toilet', or even 'I need to have a shit' which is what he means, and what you know he wants. But he'll find other ways of saying it, like 'I need to wash my hands'.

DJ: Opera is a very good testing around for this. Its linguistic forms are so condensed, so brief compared to the extended forms of a play.

JS: It's interesting, you can't translate opera as you do plays. Quite recently I did an opera in which we did a dialogue and I had constantly to intercalate phrases into the dialogue geared to cushioning the blow on the audience, like 'as they say in plays' or 'as it were', perpetually peppering the English, diluting the words so as to act as some sort of gauze between the audience and the stage. I think so much English on stage, in opera, comes at us wrapped, with implicit irony, disclaimers. That's why I admire Hemmingway so much, because his language sounds like a translation from Spanish. That's how I like to do my opera translations. . . to sound like Hemmingway.

DJ: Let me ask you about that: one of the things that Hemmingway does is preserve a strangeness in his language When you talk about this form of broken dialogue, is that procedure not tantamount to ironing out that strangeness?

JS: It depends on the piece. Certainly in opera translations there is a bedrock for translations, a sort of kit, and if you're stuck you find the same things come out over and over again, the 'pressures' and 'measures' and 'treasures', and 'emotions' and 'devotions'; all of those things come out of the opera translation box. Recently I've done quite a few operas which are French, funny, witty, ironic, and then I can really let go in English, with a verbal display, rhymes, internal rhymes. But to really get the flavour of the original is extremely difficult in opera; you can come up with the best line in the world as a translator, but unless it fits the music, fits the contours, the vowels and the singers' problems, it's worthless. I sit down with a couplet; I want to keep the sense of the original; I want to fit it exactly to the music, to make it singable; I want to be quite sure that it comes out clearly. You have to look for days and days for the answer to just one problem like that.

DJ: There must be a sizable amount in any one piece of work that you remain dissatisfied with in that case.

JS: Not dissatisfied, because it does the job. Sometimes as an opera translator you really have to take a back seat and merely provide stuff for people to sing on. The particular moment in the opera isn't necessarily about words. It's about the sharing of the sound. One has to identify the areas where you can put your emotion in, your poetry, and the areas where you shouldn't. That's no less true for the music of opera ... musically, as well, composers take a back seat when there is a plot to get across.

DJ: I'm full of admiration for this puzzle you work with because Italian, French and Spanish are so rhythmically regular in their grammatical structures that rhyme and metre are much easier to work with than is the case in English.

JS: As far as English is concerned, rhyme – if anyone who tries to do a Molière or Racine play discovers – is essentially a comic invention. Because of the many choices you can make, found-rhymes are essentially pathetic or bathetic. So in opera, and indeed when I'm translating plays in rhyme, I find the same problem; you have to find rhymes which taste like water, which are not saying or implying anything beyond the original's range of meanings. If I rhymed 'water' with 'daughter', for example, even that's clever, because they are spelt differently – it's a found-rhyme. But there is an implication in the rhyme – in that special significance created by rhyme – that my daughter has been or will be drowned, and I don't want that, and then the word slaughter springs to mind. . . and your range of implied meanings is mushrooming into incomprehensibility.

If you're working in French and you rhyme '*amour*' with '*toujours*', this is simply part of the fabric, the assonance of language. You are not doing anything essentially clever by rhyming in French; as you say, all past participle endings rhyme by definition and likewise suffixes rhyme in a very satisfying way. By rhyming in languages with a heavily structuralised phonetic system, you are not *finding* things. The idea of a found-rhyme, although it exists in German, is really the province of English and the

American musical. Listen to a Gershwin song and it is full of Cole Porter, full of gorgeous found-rhymes, word-play, and it is nonetheless emotional for that.

If you are translating a Lorenzo de Quanto script then the way de Quanto works is that he formally has three main rhymes, a big set piece that goes A BB A CC A DD, so you have to find three different rhymes that you can return to. In Italian these would include '*commenciar*' and another couple of words ending in 'ar', good old-fashioned infinitives. In English you might find 'start', 'heart' and 'part', the sort of triplet that the translator of opera guards jealously. This particular triplet is very handy because its got the 'ar' sound which you have to sing on 'commenciar', which is why he chooses that suffix – so the vocalisation is easier.

But you very quickly run out of this sort of rhyme which doesn't have the spin of irony on it. Irony control lies at the heart of opera translation because the English language is such a box of fireworks in that respect.

DJ: The reason why I mentioned dissatisfaction earlier on was because you talked about actually writing your own opera and I wondered if that had come from a growing residue of dissatisfaction over years of work.

JS: Dissatisfaction is the wrong word. It is something I have been working towards; every translator comes up with this one.

DJ: In your case, why?

JS: When I first started writing plays and translating operas my main concern was to come up with something which mirrored precisely the nature of the Italian text, or the French text, word for word if possible, and that for me was what I counted a success. I wanted to get all the words in there with all the flavour of every single one, no matter how much the result was crammed tightly and inelegantly into the text. I think now that that goal is a fools paradise, of no use whatsoever. Having said that, it's a period you have to go through to in order to come to a more creative view of translation.

DJ: An honest apprenticeship?

JS: It is certainly like an apprenticeship. You spend a lot of time doing very clever, albeit useless, things to please your masters. But it is not actually useful to an audience, unless they know it in Italian or French or German. The ideal way to appreciate an opera and certainly a play is to understand it in the language it has been written. So when I listen to French or German opera it all works well, and I appreciate it as the composer intended. To suit an audience locked into English, the translator can only be interested in something that has resonance and immediacy now; in other words in the libretto, but basically he has to take the backbone of that and write the libretto which would have resulted in that music if the composer had set it in English. . . to work backwards like that. When it comes to translating plays I try and do the same thing, which is to translate not the words necessarily but what caused the words to be written. The words are just symptoms and you have to go further back than that. It may be that you re-invent entirely. A finished text in a foreign language is like dead leaves, the end of the process. One needs to take care that when translating one is not just perpetuating a finished product. To translate a play or an opera into a living language you have to cut back into the tree and re-graft to get it to work.

DJ: That begs a series of questions about what a play actually is, and how translation can adopt a procedure that reflects the nature of theatre as a process and not simply a result.

JS: If the academic writer translates a play word for word with foot notes, is he translating the play? No. What is this play? What is this thing? It exists on the stage, it is not written to be read, it is not written to be looked at; it is written to be performed. What does it mean to say that plays still exist? Let's say we have an English audience listening to a Portuguese play written in the sixteenth century. If I translated every single word of that play straight, what on earth would that mean to a modern audience? It would mean nothing. But I wouldn't be able to do it anyhow because I would be imposing a modern sensibility on it. If you want to do a bilingual text, that's fine as an academic thing, but it shouldn't be confused with what playwrights are doing

DJ: Let me pose a hypothetical situation to you then. What if you take an opera which is very well known, say *Carmen*? How would you approach it? Would you put it in another country, would you change the elements of the plot? How would you cope with the sort of distancing that would allow a contemporary British audience to wriggle out of confrontation with the opera's driving emotions? Would you feel free to approach *Carmen* in exactly the way you wanted and, if you did, how would you warn your audience of what to expect?

JS: Of course, *Carmen* has been taken and re-invented in several ways. But perhaps we're talking about a different thing here, which is really the role of the director. In the case of opera, much more than in theatre probably, you have to translate to a clear sense of design. But let's take *Carmen*, and the famed *habanera* '*L'amour est un oiseau rebelle*'. 'Love is like a rebellious bird', he sings, 'that no-one can tame'. How do you set that in English? You could continue with the metaphor of birds being tamed, but it wouldn't cling to your music in the way you wanted it to. The real freedom of the translator is the freedom to say not 'love is a bird that can't be tamed' but that 'love is a whirlwind that can't be tamed', or love is this or that... In other words one should be quite free to change the image. The implication of that is, of course, you are writing a song about the nature of love, but the pursuit of simple meaning can lead to dross: 'love is a bird which is hard to tame' or something like that which goes 'thunk', rather than an image which captures the lyricism and the seriousness of the French line.

In opera one is falsifying the piece if in English one doesn't come up with something which clings to the contours of the music. You really are falsifying the experience in a way that is quite crucial, but if you get music and words together in the same shape and contours those two things can cut through an audience; thought and music together can really change the world. We all have snatches of music that we like best, where the words and music fit each other in such a way that it is more than one simply imposed on the other, it becomes a glowing thing, a magical thing. It sticks in your head, and it makes you laugh or it makes you cry. In translating opera one has a duty to come up with the missing half, and the more complementary you make your half, the greater the memorability, the impact, of the piece. That's very different from a play because in opera you are fitting one form to another. The other thing about opera, which is taking us into a more technical area, is that one is producing the part of the work which is the prime mover. Very, very broadly, the impact of the words leads the composer to write the music.

DJ: Is changing notes taboo?

JS: Basically it works like this. You start off with the full scene and in it you have the foreign text and lots of notes. You have to find a text which will fit those notes precisely, and you cannot change those notes except in very extreme cases; in other words, only if you are really, really stuck! Having said that, taboos are being shifted even as we speak. For my money, and for most of my colleagues' money, if the shape of the music is predicted by the words then, to give a simple example, if you happen to change the name of a character from Genevieve to Genivive I think it would be quite justified, wherever her name came up, to change the note.

DJ: Would you be more ready to change narrative music rather than the lyrical?

JS: Even that would be very extreme. There is a form of stylised dialogue – recitative – which, musically, is not of very much interest, being just heightened dialogue, a way of rotating speech. I think one would be most justified to write words of Mozart recitative, and no-one would know the difference, except musicologists and critics. But generally, as I've said, one does one's best to get the words to fit. The difficulty is this: imagine recording some dialogue with people at a dinner party and then having to write different words for it but following exactly the same intonation. It's like dubbing over a movie, where someone makes a gesture, opens their mouth, and you have to find a word that fits – if you cut that, perhaps you may save yourself a lot of trouble. But you don't change the music.

CLASSICAL YOU WIN, MODERN YOU LOSE

GUNILLA ANDERMAN

Dr Gunilla Anderman is Director of the Programme in Translation Studies in the Department of Linguistic and International Studies of the University of Surrey. She is also the Chair of the Education and Training Committee of the Institute of Translators and Interpretors. She has published on a wide range of topics related to translation, including the translation of drama. She is also the editor of *New Swedish Plays* (Norvik Press, 1992), and is about to publish *Topics In Translation* (Multilingual Matters). Her translations of Swedish stage plays produced in this country include *Seven Girls*, written and directed by Carl-Johan Seth (Open Space, 1976), P-O Enquist's *The Tribades*, directed by Michael Rudman in the Hampstead Theatre (1978), Stig-Ossian Ericson's *Haven't We Met Before*, directed by John Dove at the Mill at Sonning in 1982, *Courage To Kill* and *Munich-Athens*, both written by Lars Norén and performed at the Theatre Clwyd and the Soho Poly in 1984 and 1987. Her translation of Norén's *Autumn And Winter* was given a rehearsed reading by the RSC in the Scandinavian Festival held at the Barbican Centre in 1992. Gunilla Anderman's work for television includes a translation of Astrid Lindgren's *Brothers Lionheart*, for BBC2.

Judging from the dearth of contemporary European plays at the National, the RSC and in the West End, in contrast to the more regular revivals of Ibsen, Strindberg, Molière and more recently, Schiller, it would seem that plays in translation set in a comfortably distant past have a distinct edge over contemporary foreign drama. This, however, does not necessarily hold true for British plays translated into other languages. In many European countries, little time is allowed to elapse before the latest, critically acclaimed London stage-hit appears in translation.

Why is it then that contemporary drama in translation figures prominently on many other European theatre stages while it is only exceptionally found in this country?

English Drama in Translation
In most countries in Western Europe knowledge of English is usually viewed as a necessity. As teaching programmes tend to combine language instruction with a study of the social and cultural structure of the English speaking world, familiarity with life in this country as well as in the United States can normally be assumed amongst

speakers of lesser known languages. Unlike the British and the Americans, divided by their commonly shared language, theatre-goers in say northern Europe may, as a result of years of study, know more about the American South than a British theatre audience and find themselves in a better position to take on board the plays by Tennessee Williams in spite of the vast geographical and cultural differences.

If anything, it would seem as if clearly observable social and cultural differences make it easier for a foreign playwright to say what s/he wants to say. If, on the other hand, an audience starts feeling too much 'at home' while watching a play in translation it is also more likely to question, reject or misinterpret whatever appears unfamiliar on stage, having been lead to expect familiarity in social customs and behaviour. This, to take an example, seems to have happened initially to the plays by Alan Ayckbourn in translation into Swedish. As criticism of prevailing social and political order often takes a more direct, outspoken form in Scandinavian, the 'bite' of Alan Ayckbourn's comedies first went undiscovered and it took some time before his sardonic commentary on British middle-class *mores* emerged accurately in translation.

Another problem that may initially appear almost unsurmountable to the translator is the difficulty relating to accent or dialect, and how this may be transferred from one language into another. In the case of translation from English into a lesser known language, Josef Skvorecky, Czech novelist and translator, tells of the misguided translator of Agatha Christie's novels who, faced with the problem of translating Hercule Poirot's frenchified language into Czech, decided to draw on the divided historical past with Germany. Unfortunately – and I would say predictably – the experiment backfired, resulting in a stream of letters from outraged readers, dismayed at Hercule Poirot speaking like a Sudeten German... (Skvorecky, 1985)

Ironically, the problem is often most easily solved by simply not trying to find a solution. Following the success of *Saved* when it was first staged at the Royal Court in 1965, Edward Bond has had a following in many countries in Europe. In *Summer*, his play about the reunion of two women in an unspecified European country in the wake of a social revolution, a German tourist makes a brief but dramatically effective appearance. For comic effect his lines are sprinkled with linguistic errors commonly made by German speakers of English. But what happens then when Bond's play is translated into other languages? For an accurate impression to be created of a German speaking in a foreign language a whole new set of linguistic mistakes would have to be devised for each language into which the play is translated. Alternatively, the fact that the German is a foreigner may instead be expressed through non-verbal means such as dress or behaviour, often preferable to making use of a stilted language or dialect.

One of the most successful comedies to reach the West End in the early eighties was *Educating Rita*, Willy Russell's scouse version of *Eliza Dolittle*. In the play Rita enrolls to study English literature at the Open University and as a result much of the dialogue centres on discussions of attempted literary analyses of the list of set books. What happens then if a crucial book such as *Howard's End*, repeatedly referred to by Rita and her tutor, is not even available in translation? *Educating Rita* was translated into a large number of languages, and the problem was no doubt given a number of language-specific solutions. When the play was performed in translation in Sweden, for example, the solution agreed on was to retain the English title as, at that time, the novel had not in fact been translated into Swedish. Ironically, had the play been written a decade later the success of the Merchant-Ivory film version would probably have saved translators throughout the Western world considerable agony as the release of the film quickly turned E M Forster's novel into a household name.

Foreign Drama in English Translation

Although there are problems involved in transferring a play written in English into a lesser known language, these seem to pale in comparison with the difficulties facing the translator when a play travels in the opposite direction. The process is usually much less painful when the whole product is imported as in the case of visiting theatre companies from abroad. Whether simultaneous interpretation is provided or not does not seem to matter; the combined effort of director and actors working together on a play in their own language tends to result in an authenticity of expression to which the audience responds, whether what is happening on stage is fully understood or not. This is probably also why films from virtually unknown parts of the world seem to cross linguistic and cultural borders with considerably less difficulty than many plays in translation. The screen has a number of advantages. Not only are the actors genuine products of another culture, but the social, cultural and geographical setting can, as a rule, also be more convincingly conveyed by film. Without such visual clues and with only the help of set and props to provide local atmosphere, it is much more difficult for a theatre audience, watching a play in translation, to feel transported to another, culturally unknown setting. Given these difficulties, it is hardly surprising that it has become increasingly common for plays in translation to be staged in so called 'versions'.

A highly successful example of such a version, or what Michael Billington (1984) has referred to as a 'creative rewrite', is *On The Razzle*, Tom Stoppard's 1981 version of Johann Nestroy's Viennese comedy *Einen Jux will er sich machen* for the National Theatre. Originally written in Viennese dialect, Stoppard's English stage version, already preceded by other adaptations such as Thornton Wilder's *The Matchmaker* (1954), which served as the basis for the Broadway musical *Hello, Dolly* (1963), makes no attempt to draw on dialect, providing in its place Stoppard's own, well-known verbal acrobatics. His method, he professes in the programme note, may most closely be compared to 'cross-country hiking where one takes the bearing on the next landmark and picks one's own way towards it'. 'The particu-larity of a writer's voice', he continues, 'is a mysterious collusion of sound and sense. The certain knowledge that a translation will miss it by at least an inch makes it less dreadful to miss it by a yard. I have aimed in the general direction' (1981).

Unfamiliar with the particularity of Nestroy's voice in the original, I am unable to comment on the extent to which it has been retained in translation. What has quite clearly been retained, however, or perhaps better put recreated, is a sense of the social and cultural atmosphere of Vienna at the time, be it through the use of original street and place names or Stoppard's own imaginative coining of new, evocative alliterations such as 'It's enough to make one burst a bratwurst'.

But it is not a common occurrence for a foreign play to be a box-office hit. In the case of *On The Razzle*, the play had, in addition to Stoppard's brilliant adaptation of the text, a couple of other factors working in its favour. It was set in a Central European city which, if not familiar, at least was not completely unfamiliar to the audience and, perhaps even more importantly, it took place in a comfortably distant past. As a result, anything puzzling or unusual, not sounding or looking as expected, may still be taken on board by an audience, able to suspend disbelief because the events belong to the past, to a period of time of which they have no first-hand experience. If the time of the action of the play is the present, however, an English audience is instead being asked to make allowances for say a Swede, a Finn or a Dutchman who are almost but not quite the same as they are themselves. And the fact that they are not is easily overlooked, making any divergence in behaviour, views and actions at best puzzling, or leading at worst to misinterpretation.

While speakers of smaller nations are likely to spend years devoted to the study of the customs and mores of countries where major languages are spoken, the opposite is rarely true. This in turn makes it, as Skvorecky has observed, a far better proposition for a budding writer to have been born a citizen of one of the bigger nations. In his musings on the undeservedly hard lot of writers of smaller nations, Skvorecky speculates on the probable fate of Mark Twain, had he been born in Bohemia instead of the United States. He might, Skvorecky suggests, have got involved in the revolution of 1848, and like many of his compatriots have emigrated to California, where he would have settled down and written in Czech. Translated into English by one of the many war veterans of the Civil War he might then, with some luck, have become the star writer of the August Geringer Bohemian Publishing House in Chicago. In all likelihood that is where he would have ended his days, a penniless but popular raconteur of Czech tales in the pubs of the Windy City...

I first became aware of the problem of transferring contemporary European drama into English in the Seventies when I translated a Swedish play for production at the Open Space, Charles Marowitz's old theatre in London's Tottenham Court Road. The play, *Seven Girls*, by Swedish playwright Carl-Johan

Seth, was set in a sort of Community Home in Sweden, catering for 14-16 year old girls referred for problems such as alcoholism, drug addiction or prostitution. The action of the play takes place during an event-filled weekend which sees the return of some runaways as well as fresh attempts at escape from others, and includes a visit from the Secretary of the local Child and Youth Welfare Committee. This representative of the ruling establishment, a well-meaning but ineffectual Social Democrat with his heart in the right place, never failed to make the audience smile in instant recognition during the play's successful run throughout Scandinavia. For a British audience, however, lacking the Swedish frame of reference, this character never came over as anything more than a somewhat eccentric bureaucrat, losing in part the author's commentary on aspects of the Swedish welfare system. This, in turn, was probably one of the reasons why all too often the wrong questions were asked. 'Why, in a home for girls, were there so many men amongst the wardens?', one critic asked, a question of interest only in a country which favours single sex schools but not in a country like Sweden, where mixed education is the norm. Given present day discussions about law and order and overcrowded prisons, it is even tempting to speculate to what extent the tenet of the play – you can always lock people up but the problem which brought them there won't go away – was ahead of its time, and that concern with minutiae became the defensive response to a problem that no theatre performance was likely to resolve.

Considering the difficulties involved, it is not difficult to see why it might be tempting to try to adapt a text in translation, making it more accessible to an English audience, as is often done in the case of the classics. One such attempted rewrite with which I was involved occurred during the period leading up to the rehearsal of *Courage To Kill*, a play by Swedish playwright Lars Norén which I had been commissioned to translate in the early eighties. Money matters were handled in terms of 'fivers' and an evening meal, pivotal to the play, had been reworked to offer a wide range of items originating from different parts of the world. While in the original Swedish version a father and his grown-up son have an argument about whether or not to have dinner, the son declaring he doesn't want anything because he isn't hungry, the English version offered a menu composed of an assortment of vegetables and other dishes in current vogue in English yuppy circles:

The Father: Peas?
The Son: No, let's have some courgettes. And some asparagus. Fresh. Avocados to start with? No, how about some globe artichokes? Yes. And then some aubergines to go with the courgettes. Some Swiss chard, stir-fried in garlic, it's delicious. And a few okras if you can get any.
The Father: I was thinking more about...

The reason why the father-son exchange had undergone a change to take on its new form was not difficult to find. The original translation of the dialogue had accurately reflected the short, direct answers, commonly found in normal, polite discourse in northern Europe. To an English cast, however, the lines, consisting of virtually monosyllabic questions and answers must have seemed too curt and abrupt for a socially accepted exchange. Just as Alan Ayckbourn's characters may appear too 'nice' on the surface, leaving the undercurrents to go undetected by Scandinavians, an English theatre audience might be just as likely to misinterpret a direct, seemingly abrupt discussion, as aggressive, even threatening. One way of getting out of this dilemma then appears to have been to let the son show his rejection and his defiance of his father through other means, by letting him know that his taste in food is at odds with that of an older generation. However, while the introduction of a new, imaginatively composed menu might have helped to solve one problem, it also succeeded in creating another one. Every time a new set of associations is conjured up, a text in translation moves further away from the original and given too many such moves the final product can easily end up, literally, in no-man's land. The most successful production of a contemporary play that I have translated was probably due, in addition to the combined efforts of the playwright, cast and director, to the quite legitimate absence of a cultural setting. The play, again written by Lars Norén, was staged at the Soho Poly Theatre in London in 1987, and was called *Munich-Athens*. Literally set in transit, it took place during a forty-eight hour train journey from Stockholm via Munich to Athens, reducing the need for local atmosphere and references to a minimum.

This is not to say that it is only contemporary drama that is beset with problems. A frequent difficulty when translating the classics, whether written in Germanic, Romance or Slavonic languages is the problem related to the two pronouns used for formal *vis-à-vis* informal address such as '*tu/vous*' in French and the absence of a corresponding distinction in modern English. Writing as he did when the T/V distinction was still observed in English, Shakespeare's use of thou/you, the two pronouns of address in English, has attracted considerable attention amongst scholars (cf., for instance, Barber, 1981). But although the problems related to the translation of this distinction in Russian has been acknowledged (Lyons, 1980) it is somewhat surprising to find that the difficulties involved in the translation of so called pronominal switching (Friedrich, 1966), used to signal differences in social status as well as varying degrees of emotional commitment, in e.g. Ibsen and Strindberg, have on the whole not been widely acknowledged. In the case of Ibsen it has been shown by Amundsen (1981) how pronominal switching, first used in *A Doll's House,* is used consistently in *Hedda Gabler* to reflect the two different sides to Hedda's personality. When her public personality is speaking it expresses itself through the use of the formal '*De*' while her other private self, emotionally undeveloped and, as a result, frightening to her, is manifested through the use of the informal '*du*'. Consistent change in the use of the T/V distinction in Swedish is also found in Strindberg as in, for instance, *Miss Julie*, to mark the different stages in the psychological and sexual power struggle between the lady of noble birth and her father's valet (Anderman, 1993). Here too, an accurate rendering in translation of the shift in power, reflected through the use of the different pronouns of address, is virtually impossible.

Still, as *Hedda Gabler* and *Miss Julie* have both succeeded in holding their rightful place in the league of world drama through the ages, it would seem that survival is possible in spite of occasionally unremedied translation loss. It is interesting, however, that this loss appears to manifest itself much less markedly in the writing of the past than in the work of contemporary dramatists in translation. Thus, a reviewer of a relatively recent Off-West End production of a contemporary French play points out that for all the excellence of the translation 'it is difficult to convey in English Duras's musicality and subtle shifts of tone from "*tu*" to "*vous*" '.

It is indeed, but it has been ever thus. And unless the scale of the problem of transferring the work of contemporary writers working in other languages is fully understood, little can be done to help open the doors to playwrights who can tell us what is happening in other parts of Europe. Right now, not a hundred years ago.

TRANSLATING THE FAMOUS DEAD, THE DEAD OBSCURE, AND THE LIVING

JACEK LASKOWSKI

A former Literary Manager of Leicester's Haymarket Theatre, Jacek Laskowski now teaches European Literature, Creative Writing and Drama in the Adult Education Department of Nottingham University. His extensive dramatic work includes original work for radio (*Dreams To Damnation, Pawn Takes Pawn*) as well as adaptations (*The Secret Agent*, a six-part version of *Nostromo*) and translations. His theatre work has included *Galatea* (winner of the Michael Codron Award in 1978), *God's Own Prophet* and *Silver Lining*. Stage adaptations include *Under Western Eyes*, *The Idiot* as well as free versions of Witkiewiez's *Crazy Locomotive*, *The Mother* and *Them*. He has made numerous translations from Polish, including poetry and novels. Among these translations are more than a dozen plays by Slawomir Morzek (most recently *Love In The Crimea*), other contemporary playwrights such as Jerzy S Sito (*Hear, Oh Israel*) and Tadeusz Slobodzianek (*Merlin*). His translations and adaptations from other languages include version of Euripides's *Electra* and *Orestes*, of Molière's *The Phoney Physician* and *Wiseguy Scapino*, as well as from Russian.

D is a lover of the theatre, is a native French speaker, and is a good friend of mine. Loyally he has attended all the productions of plays by Molière which I have translated. When we meet after the show, he always chuckles knowingly. He says: 'You should come clean, you know. Just have them take Molière's name off the posters. It's about time that the world knew that the piece is an original Laskowski'. I know I'm supposed to take this as a compliment. As I'm mulling over my reply, he adds that I could revive my quiescent career as a dramatist by passing off more of my plays as translations of Molière. 'You could say you've discovered a hitherto unknown piece in some attic'. D has a house in France. (He is, after all, half-French). He offers it to me as a front. He says there's a huge attic in the house which could easily contain all sorts of obscure bits and pieces. It's so vast and so cluttered nobody's even dared to start wading through the detritus gathered there over the centuries. 'You could be uncovering new Molières for the rest of your life. It's a gold-mine'.

I can see D's point. Bookshops are crammed with translations of Molière, most of them not only accurate but easy to read. Why would any self-respecting translator bother to add yet another translation? Especially as this new translation is both funny and enjoyable, whereas anyone who has studied *Tartuffe* for French A-level knows only too well that Molière is Gallicly pretentious and with as many laughs as a visit to the dentist. In addition, producers have to pay the same money for a new translation as they would for an original English-language script, whereas an old, already published translation would be a tenth of the price for the royalties. My friend D is an accountant, and he knows why new translations are commissioned. 'It's because new plays are box-office death', he says. 'Unless they're by Alan Ayckbourn. So new plays are disguised as translations and people flock to see them'.

He points to the plethora of plays calling themselves 'versions' of Ibsen, or Chekhov, or Strindberg. 'New plays all of them', he states categorically. 'At least these so-called version-makers are coming right out into the open. I've read interviews with them. They don't even pretend to know the language the play was supposed to have been written in'.

My head is always left spinning after these post-Molière meetings with D. His arch insouciance always raises teleological questions which I find hard to resolve. One the one hand I'm a trifle affronted that he thinks my command of the French language is so feeble that I couldn't possibly concoct a funny and *accurate* version of *Les Fourberies de Scapin* (the title itself being enough to cause a migraine). On the other hand, I'm deeply flattered that he thinks the production was hilarious and that I was its sole begetter. Who wouldn't be? I begin to understand how devastatingly effective my friend D must be in his dealings with the Inland Revenue.

It's not that I don't consider the folly of attempting another version of a moderately well-known text when I am commissioned to do it. Every time it happens I have to reassure myself that in a theatrical context the translation exists in the same unique and unrepeatable relationship to the original as do the set design, the costumes, the lighting design and the sound effects. In other words, the translated text belongs specifically to the one production and to no other.

This is how I argue my self-justification. I refer to the translations that Michael Frayn has done of the plays of Chekhov. If a translation can ever transcend a particular and unrepeatable production, all four of Frayn's anglicisations of the major Chekhov plays can. And maybe do. In them, Frayn has achieved as close to perfection in the translator's art as it is possible to get. Probably. The English is exquisite, the rendering of the Chekhovian mood and temper is virtually indistinguishable from the mood of the Russian original. If Chekov had written the plays in English, they would have been Frayn's translations. So, naturally, every other production of a Chekov play in English reaches for his translations. And every other production commissions a new one.

This is what a director told me about the Frayn translations: 'They are very good, of course they are. But they are *too* English. Reading his translations, I get no sense of otherness, no sense of foreignness'. Exactly, I replied. They are perfect anglicisations. 'Exactly', the director sighed. 'So I get no sense of Russia. And if I get no sense of *Russia*, then the plays themselves make no sense to me. The plays are about Russians living in Russia. If the English is so flawlessly, idiomatically English then my audience will not perceive its fundamental nature: its Russianness. The audience will be baffled by the play'.

The director and I agreed to differ. But the fact remains that her productions of Chekov will eschew what, by common consent, are translations of near-perfection. Her productions will reach for other translations, or will go to a tormented translator who will wonder what possible justification he or she can find for venturing into territory already gloriously captured by Frayn.

What he or she, or I, have to remind ourselves is that translating well-worn texts is a little like mountaineering: just because someone has already conquered the peak does not mean everyone else has to abandon the climb. You may not be the first to get to the summit, you may not even do it most gloriously, but there is a purpose to your journey. The purpose is in the need of the moment. And theatre is the art of moments, of infinitely variable evenings within the same production, of infinitely variable stagings of the same play, of infinitely mutable gestures, grimaces, costumes and masks. I have never designed a stage production, but I presume that the temptation to peek at previous solutions to problems offered by a much, or recently, produced play are fairly strong. Especially if the problems appear to be intractable and time is running short, as it invariably does in the theatre. I know that, as a translator, when the word-processor stops processing because a scene isn't working, or because the language has stiffened to incomprehension as all the characters are suddenly struck down by some as yet uncatalogued tropical disease which causes their tongues to swell, making every noise that issues from their mouths sound like a primeval and untranslatable grunt, I know that in such circumstances the dog-eared paperback of Molière translations just happens to catch my eye because of one temptation too many. Do I rush through the pages and find out how previous translators have unravelled this impossible knot? Of course I don't! I'm doing my own translation and it would be unprofessional of me to reach for colleagues' work.

Well, if you believe that you'll believe anything. Along with my good friend D. you might even believe I wrote the plays myself and stuck Molière's name on them. Yes, I confess it: I do glance at other people's solutions to problems. Do I ever use their solutions? I have been known to, yes. Rarely, reluctantly, remorsefully, but I have done it. *Mea culpa, mea maxima culpa.*

On the other hand, of course, there is much preciousness talked when the subject is writing. And translating is a branch of writing. I have even come across handbooks of advice which state authoritatively that the *real* writers don't, shouldn't, mustn't use a Thesaurus to find the *mot juste* when it has evaporated from their fevered brain. These same mentors would, I've no doubt, sniff at the idea of using a dictionary when translating. They would certainly consign me to perdition for reading what others have written. It's a strange thing, but very often just the mere activity of dipping into a Thesaurus is enough to unlock the word I'm looking for. As often as not, I don't even reach the section I've been sent to by the index (parenthetically I might mention that every time I do open the Thesaurus I'm convinced the index has been compiled by someone who wilfully misunderstands every thought I've ever had and offers me a choice of meanings none of which is applicable to the word I've forgotten or maybe never even known). A similar process seems to be working when I look at previous translations. Suddenly, the solution appears as if by magic (it probably is magic): it's not what the previous translator has done, nor is it very close to that version. But seeing it, or, just as often, seeing three lines before it or glancing at the next page, is enough to disclose what was previously closed. Easily explained, I've no doubt, by neuro or psycholinguists, but mysticism of a high order to me. Like mountaineers who talk of being 'shown' a way towards the top by the spirit of previous climbers, so it is with us more modest translators: others have indicated a path which avoids the drop. We would be daft as goats if we ignore it simply because someone else had gone there before and insisted on falling off instead, consoling ourselves as we fell with the knowledge that we are the first to have chosen *this* particular path.

On the basis of this admission, another friend of mine, F, argues that not only should I keep Molière's name on the posters, I should insist on adding the names of the dozens (if there have been dozens) of previous translators of the same text. He says that theatre is an overtly collaborative venture and it's simply not right that any one name should be printed in letters bigger than the others. He says that, alternatively, we should return to the pre-Renaissance days when artists never put their names to anything, thereby tacitly admitting that their work was produced as much by the society and its culture as by their own individual effort. He says: 'You use other people's work all the time. I've seen you read books. You don't read books, you rip them to shreds. You're always on the lookout for clever ways of saying things. You read the newspaper from cover to cover every day. You watch telly, you listen to the radio, you eavesdrop on people in trains. I've seen you doing it: it's embarrassing. You've got more dictionaries of one kind or another than most people have got books. And what's more you read them! Why would anyone read a dictionary if they weren't going to steal the words out of it? You should admit it and either put *all* those names on the posters or none at all'. I walk down Shaftesbury Avenue and see the actors' names in huge neon lights dwarfing the name of the play and find myself feeling in some sympathy with my friend from the Dark Ages. He may not know much about marketing, but he certainly has an insight into the creative process.

Theatre, he knows as we all do, is a collaborative activity: every part has to *fit* into a whole. Just as you could have a handful of priceless gems lying on a table-top and, despite their being fiendishly expensive, they still wouldn't add up to a tiara, so you can easily have lots of vignettes that don't add up to a performance. The translation, just like an original script, is part of it. And if someone wants to set *The Cherry Orchard* in Ireland, they will hire Irish actors to play the parts, they will work with the designer to give the set an Irish feel, they will make sure the sound effects are consonant with the sounds one could hear in Ireland. And, despite the fact that Frayn's translation is probably as near perfect as you could get, they would, very reluctantly, put it to one side and commission a new, more Irish-sounding translation.

That's how I came to work on Molière. Directors wanted a certain slant on the plays. They wanted, for instance, to set *Les Fourberies de Scapin* (the title still giving me a migraine) in a Mafia-dominated Naples. What was needed was for the two old men plotting their children's unhappiness to be Mafia-style godfathers, with acknowledgements to Marlon Brando. Previous translations had been used to make different, but probably equally specific, productions. To use them simply because they were miraculously close to the original (as I'm sure some have been) would have been like using the same props, or the same sets, simply because they are similar to those used three hundred and more years ago by Molière himself.

So we (and I do mean *we*) set about creating a Naples-based Mafia-encrusted version. We threw out the rogues and wretches which are perfectly reasonable translations of the French insults and threw in a few dipsticks and palookas. We ignored old solutions of conveying the speech of a simpleton that exploited rustic diction and gave them an urban monosyllabism instead (in a version of another play by Molière the team went for rural proverb-speak from somewhere north-east of Sheffield to convey the same dogged simplicity for which Molière used his provincialisms); for some talkative characters (the young hero, for instance) we provided versions of the same sense but expostulated in the exaggerated style of an undergraduate turning his back on his roots and using four syllables where one is already too many. Oh, yes, and we took some aspirin for the migraine and called the piece *Wiseguy Scapin*. It isn't a precise, word-by-word translation of *Les Fourberies de Scapin* but it gives a clear indication of the nature of this particular production's provenance.

Not many of the solutions found for that production would work in a version setting the play in, for instance, South Africa. Even the title would have to be changed. Does that make it, as my friend D would have it, my play, written by me? I don't think so. It makes it Molière's play interpreted by me for use in a particular production. That's all.

And that, after all, is everything.

This needs to be underlined because my main translating-from language is not French, it's Polish. I am bilingual in Polish and English, which means I dream (and count) in both languages (sometimes simultaneously, which can be confusing for the monoglots who appear in my dreams). Unlike French dramatic literature, which is full of plays, fascinating and indifferent, that have been translated many times over into English, Polish dramatic literature is full of plays which have never found an English audience. Not many *writers* have known, or even shown any great interest in Polish dramatic literature so most of the plays that have found translators have been consigned to academic presses with editions crammed full of learned footnotes and without any consideration of the possibility that, one day, a living actor might actually need to speak the lines.

Lovers of Polish drama with whom I have spoken about this dearth of English-language productions of the Great Tradition, mostly what we would call heritage workers of one kind or another, have, in the past, pestered me about this absence of Polish drama in the English theatre tradition. They have deemed that I use my skills (for drama) and my knowledge (of two languages), not to mention that I should follow the dictates of my heart (viz. my affection for certain Polish dramatists), and produce readable, speakable, performable English language versions of the Polish classic repertoire. 'It wouldn't cost you much', they said. 'After all, you translate so quickly it would be like simply re-typing the original. And then Polish drama would have arrived!'

It was a good argument in some ways (though not so good when you realise that many of the great classics are tragedies in verse, nearly always rhyming verse, a form of presentation which has few examples in the current repertoire of English-language theatres, and for which it might, therefore, be difficult to find a suitable stylistic equivalence). It was certainly persuasive enough to make me feel pangs of conscience about not using a gift which I have done little to deserve but which has been thrust on me by a profligate providence. Thanks to my good fortune I could do the very thing a translator is supposed to do: I could bridge the gap in understanding between cultures by showing the English-speaking community some masterpieces of Polish dramatic literature, with mutual benefit to both the Polish and English-speaking communities in terms of understanding, extensions of horizons, exposure to new and daring ideas.

Easier said than done. Theatre, we have agreed, is a collaborative venture. In order to discover, or re-discover, obscure dead writers for the theatre one needs, really, to set up an expedition consisting of a producer as barmy as oneself, and a director, and a designer, not to mention the actors who, as a rule, have the heart-breakingly enchanting gift of summing up child-like enthusiasm for the most bizarre undertakings (so who could, to a large extent, be taken as read). But these barmy folk are not easy to find. They have their own obsessions, their own private pangs of conscience about their own fields of unjustifiably lavished gifts.

The heritage workers in Warsaw and Krakow remained unimpressed by what they saw as my sloth in this matter — what, indeed, I too, saw as my sloth. 'Just do the translation', they insisted, 'and show it round the theatres as you would a new play'.

People who have been in artistic directors' offices anywhere in the country will now smile. They have seen the huge hills of scripts growing round the P As' desks, hills that are dwarfed only by the mountains of letters and photographs submitted by actors, recently (and often not *that* recently) qualified graduates of drama schools. They have seen the dust gathering on those hills: they know that even the *cleaners* don't touch the scripts.

'But new plays are still done', the heritage workers insisted. 'Somebody must read them. And the Polish plays are so wonderful that as soon as somebody reads them they'll want to do them. Send them in like you would a new play!'

They're right: the plays *are* wonderful (some of them; certainly the plays I would want to translate are). But the rub is that they are not new plays. They do not stand in the same relationship to the theatre and its producers as does a new play. A new play is produced (on the rare occasions that it is produced) because it is dealing with subjects and in a way which is important to people *now*. We are at present, constantly exposed to plays about AIDS; in twenty years' time *none* of them will *ever* be produced. The better ones will be studied at colleges and universities, and the handful of the best plays will be re-interpreted in the light of, say, a brand-new, sexually transmitted disease which might be afflicting the lumberjacks of outer Siberia. That is how vibrant theatre works, I tell my distraught heritage workers. They mutter: 'Mickiewicz did not write about sexually transmitted diseases...'

They are disappointed. I am disappointed. The handful of translations worthily and devotedly carried out by academic enthusiasts has proved more of an obstacle than a help in staging. They are like the Samuel Beckett estate, giving us the official version of the play, not letting us interpret it in a new, vibrant, relevant-for-today way. They are like the old D'Oyly Carte company in the days when Gilbert and Sullivan were still in copyright that gave arthritically creaking pieces which performed the function of a travelling and mobile (though scarcely that) museum. They are *translations* which have no home: they were prepared without a theatre in mind, without a *specific* production in mind, with a reverence which is out of keeping with the nature of theatre, though it may well be appropriate for the field of literature. In these translations the plays are stifled by the reverence, and their obscurity is preserved like onions in vinegar. When they are opened, you can taste only vinegar. The answer, my heritage workers explained to me, is to play the part of producer and director yourself. Persuade actors (professional or amateur) to work for nothing, show them a version of the obscure Polish play and convince them that, with the right marketing, it will bring floods of fascinated viewers into the theatre. And yes, I have done that, too; and yes, it was exhilarating to see Witkiewicz's *Crazy Locomotive* staged in a quite unsuitable hall where a personal assistant with whom I wasn't even on speaking terms at the time (and who is now my wife) had to lie perched on a catwalk clutching the ballcock of a cold-water cistern for an hour and a half. This was to prevent the noise of water drowning out the actors' words as it filled the cistern each time someone in the adjacent student bar flushed the toilets. And the actors (all students) threw themselves into a weird and wonderful world of pre-absurd drama with enthusiasm and no little skill. And, yes, the audiences did come.

So the heritage workers in their yellowing offices in the centres of Warsaw or Krakow are right, it seems. The one sure way to promote the works of obscure dead Polish playwrights onto the stages of Britain, or America, or any other English-speaking part of the world is not just to translate, but to produce the pieces yourself as well. Just like new plays. What is frustrating for the translators of these apparently obscure Polish playwrights is that their plays are not obscure: they permeate the whole of subsequent Polish dramatic writing, they are staged and re-staged not only in Poland, but in Russia, in Germany, and in other countries east of the Rhine.

And, most frustrating of all, they are not new. There is no disguising their venerable old age. They *need* to be re-interpreted for the present, for the moment. But they are in competition for the translator's attention with their successors, their descendants, their inheritors of the tradition they have created. They are up against the demands of the plays that *are* being written now.

Contemporary playwrights in Poland or (in the case of Slawomir Mrozek, the greatest living contemporary Polish playwright) Mexico are responding to, commenting on, criticising and shaping (to a tiny extent, of course, but shaping nevertheless) the very events that are tormenting, amusing, baffling, and irritating people in the world today. They are as close to the events that form their obsessions as their audiences are. When a translator looks at their work there is no room for the kind of interpretation that I've been talking about. We are presented with a raw, maybe considered, maybe ironic, but nonetheless raw and pulsating response to events. And we, the translators, can only respond to the original in the same direct way. We are unable to look back on the piece and take from it what is relevant to us now, fifty, a hundred, three hundred years later. We cannot interpret afresh; we interpret for the first time, and we are hamstrung by the responses we have to the very same themes with which the writer is dealing. Everything in the play is relevant but at the same time, we take up positions, we have our own responses to the events which have fired the playwrights' imaginations, we have our own way of interpreting reality.

And yet we can't interpret. We can't lay stress on one aspect of the play when the author insists on having it as just one part of the whole. For instance, in his most recent play, Mrozek tackles an easy enough subject: the history of Russia in the twentieth century from pre-revolutionary times to the fall of the Soviet Union and the collapse of Russia's economy. Doing so, he parodies Chekov (pre-revolutionary Russia), Bulgakhov (post-revolutionary Russia), and to some extent, himself (contemporary Russia). *Love In The Crimea* is a piece of stunning theatrical genius. As a member of the audience, and a reader, I focus on those parts of the play which I find most congenial to me, the ones in which I detect the most accurate perceptions, the wittiest interpretations of reality, the most satisfying metaphors. If Mrozek had died a hundred and fifty years ago I, in my role as translator, together with my director and producer (maybe in the same person as translator, of course) would try to emphasise those aspects of the play which we found most pertinent to us and, therefore we would hope, to our contemporary audience. It's not that I would ignore the less pleasing, or less pertinent parts of the play: but I would certainly not allow them to distract from those parts I considered important. Indeed, I would try to translate them in such a way that they reinforced the most pertinent aspects. I'm sure that when Mrozek's play is re-translated in a hundred and fifty years time, that is exactly what the translator will do. But what the translator of the piece hot off the presses has to do is something very different. And the problems which that brings with it are very different, too.

I'll leave to one side the mere linguistic problems involved in translating a contemporary piece; the fact that languages are changing so rapidly that you have to be in instant and constant contact with at least two cultures (and if English is one of the languages then, realistically, with at least three cultures); the fact that each of those cultures has a different perception of the importance of events in the great world outside, and sometimes those perceptions overlap and sometimes they don't come within each other's orbits at all so that when something is mentioned in the source language the effect is supposed to be devastating, but when rendered into the target language it has no effect at all because the event and its linguistic description is of variable vitality in the various cultures; the fact that the theatrical traditions from which the original piece and its translation come are different even when they *appear* similar (Chekhov and Bulgakhov are, of course, common to all three cultures, though probably in slightly altered shades of colouring; but when another brilliant playwright, Tadeusz Slobodzianek, draws on Byelorussian, Russian and Polish devotional literature, the translator's difficulties become even more discomforting).

No, the main problem with translating contemporary writers lies not in the language difficulties (language difficulties are, after all, the translator's stock-in-trade, they're why we exist, they're what makes our work worth doing, my friends tell me): it lies in the mere fact that the writer is alive.

The living writer is not as bad as the Beckett estate: indeed, I'd rather deal with ten living writers than I would with one Beckett estate. In fact, if I have to be truthful, the living writer is often a useful, sometimes an indispensable, ally. Who but the living writer can resolve a problem of meaning if the meaning escapes me? From time to time I have contrived to misunderstand a word, a sentence, even as a consequence, a whole passage of dialogue. Sometimes, without misunderstanding the surface meaning, I have missed the subtext of a line being phrased in this way and no other. What I have given is a perfectly *acceptable* translation of the surface meaning but, by drawing my attention to the multiplicity of intended meanings, the living writer can point me to a more fertile choice of words which might propagate more of the subtext. And I have to say that, in the overwhelming proportion of interventions that have come from the living writer about my translations (and it is both a blessing and a curse that English has become a *lingua franca*, because everyone thinks they know more English than, quite often, they really do) the effect has always been beneficial.

But not always. Sometimes the intervention can save the line but ruin the passage or scene. It can be difficult to convince the living playwright that the sacrifice of some of the line's subtlety can be necessary to salvage the scene. Like all authors, living playwrights can become unreasonably attached to a choice of individual words. Not to mention jokes. For a translator to change, or even throw out, an author's joke because it is so bad that the translator can't bring himself to repeat it could, I've no doubt, destroy friendships and ruin exemplary working relationships.

And it is the relationship with living writers and their work which creates those problems (or opportunities, as we've all been taught to regard them by the power of positive thinking) which makes the task of translating the living so different from translating the dead, and the long-dead especially. As a translator, what you are trying to give the living writer is an English-language voice.

You're also, of course, having to do all those things with the text when it has been rendered into English as you would with a new play; cajole, persuade, convince the producing team, argue the merits of the piece and its component parts with directors, designers and actors who have difficulties with one aspect or another. You don't overwhelmingly mind doing that. You know it's part of the joy of translating a piece for theatre and you do know that there are times when you have to accept that a difficulty is insuperable and, just as in a play that you yourself have written, you acquiesce to the demands of the director, or designer, or the actor and change a line, or a passage, or (heaven forbid!) a scene.

But when you do so, you do so with greater than usual squeamishness. Even if you acknowledge that the decision is, theatrically speaking, the right one, you find yourself uncomfortable, even starting to hope (if these little concessions have been numerous) that the living writer will be forced, by something like a prolonged strike of air-traffic controllers, to miss the entire run of his translated piece. Because you feel that, however justified it has been, every surrender to the needs of the production has been a kind of betrayal. And, naturally enough, nobody wants to be seen to have been disloyal.

A barrister friend of mine tells me that, in effect, what he has to do in court is give his clients the words which they would have used if they'd been trained in the niceties of the legal system – and no others. If, at the end of the trial, a client feels that his case and arguments have been mis-represented, then naturally he feels aggrieved. My job as a translator of a living writer is not dissimilar; if the writer feels that he wouldn't have said it like that in a thousand years, he feels aggrieved. And rightly, too.

There are two really exciting, but sometimes problematic, bonuses for the translator of the living writer. The first is that the living writer is alive – and writing. This means that every so often a new piece comes off the typewriter and is sent to the translator to put into English. There is no canon with a living writer. As a translator you can suspect how a playwright might develop, what kinds of plays he might come up with. You make a kind of commitment to a living writer which you don't need to make with one who is dead; you offer him your English-language voice for better or worse. He may not like your voice and may decide to try another, or do without one altogether. At the same time, you may not like some of the things he has to say and that you have to anglicise, and if you start disliking more and more, you might ask for a divorce, with all the acrimony that that entails. But, fundamentally, when you enter into a translating relationship with a living writer you try to commit yourself for better or for worse...

When you do it, it's with the hope that you will manage to grow in the same directions as the living writer will grow, though that can never happen. You hope that the plays you have admired and which have caused you to offer your voice to the playwright will be followed by plays you can admire just as wholeheartedly. It's an impossible hope, just like the hopes of a perfect marriage are quite impossible. Sometimes you find the hot-off-the-typewriter work that arrives at your door depressingly familiar; same old stuff, you sigh to yourself, I could have guessed he was going to write this, I wish he'd find somebody else to do this one piece for him...

But you don't make those particular wishes fathers of your deeds. You sit down and you do what you can to make the piece vibrant and exciting, just as it was to the living writer. You do it because you have a loyalty to the writer, because you are just the writer's English-language voice, because you are constantly trying to be that writer in his or her English-language incarnation.

You search for other writers, other marriages. You become excited by the discovery of a new voice that is missing only one component: its English sounds. Recently, one such discovery led me to a quirky, difficult, probably impossible-to-translate writer called Tadeusz Slobodzianek, who is tackling the big themes of loyalty, honesty, spiritual needs and many of the other things that, as a human being who is also a playwright and translator, I feel are important, in a way which is bitingly funny and theatrically overwhelming. He has written a play about Merlin, he has written a play about the East Polish inter-war drifter who proclaimed himself, and allowed himself to be crucified as the new Messiah, he has written how ordinary people live when the only certainties are lies. He has written them in a language which is vibrant, funny, poetic. He has used theatre to stunning effect. The translator in you itches to get his hands on the text and turn it into English, can't wait to hear English-speaking actors say those funny lines, to watch an Anglophone audience be moved by the dilemmas facing the ordinary yet extraordinary characters the playwright has created.

So, reader, I married him. But I didn't divorce the other writers first. No, I became a bigamist. And all the problems of one marriage became multiplied by the problems caused by this and other marriages. Who, you might ask, would want that?

But then, just as in any marriage, miracles happen. A living writer, unlike a dead one, can always produce a new piece that makes your heart sing with joy. A piece that makes you shake with excitement as you turn the pages. Makes you weep with the pleasure of being witness to the birth of a masterpiece. And then makes you shake with trepidation, knowing that this masterpiece's immediate future in the English-speaking world is relying on your voice so that it can be heard.

I've been translating Slawomir Mrozek's plays for close to twenty years. If most of them have been good experiences, as they have, I can't deny that there has been the occasional moment of dissatisfaction. And then, suddenly, out of the blue, completely unexpectedly, he sent me *Love In The Crimea*, which I've already mentioned, a piece of pure theatrical genius. I spent days walking about in a state of hyper-excitement. *It was as if I myself had written a masterpiece.* Even though I hadn't even begun to translate it, hadn't even begun to dare to translate it, I felt as if I had personally created a work of genius.

When I started to translate the piece, it felt as if I were, indeed, writing a masterpiece myself. And when I had finished translating it, I felt as much (if not more) satisfaction as I would have done with any of my own pieces of work. It felt as if it had come out of my own head, out of my own heart.

Perhaps my friend D is right after all. Maybe I should leave Mrozek's name off the posters and claim it as my own.

TRANSLATING INTO DIALECT

BILL FINDLAY

Bill Findlay is currently working on a research project on Scots as a theatrical language in the Drama Department of Queen Margaret College, in Edinburgh. The Scottish Cultural Press is about to publish his volume of essays *The Use Of Scots In Translation*, and he has just finished editing *A History Of Scottish Theatre* for Polygon. With Martin Bowman, he has translated into Scots five plays by the Quebec dramatist Michel Tremblay, once described by the *Guardian* as the 'best playwright Scotland never had': *The Guid Sisters, The Real Wurld?* and *Hosanna*, all staged by the Tron Theatre, in Glasgow; *The House Among The Stars* (Traverse Theatre, Edinburgh, and Perth Theatre); *Forever Yours, Marie-Lou* (Ladderman Productions, in association with the Tron). His translation of Gerhart Hauptmann's *The Weavers* was staged by Dundee Rep in 1995. Bill Findlay's Scots versions have also been performed abroad, including in Tremblay's native Canada, where the special qualities of Scots were relished and proclaimed as 'a revelation' and 'startlingly fresh'.

This piece will be in two related parts: the first part will comprise general discussion of dialect translations of plays, with reference to the Scottish experience; and the second will offer some specific examples of effects which can be achieved using dialect as a translation medium, drawing on the five translations into Scots which Martin Bowman and I have had staged of plays written in Québécois by Michel Tremblay.

1

As I write this, the Glasgow novelist James Kelman has recently been awarded the Booker Prize for his novel *How Late It Was, How Late*. The award has provoked some controversy, partly because some critics profess to find Kelman's Glasgow working-class dialect incomprehensible, and partly because some would deny literary sophistication to a work in such a medium. Due to time constraints, Kelman's speech at the award ceremony was cut short but the full text was subsequently published in a Scottish newspaper. In it, Kelman attacked the élitist cultural values of critics who disparaged his work because of supposed linguistic – and therefore artistic – limitations inherent in his chosen medium:

...the gist of the argument amounts to the following, that vernaculars, patois, slangs, dialects, gutter-languages, etc., etc., might well have a place in the realms of comedy (and the frequent references to Billy Connolly or *Rab C Nesbitt* substantiate this) but they are inferior linguistic forms and have no place in literature. And *a priori* any writer who engages in the use of such so-called language is not really engaged in literature at all.

Part of the problem with some of the critical comment by London-based reviewers on Kelman's work is that dialect writing stands outside the English literary mainstream, in both historic and contemporary terms. A serious literary work employing dialect in a sustained manner is therefore viewed as an oddity in England. England does of course have a dialect inheritance but it has not been given literacy or social legitimacy. It is, for example, this illegitimate status – and the class bias behind it – which the eminent poet and theatre translator, Tony Harrison, bitterly laments in his collection of poems, *The School Of Eloquence*, one of whose themes is how his education placed no value on his native Yorkshire vernacular and encouraged an inferiority complex in speakers of it. In one poem, 'Them & [uz]', Harrison relates how, in a school production of *Macbeth*, he was cast as the Drunken Porter because of his vernacular speech:

'Can't have our glorious heritage done to death!' chides his English teacher.
'Poetry's the speech of kings. You're one of those
Shakespeare gives the comic bits to: prose!
All poetry (even Cockney Keats?) you see
's been dubbed by [ʌs] into RP,
Received Pronunciation, please believe [ʌs]
your speech is in the hands of the Receivers'.
'We say [ʌs] not [uz], T.W.!' That shut my trap.
I doffed my flat a's (as in 'flat cap')
my mouth all stuffed with glottals, great
lumps to hawk up and spit out ... E-nun-ci-ate!

Speakers of Scots dialects – and particularly urban varieties, as James Kelman would doubtless testify from Glasgow experience – have often suffered at the hands of the same syndrome described by Tony Harrison. Nevertheless, a key contrast between England and Scotland is that works in or featuring Scottish dialect stand in the literary mainstream, stretching back almost a millennium. The canonization in Scotland of Robert Burns in poetry and Walter Scott in fiction testify to the language's literary status. Also, the use of the term 'dialect' when applied to Scots is problematic in that it can seem to mean, wrongly, both that Scots is but a regional dialect of English and that there is only one undifferentiated Scots dialect. The word 'dialect' can therefore be unhelpfully reductive here and serve to obscure a richer reality so far as the linguistic culture of Scotland is concerned. To help explain what I mean here, I should offer some very brief historical background.

In the twelfth century, Scots developed out of the northern dialect of Old English, whilst the contemporaneous development of English was based on the southern dialect. Although Scots and English therefore had much in common, the differences between them increased in correspondence with the separate political development of Scotland and England as independent kingdoms. Prominent among the distinguishing features of Scots from English by 1500 were the retention of a strong Scandinavian colouring in pronunciation and vocabulary, and a distinctive infusion of French and Dutch loan words (the consequence of political and trade alliances). In illustration of the differences between the related languages of Scots and English by 1500, when a Spanish ambassador visited the Scottish Court in 1498, he likened the languages of the neighbouring kingdoms to Aragonese and Castilian. A number of subsequent events, chief among which were the union of the two countries' monarchies and parliaments in 1603 and 1707 respectively, led to Scots losing its national status as well as its written register; thereafter it fragmented into its local dialects (one of which, Ayrshire, formed the basis of Robert Burn's poetry). Gradually, Scots was replaced by the sister language, English, as the language of officialdom and the higher social classes. Whilst space requires that I paint with a broad brush here and telescope history, suffice it to say that, today, English predominates in Scotland but also that it co-exists with rural, urban, and regional varieties of Scots dialect (and with Gaelic in some areas). Indeed, I think that one could fairly say that the tenacious survival of Scots in its various dialects – in daily life as well as in literature, theatre and popular culture – has contributed to that cultural differentiation from England which has helped secure a continuing sense of Scottish nationhood within the political fabric of the United Kingdom. (On a small scale, we can see that 'differentiation' at work in the respective linguistic options available to theatre translators in Scotland and England, which I will discuss a little later.)

It may be that James Kelman would not choose to locate his work in the above linguistic tradition – particularly as admission to the Scottish literary mainstream of writing in a realistic working-class Glaswegian idiom has only been achieved in the past twenty-five years. Also, I suspect he would have strong political objections to the word 'dialect' being applied to his language, since the term implies that what he speaks and writes is not 'standard', whereas for him it is 'standard'. But the point I wish to draw out is that, in contrast with England (witness the critical response to Kelman's Booker novel), a Scottish writer's decision to use one of the many dialects of Scots is regarded by critics and the public in Scotland today as a natural rather than an eccentric choice. Evidence of this can be seen in the fact that, in the week that I write, the ten best selling books in Scotland include not just Kelman's *How Late It Was, How Late*, but two books of fiction by Irvine Welsh featuring Edinburgh dialect (*Trainspotting* and *The Acid House*), and a novel by Duncan McLean featuring Aberdeenshire dialect (*Blackden*). The recent list of the most promising 'New Generation' poets in Britain included W N Herbert, who writes in Dundee dialect, and Kathleen Jamie, who sometimes makes use of a generalised Scots. John Byrne's *The Slab Boys* trilogy of plays in Paisley dialect, is currently running at the Young Vic in London; and Bill Bryden's theatrical 'spectacular', *The Big Picnic*, written mainly in Glasgow dialect, is nearing the end of its run in the cavernous engine shed of Harland & Wolff shipbuilders in Glasgow, where it looks set to have drawn a total audience of 40,000. And in popular culture, a new series of *Rab C Nesbitt*, in Govan dialect, is currently running on television.

Whilst I do not want to pretend that Scots dialect speakers (particularly urban ones) have not experienced, and do not experience, some social stigmatisation because of their speech, it is nevertheless the case that, as the above demonstrates, in Scotland the translator into dialect works in a more hospitable climate than seems to pertain south of the border. An important consequence of that fact is that the Scottish translator has *potentially* a richer linguistic source to draw on than has conventionally been the case in English theatre (I will explain later why I emphasise 'potentially'). Not only do we have standard English and its varieties at our disposal, but we have the many regional varieties of Scots, whether urban or rural, contemporary or historic, and we can also draw on a more 'literary' register of Scots, whether borrowed from an earlier period of the Scots Literary tradition or created 'syntheti-cally' by writers for their individual purposes. Fine examples of the rich linguistic brew which a translator can concoct from such a resource are Liz Lochhead's translation of Molière's *Tartuffe* (1986) and Edwin Morgan's translation of Rostand's *Cyrano de Bergerac* (1992). Lochhead's introductory note to her translation offers a description of her chosen medium and supports the point I am making here:

> It is a totally invented and, I hope, theatrical Scots, full of anachro-nisms, demotic speech from various eras and areas; it's proverbial, slangy, couthy, clichéd, catch-phrasey and vulgar; it's based on Byron, Burns Stanley Holloway, Odgen Nash and George Formby, as well as the sharp tongue of my granny... There seems to be a sensuous and sensual earthiness in Molière's masterpiece, a comedy both classical and black, and with an ending of quite political satire which bland English translations totally lost.

Lochhead's last comment points up an important consideration for the Scottish translator in the choice of a translation medium which might include dialect in part or whole: how can one most effectively render the original work? It would plainly be daft and counterproductive to use Scots indiscriminately for translation purposes in accordance with some kind of manifesto. The choice of a translation medium must be one of 'horses for courses' depending on the nature of the original work. Thus, English might be appropriate in one instance, a Scots dialect in another; or a contrasting combination of the two; or a commingling of the two either straighforwardly or experimentally (as in the case of Lochhead's *Tartuffe* and Morgan's *Cyrano*). Whilst translators everywhere will of course begin by asking how best they can render a work, so far as the related question of 'horses for courses' is concerned, the Scottish translator is potentially at an advantage in the English-speaking world in having an unusually rich variety of language options to draw on, including dialect.

To return to the example of Liz Lochhead's *Tartuffe*, the availability of these languages options is perhaps one reason why Molière enjoys a widespread popularity in Scotland unknown in England; that is, it may be that a Scots translation releases qualities in Molière that standard English does not. For it is noticeable that Molière has never quite enjoyed the popularity on the English stage that his status warrants. As one reviewer asks, in a review in *Plays And Players* (December 1987) of a production of Molière's *Le malade imaginaire*, 'If truth be told, is he not in English the most uninteresting of world dramatists?' In contrast, the popularity of Molière on the Scottish stage in the post-war period has made him almost a Scottish playwright-by-adoption, as evidenced by the extraordinary number of productions listed in Noel Peacock's book, *Molière In Scotland: 1945-1990* (Glasgow, 1993). Not only have Scots translations of Molière's work by writers such as Robert Kemp, Victor Carin, Hector MacMillan and Liz Lochhead enjoyed great success but they have helped define the distinctiveness of modern Scottish theatre. It could be argued that, in large part, Molière's success in Scotland can be explained by how well he translates into a Scots idiom, and how alive his work thereby becomes for Scottish audiences.

Something similar can be seen in the recognition enjoyed in Scotland by a major contemporary foreign playwright who remains relatively under-appreciated in England: the Quebec dramatist Michel Tremblay. Between 1989 and 1994, there have been staged five translations into Scots by Martin Bowman and me of plays by Tremblay, and in some cases there has been more than one production as well as foreign tours. Tremblay has thereby become the most regularly staged playwright in Scotland in recent years; and he has been awarded an honorary degree by Stirling University in recognition of both his international stature *and* his contribution to Scottish theatre. The *Guardian* has described Tremblay as 'the best playwright Scotland never had'; and The *Scotsman* has said, 'if Scotland is to adopt a playwright there could be no better candidate than Tremblay'. The *Glasgow Herald* has summed up Tremblay's appeal thus: 'In the translations into Scots. . . the plays of Tremblay achieve an astonishing affinity of class, religion, voice and emotional oppression for

Scottish audiences'. That is, as with Molière, the use of Scots as a translation vehicle releases qualities in Tremblay lost in standard English translations.

The availability of dialect in Scotland, then, rather than being a constraint on writers and translators in their artistic ambition (as some of the critical response to James Kelman holds) presents, rather, special opportunities. Of his translation of *Cyrano de Bergerac*, Edwin Morgan said in the programme notes to the Communicado production:

> I decided that an urban Glaswegian Scots could offer the best basis, supplemented where necessary, to meet the range of tones and tongues in the original, by other kinds of Scots and English.

That reference to 'the range of tones and tongues in the original' is interesting, for it lends support to my belief that the long-standing predominance of standard English translations in British (and to a degree, Scottish) theatres – more often than not delivered in the class-associated accent of received pronunciation, with the 'mechanicals' sporting regional accents – has misrepresented both the 'non-standard' linguistic nature of much Western drama and its rootedness in the texture of a particular national or regional culture (in the case of *Cyrano*, for example, that of Gascony).

Wonderful though the English language is, as a translation medium it can have a homogenising effect on foreign work translated, which can in turn disfigure the original work. To take the German theatre tradition, for example, one would not know from existing English-medium translations that such seminal plays in Western Drama as Buchner's *Woyzeck* and Hauptmann's *The Weavers* were written in dialect. The translators, of course, know this but they do not have an equivalent dialect resource available, as they often lament. For instance, in his introduction to *The Plays Of Georg Buchner* (Oxford University Press, 1971), Victor Price says of Woyzeck:

> The play is largely written in Hessian dialect and steeped in the atmosphere of Hessian folk-songs. Standard English cannot cope with this combination. Even a colloquialism which corresponds exactly, like 'one damned thing after another' for '*eins nach dem anderen*', is totally different in mood from the German. I have tried hard to match Buchner's concision; but what can one do with the dialect? Perhaps the ideal translation would be in dialect too – a latterday Robert Burns might be able to render the roughness and poetic qualities of Buchner's idiom.

The inference I draw from this is that Victor Price acknowledges that there is no dialect resource on which the English translator can draw, but that there may well be in Scotland, and that could place the Scottish translator at an advantage in certain circumstances.

The lack of such a dialect resource is, I think, a contributory factor as to why an important world playwright like Gerhart Hauptmann remains little known and little produced in Britain. It is also, I believe, the chief reason why the genius of another nineteenth-century dramatist, the satirist Johann Nepomuk Nestroy, remains locked in the Viennese dialect he employed (notwithstanding Tom Stoppard's adaptation of one of his plays, *On The Razzle*). As Martin Esslin has remarked, Nestroy is thus 'one of those great playwrights whose fame, it seems, is doomed to remain founded on mere hearsay' (*Theatre*, XII, 2, Spring 1981). That such translation problems impact on contemporary work, too, and lie not just with the historic repertoire, can again be seen from German language theatre. Use of dialect is a major feature in the work of leading contemporary writers who have been translated into English such as Martin Sperr and Franz Xaver Kroetz. For Kroetz, for example, the use of dialect in his plays set among the modern Bavarian underclass is 'part of the armoury of the plays and crucial to a fair interpretation'. For him, it is intimately bound up with the environment he depicts, hence he says, in *Plays And Players* (August 1987)

> Dialect is connected with work, with nature and landscape, with money, even. Dialect is man's dirty underpants.

I would argue, then, that the linguistic resource available to us in Scotland, and our dialect inheritance in particular, provides the theatre translator with special opportunities as regards classic and contemporary foreign drama. Whereas that living dialect inheritance, in life and in literature, might seem curious from an English perspective, it should be emphasised that it is a common enough past and present international norm – as reflected in the dialect usage of many historic and contemporary foreign dramatists. In short, what might strike some as linguistically odd about Scotland in British terms is not necessarily so when viewed in an inter-national context. Of course, an objection to a medium drawing on dialect might be, why translate from one foreign tongue into what for many English-speakers outside Scotland is another incomprehensible one? The simple answer is that Scottish theatre cannot function by looking over its shoulder for approbation from elsewhere. As with any national theatre culture, Scottish theatre has an obligation towards its own audience; and that obligation must entail reflecting to a significant, though not exclusive, degree the diversity of voices which are the daily (and at times, past) reality of life in Scotland. Whilst there are many schools of translation, I identify with the view that the translator translates for his own time, place, and audience; and it is not therefore a controlling concern for me that a translation should have 'marketability' in the sense that it can travel beyond the culture for which it was fashioned.

That said, I would like to think that translations featuring Scots dialect *can* travel, and be sufficiently well understood in the English-speaking world without the language needing to be diluted to a more 'standardised' form. My experience with plays by the Quebec playwright Michel Tremblay suggests that audiences can cope surprisingly well and that the difficulty can be overstated. Glasgow's Tron Theatre took *The Guid Sisters* to the World Stage International Theatre Festival in Toronto in 1990, and *The Real Wurld?* to the Stony Brook International Theatre Festival in Long Island, New York, in 1991. Also the Tron took *The Guid Sisters* back to Canada in 1992 for a four-week run in Montreal as part of the official British contribution to the city's three hundred and fiftieth anniversary celebrations. None of those invitations would have been forthcoming if the language of the translations had been considered impenetrable for English-speaking audiences. Moreover, those productions would not have proved the popular and critical successes which they did in both Canada and the USA if the language had turned out to be incomprehensible. As the *Toronto Star* said of *The Guid Sisters*, the language 'is not unduly difficult for Canadians to understand'; and as *Newsday* (USA) said of *The Real Wurld?*, 'concentration makes nearly everything comprehensible'. Hearteningly, too, the special qualities of the language were singled out for comment. For example, reviewing *The Guid Sisters*, the critic in the *Montreal Gazette* found the Scots 'a revelation', and the *Toronto Star* described it as 'startlingly fresh'.

Aside from the language's 'freshness', a further reason why Canadian critics responded so positively was that many had previously lamented the inadequacy of standard English translations in conveying Tremblay's genius with Québécois. The fault lay not with the translators' proficiency but with the limitations of English. As one critic remarked, 'Contemporary homogenized English offers no obvious equivalent to the various accents and locally rooted vocabulary of Canadian French'; and as another said, 'In English Tremblay's plays reveal little of the colour, resonance and musicality of the originals'. That Scots could be recognised in this way as getting closer in letter and in spirit to Tremblay's language – mainly the east-end dialect of Québécois – helps confirm me in my belief that the availability of dialect can be harnessed to unusual advantage by Scottish translators. Dialect presents us with special translation opportunities not just in regard to certain contemporary playwrights but certain historic ones as well. For example, Scots translation of historic plays such as Buchner's *Woyzeck* and Hauptmann's *The Weavers* afford a unique opportunity to get closer to the texture of the original work and thereby to reveal a wholly fresh perspective to audiences within and beyond Scotland (as happened with Edwin Morgan's Scots translation of *Cyrano de Bergerac*).

I use the word 'opportunities' here for the same reason that I emphasised the word 'potentially' when I said earlier that the Scottish translator has a potentially richer linguistic resource to draw on than has conventionally been the case in English theatre; namely, because I do not want to create the impression that I am speaking from a position of strength so far as the depth of repertoire of Scots translations is concerned. The translation repertoire dates only from the immediate postwar period when Robert Kemp, who prepared the acting text of Sir David Lindsay's *The Satire Of The Three Estates*, performed at the 1947 Edinburgh Festival, translated in the following year Molière's *L'école des femmes* as *Let Wives Tak Tent*. As mentioned earlier, Molière-into-Scots subsequently became a commonplace on the Scottish stage and a number of his works have been translated by different hands over the past forty years. The relatively few other translations into Scots of classic work include plays by Goldoni, Kleist, Holberg, Aristophanes, Beaumarchais and Rostand (as well as a recent adaptation of Hasek's novel, *The Guid Sodjer Schweik*, and a translation of the major cycle of *The Oresteia*). As regards contemporary foreign plays, extraordinarily, it was only in the 1980s that translations drawing on distinctive Scottish speech began to appear. Since then there have been translations of single plays by, for example, Michael Vinaver, Enzo Corman (this by James Kelman), Ludmilla Petrushevskaya, and Alexander Gelman; and translations of a number of plays by Michel Tremblay and Dario Fo (plays by Fo translated into an urban Scots idiom proved hugely successful in Scotland in the 1980s).

I would also not wish to suggest that, historically, there has been wholesale acceptance in Scotland of the validity of dialect as a medium capable of artistic sophistication in theatre translation. In the past, we have suffered from the unexamined assumption that translations into standard English of, say, Chekhov or Ibsen, delivered in received pronunciation (and thereby suggesting an English setting), need not be adapted to England, whereas translations into Scots must be adapted to Scotland. Part of the problem here, too, has been the genuine difficulty some have experienced in divorcing Scottish voices and language from Scottish culture. But the experience of the past fifteen years suggests that we have largely overcome such difficulties and that Scottish audiences are now being credited with the maturity to cope with non-adapted Scots translations. Of assistance to this has been not just the increased frequency and popularity of performed Scots translations, making them a regular feature of our theatre scene, but the new-found confidence displayed by a younger generation of theatre practitioners in asserting the validity of Scottish voices in performing plays written in English but not set in Scotland, and ranging widely in time and place from Shakespeare to Mamet.

My hope for the future is that the repertoire of Scots translations will be extended, to the enrichment of Scottish theatre in particular and English-language stage translations generally. I hope, too, that some productions of those translations will have exposure outside Scotland and thereby assist recognition in the wider English-speaking world of both the artistic potentialities which reside in Scottish dialect and its special effectiveness as a translation medium, in whole or part, for certain classic or contemporary plays where standard English proves an inadequate match. The low profile of dialect in English writing and translation, which I discussed at the outset, should not cause us to question the validity of drawing on our Scots dialect inheritance for stage translations any more than, say, James Kelman should 'standardise' his literary medium because some London critics find it incomprehensible and supposedly lacking in literary sophistication. Indeed, so far as work for the stage is concerned, should we in Scotland not be more assertive and voice the view that the National (sic) Theatre in London live up to its name and show willingness occasionally to programme work reflecting the linguistic diversity of the United Kingdom? Perhaps the mould could be broken with a translation. . .

2

In the speech defending his chosen medium, from which I quoted at the beginning of this piece, James Kelman lambasted those critics who made the *a priori* assumption that 'any writer who engages in the use of such so-called language is not really engaged in literature at all'. At the point I ended the quotation, Kelman continued:

> It's common to find well-meaning critics suffering the same burden. While they strive to be kind they still cannot bring themselves to operate within a literary perspective; not only do they approach the work as though it were an oral text, they somehow assume it to be a literal transcription of recorded speech.

In offering the following examples of some of the effects which can be achieved using dialect as a translation medium, I hope to demonstrate at the same time that dialect does, as Kelman argues, have the capacity for literary sophistication.

My examples will be taken from the translations by Martin Bowman and me of five plays by the Quebec dramatist, Michel Tremblay. Chief among the reasons why we chose to render Tremblay into a Scots idiom is that he has written some twenty plays in Québécois, which stands in something of the same linguistic and sociolinguistic relationship to standard French as Scots does to standard English. The variety of Québécois most commonly found in Tremblay's work is Montrealais, the working-class dialect of Montreal's east-end; but where required he has also drawn on a rural dialect, and a more standard register for middle class/professional characters. Tremblay's plays reveal a sustained creative engagement with Québécois and demonstrate a sophisticated exploration of the language's theatrical possibilities.

When Tremblay started writing in the 1960s, his native Montréalais dialect was dubbed '*Joual*'. '*Joual*' is the Quebec form of the standard French word for 'horse', *'cheval'*; hence, the speech of Tremblay and his community was pejoratively dismissed as 'horse language'. Whilst the subsequent nationalist 'Quiet Revolution', which took place in Quebec in the late sixties and early seventies, in time brought about a sea-change in attitudes towards Quebec-French and its varieties, Tremblay's first play in *'Joual'*, *Les belles-soeurs* (*The Guid Sisters*), proved a *succès de scandale* when premiered in 1968 because of its language. Traditionalists, who looked to France for their standards in taste, were shocked and ashamed by Tremblay's realistic representation and public exposure of what they regarded as the language of the gutter. The one socially aspiring and would-be standard-speaker among the working-class women characters in *Les belles-soeurs* embodies the attitudes which Tremblay challenged, as can be gauged from this abstract from one of her speeches:

> And as for Europe! Everyone over there is so well brought up. They're far more polite than here. You'd never meet a Germaine Lauzon over there. Only people with class. In Paris everyone speaks so refined. There they speak proper French. No like here. Leopold [her husband] was right. These people are inferior. They're nothing but keelies. We shouldn't be mixing with them. We shouldn't even waste breath talking about them... They should be hidden away somewhere out of sight... My God, I'm so ashamed of them.

They irony here, of course, is that the character, Lisette de Courval, attempts to speak 'well' but cannot avoid tell-tale slips into dialect ('No like here' and 'keelies'). In its clash with the rest of Lisette's language, the Scots dialect word 'keelies' ('a keelie' is a dismissive term for a vulgar lower-class person) attempts to convey the similar effect which Tremblay achieves with the word 'cheap': *'C'monde-là, c'est du monde cheap'*. 'Cheap' is one of the many borrowings from English which one finds in Québécois through the language having to co-exist with North-American English. Quebec-French has adopted many anglicisms such as this but they have been transformed through pronunciation and specific usage into words uniquely Québécois. 'Cheap' has thus taken on a particular meaning in Québécois, and no other word carries as dismissive a connotation in Quebec-French as it does. For language 'purists' in Quebec, such borrowing from English was additional cause for disparagement of *'Joual'*, which gives a further twist to the aspiring Lisette's use of the word. Whilst 'keelies' is not an exact equivalent for 'cheap', since it is not a word imported into the dialect in the way that anglicisms are in Québécois, it posits a word into the text that has similar resonance in its clash with the rest of Lisette's language, in its undercutting of her attempt to speak 'well', in its dismissive suggestion of someone vulgar and worthless, and in its onomatopoeic quality of disdainfulness.

Aside from assisting Tremblay satirise views such as those held by Lisette de Courval, having her speak in a more standard form than the other characters (and with a degree of affectation) helped him to throw into greater relief the earthy vigour of the other woman's *'Joual'*. We were able to convey this in translation through our Scots dialect resource, as seen in this example:

> Lisette De Courval: As far as I'm concerned there'll never be a substitute for real fur. By the by, did I tell you, I'll be getting a new stole come the autumn? The one I have just now is three years old and it's starting to look... well, just a wee bit tired. Mind you it's still quite presentable, but...
>
> Rose Ouimet: Shut yir gub, ya bloody leear ye! We know damn fine yir man's up tae his erse in debt acause ae your mink stoles an yir fancy trips tae Europe. Yae cannae take us in wi aw that shite aboot bein weel-aff. Ye've nae mair money nor the rest ae us. Christ, ah've hud it up tae here wi that slaverin bitch bummin her load!

Another example of register contrast in *The Guid Sisters*, but of a subtler variety, can be found in the differentiation between different generations of dialect speakers. The ages of the fifteen characters range from fifty-nine to twenty, and the play was written in 1965, so a strict reading would lead one to conclude that the two oldest characters, the fifty-nine-year olds, were born in the first decade of the century. This explains, in terms of the plays urban setting and language, some apparent anachronisms in the older women's speech, as evidenced in this exchange between them:

> Angéline Sauvé: ... Here, did ye notice that deed man's lassie? Monsieur whit's his name? She looked like daith waarmed up.
>
> Rhéauna Bibeau: Ah ken. Pair Rolande. She's gaun aboot tellin awbdy she killt her faither. It wis acause ae her he loast his temper at the tea-table, ye see...Ah, aw fel sorry fur her... and her mither. It's a cryin shame, so it is. It's a sair loass fur thum aw... a sair loass...
>
> Angéline Sauvé: Aye, the heid o' the hoose, the faither... you're tellin me. Mind you, it's no as bad as loassin the mither, but still...
>
> Rhéauna Bibeau: Richt enough. Loassin yir mither's worser. Naebdy kin tak the place o a mither.

Although *The Guid Sisters*, like all our translations, retains the Quebec setting and is not adapted to Scotland, we had to settle on a Scottish linguistic equivalent to Tremblay's Montréalais, so we used an urban working-class – and essentially Glaswegian – dialect of Scots. However, in the exchange above, certain words and forms (e.g. 'ken', 'richt', 'tak', 'worser'), as well as the different accent which these invite in the delivery of the two characters' speech, signal a more rural and 'period' dialect, and thereby a generational difference from the other characters. A gain in being able to achieve this differentiation is that it sits with the Montreal experience. Montreal was late in being industrialised, and mass migration from the country to the city occurred at the beginning of this century. A consequence of this was that urban Québécois for long reflected strong rural influence. Angéline and Rhéauna are of a generation who may either have migrated to the city with their parents or they may be first-generation urbanites whose speech reflects their parents' roots. In dramatic terms, a further gain from this rural-urban differentiation is that Angéline and Rhéauna's dialect and accent, in contrast with the other characters' more urban speech, are an aid to characterisation and help convey that their views are traditional and conservative, that they have lived narrow lives, and that (a source of humour) they are somewhat out-of-touch and naive.

In his play *La maison suspendue* (*The House Among The Stars*), Tremblay makes a more extended use of contrast between registers of language in distinguishing between three sets of characters from three different periods in time and three social groups. Each of Tremblay's registers finds an unforced Scottish equivalent: the nineteen-ten characters, who live in a remote country area, speak a lyrical, rural Québécois/Scots: their children, the nineteen-fifty characters, are working class Montrealers who speak a sharp, urban Québécois/Scots; and their grandson and his male lover, the nineteen-ninety characters, are middle class Montrealers who speak a relatively prosaic standard French/English with some Quebec/Scottish features. The language contrasts have a poignancy which complements the play's elegiac tone and its thematic concern with change and with how geographic and social mobility can lead a later generation to a troubling sense of deracination, loss, and aridity.

The three generations of this extended family appear on stage simultaneously but on different time-scales, so the three registers of language are important for the audience in distinguishing the different generations and in suggesting the passing of time and the loss of roots. Tremblay often counterpoints these different characters and their speech patterns with carefully crafted exits and entrances, as in the following example where the fifty and ninety generations make their separate arrivals at the family cabin in the country (the ten generation is already there). In order of appearance, Victoire is a nineteen-ten character, Sébastien and his father Mathieu are nineteen-ninety characters, and Edouard and his sister Albertine are from the fifties (it may also help to know that Edouard is a camp transvestite).

> Victoire (*to herself*): Ah'm guantae feenish up hinkin it's true he gars the mune come oot at nichts! That brither ae mines is jist a damn twister. He must be keekin intae the almanac oan the fly. (*The door of the house opens. Sébastien comes out running.*)
> Sébastien: I've left it in the car!

Mathieu *(offstage)*: What a numpty! You harped on about that damn Nintendo all the way here in the car and then you go and forget to bring it in with you! *(Exit Sébastien through the garden.)*

Victoire: The black fly season's owre. We'll kin sit oot oan the verandah again. Josaphat's pipe'll keep the mosquitoes awa'. *(She looks at the sun. She smiles.)* Aye, oan ye go, awa' tae yir bed, ya auld besom. Yir darg's duin fur the day. Same's oorsels. *(She looks in the direction of Josaphat.)* Or same's me, onywey. *(She sits on the first step of the verandah.)* It's a braw tae sit stracht doon oan the bare wid when it's still waarm like this. It's no burnin hoat like it gits in the middle-ae-the-day, an somehoo it feels saft tae the skin. The day's near owre when it's like this. Ah'd like it fine if it could aye be a hauf-hoor afore the sun gaes doon. The warld wid be aa the better a place fur it. *(After a few seconds the fiddle ceases. Enter The Fat Woman, Albertine and Edouard, collapsing under their luggage. They are dressed very much in the style of 1950.)*

Edouard: Anither half-hoor an ma erse wid've been fit fur nuthin!

Albertine: Cut that oot, Edouard! You promised me ye widnae make any fulthy remarks this week. Ye behaved yirsel in the caur so jist cairry oan that wey...

Edouard: What makes ye think it's so fulthy? If ye ask me, ma wee sister, ah think your mind's no as clean as you'd hiv us believe! Ah meant nuthin mair thin ma bum's paralysed, that's aw! Ah'll hiv ye know it kin happen tae any man's been sat fur six hoors in an auld motor-caur... an tae any wumman, come tae that! D'ye mean tae tell me your bum's no paralysed?

The Fat Woman: Am ah gaunnae hivtae keep the peace atween youse two awready? *(To Edouard.)* Instid ae you tirin yirsel oot actin the eejit, go'n cairry the suitcases up oantae the verandah... *(Mathieu comes out of the house.)*

Mathieu: Sébastien, what are you doing? Why's it taking you so long?

Sébastien: *(offstage.)*: I can't get the door open!

Mathieu: Oh, just great! We've only just arrived and already you've started your carryings-on!

In *Le vrai monde?* *(The Real Wurld?)* Tremblay again makes use of contrasting varieties of dialect, but here the contrast is between a realistic dialect and one which has a certain 'inauthenticity' about it. The reason for this is that the work has a play-within-a-play structure, and the fictional play – written by one of the characters – is meant, in Tremblay's words, to be 'a bad play'. Through this device, and as hinted at by the title, *The Real Wurld?*, Tremblay is asking what right he has as an artist to exploit his family's experiences in pursuit of his art and whether his interpretation of events can only ever be partial and flawed. Thus the outer play seems to represent the 'actuality' of one family's relationships (father, mother, son

212

and daughter), whereas the inner play gives the callow twenty-three-year-old son's dramatic version of how he perceives his family. In contrast with the language of the outer play, that used by the son in his play has a self-conscious quality and a certain lack of colloquial authenticity. The language thereby complements the son's rather grotesque portrayal of his family.

In attempting to communicate Tremblay's intentions through translation, we used two slightly differentiated dialect registers: one which is realistic and energised, and one which is slightly wooden. This can be exemplified by comparing the speech of the two fathers. In this first excerpt, the 'real' father, Alex I, needles his son Claude, characteristically veering between the aggressively threatening and the flippant in his belittling dealings with, what he considers to be, his over-sensitive son (an aspiring writer and author of the inner play):

> · Alex I: D'ye stull go oot tae work wi yir wee briefcase, actin the intellectual? Whit d'ye pit in it? Yir piece? *(Claude lowers his eyes.)* Yir piece and yir bits ae scribbles? When're we gaunne git a kike at the master-piece, eh? When it's a blue moon?... Anyhow, if it's poetry, ye kin keep it tae yirsel... Ah've hid it up tae here wi aw you bloody beatniks scrapin guitars in every bloody hotel ah go intae in the province... How come yese've taken tae twangin away at guitars aw ae a sudden, eh? It's spreadin like the bloody plague! Ah jist seen wan ae yese Setterday night thair in Saint-Jerome... Jesus Christ, even yon Felix-bloody-Leclerc insnae as sair oan the lugs as thon wis...
>
> Claude: Aw keep the heid. What ah write's goat nothin tae dae wi guitars.
>
> Alex I: Well, ah'm gled tae hear it... that's a relief, ah'm shair! *(He laughs.)* Ah think ah know you well enough, oor Claude, tae know thit anythin you write couldnae tickle wan ae ma baw-hairs.

In general, Claude's inner play lacks the verve of exchanges such as this in the 'real' play. This a particularly evident in his depiction of his father, whose dialogue often comes across as clichéd and gauchely written. For example, in the inner play, Claude accuses his father of being a philanderer and of sexually abusing his sister (now a go-go dancer whom the father watches voyeuristically). After the mother and daughter have confronted the father about his behaviour, he reflects to himself:

> Alex II: Things used tae be that simple! That straight-forrit! When ah wis wee, ma mither used tae say tae me that every sin gits fund oot, every sin his tae be peyed fur. Ah used tae make fun ae her. An ah've led ma life so's tae prove her wrang. Ah've been smert enough tae oarder ma life so's ah've hid ma freedom tae dae whit ah waant an ah'm damn sure ah'm no

gaunne loass it! Ah'm no gaunne start peyin noo fur somethin happened in the past. Thurs nae wey ah'm gaunne pey! Nae wey! They'll can pit up wi me as ah am, lump it or leave it. Jist who's the gaffer aroond here? Eh? Ah'm no gaunne be led aroond bi the nose bi some hysterical, slaverin wumman an a go-go dancer disnae waant folk tae go an watch her dance! Ah'll watch her dance when ah waant tae! If she waants tae show aff her flesh, lit her git oan wi it!

In the play *Hosanna* (same title in translation), the eponymous Hosanna (Claude, a transvestite) and his live-in lover (Cuirette, a leather-clad biker) enjoy a stormy relationship. Their repartee is caustic and peppered with expletives, puns, and gay and camp words and expressions. Hosanna in particular has a special way with language, as the following attempts to show. Hosanna's rival, the arch-bitch Sandra (another transvestite), who earlier in the evening humiliated Hosanna in public, has telephoned at 3.30 a.m. to rile Hosanna further by inviting Cuirette over to her place:

> Cuirette: Naw, ye cannae tempt me... Ah'm no in the mood... Ah'm steyin put here...
> Hosanna: Too bloody tootin yir steyin here... *(She takes hold of the telephone.)* 'Ello, Sandra, comment allez-vous, mon petit chou? Je suis jist fine, merci buckets. But it's half-past three, ah've goat work the morra, an ah need ma bed...The fun's finished... It wis awfie nice ae ye tae invite Cuirette owre tae spend the night, but good hubbie that he is, dear Cuirette's elected tae stey here. Oh, and Sandra, you've been chasin him that long that ah'd've thoat you'd've goat the message bi this time thit he funds you pathetic... In fac', you're that pathetic you gie us baith the boak! Admittedly you were awfully funny this evening, and clearly you were tickled pink that everybody laughed at your putrid jokes, but did you not notice, dearie, how everybody laughed hardest when your back was turned? That wis because your dress wis that tight yir belly'd burst oot at the seam. Yir spare tyre wis hingin oot like a big shooglie lump ae pink meat! An as fur that yellie froak! His naebdy ivir tellt ye how yellie clashes wi peroxide hair? *(She hangs up.)*
> Cuirette: What a tongue! Here wis me thinkin she wis gaunnae tear intae you! Ah go aw limp when ah hear you talk like that!
> Hosanna: It's nothin new fur you tae be limp, Queen-ette... Oh, sorry, Queer-ette...

The changes in register here – from the pseudo-sophistication of the French, to the downrightness of urban Scots, to affected poshness, to colloquial English of a 'matronly' variety for camp effect – allow Hosanna to adopt different tones of voice the better to communicate his/her distaste to Sandra. But the blustering bravado of these switches also suggest Hosanna's unease in dealing with a rival who has won a shattering triumph over him/her earlier that evening; and at a deeper level these switches in register reflect the issue of identity which is at the heart of the play. Also, the richness of Hosanna's language and his/her command of different registers help define who he/she is as a character; that is the richness of his/her language is a key aspect of his/her complexity as portrayed by Tremblay. In the original play, Hosanna and Cuirette are lower-class Québécois speakers, so we used an urban Scots as the basis for their speech but drew on other varieties of language as demonstrated above. An aspect of this worth mentioning is that having the gay lovers as dialect speakers was, for us, a welcome departure from the way in which gay characters tend to be socially, and therefore linguistically, stereotyped on the stage.

My last example comes from our most recently staged translation, *Forever Yours, Marie-Lou* (*À toi, pour toujours, ta Marie-Lou*). The play is a bleak tragedy of family breakdown, with occasional shafts of grim humour. It again shows Tremblay's experimentation with form, for the two sets of characters (a mother and father make up one set, and their two daughters the other) inhabit different time-planes, ten years apart, but are on stage simultaneously. All remain virtually motionless for the duration of the play, which has the effect of focussing attention on the play's aural qualities. Tremblay has acknowledged that the play reflects his love of chamber music, and critics have seen it as a cantata of sorts. The 'musicality' of the piece is evident not just in the way that the different voices counterpoint and overlap but in how Tremblay makes use of effects such as rhythm and repetition.

In the early part of the play, a petty but rancorous argument develops between the husband and wife (Leopold and Marie-Lou) about the affordability of two kinds of peanut butter. It is an argument indicative of both the banality of their lives and the bitterness underlying their tortured relationship. This extract is one of the first moments in the play where the supposedly prim and devout Roman Catholic, Marie-Lou, swears:

> Ben oui, j'le sais que tu fais un salaire de crève-faim, mais c'est pas une raison pour se priver de beurre de peanuts crunchy! Quand tu sues comme un Christ en croix en arrière de ta Christ de machine, dis-toé qu'au moins demain tu vas manger du beurre de peanuts crunchy au lieu du beurre de peanuts smoothy! C'est déjà mieux que rien, bâtard!

Tremblay's musical sense is evident here in the rhythm of the writing, in the use of alliteration, and in the repetition of 'Christ' and the anglicisms 'peanuts' and 'crunchy'. A Scots dialect medium is able to accommodate these aspects of Tremblay Québécois. The cultural oddity of peanut butter in a Scottish context –

and particularly in a dialect context – creates the same absurd banality as do the English words in the original; and, although we found it necessary to reverse the swear-words and to introduce a third swear word, the 'musicality' of the original speech is maintained without sacrificing the rancour:

> Fine well ah know it's starvation wages ye bring in but that's nae reason fur us tae go wi'oot crunchy peanut butter! When you're sweatin yir guts oot behind yir bastardin machine, tell yirsel at least the morra ye kin eat crunchy peanut butter instid ae smoothy peanut butter! It's better than bugger all, fur Christ sake!

Sometimes Tremblay achieves a musical effect through more insistent and extended use of swear-words. These are often religious words – such as '*tabarnac*', '*hostie*', '*cibiore*', '*sacrement*' – which in Scotland lack the capacity for profanity that they have in a Roman Catholic society such as Quebec, so we frequently have to adapt them to Anglo-Saxon expletives. (In passing, it is interesting to note that James Kelman's use of swear-words has stirred some strong reactions but one of his ripostes is that he is not a mere translator of vernacular speech but an artist manipulating his chosen medium for a literary end.) The following extract from Leopold's bitter reflection on his wasted life shows our attempt to replicate Tremblay's manipulation of naturalistic dialogue to achieve a rhythmic 'beat' (for the reason just given, we had to provide an Anglo-Saxon substitute for Tremblay's profanities):

> Leopold: ... Ye spend yir hail fuckin life workin in the same fuckin machine makin the same fuckin thing!... Yir hail life!... Aw, but you've hid special trainin, they tell ye; you're lucky; you're no a part-timer; you've goat a steady joab!... The be-all and end-all, eh, a steady joab!... Is thur anythin mair fuckin awful in this world than a steady fuckin joab?... Ye git tae know yir joab ootside in an back tae fuckin front!... Ye get so's yir jist a cog in the wheel, a cog in yir machine... The machine's the gaffer an you're the worker... You dae whit it tells ye... Turn yir back fur a minute an it grinds tae a fuckin halt... You're at its ivry beck and fuckin call... It's as if it's yir twin; it knows ivry move ye make, and you know aw its tricks

By way of concluding comment on the effectiveness of Scots dialect as a translation medium for Michel Tremblay's Québécois, my Montreal collaborator, Martin Bowman, has written in an article on our translations:

> Over and over we have found that the problems arising in the translation of Tremblay find relatively easy solution in the Scots language.

Scots seems able to duplicate the effects of Tremblay's style — its rich vernacular, its musicality, its almost lyric despair — and gives another true voice to this great writer who, against all the odds, has made his people sing in their own music... We are fortunate to have been the Scots agents of this song.

EDWIN MORGAN: LANGUAGE AT PLAY

IN CONVERSATION WITH JOSEPH FARRELL

Edwin Morgan, born in 1920, has a strong claim to be regarded as Scotland's finest living poet and as one of the most versatile poets anywhere. His *Collected Poems* (Carcanet, 1990) contains the disarming assertion that he has excluded those poems which would have 'required colour reproduction'. However, he did include his 'newspoems', which consist of words taken from newspapers, arranged in a pattern and photographed, as well as his concrete poems, his 'instamatic' poems and works like *The Loch Ness Monster's Song* which contains no words in any known language. It also contains *The Whittrick,* subtitled 'a poem in eight dialogues', which includes dialogues between Joyce and MacDiarmid, Faust and Bosch as well as between Charlotte and Emily Brontë. His poems are known for their linguistic exuberance, their impish inventiveness as well as their devastatingly sudden moves to moods of deeply held emotion. He writes in Scots and English, and the writers he has translated include Mayakovsky, Leopardi, Sandor Weores, Montale, in addition to other poets who write in Hungarian, Russian, Italian, Spanish, early English Saxon and other languages.

JF: You are known principally as a poet, so I presume that your first work of translation was of poetry. How did you become involved in theatre translation?

EM: Yes, my first translations were poetry translations. As far as theatre is concerned, it began in two ways. The most important was my contact with the Medieval Players, now unfortunately disbanded, but dedicated to the idea that pre-Shakespearean drama was something a modern audience could enjoy. Although they did quite a number of plays which had originally been written in medieval English, they also staged various anonymous plays from other countries. They asked me to take a hand in translating these and preparing them for performance, which I did. I did two plays with them, and they seemed to work all right on the stage. That was probably what got me interested in the stage.

JF: Where did these plays come from?

EM: The titles were *The Apple Tree* and *Master Peter Pathelin*. The first of these was Dutch, and I worked with a Dutch translator. The other was a French farce, written in medieval French. *The Apple Tree* is a morality play, with a decidedly grim morality, but the other was quite a famous work of farce, with lots of scope for linguistic play, which is why I got so much enjoyment from doing it.

JF: What kind of work did you actually do with the plays? I start from the premise that the distinction between translation and adaptation is fundamental. Were these translations in a conventional sense, or were you doing an adaptation for the tastes of a modern audience?

EM: No, these were fairly faithful translations. That was how the company wanted to present these plays, so both translations are close to the original. With *Master Peter Pathelin* there are no substantial changes in the text or action, and I kept as closely as possible to the form. The translation has metre and rhyme, as had the original. It was much the same with the Dutch play. Both the plays were translated into standard English, although there were occasional bits of Scots, and other languages too:

PATHELIN
Paid? You don't pay such grasping men.
The devil gets *mafeesh faloos*.
He's coming here to eat a goose
And this is what we have to do.
Long before he starts to chew
He's going to cry to be paid pronto.
The bed is what I must get onto.
You understand? I'm a sick man.
He knocks, you open, lift your hand
To your lips, say "Shush!" You sigh
You're sad, you say, "Don't even try
To see him, poor man, ill in bed
For two months, oh, with what a head!"

EM: There is quite a lot of linguistic play in them, but the basic language is English. It was much the same with *The Apple Tree*. Being a morality play, I gave them names which reflected this, names like Frank Goodheart, Faith Trustwell, Willie Wildoats, or Jenny Joycat.

JF: I'm assuming you don't speak Dutch, so how did you work when you were translating that play?

EM: You are correct in your assumption. I had a translation given to me, a direct word-for-word translation into English.

JF: I would be curious to know how you actually worked in these circumstances. Was it a joint enterprise, did you work together, did you have him there at your elbow, or did he simply send you the translation?

EM: He sent me the translation, and I got to work on it, and thereafter we kept in correspondence. There are problems in interpretation or intelligibility, as there always are with any translation, but perhaps they were more severe in this case because of the age of the text. It is obviously frustrating not to have a knowledge of the original language, and it can never be the best way. I did it in this case because I was invited, it was a pleasing challenge, and I thought I would enjoy doing it. I seemed to get into the spirit of the piece, and it worked well on stage. Plainly I much prefer to work as I did with the French play, seeing it as I would see it and knowing exactly what the words meant. With *The Apple Tree*, it was not unduly difficult, because it was a short play and fits into a known genre – you know what medieval morality plays are like. It is similar to various early English morality plays. You are not entirely at sea. You are not hopelessly distant from the text.

JF: Your part, when you are basing yourself on a literal translation, is to devise speakable dialogue.

EM: It is no use – ever – having a translation which might be pedantically accurate or scholarly if it cannot be spoken on stage. Any translator has to bear that in mind, always. As it happens, I relish thinking in those terms and working in that kind of way. I find myself speaking the individual lines to myself. I knew that with the Medieval Players, actors and actresses would be working on those lines very soon after I had finished putting them on paper:

FROM THE PREFACE TO *THE APPLE TREE* (1982)

Clearly, it would not do to turn the Dutch text into an imaginary English version contemporary with it (i.e. about 1500); any such historical pastiche would seem forced and fraudulent. At the same time, the whole nature of the play resisted absolute modernisation. The solution adopted was to make the language itself modern, but set within the structure of a four-stress alliterative line which would hold associations with the earlier English drama and poetry. The Dutch original is written in a rough four-stress line, in rhyming couplets, and the use of alliteration in English may be taken as some kind of equivalent for the use of rhyme in the Dutch text. It can give a certain shape, a certain formal interest, to the colloquial language, without destroying the raciness required. Not all the speeches have this quality of raciness. Some lines and couplets have more 'set', chorus-like, proverbial character, which has to be indicated. Also there are on three occasions examples of a more marked formality, a sort of interlacing 'round' of repeated phrases suggesting something ritualistic, perhaps musical, perhaps gestural. . . . It was important that these features should be reproduced as far as possible, since they are part of the linguistic variety and verve of the play.

EM: I said at the beginning that there were two factors which had induced me to take up translation for the stage. The second was that I had been writing opera libretti just around that time. I worked with Thomas Wilson, and did a script based on the life of St Columba. It was very lively, because Columba may have been a saint, but he was a very forceful character who made his presence felt.

JF: Your poetry too has a quality which lends itself to theatre.

EM: I think that lies at the back of it all. The kind of poetry I write is often incipient theatre. I like dramatic situations, and characters, and the poem is often like a scene from a play, so I found it natural to take the extra step. I have always liked the presence of the voice in poetry. Long before there were books, poetry was spoken or chanted.

JF: Do you use a different technique for translating poetry, compared to what you would use when translating for theatre?

EM: The difference lies entirely in the realisation that dialogue has to be spoken. I have never translated plays for publication, or not primarily for publication; there was always some company waiting for the script. With a poem, there might be a complex concatenation of ideas, or the images might be unusual, so you would have to think of the best way of rendering them, but without the urgency of producing words to be spoken aloud. I probably enjoy best poets from other languages like Mayakovsky who, like myself, believe in the primacy of voice.

JF: Your best known translation, or perhaps it is just the most recent, was the *Cyrano de Bergerac* you did for the Communicado Theatre Company. Had you always had a special fondness for this play, or was it just a telephone call?

EM: I was asked to do it. Communicado wanted a new version for the Edinburgh Festival in 1992, and they asked me to think about it. I have to confess that I had never read the play before. I knew the story, but I had never read the play. I read an American version, and decided it was something I would like to attempt. Gerry Mulgrew, the director, wanted a Scottish version, although he did not specify it absolutely. There was no time for theorising about the type of Scots to be employed, because it had to be done very quickly. Rehearsal schedules meant that I only had three months to do what was a full five act play.

I concluded that it should be in Scots, but not the kind of 'historical' Scots used by the playwrights of the thirties and forties like MacLellan and Kemp, which was a deliberate attempt to reproduce a older Scots language. These plays have mostly fallen by the wayside now. I felt that it would have to be a Scots which could be spoken today by actors, and since it was me who was writing it, it would need to be a Scots with a strong Glasgow basis – a Glaswegian Scots if you like. It uses words from other parts of the country, but I was not too worried about purity of the language. I wanted something which would meet the demands of the play, while always being speakable. The main part is very long and demanding, so it was vital that the actor playing that part had a language he was at ease with. Tom Mannion is from Glasgow, and that did work for him. We experimented with the first act, and it was felt to be successful. I was there during rehearsals, and if they felt I had used a word which was too obscure, I met their objections. There is no point in being too precious about this.

I wanted to keep it racy, but formal. I kept the original metre. The original has metre and rhyme, and it seemed to me that there was no point in abandoning that, because part of the joy of the play is in the rhyme. The play itself is linguistically sparkling, and I felt that to do it in some kind of free verse or blank verse would not meet the case. The actors were initially surprised to be confronted by metre and verse, because so few plays today are written in that style, but they rose to the challenge:

FROM THE INTRODUCTION TO *CYRANO DE BERGERAC* (1992)

In the age of Ibsen, the play came as a delightful release. The hero was a poet, and the brilliant verse of the play, full of pyrotechnics and wit, but racily colloquial also, and capable of a moving lyricism when the need arose, was a reminder of what poetry can do in theatre. The play was robust and boisterous, yet sad also, and it at once inhabited a territory of its own, escaping gritty naturalism and *fin-de-siècle* decadence. That robust quality, theatrical yet human, is what keeps the play alive today.

Various English translations of the play have been made, but it is one of those plays which need to be translated again and again, in different circumstances and for different purposes, readerly and actorly. The time seemed ripe for a Scottish version, but one that would be thoroughly stageworthy and not incomprehensible to an international audience at the Edinburgh International Festival. I decided that urban Glaswegian Scots would offer the best basis, since it is widely spoken, can accommodate contemporary reference, is by no means incapable of the lyrical and the poetic, and comes unburdened by the baggage of the older Scots which used to be thought suitable for historical plays. I kept English for the Count de Guiche, and for some of the minor characters (the fops, the nuns, Roxane's duenna).

JF: Did you change the play, not in its structure or plot, but in its tone? The Communicado production was uproariously funny in parts, but I once saw the play done by the Comédie Française. It was an infinitely more stately production, especially the famous speech about Cyrano's nose, which was delivered by an actor in the grandest of classical styles, and stilled the entire audience. Were you trying to write as you thought Rostand intended, bringing out a comedy others might have missed, or were you consciously altering the style?

EM: Well, I have never seen a French production, so I cannot judge that. I thought I was getting into the spirit of the play, which seemed to me both comic and serious, in different ways and at different moments. Obviously you can be serious by being funny, but in that long speech about noses, it seemed to me that the joy with which the character spoke about all the ways in which someone could have spoken about his nose, if they had the language to do it, must communicate itself. It is a very funny speech, and this must be brought out. Cyrano is not only a swordsman, but he is a poet, and the translator must address himself to the problem of getting the poetic verve across. That was my aim in that speech – to forge a kind of poetry which would show how his mind worked, how it leapt from one subject to another very rapidly and very convincingly, while at the same time bringing out the comedy:

Yer *canto*'s no *bel*, young man.
Ye could have said – oh lotsa things, a plan
For each, tae suit yer tone o'voice, like so:
Thuggish: 'If Ah'd a nose like yours, Ah'd go
Straight to the surgery fur amputation'.
Freen-like: 'Dinnae dunk it in a cup, fashin
yersel a Munich tankard for tae slurp fae'.
Descriptive: 'A rock? A peak? A cape? the survey
Shaws the cape's a haill peninsula!'
Pawky: 'If it's in a boax, and no a fistula,
Whit's in it, pens or pins or penny needles?'
Gracious: 'Ye're a right Saint Francis, ye weedle
The buds o the air tae wrap their gentle tootsies
Roon yer pirch and rest their weary Guccis'.
Truculent: 'Puff yir pipe until the smoke
Comes whummlin oot yer nose, and the big toke
Has awe yer neebors cryin – Lum's on fire!'
Saft-hertit: 'Whit if it fadit at high noon?
Make a wee parasol tae keep the sun aff!'
Bummin: 'Nae wind, O hypermacho nose,
Could give ye snuffles but blasts fae Muckle Flugga!'
Dramatic: 'Bleeds a haill Rid Sea, the bugger!'

EM: In other parts of the play I aimed to bring out the lyrical note, which clashes with the more boisterous parts of the play, for ultimately we are dealing with a tragic love story. It would be easy to overlook the moving, touching mood which emerges most strongly in the latter part of the play. I suppose I was after a flexible kind of language which could be funny when needed, yet straight and serious at other times.

JF: Are you tempted to improve on the original, to write in jokes when you think that Rostand, or any other author, could have, or should have been funnier than he actually managed to be?

EM: I think to some extent, because theatre is a living process, some changes are necessary. Some characters have to be dropped or amalgamated, or little bits have to be added. For *Cyrano* I was asked to write a nuns' song at the beginning of the last act, and this too I did. In addition, when the director, or some actor, found some part appealing, he asked me to write a few extra lines, which I did. So there were some changes.

JF: As an instance, the *distributrice* of Rostand's original Act 1, sells nothing more remarkable than 'oranges, milk, strawberry water, lime juice', while the 'usherette' of your version offers:

Ices, ginger, tea,
Raspberry yoghurt, Greek yoghurt, aw the yoghurts,
Lovely Turkish delight, licorice awsorts,
Popcoarn, hote chestnits, marshmallows,
Chewin gum, candy-floss.....

EM: However, I decided not to change the main setting of the play. It was tempting to switch the action to Scotland, and make it a Scottish historical play, but the work needed its French environment. Cyrano, after all, was a character from history, his life is documented so it seemed to me important to respect that element. The play remained set in seventeenth-century France, even if the language used was Scots.

JF: Do you have any feelings about that in general? There are many Scottish versions of Molière or Goldoni which have been transported holus bolus to Glasgow or to Edinburgh's New Town. There are two points of view on this – one that it makes the work more immediate for an audience, or alternatively that is is a refusal of the challenge of foreign, unfamiliar ideas and an invitation to couthy provincialism.

EM: I think it varies. At times it can be illuminating to have the play in a very different setting, but on the whole I prefer to respect the original. In my *Cyrano* I have some anachronistic references to Gucci shoes, for instance, or to the Body Shop, but paradoxically these references may have a very limited lifespan. But a play is a very fluid thing.

JF: The voice that people are getting is yours and not that of Rostand, or of the anonymous authors of medieval morality plays.

EM: Is it?

JF: I put that as a general point. I don't know if it is any more strongly true in your case, although I suspect it is.

EM: I don't know about this. I suppose in general that must be true. I suppose that you as the writer are responsible for the words and the arrangement of the words, so it is inevitable that something of yourself must get into it. On the other hand, I don't try to do this. Some translators make a deliberate effort to make the translations an integral part of their own output. I am thinking of Ezra Pound or Robert Lowell. Their translations are just Pound poetry or Lowell poetry. But I do try to be fair to the other writer, to reproduce the effects of his or her style as far as I can. Where I have published translations of different authors from different periods, I would hope that this would appear as an anthology of writings by different people.

JF: So you regard that as a value of your translation, or an aim of translation in general – the retention of the flavour, the voice of the original author, as against the contrary view which would be, more or less, that all that counts is producing something which reads well or works on stage here and now.

EM: Yes, I think I am with the first view. It is hard to be exactly sure of what was in the original author's mind. Rostand belonged to another century, but I think I got into his way of thinking fairly well. I did a lot of research, I read others of his plays... But theatre is still something else. If you read the play in a book, you still have not seen the play as it was presented on the French stage in 1897. I would love to have seen that!

JF: Do you find you have greater liberty when you are writing in Scots, as against writing in English?

EM: I think the answer has to be 'yes'. It is a strange thing that it should be so, but it is. It may just be because you are doing something uncommon. Quite a lot of my poetry is in Scots, or other languages – invented languages – but it is true that you do have more liberty precisely because of the freshness of the enterprise. *Cyrano* does not use many words which would not be known to people in Scotland, but there is another curious thing: people seem to get a disproportionate delight from hearing Scots words which they use frequently enough, but which acquire an extra dimension for them when they hear them in the theatre. Also, there is a stimulus for the writer to be writing in Scots. If I translate into straight English, as I did with French and Dutch plays, it works all right, but they lack that spice which you get from something slightly different.

JF: Another topic. Both in poetry and theatre, what are you ultimately translating? Is it some inner core of meaning you believe you have identified, and how do you work out the balance between the desire to deal with the emotion or thought contained in a poem or speech and the need to keep some sense of the linguistic richness present in the original?

EM: That is the hardest thing of all. You are working as you go, and it is very difficult to start from a theory. It is very much a question of practice. I like to do it thoroughly. I like to get to know the original poem or play as deeply as possible, and this means you have a double task. You have to understand, if you can, the semantic part of the meaning, but you also have to do a different kind of reading.

You have to soak yourself in it, to let it float into your mind at different times until you get a feeling for what the work is like at levels other than that of the literal meaning. Not all poems are amenable to this kind of treatment, but if a poem is at all complex, it will have both an intellectual and an emotional dimension, and you must aim to transmit both of these aspects, which is not easy, but I think it can be done. It is a slow process, unless you are lucky.

JF: Since you have translated both from languages you know, and from languages where you had to rely on the 'literal' translation, can you draw up some kind of balance sheet of the advantages and disadvantages of these processes? What do you lose by not being able to read the words of the original writer?

EM: Obviously you do lose a lot. *The Apple Tree* seemed to work, and everyone was pleased with it, but from my point of view, I really want to be able to read the text – play or poem – and get to know it as deeply as I can. But there is an important qualification to be made. As well as the Dutch translation, I have worked on quite a lot of Hungarian poetry. Modern Hungarian poetry is of a very high class but because their language is so isolated, the Hungarians find it hard to persuade people of this. They are very keen to have their literature translated, especially into English. I have visited Hungary, I know a bit of the language, so I am not totally ignorant of what the language is like, but I need assistance. Even if I have a literal translation, I go through the text for myself, I know the sounds and know something of the background. With all these qualifications, I still am reliant on others for access to the text, but I think that in certain circumstances that is unavoidable, and it is preferable to not having valuable work made available in other countries.

TRANSLATING (AND NOT TRANSLATING) IN A CANADIAN CONTEXT

DAVID EDNEY

David Edney is Associate Professor of French at the University of Saskatchewan in Saskatoon. He has both directed and acted for many years in amateur and professional theatre. Several of his translations have been performed on Canadian stages, and his translation of Brigitte Jaques's *Elvira 40* was presented at the Chichester Festival in 1993. This script, together with his translation of Molière's *Don Juan*, is to be published by Nick Hern Books. Other translations, including the bilingual *Scapin*, have been or are about to be published in Canada. David Edney's work as a translator is characterised by his acute sense of the dramatic possibilities as well as political tensions inherent in Canada's bilingual situation. A very useful publication in this respect is *Modern Canadian Plays* (Vancouver, 1994), containing the texts of *Balconville* and *Polygraph*, as well as eight other plays and comprehensive notes and bibliography.

Working for the stage, particularly in productions of classical plays, involves the translator in a particular series of problems, which are not found in other forms of translation. Publication and performance are different modes of transmitting a text with different sets of rules and different goals. In a book, obscure allusions and culture specific items can be explained in notes; a text spoken on stage must be immediately accessible to the listener. A student reading a published text as an example of an author's work is interested in the original play and wants the translation to convey it as accurately as possible, to be transparent. Spectators in a theatre are looking for something quite different: to be moved or entertained, to be struck somehow in a compelling way. They want a good show, and the translator must accept part of the responsibility of providing it. Here, the translator is not only a writer, but also a theatre person, working with other theatre practitioners – directors, actors, designers, and so on – to create a stage piece. Can one translation be effective in both publication and performance? Can it satisfy both the student and the spectator? While I have pursued these two different goals in most of my work, I sometimes wonder if it is not a mission impossible. In the case of Beaumarchais's *The Marriage Of Figaro*, the need to adjust the text for performance seemed so overwhelming that I made two versions, an 'exact' translation for publication and a 'performing version', which is about ten percent shorter than the full text.

Should works destined for the stage, then, be 'adaptations' rather than translations? The former term seems to enjoy greater prestige among theatre people than the latter. Although I always call my scripts 'translations', directors often refer to them as 'adaptations', (or as 'translations/adaptations'). I take this to be an expression of approval, indicating that the text seems natural and playable: 'It does not read like a translation'. Spectators as well as directors think along these lines. Even though the programme and publicity for my version of Molière's *Don Juan* used the term 'translation', several audience members commented on the 'adaptation'; one even asked: 'Who made the adaptation, you or the theatre?' I surmised from these remarks that they did not imagine that classical seventeenth-century dialogue could be lively and entertaining without being adapted somehow to modern tastes. I believe that these directors and audience members use the term 'adaptation' to describe a text that stands on its own as an effective piece of theatre, whereas they consider a 'translation' to be a reflection of something else and inevitably inferior to that other object, the original text. If one accepts this definition, then, of course every translation for the stage should also be an adaptation. I believe, nonetheless, that the distinction between the two things is worth making, and, with one exception, I do not describe my work as adaptation. Even my *Marriage Of Figaro* script destined for the stage I label 'performing version' rather than 'adaptation'. In my mind, the distinctive feature that sets an adaptation apart from a translation is the presence of effects, conceived by the adaptor, which are not found in the original. Humour offers the most evident examples of this; many translators find it difficult to resist the temptation of trying to add to the humour of a play.

My practice in this matter has changed over the years. My first effort at translating a play, a commission, was billed by the theatre as 'a new adaptation'. In going over early drafts, the theatre manager who had commissioned the translation, encouraged me to be very free with the dialogue, to 'have fun with it', to make it my own rather than slavishly following Molière's text. Director Jean Gascon, on the other hand, a French Canadian who knew Molière extremely well and consulted a French edition of the play throughout rehearsals, kept steering the text back towards the original. These two opposing sets of advice which I received from the manager and from the director sum up the dilemma of the translator, who must always chart his or her course somewhere between them. The experience of seeing my scripts rehearsed and performed helped me to move away from free, personal expression towards fidelity to the original text. In watching directors and actors working with my original scripts, I appreciated more fully that Molière really did know what he was doing and that what came from David Edney did not measure up to the master. I also observed that audiences have more acumen than I had given them credit for, and that I was wrong to want to make everything easy for them. Immediate accessibility does not imply simplicity. In my first attempts at making Molière accessible to modern audiences, I tried to smooth everything out, I reduced unusual expressions to standard speech to make sure that they could be easily understood. By going too far in this direction, I diluted Molière's richness and produced a text that was homogenized and rather bland.

One instance where I went back on a previous simplification is my translation of Brigitte Jaques's *Elvira 40*. In this play, the French actor, director, and teacher, Louis Jouvet, coaches a student in the role of Elvira in her scene in act four of Molière's *Don Juan*. The scene is presented in full, and Jouvet comments on it. It is important that the passages from Molière presented within the modern play live up to Jouvet's description of them. One of his main ideas concerns sentence structure; the length of the sentences in which Elvira pours out her emotions reveals her character. There is a relationship, he says, between the sentence, the feeling, and the breath (Second Lesson). In my Molière translations, I have often broken up sentences which I found too long and complicated, and I sometimes did so in *Don Juan*. Francois Regnault, a collaborator of Brigitte Jaques and a translator himself from English to French, criticized my translation of Elvira's speeches for the liberties I had taken with the sentence structure. When I re-examined the scene in the light of his remarks, I discovered that, indeed, it was possible to retain the long sentences in English, and I revised the scene accordingly. When I reviewed the rest of *Don Juan* from this perspective, however, I restored only a small number of the long sentences; I retained the liberties I had taken with Molière's syntax whenever long sentences would seem awkward and unnatural in the context of my script.

While the phenomenon of performance poses many problems for translators, it also offers us precious assistance. The director and actors constitute a team of collaborators that I am always keen to take advantage of. The text I give the company for the first staging of a script is a provisional, working version that is still in progress. I consider the contributions of director and actors, and the text not finished until it has gone through the process of rehearsal and performance.

Even when actors accept without question the text I give them, their work on the script helps me. Hearing the text spoken over and over in rehearsal allows me to spot awkwardnesses, obscurities, things that are difficult for the actors to say or the audience to hear. Following the original text while listening to the actors speak the lines in English is an excellent way to compare the translation with the original. In the course of learning lines, actors give the text inaccurately, and their paraphrasing, and even their mistakes, can provide useful alternatives. A delightful example of a misreading which I adopted was when an actor stumbled over an expletive, 'By Jiminy!' and let out: 'By Jimmy!' instead. If an actor has difficulty learning a certain passage, that is often a sign that the passage is badly written and needs to be revised.

Actors who do not question the text are not intending to participate in the creation of the script, but in fact, through their work at rehearsals, they do.

Those actors and directors who play a more active role by challenging parts of the script which they find unclear or inappropriate help the translator even more. To facilitate this process of criticizing the translation, I always give the director a copy of the original text. Tibor Feheregyhazi, in directing *Don Juan*, was also able to compare my script with a Hungarian translation. While he was amazed at the similarity between my English and the Hungarian, he noticed that the exchange, 'Was it him? – Yes, it was' ('*C'est lui? – Lui-même*'), was very flat where the Hungarian version used a vivid expression to denote the whole person. I came up with: 'Was it him? – In body and soul'. While this rendering does not follow the French exactly, it conveys the buoyancy of Sganarelle's reply, which my first English version did not. This change of mood is useful dramatically, as it helps to enliven Don Juan's first entrance in the play.

While it is generally acknowledged that directors should offer some textual advice in working on new scripts, I have often found that questions and remarks from actors can be of great value as well. When the Marquise in De Musset's *A Door Must Be Open Or Closed*, dismisses love as always being the same, the Count, in the course of his reply, says: '*Si vous ressemblez à votre grand'mère, est-ce que vous en êtes moins jolie?*' Actor Tom Rooney complained that 'you look like your grandmother', a wrinkled old woman, is not an image of beauty as the Count intends, but practically an insult. I rewrote the line (revision underlined): 'If you take after your grandmother, are you any less pretty for that?' The actor's point is indisputable, but I would probably never have noticed it myself.

The work I do on a script in rehearsals is not only for the upcoming performances, but also for future productions and publication. In fact, many of the revisions that come from the rehearsal process, never find their way into the production being worked on; once actors have learned their lines, I rarely ask them to make changes. In the case of Brigitte Jaques's *Elvira*, however, we were able to implement many changes in the script thanks to the method of work of Tom Bentley-Fisher, the actor who played Louis Jouvet. An artistic director who devotes himself to workshopping and producing new scripts, and collaborating with writes in the final stages of composition, Bentley-Fisher had behind him a wealth of experience in script-writing, which I found rather intimidating. My apprehensions, however, were groundless. Like every other actor and director with whom I have worked, he wanted to be as faithful as possible to the original text, not to create something different that bore his stamp. During the rehearsal period, he studied each section of the play before memorizing it and indicated to me any passages that did not seem right to him. The next day, I brought the changes I had made, and he learned the revised version. In this way, the text of *Elvira* was modified in rehearsal more than any other of my scripts, and the production benefited greatly from the changes.

While I have never pushed the collaborative process as far as workshopping a translation with a group of actors and a dramaturge, I came close to doing this with my translation of Molière's *Don Juan*. This play raises the thorny and intriguing problem of dialect. The peasants in act two speak a patois that is so different from the standard French of the other characters that abundant notes are necessary to enable modern readers to understand it. How can one translate that for modern English-language audiences? Some radical form of departure from standard speech is necessary to convey the effect of the dialogue. In approaching this problem, I was guided by the example of a French-Canadian company who scored a great success with this act by using a French-Canadian accent for the peasants and international French for the other characters. I tried to find a similar device in English. I was familiar with only one way of speaking in Canada that was sufficiently different from standard Canadian English to qualify: the dialects of Newfoundland; so I decided to base my translation of the peasant speech on Newfoundland speech.

In performance, these scenes proved to be very effective. I came to realize, however, that the dialect I had written was not really authentic, and I decided to travel to Newfoundland to have the peasant scenes workshopped with Newfoundland actors and a dramaturg versed in the dialects of the region. I eventually relinquished this project for reasons that were political rather than artistic. While it was legitimate for French-Canadian actors to use their regional accent in playing to their own audiences, in effect making people laugh at themselves, I came to see that it was inappropriate to borrow another people's speech when it might appear that they were being made the butt of our laughter. It is healthy for us to laugh at ourselves, but do we have the right to use the speech of an identifiable group of others so that *we* may laugh at *them*? To satirize the rich and the powerful is fair enough. Newfoundland, however, is not a wealthy part of Canada, and the people of the province are often made the target of facile 'Newfie jokes', which characterize them as quaint, folkloric, and dim-witted. Fearing that my use of Newfoundland speech in *Don Juan* might be taken as similar mockery, I decided that my choice of dialect was injudicious, and I accordingly removed from my translation anything that might strike the reader or spectator as specifically Newfoundland. In rewriting the peasant scenes, I attempted to create a colloquial speech which maintained some of the richness and verve of the Newfoundland version but could not be identified as belonging to any one group. I hope that the resulting text gained from having passed through a Newfoundland stage, and that this version of the script will allow actors in various places to draw on the speech of their region to create believable and interesting characters.

This experience showed me that political propriety can pose a problem for the translator as it does for other theatre people. When translations of Feydeau poke fun at a speech defect, a physical deformity, or a German accent, the translators can disclaim responsibility on the grounds that Feydeau wrote these things. I did not have that line of defence in my translation of *Don Juan* because Molière did not depict his peasants as Newfoundlanders.

Sometimes it is not necessary to translate. I collaborated on a bilingual production of Molière's *Les Fourberies de Scapin*, in which unilingual spectators from both language groups were unable to understand part of what was being said. Bilingual shows have appeared now and then in Canadian theatres in recent years. The first big success in the genre was David Fennario's *Balconville*, which premiered in 1979 at the Centaur Theatre in Montreal, directed by Guy Sprung.

The use of two languages in this play was not an imagined literary device; it reflected the reality of the society being depicted in the play. Two English-speaking families and one French-speaking family share the same two balconies of an apartment building in a poor working class district of Montreal. Of the eight main characters, four are francophone, four anglophone. As this play was conceived for an English-language theatre company, more of the dialogue is in English than in French. Three of the anglophone characters are unable to speak French, and so exchanges between the two languages groups are almost entirely in English with the occasional interjection of French words. The use of French, however, goes far beyond the picturesque; the francophone characters speak to each other in their own tongue, expressing some complicated and subtle relationships which almost no use of English apart from occasional anglicisms, which are characteristic of Montreal speech: '*J'ai un flat tire sur mon bicycle*', '*Diane veut un lift pour aller a l'école?*', '*Il a sacré un peu après moi, but so what, eh? il est jamais content anyway*'. One of the climactic moments, the revelation that Paquette has lost his job, is expressed first in French and is not explained in English for some time. No attempt is made to render the French dialogue intelligible to unilingual anglophones. Three expressions are translated for a character who has not understood, 'small cocks', 'magnet', and 'faggot', but the translation from English to French is of no help to anglophone spectators. The last line of the play is declaimed in both languages:

The four anglophones: What are we going to do?
The four francophones: *Qu'est-ce qu'on va faire?*

Apart from those rare instances, there is no translation in the play; each language is spoken without being explained in the other.

As the Centaur Theatre, for which *Balconville* was written, is located in Montreal, a predominately French-speaking city, some of the audience members were francophone, and many of the anglophone spectators were able to follow the dialogue spoken in French. After its initial success, however, the play was performed in several cities of English-speaking Canada, and in Belfast, in Bath, and at the Old Vic in London. In all these locations, most of the spectators did not understand French. David Fennario reports that audiences in England reacted differently from those in other places. He had the impression that the English tried seriously to decipher the French words, whereas elsewhere, spectators accepted that they could not understand some of the dialogue, followed the body language and the musicality of the speech, and enjoyed the humour. Throughout English Canada, the show was invariably received with great enthusiasm. Tibor Feheregyhazi, Artistic Director of Saskatoon's Persephone Theatre, reports that the audience reaction to his production of *Balconville* was 'unbelievable! unbelievable!' and that not one audience member complained about being forced to listen to French for a good part of the evening. This is in a region of the country where many people are hostile to official bilingualism and suspicious of measures to promote French in their area. Since this highly successful experiment with languages, other theatre people have made efforts to use more than one language on stage. Robert Lepage has used not only French and English in his plays, but also other languages such as German, Chinese and Mohawk.

The bilingual production of *Scapin* (a title that works in both English and French) on which I collaborated was mounted by La Troupe du Jour, a French-language company in the predominantly English-speaking city of Saskatoon. After a happy experience with *Balconville*, the second production of the play in that city, the Troupe did a bilingual adaptation of Rick Salutin's *Les Canadiens*, a play written in English about the Montreal hockey team; as in *Balconville*, the action was set in a Montreal milieu where both English and French are in fact spoken. These bilingual productions were mounted by the Troupe to reach out to the anglophone community around them and attract English-speaking spectators to their theatre.

The adaptors of *Scapin* took the idea of mixing languages, which had been used to good effect in *Balconville* and *Les Canadiens*, and applied it to a classical play written in French and very far removed from any Canadian context. It was not the first such endeavour in Saskatoon. In 1989, the Shakespeare on the Saskatchewan Festival produced a bilingual *Romeo & Juliette* (sic), co-directed by Gordon McCall and Robert Lepage, with French translation by Franco-Ontarian playwright Jean-Marc Dalpe. The action was set on the Trans-Canada highway; the Capulets were francophone, the Montagues anglophone. For the bilingual *Scapin*, on the other hand, performances and design were inspired by traditional *commedia dell'arte* style; no attempt was made to evoke a Canadian setting. As La Troupe du Jour is a French-language company, French was the dominant language of the show; English was introduced to allow unilingual anglophones to follow the plot.

Les Fourberies de Scapin was chosen for this experiment because, as in *Romeo & Juliette*, the characters of the play are divided into two families; this production made one francophone, the other anglophone. Unlike the Montrealers of

Balconville, all characters in this Scapin speak both languages, and they often mix them together as bilingual people commonly do. They sometimes maintain their own speech habits when speaking to a member of the other linguistic group, so that a question asked in one language might be answered in the other. The pattern was varied to avoid monotony; both speakers might move into one language and then the other. In one instance, in an effort to accommodate the other, a francophone speaks English while the anglophone answers him in French.

Whereas translation is generally avoided in *Balconville*, it appears very frequently in *Scapin*. In passages where both languages are used in alternation, a speaker sometimes repeats in translation the words just spoken while answering or commenting on them in the other language. For example, when Argante talks to himself out loud, Scapin comments as follows to his crony, Sylvestre (underlinings indicate translated interpolations):

Argante: *(thinking he is alone) 'Je voudrais savoir ce qu'ils me pourront dire sur ce beau mariage.'*
Scapin: *(aside)* We've thought of something <u>to say about this fine marriage.</u>
Argante: *Tâcheront-ils de me nier la chose?*
Scapin: No.I don't think <u>we'll deny it.</u>
Argante: *Ou s'ils entreprendront de l'excuser?*
Scapin: We might <u>try to excuse it.</u>
Argante: *Prétendront-ils m'amuser par des contes en l'air?*
Scapin: <u>Spin you a tall tale?</u> Yes, we may very well.
Argante: *Tous leurs discours seront inutiles.*
Scapin: We'll see <u>if it's useless or not.</u>
Argante: *Ils ne m'en donneront point à garder.*
Scapin: Don't be too sure; <u>I bet you will fall for it.</u>
Argante: *Je saurai mettre mon pendard de fils en lieu de sûreté.*
Scapin: <u>You won't be able to put your son in a safe place because</u> we'll do it first.

Without the underlined passages, the responses in English would make no sense to those who did not understand Argante's remarks in French; the interpolations allow these spectators to follow. While the French parts of the bilingual *Scapin* use only the words of Molière, the adaptors added fragments of their own in English to ease transitions and to facilitate the comprehension of anglophone spectators.

Some attempt was made to use the languages in ways that were psychologically true; under the pressure of emotion, for example, a character might revert to his or her own tongue. Scapin, however, is a farce, not a realistic play, and the adaptors did not hesitate to use the languages in an artificial way, sometimes even calling attention to the device. Some scenes were played twice, usually the French text first, immediately followed by the English translation. While the main purpose of these instant translations was to ensure that unilingual spectators of both languages received information vital to the plot, it also heightened the ludic nature of the farce and enhanced the comic effect. Two techniques for this doubling were used: the instant replay and the action loop.

To execute the instant replay, the actors suddenly freeze; then, accompanied by strobe lights and atmospheric music, they retrace their steps and gestures, walking backwards like a videotape rewinding, to their positions at the beginning of the passage and repeat the scene in the other language, duplicating movements, gestures, and vocal inflections as exactly as possible. This procedure was employed at the beginning of the play to establish the convention; the first scene and the first five speeches of the second constitute the first passage repeated by instant replay. By calling attention to itself in an obvious and rather sensational way, this device became a kind of game, which, after the astonishment caused by its first appearance, was instantly recognizable each time it was employed thereafter.

In the action loop, the second method of effecting a repeat, the characters find themselves, as if by accident, in the positions they occupied at the beginning of the passage and repeat the passage in the other language without a break. As a variation of the device, the second version was sometimes a mirror image of the first, with the characters on opposite sides of the stage. As the transition from the first version of the passage to the repetition is not marked in any way, the action loop is a subtler device than the instant replay. In these cases, it sometimes takes a few moments for the audience to realize that they are watching a repeat; their recognition of the device is an additional form of enjoyment.

The juxtaposition of two versions of the same passage draws the audience's attention to the translation, which is exposed to view as it normally never is on stage. Translation is shown to be a means of conveying information and also a form of playing with language. The spectators are invited to participate in the game according to their language abilities; alert bilingual audience members can assess the merits and flaws of the translation by comparing the two versions; unilingual spectators can pick out at least a few words in the language they do not know. Repetition and parallelism are two of Molière's favourite comic techniques; as an extension of those devices, the use of translation to repeat certain passages suits the style of the play. Such repetitions must be used sparingly, however; the instant replay appears four times in *Scapin*, the action loop three times, and not more than one tenth of Molière's text is repeated by means of these devices.

The making of the bilingual script of *Scapin* was an interesting example of collaboration between translator and director. Before receiving any of the English translation, the director, Ian C Nelson, studied Molière's text, determined the techniques to be employed for using two languages, and selected the passages to be given in English, in French, and in both languages through instant replay and action loops. I independently translated the whole play as I normally would in making an English version of a text. Passages from the translation were fitted into the French text to make a bilingual version. I created interpolations as in the passage quoted above from the fourth scene of act one, according to the director's instructions. Once the bilingual text was assembled, both director and translator freely suggested revisions and extensions of the bilingual techniques. I found that I had to make some revisions to the translation to accomplish the effect of parallelism. For example, I had first translated '*J'ai cette insulte-là sur le coeur*', from act two, scene four, as 'His insults really hurt'. Seeing in rehearsal that the actor made a gesture towards his heart on the word '*coeur*,' I changed the line to read: 'His insults lie heavy on my heart' so that the gesture conceived for the French text would also make sense in the English version. I have maintained the first phrasing in my English translation of the play and the second in the bilingual script.

The use of languages in *Balconville* and in *Romeo & Juliette* is, above all, political. The creators were attempting to represent in their work the Canadian duality, a clash of cultures that in both plays eventually leads to a kind of reconciliation. *Romeo & Juliette* is a tragedy; *Balconville*, in spite of its comic moments, is a drama; both speak very seriously to Canadians about the essential nature of their society. *Scapin* is a farce, and the use of two languages here is ludic rather than political. The juxtaposition of two versions of the same passage is not a source of tension and conflict, but rather a form of game that corresponds to the stylized comic devices of the play and heightens its madcap mirth. While not intending to be political, however, the bilingual Scapin does have political implications as well. Its first production brought together two cultural groups, both in the troupe and in the audience, enabling them to speak to each other and to participate together in a project. The joyful nature of the play, which celebrates human ingenuity through its title character, made the coming together a kind of festive occasion and a celebration of human ingenuity in its own right. Anglophones took delight in hearing a language that some rarely encountered in any sustained way, in seeing a French play performed by a francophone company, and in being able to understand it. Many spectators of both languages felt that, far from being an awkward device, the use of two languages was a positive quality that enhanced their enjoyment.

Translating plays is a great adventure. Before the first preview of *Don Juan*, I wondered anxiously whether any of it would get across. I found, however, that audiences are very willing to cooperate in the enterprise, just as I have found that actors and directors are eager to get to the heart of the original text and to express it. Theatre is a collaborative endeavour that works only because people agree to listen to each other. By enabling us to hear voices from another culture, bilingual plays and plays translated from another language extend that theatrical process of breaking down barriers and making connections between people.

ADRIAN MITCHELL: POETRY ON STAGE

IN CONVERSATION WITH DAVID JOHNSTON

How does one write a half-page biography of Adrian Mitchell, other than to say that he is an extraordinary writer of novels and plays, of filmscripts and strories, of lyrics and music theatre, a performer and, above all, a poet in all that he does? He has published ten books of poetry since 1955, including *Blue Coffee*, a collection of poems written between 1980 and 1996. In addition to innumerable plays, many of which contain original lyrics or are sung throughout, he has adapted fourteen plays and librettos. These include *Marat/Sade*, performed by the RSC in 1964; *The Magic Flute*, for Peter Hall's Covent Garden production in 1966; *Peer Gynt*, performed at the Oxford Playhouse in 1980; and Goldoni's *Mirandolina*, for the Bristol Old Vic in 1987. In particular, Adrian Mitchell has done much to put Calderón and Lope de Vega back exactly where they belong in this country: on the stage. His adaptations of Calderón's *The Mayor Of Zalamea*, *Life's A Dream* and *The Great Theatre Of The World*, and of Lope's *Woman Overboard*, *Fuente Ovejuna*, *A New World*, *The Tears Of The Indians* and *Lost In A Mirror*, have been of crucial importance in establishing Spanish Golden Age theatre within the repertoire of the English-speaking stage.

DJ: Why does a creative writer, who has such a considerable reputation as yours, translate?

AM: Why do I *still* do it, because I didn't have any name at all when I started doing it? There are many reasons. One is that I have a limited number of stories to tell, I find writing original stories hard and I think most of my work has been based on other people's stories in the first place. I've just done two new versions of Hans Andersen's stories because I love them so much, because I'm interested in getting them into the most perfect English possible, and those are very good reasons. It's a delight to do *The Ugly Duckling* and *Steadfast Tin Soldier* in the confident knowledge that they are absolutely great stories.

DJ: When you did *Fuente Ovejuna*, even bearing in mind the Joan Littlewood production, there was a sense that although somehow Lope was seen as a great dramatist, the greatness accorded to him was empty because his plays were rarely or never performed. One of the things that I noticed in your introduction to the play was that you believed crucially that 'it worked'. Did you feel as though you were functioning as a cultural enabler at any point?

AM: I think it is a description of somebody who makes things work, and although I do like to make things work, I am not sure if I would apply it to myself. If there is a joke, and the person who has done the literal translation assures me that Lope really did mean it to be a joke, that it was funny in those days, my job is very much to get a joke there that works. If Lope's original joke is so far away from our time that it can't possibly work then I have to find a kindred joke that will work with a modern audience, hopefully anywhere English is spoken today. The same applies for *The Government Inspector*. But most of the plays I have taken on have been verse plays because I think that is my field; making verse work with an audience. I think I know how to do that and I have acquired a whole baggage of technique because I have been writing verse seriously most days since the age of fourteen. So I can write in a lot of different styles. Usually it would be a verse play done into verse, with various verse forms, not necessarily those of the original. But *The Government Inspector* is a play of which I have done three versions. It's one of my favourite plays – one of the funniest plays in the world, also a very profound one. So, I have had all those bashes at it, even though it's not a verse play, and the job has been to make the characters and the jokes really work.

DJ: Do you speak any other languages?

AM: None at all.

DJ: I know you are scrupulously fair about giving acknowledgement to your literal translators; I think that's refreshingly honest, but unusual.

AM: Theatres tend to militate against it. I think literal translators should be accorded more credit than they are. When I did *Peer Gynt*, for example, the credit line ran 'Adrian Mitchell's adaptation from Karin Bamborough's translation', which had the merit of rhyming, I might add. It also gave Karin a proper credit. . . and I think she was on a percentage too. I think that should happen.

DJ: Even more unusual.

AM: Very unusual, because normally you 'buy' the literal translation outright. I had a bigger percentage than she did, but on the other hand I think that is the nearest I have seen to translators being treated fairly. I have to work from literal translations.

DJ: How do you work with your literal translators? Presumably from what you've been saying about being reassured by your literal translators that such and such was originally conceived as a joke, you don't just take delivery of the script and that's it.

AM: I'll meet with the literal translator usually and talk over and explain what I want, and generally what I get is a line by line literal translation with notes on the opposite page explaining the peculiarities in the text, or sometimes saying 'this is a joke', or pointing out the rhyme scheme if it's of particular significance. Then I look at it and at a certain point, although this varies, I will have to go back to the literal translator and say 'Look at this. This is what I want. What do you think? Is it OK?'

DJ: So you would use your literal translator almost as a linguistic and cultural guide?

AM: It would depend on the literal translator because I am closer to some than to others, and some are more interested in cooperating than others, and some are better at it. I've never had a bad one; they have always been good, and they have always understood that I am going to take liberties with the text they provide. It would be no good for me to have somebody who is highly academically qualified but didn't know about theatre at all, who wasn't able to make allowances for the sort of rough and tumble of theatre, and the sort of process that a play has to go through on stage.

DJ: So you think a knowledge of how theatre works is a much more important piece of equipment than academic or linguistic expertise? That's not entirely a leading question, by the way.

AM: In an ideal world, I wouldn't be – I'm not – really qualified. But I don't know many people who are. Usually people fall down on one thing or another. You may be very good with language but you may not know how theatre works, and you may not be a poet and understand how verse works. Very few people are both real poets and real linguists... even if they are both, it sometimes still goes wrong. I can't stand Roy Campbell's translations, for example. . . I can say that because he's dead.

DJ: Taking equal advantage of that, let me say that Roy Campbell's translations are also filtered through an ideology which casts a particular colour on every thing he does.

AM: Yes. But it's really his poetics which colour his translations. I don't like his rumpty-tum – he's very heavy handed as a versifier. The play I want to do more than any other is Cervantes's *Siege Of Numancia*. I've only read it in Campbell's translation and through that I can see what I believe is a great play. But it is behind bars to me, behind the bars of that translation, and partly because of that I haven't been able to persuade any theatre to commission me to do it yet.

DJ: I'm sure that this is the right moment for Cervantes.

AM: I would have thought so. But I haven't been able to persuade anyone. Richard Eyre at the National Theatre said he didn't like plays with Roman soldiers, which seemed to me a slightly flip reason for not doing it. They don't have to be dressed up in metal skirts – I know what he means – there *is* something really silly about togas and metal skirts. But it doesn't have to be done in that costume anyway. And it has immediate resonances of Sarajevo and Bosnia; it illuminates them.

DJ: Let me use that to lead into another question. Would you take Cervantes's *Siege Of Numancia* and modernise it totally so that its principle framework of reference was Sarajevo, or whatever the burning issue of next year or the year after happened to be?

AM: I think I would probably do it like the version of *Fuente Ovejuna* done by the RNT. If I was directing and designing I don't think I would have it in historical costume so that the play's frame of reference would be made more universal.

DJ: One of the interesting things about the language that you use both in *Fuenteovejuna* and the Calderón plays is the way that it spans the centuries, it moves backwards and forwards in a sense. It has an historical dynamism in it that takes you back and brings you forward all the time. Was that something you worked in deliberately?

AM: Yes. I took two goes at *Fuente Ovejuna*. The first time I did what you were asking about *Numancia*, that is, I set it in a Latin American country, probably Chile, though that was never stated. I also called it *Sheep Spring* because I am sure some people were put off by not knowing how to pronounce *Fuente Ovejuna* to buy a ticket. But I didn't change the play essentially; it was more that the surface details of the political scenes changed, so that when they were reporting a battle it was with tanks and helicopters and so on. But the peasants are still the peasants, and they didn't change much. It wasn't all that different from the version that was done, but nobody at the National liked it. Everyone said 'People will make the leap' and, in fact, people did. I remember two people talking to me about South Africa after the first night, because at that time it was very relevant to South Africa. I have always been bothered about people evading or not seeing the political point. In a play like *Fuente Ovejuna* politics is certainly not the only point but if you miss the political point, you are missing a lot.

DJ: Is it the job of the translator or the director, or an amalgam of them both, to bring out these political points expressly?

AM: I think linguistic clarity is the job of the adaptor and then, of course, it should be a real cooperation with the director. It is both their jobs, and the actors', to clarify what the play is about.

DJ: How do you work with directors?

AM: That's varied. Peter Brook was absolutely tremendous to work with, on Peter Weiss's *Marat/Sade*, which I adapted from Geoffrey Skelton's literal translation. He is marvellous in the early stages of rehearsal. He does a lot of listening, very little talking and encourages everyone else to talk. Just because you are a writer or an actor doesn't mean you can't make suggestions about set or music or staging or ice-cream flavours for the intervals or whatever. All ideas are welcome and he sits sponging them in, and he selects them from everybody's creative imagination, and then adjusts them. But I also learnt theatre discipline from Peter. I once rewrote a line and gave it to an actor without showing it to Peter first, and I was subjected to the glare of these twin icebergs he uses for eyes when he feels like it. I've never forgotten that, and I have never done it again. I am very well behaved. I write, I go home at night, I don't whisper into actors' ears. At home in the evening I write a long memo to the director about anything that has happened that I like, don't like, any word suggestions I have and my rewrites and things like that. I then give it to the director. This is a really good way of working because the director, however busy, can always choose a moment to read through what Nutter Mitchell has suggested today and he can tick off the things that he would do. Normally we go through the memo together and the director tells me what he thinks. If he tells me he doesn't agree with a point, then I don't belabour it, I just drop it. I think I work well with directors, when I get the chance.

DJ: Were changes made when you weren't at rehearsals? Your writing is so tight that it would be worrying if changes were made without very strict consultation.

AM: I try and make that clear right at the beginning, to any director, that I am absolutely not adverse to making cuts, but I want to be consulted. If they want a cut then they should tell me how much and let me do the cutting. If it is a specific cut then we can talk it over and find a way of seeing how it would work with the cut. It is your right not to have cuts or alterations made without your agreement, and you really have to stand up for that right.

DJ: I noticed that when I said 'translator' a moment ago you said 'adaptor'. When you get your literal version do you consider yourself as a creative writer developing a new piece of work from that literal version? Or, do you consider yourself as a creative writer working within the restrictions of that literal version? I'm trying to understand what we might mean by adaptation as opposed to translation.

AM: I don't feel like an original writer writing a new piece out of this material. That is not the idea of doing it. The idea of doing it is to take a great play – usually it is a great play – and reveal it. That's all. That is all that stems from you. Of course, it shouldn't have any of this dead stuff hanging from it, archaic stuff that makes people stop and say 'I don't know what that means'. In *The Mayor Of Zalamea*, for instance, there is some explanation about honour in the dialogue that isn't in the original. Explaining within is sometimes necessary. But it's not just a question of context. Language has to be adapted as well. For example, I don't really know how Spanish peasants talk. However, I did live for five years in the Yorkshire Dales. So I modelled Pedro Crespo on the Yorkshire Dales' farmer, but without telling anyone. Curiously, I found Michael Bryant was giving it a slight Yorkshire accent. He'd picked up the patterns, the sentence shapes, the odd Yorkshire word, because he has an infallible ear.

DJ: That's a good example of speech colouring. But presumably your sense of how Pedro Crespo speaks comes from your analysis of character because it couldn't have come from linguistic analysis.

AM: It came from character and situation. The sort of humour I thought I picked up in Pedro Crespo seemed a very wry kind of humour, very Yorkshire Dales.

DJ: Can I come at this point to translation taken in its most literal, faithful, or conventional, sense (choose your own word). Is there anything that you would consider to be bad practice, taking too much liberty?

AM: I can hardly say that, having once set *Hamlet* on a double-decker bus.

DJ: Hamlet survived the experience?

AM: Yes he did, but that was partly why I could do it. If it had been the first production of *Hamlet* in English I wouldn't have done it. Neither would I have done it with *Fuente Ovejuna*. Even when I considered setting it in a different period and country, I was sticking very, very closely to the story. When every schoolchild knows the play, then I will be able to take liberties with it. I think with a play of that importance, when it is being staged for the first few times, until it is really in the canon, your main duty is to let the play speak for itself, let the playwright really speak and be heard properly. At least that's the theory.

I did the play *The Gardener's Dog* (Lope's *El perro del hortelano*) in a very free version under the title of *Women Overboard*, at Watford, and it was not a great success. I don't know why, I really liked it. I set it on a yacht in the Bay of Naples. The play is a silly comedy about a woman who is always changing her mind. I thought it would make a good sort of thirties musical. And I'd never written one, so I set it on the yacht and we had lots of songs and music. At the end of it all, Lope de Vega came on stage and said how much he liked the show. We gave him a big speech along the lines of 'Go and write this down', because one of the characters in the play was actually trying to write a musical. In fact, I played Lope in the last two performances myself, so I got my Equity card. I took a lot of liberties with that one, and I really forgot about the original play after a time. I couldn't have done a straight version of that, I wouldn't have enjoyed it because, frankly, I didn't like the play much.

DJ: You have a noticeable tendency to adapt through creating song, setting plays to music, so to speak. I'm thinking as much of your very exuberant *Peer Gynt* as of Lope.

AM: One of the things in that, and certain other plays, is that sometimes you come to a series of very long speeches. I tend to rephrase these in song because I have found that in a song I can concentrate the content of a long speech, and I am part of the majority of modern theatre audiences that really enjoy songs. It's an inheritance from Brecht as much as *Guys 'n' Dolls* and *Oklahoma*. Joan Littlewood nearly always had songs in a show. I like songs in plays, and quite often I find that it's a good way of cutting those amazingly long speeches which must have been very popular at the time, but which are less so now.

DJ: Brecht was very aware of metatheatre, all of those bits of theatre that are beyond language. I think one of the primary problems of, if you like, the non-theatre translator/adaptor is that they try and translate everything, they make things top-heavy. For example, the opening lines of *Life's A Dream* in Spanish are just impossibly baroque. Your opening lines, while capturing the essence of Calderón's, and being beautiful in their own way, are also a clarification of the original. Is this a principle that you would work to: clarification without dilution?

AM: I'd like to. Clarity is one of the words I think will be found to be carved upon my heart when I am cut up. Clarity is a beautiful word. Sometimes some things have to go in order to make other things stand out; that applies to adaptations as well as to one's own creative work. It really isn't a loss. Instead of saying the same thing three times, once very beautifully and twice not really so interestingly it is better to say it just the once, beautifully.

DJ: When you were working on your translations did you stick to your literals or did you look at other translations as well in your search for the ultimate beauty of expression?

AM: No, I stuck to my literals. I didn't look at other translations for the plays, although with the Hans Andersen stories I did look at a whole lot of translations. I've also done some collaborative work. On *Life's A Dream* I worked with John Barton. I was originally commissioned to do it for the National. When I gave it in they liked it, but then they phoned me up and said 'Sorry Adrian, the Royal Shakespeare have announced that they intend to do *Life's A Dream*, and we have an agreement with them that if one of us announces it first then the other doesn't do it'. I asked who was doing the translation and it was Professor John Barton, and to make sure that they were going to do it, I rang John Barton. When I told him I had done a version he looked at it and generously suggested we should do it together. We took bits from his version and bits from my version, and in the end we did about half each.

DJ: When it was performed were you not worried that it would lose its voice, its coherence?

AM: Yes, but then I was pleased that we had actually got the play on and that it contained some of my favourite bits, and we had it published. To me it seemed important to get more of these plays onto the stage. I was glad to be part of *Life's A Dream*; it was a very happy experience, and I was happy with the way it worked out on stage in the end. It was first performed at The Other Place in Stratford. John had this idea, because of the play of illusion and reality, that when Rosaura first came on, on the horse, that it should be a child's hobby horse. Then right towards the end of the play, a real horse came on – it was a fantastic *coup de théâtre*. It stayed on for about two minutes, then trotted off.

The very first night I was sitting watching the play and I could see the audience very well. I could see a couple who were talking through the whole first half. When the interval came I thought they would go away. But no, they came back, chatting away. I was going spare until the horse came on and they finally stopped. They stared at the horse and when the horse went off they started chatting again. It wasn't until afterwards that I found out that they were the people who owned the horse. That really taught me a lot. Now when somebody in the audience isn't reacting in the way I would expect, I think 'It's the couple who own the horse'.

DJ: Would you collaborate on another translation again?

AM: If it was the right person, the right play, the right reason, certainly. The last one I did was interesting because it was very different from all of this; it was another brave emergency poet job. I was called in to rewrite a lot of the translations of the Piaf songs for Elaine Paige. Some of the originals of the Piaf songs were tremendous, very down to earth and tough and sort of sexy in a genuine way. A lot of them had been cleaned up and turned into English pop songs, totally bland, with no physical details at all, just abstract and sugary. My job was to work on these and try and get back to the original; it was fantastic because it was very high pressure. I had to come home to work in the evening and next morning go and face Elaine Paige across a table, with Peter Hall and Pam Gems also sitting there. It was like Roosevelt and Stalin and Churchill. Then she sang the new versions to me and showed me what she didn't like, so I had to go back and change it. It was a very exciting job, I really liked doing it. Elaine is amazing doing those songs; she was born to do those songs... a fantastic performer.

DJ: I found it interesting that when you talked about John Barton you talked about interpretive processes. Your working processes seem to be either functional, in terms of how theatre works, or poetic, in terms of how you create a poetry that will work on stage; not a poetry of the page but one that, as Lorca said, requires a living performance (which you're echoing in your description of the talent of Elaine Paige). It's always surprised me that you've never done any Lorca.

AM: I nearly did but I couldn't quite come to terms with it. I don't find myself very close to Lorca. I feel very close to Lope, and also to Cervantes. Lorca's more distant even than Calderón. I don't think that to know him is to love him. I don't think he'd be my best friend if we knew each other. I would respect him and I do respect him.

DJ: You don't find Calderón as cold as other people seem to.

AM: No, I certainly don't. Not in The *Mayor Of Zalamea* and not even in *The Great Theatre Of The World*. I think there is a warmth there, although he's more restrained about it than Lope. Lope's a marvellous animal of the theatre. But to go back to Lorca.. somehow he and I never really became friends.

DJ: Calderón and Lope were Lorca's great masters. They all have a tremendous ability to create a poetry which is the theatre's alone. This is where Adrian Mitchell the poet and these dramatists as poets perhaps find their common centre.

AM: For a long time I have been interested in writing poetry that can be performed, a poetry that isn't just for the head but is for the body as well. It's very old fashioned, but there it is. Perhaps that's why I've always loved theatre and been tempted by it. Poetry's at the heart of it for me.

DJ: How worthwhile do you think it is to attempt to recreate the varied poetical forms that Lope and Calderón use for an audience in the 1990s? So that if you are not following their forms exactly you are following them in design at least?

AM: I try to follow the characters and the action in design and if the mood is one of 'Come on let's get on with it', then I try and give the verse a form that's saying the same.

DJ: Was that a preoccupation at the front of your mind when you were working on these plays?

AM: No, that is just part of the process really. Part of the way of giving characters depth is to give each one of them their own rhythm. When I was a very young poet I gave a reading in New York at which Alan Ginsberg was one of the twelve people there, and he criticised much of the stuff I was writing at the time. He said 'You should listen to your own voice and hear the rhythms of it. Start with that music and use it'. I don't mean to be a slave to that, but I do think that people have their own music, and that it's important to establish that in a play, whether it's a verse adaptation or a prose play or, for that matter, your own...

DJ: You say that you use rhythms that are not based on syllable counts but on spoken language, so I presume you read your work out loud, rather than beating out syllables on the palm of you hand?

AM: I did a lot of syllabic count in the first Spanish play I did, which was *The Mayor Of Zalamea*, but when I moved on to the next play I thought 'What the hell'. Nobody knew it was syllabics anyway; not one of the reviewers knew the lines were carefully syllabic. All they notice is if you are trying to use half rhymes; I know that if I use half rhymes then I am going to get at least two reviewers who quote these as examples of how I can't rhyme. So I have to react to them and say 'Look, you should read some Wilfred Owen sometime and see how he can't rhyme either'. That really is a bit basic, I'm afraid, but there again, theatre critics are not renowned for their knowledge of the technicalities and techniques of good poetry.

RANJIT BOLT: TRANSLATING VERSE PLAYS

IN CONVERSATION WITH DAVID JOHNSTON

Having read Classics at Balliol College, Oxford, from where he graduated in 1982, Ranjit Bolt worked as an investment advisor until 1990. At that point he decided to give up his job in order to translate for the stage. He is now universally recognised as one of the most accomplished translators of verse, and among his productions are *The Liar* and *The Illusion*, for the Old Vic (under Jonathan Miller), *Tartuffe* and *Lysistrata*, for Sir Peter Hall, *The Venetian Twins*, for the RSC, and *Le Cid* and *Arturo Ui*, for the National.

DJ: Which languages do you speak?

RB: I speak a bit of Italian and fairly good French.

DJ: Those are the languages that you translate from most easily?

RB: I would say yes. French is by far and away the easiest. I'm now doing my second and third Greek plays, In the past I've done a Spanish and a German, without knowing any Spanish at all, but using the original Spanish and trying to work it out on the basis of my Latin and French and Italian. I did a year of German at school, so I did the Brecht at the National Theatre.

DJ: To some extent you're giving me the answer to my next question. How important do you think it is to have at least a very good reading knowledge and, if you like, sense of cultural background?

RB: I think I'm lucky because I've studied Classics, and I think Classics is important in two ways. Firstly, it's the root of many languages and, secondly, it is very good, especially Latin, as a linguistic model; if you can grasp Latin I think you can pick up other languages very quickly. It might sound a little bit pretentious but I think that that's probably true. So, that's the first point. The second point that I would make is that I don't think it's terribly important to get all the nuances. Being acquainted in some way with the original texts far outweighs whatever disadvantages there might be in your not actually being a scholar or fluent speaker who knows all the different implications of each word. I think on the whole I would rather be, however darkly or obscurely, acquainted with the original if I could. I've only worked from a literal once.

DJ: Yes, that was one of the Goldonis wasn't it?

RB: That was *The Twins*. For special reasons it was done very rapidly, in about four weeks, and even then I did some of it from the Italian, just to see what it felt like and what the dialogue felt like.

DJ: Is the play written in Venetian dialect?

RB: In some of his plays Goldoni writes in dialect. I think *The Twins* is probably Burgamese dialect, because the twin, who is a yokel, and his servants speak in a very different dialect from the other characters. What I imagine the other characters are speaking, and almost certainly what the audience would have spoken, is what one might call 'BBC Venetian'. I used Lancastrian to reflect the dialect form. I think the big strength of my translation, because it wasn't a great creative work of translation, as it was done, as I said, from a literal, was this use of 'trouble at mill' stuff... all this 'nowt' and 'owt', 'appen as reckon as 'appen as like', that kind of dialect. I think it was true to the spirit because you had these two Lancastrians in the middle of all these rather upper-class chaps. This character differentiation through linguistic texturing also gave an opportunity for a '*tour de force*' of comic acting in that one minute this chap, the same actor, is completely upper-class and Etonian and 'I'm a man of honour' and the next minute it's 'Eeh, eha's a right chump'.

DJ: So you're not hostile to the use of literals?

RB: People have translated from literals and what they've produced has been said to have been closer to the original than the literal translation. It can be done by feeling how the play works and how the characters work. I'd like to think *The Twins* was quite lively and captured the spirit of the original, and it was done from a literal.

DJ: So what matters is your knowledge of how theatre works?

RB: What matters is a sense of theatre and character and the functioning of stage-language, more than an academic knowledge of language, words pinned to meaning in its most literal sense.

DJ: You mentioned the idea of a 'creative translation' a moment ago. What do you mean by that?

RB: One of my tags is that if poetry is what is lost in the translation it's also what's added. You can't really translate poetry and be totally literal, totally faithful. A verse translator, working about the same time as Dryden, said that it is possible to 'grow unjust by seeming overnice'. In other words, if you are too particular about getting the words right you'll lose the spirit of the poetry. You won't do your author a favour. In prose it's less true, certainly of prose writers like Goldoni, or Tolstoy. Russian friends tell me 'Pushkin you'll never know, you'll never understand. But with Tolstoy, you won't lose a lot by reading the Rosemary Edmunds translation'. Goldoni and Marivaux to my mind are in that same boat. They don't lose a great deal (although Marivaux probably loses a bit more than Goldoni, in that he is an elegant writer of prose. But then you can write elegant prose yourself, if you try).

DJ: Is there not the fact as well that, unlike in the novel, what you're doing in theatre is engaging in a constant negotiation? What you sometimes lose with words, you create through other aspects of theatre.

RB: Yes, and you are also adding words. Dryden says that in translating verse he would often find that a rhyme would suggest something extra to him which he thought was interesting and not out of keeping with the original, although different from it. So he would put it in.

DJ: So translation is a process of constant interrogation?

RB: You are constantly making decisions, certainly, and especially in verse where you have a line, a metre which you have to fit. I always say with the French alexandrine you have a problem because it is a longer line, and often that length will foist more information on you than a single English pentameter will carry; I definitely think that's the line, the Shakespearean line, you should use. You can't use a six foot line. So, you say 'Well, what do I want to do? Do I want to do two and a half lines to get this, or do I want to cut, because if I go on like this I'm going to be expanding the play and probably making it woolly'. So, often you find you drop things, deliberately drop one detail and keep what you think are the most important parts of the line, the most important details in a line or a couplet, and render that as a new couplet. The English version might be rather pared down, but you feel you've made the right decision.

DJ: How important do you think it is to use appropriate verse forms for translations of plays which are originally in verse?

RB: I feel that Molière or Corneille, for example, lose a great deal if they are translated either in blank verse or in prose. I think it's something to do with the way the couplet form reinforces the ethos of the play, the message of the play. There is often a rhetorical use you need to fathom; for example, you'll have antithesis A,B – on the one hand this, on the other hand that – which the couplet suits particularly well. Or again, a joke will be of an A,B, form, and if you have a couplet it works better because the feedline ends in one rhyme and the punchline ends in the second and you have that same clipped aphoristic quality that Molière or Corneille would have been aiming at. With Sophocles, on the other hand, I'm using rhyming couplets because I feel that his verse is so formal and stylised that if I were to use blank verse, my blank verse being what it is, it would be very, very ordinary. So, I've done it in couplets to try and get a feeling of its being rather special, of its being different, heightened. Sophocles's verse, unlike Molière's, is extremely stylised, and beautiful with it. I'm aiming for something special here, something perhaps not lovely, but that will make people sit up and think, 'This is heightened, there is something special going on here'. My blank verse, at any rate, could not do that. My blank verse is just like me speaking, except it scans. It's not quite that bad but when I get into couplets, for some reason I find myself doing much more interesting things.

DJ: You obviously have a good ear for picking up dialogue and then transforming it into verse.

RB: Transforming everyday colloquial dialogue into couplets is my thing, at any rate with comedy. My golden rule is that if you wrote it out, it should just sound just like prose dialogue without a single seam or stitch dropping. It's not quite the same for tragedy because for tragedy you can use a slightly more heightened 'poetic' form. I'm sure my version of a comedy like *The Liar* would read as just people talking if you wrote it out and didn't break the lines.

DJ: It takes a very special translator to be able to create verse which is the speakable poetry of the stage.

RB: It is tricky. There are people, dare I say, who don't manage it. One slip is bad but several slips are terrible when you are in verse or in prose; they tend to stick out more in verse because they are usually to do with the rhymes. You suddenly find this word sticking out like a sore thumb, and you know it's there to keep the thing going, to keep the rhymes going – only as a rhyme it won't do.

DJ: So, on one level verse imposes a discipline on your writing? It forces you, to some extent, into a form of clarification as well?

RB: The writing of conventional, non-free, rhyming verse imposes a set of rules that have to be obeyed. With conventional rhyming verse the rule is clear: the rule is the rhyme and to make rhyme fit metre. If you are in blank verse: 'I'm going to take the bus tomorrow night, I want to have some tea when I get home'; all that is in pentameters. You could just do whatever you like, but it doesn't really say anything.

DJ: I was very taken by how easy it was to read *The Liar*, and how good it sounds. How did you find your actors did it?

RB: They didn't do it in a consciously poetic way, and I think that was right. They did it just as I like to write it, making it sound like people chatting. Then gradually the audience realises 'Hello, there's something else happening here; it's in verse, and it's not just in verse, it's in rhyming verse, and yet this is the the kind of thing I might easily say to someone'. If you just did blank verse in that way, it wouldn't be nearly so intriguing. If you are pulling off some kind of poetic stunt by making it rhyme and fit the meter as well, then you are starting to interest people because they think 'Gosh, that's just like me asking for a cup of tea, but it rhymes and scans!'. It lends a comic dimension to the whole thing, an excitement, because then they start to think 'What's coming next, what rhymes are coming next?' Talking about rhyme and what rhyme can do, one of my favourite things in *The Liar* happened in rehearsal, just before we started the show, when I suddenly thought, 'Oh, I've got a joke here'. It went:

'Why did he bother spouting all that tosh?
He surely must have known it wouldn't wash.
He lies to everybody willy-nilly.
Whoever heard of anything so stupid?'

The audience burst out laughing every night at that. There are two things there.

One, it wasn't in the Corneille, and two, it was funny precisely because the last line obeyed metre, but not, of course, rhyme.

DJ: And it was also the translation being aware of itself.

RB: Exactly. You are almost saying to the audience 'You know this is verse don't you, and you are enjoying it'. To some extent it is Bolt and not Corneille, and yet it works because it's frothy comedy, it's light and it's fun, and it's what Corneille would have liked. I like to think he was looking down and saying '*ce n'est pas Corneille, mais ça marche*'.

DJ: Are you comfortable with the idea that the translation shouldn't be invisible; that is that people notice the translation, that it's not just a window into a play?

RB: I'm happy with that in this case because I do think I can do things in verse which are funny. For something like *The Twins*, or say if I were to do a Feydeau, which I have never done, it should be much more transparent because the point there is much less to do with elegance and rhetoric and wit (as it is with Corneille and Molière) than with slick farce, so that all you need there is prose that speaks well, just fizzes along. My reviews hardly ever mention me when I'm doing a prose play. They'll say 'Ranjit Bolt's flashy translation' or 'Ranjit Bolt put "Bugger off!" too often'. However, with the verse there'll almost always be a paragraph about the translation, and that is interesting, They'll always spend more time on the translation if it's in verse.

DJ: Because clearly the translator there has played more of a key role. What do you think of the famous quote describing you as 'the translator as star'? Does that put the translator at too high a level in the whole process?

RB: I suppose it probably does. It's nice to read in the newspaper, but I think it does put the translator above himself. I do think that translators get above themselves, I used to get above myself when I started off. I now find myself much less impressed by being a translator. One day I hope I will write something of my own, either a novel, or a film script. Until I've done that I won't be totally pleased.

DJ: Working in translation is pushing you towards wanting to write your own stuff?

RB: I started off because I always wanted to be a writer; my uncle is a writer and my father has written books as a literary critic. I've always wanted to write, but I didn't think I was ready to say anything totally of my own. The nearest I come to being me is when I'm doing a verse play and there you can have all of the fun of contributing and none of the hassle of trying to work out a plot, and all the rest, from a to m to z. I think translating is a very good way to learn how to write. There are always decisions to make, as I've said, about what to leave out, when to add a touch.

DJ: I gather, from what you're saying that, as a translator, you don't work to a consistent set of principles, but that you make decisions provisionally and circumstantially, according to what you are doing, what play you are working with and so on?

RB: Yes, I think that's probably right. *The Cid* makes a totally different set of demands on you than a Molière, and is basically harder. The reason for this, in my view, is that rhyming verse in English tends to be funny. I don't think it *has* to be and, quite clearly, there are many poems that aren't, but English rhyming verse does have a very strong comic and satirical tradition. In any event, in a tragedy it is very easy to strike a wrong note by choosing an infelicitous rhyme. You have to be very careful. One of the things the director was always saying to me was 'I think they're going to laugh here. You have to change this rhyme We are on very portentous ground, there are people offering swords to other people to kill them and if you say the wrong word at the wrong time you'll be in trouble'. On the whole, I would say that posed a harder problem than the comic problem, which, essentially, is how to be as funny as possible.

DJ: So you feel more at home in comedy?

RB: Yes. It's much easier to work in rhyming verse because, for the reasons I've given, its much harder to make a real *faux pas* in comic verse. English rhymes are very difficult to find whereas the French would happily rhyme 'constatation' with 'proclamation'. We wouldn't allow that sort of thing. If I rhymed 'proclamation' with 'sophistication' it wouldn't really be very interesting; it's a kind of half rhyme, if that. There are rhymes like to/you and me/see, which will trot along and pass muster, but you're always trying to twist the language. The interesting ones, might be compound rhymes, like Byron's 'prided' rhyming with 'I did'. Those are funny. You can't do that sort of thing in tragedy – it's too undignified.

DJ: As well as that, of course, the timing of comedy is everything, and, as you have said before, your timing is imposed upon you by your metre – your rhyme comes at just the moment you'd expect it. It has to work like that. Going back to the original starter to this question, which was not working to a consistent set of principles, are there any examples of what you would call bad practice, what you would avoid at all costs? Is there anything that you would consider, to use a grand word, unethical?

RB: I said earlier that a critic might say Bolt said 'Bugger off!' too often, but in fact I've never used the term 'Bugger off!'. I would never use phrases that make people laugh automatically and in a very base way. It's very easy to make a hundred people out of seven hundred laugh just by saying 'You silly fat bastard'. You *could* do it and someone *would* titter. But my primary rule is to avoid such easy laughs.

DJ: And if the original has the equivalent?

RB: If the original has the equivalent yes, but otherwise no. If it goes with the character – say Zanetto, in *The Twins*, fine. Another rule of mine is that unless you are really stuck, don't do anything just for the sake of the rhyme, because you will be found out. If you are stuck for a rhyme, you just have to work until you find the right one. If you start putting 'shoe' in to rhyme with 'do' when there are no shoes around, you're cheating, and you'll be found guilty.

DJ: The two principles you've articulated actually come from the same area, don't they? You are talking about being very faithful to the spirit of something, to what is there, rather than imposing something on it. There is a very good example of what you are saying in Peter Luke's translation of *Yerma*, where Yerma has heard this man singing and has been stirred by his voice. Her husband reprehends her, warning that 'people will start talking if they see you out and about like this', to which she kneejerks 'Fuck people'. Yerma simply wouldn't say that; it's not in her character, it's not in her nature. Hers is the tragedy of the ultra-conservative woman. This is really a failure to interrogate character, on one hand, and a cheap playing to the gallery on the other.

RB: Yes, and as far as technique goes, if you look at verse translations, either mine or anyone else's – and I'm sure I do do it – you can always tell where someone has changed the word order etc., so that it doesn't really work naturally, just to make it rhyme. One minute you'll have people taking quite fluently, collo-quially, and then something will come marauding out of another century, hymn book-style. And you know that they've twisted it, and if the audience is on their guard, if they are alert, then they'll spot it.

DJ: How do you feel about other practices of translation, like collage translation, when you take four or five of the translations on the market and put them together to form your own translation? Have you ever come across that?

RB: I've never done it, but I don't see why not, if it produces something interesting.

DJ: So the end product is what you judge something by?

RB: Yes, I think I would judge by the quality and effectiveness of the end product. If it worked and everyone was happy, then fine. The only time that has happened to me was once in a particular show when people put in bits of another translation. I didn't like that other translation, so I was quite annoyed. But if they had been good bits, it would have been fine.

DJ: What took you into translation in the first place? In one of your introductions you talk about when you were an investment adviser.

RB: It goes back to something I said earlier about having a beginning, a middle and an end when you're translating. If you have a full-time job then I think it is easier to start off as a translator because you are not working around the clock. My uncle was a school teacher who had long holidays in which to write, and he started writing plays. I couldn't have done that. I think translating was the best way I could have started. It meant I could do twenty lines every day, even work on the bus on the way home, because I never had work to take home. It was the ideal way for someone with a job, and for someone who I don't think would have managed a play, for example, first off. If you are someone working full-time, translation is a lot less demanding than spending two years on a play, planning it out and trying to do it in your spare time. I have friends who've tried this and it hasn't worked for them.

DJ: You see translation as some sort of apprenticeship in writing, in a way?

RB: Yes, I'd like to think it was. What I would really like to do is to write a novel. In fact, best of all would be to invent a detective and produce, say, one 'Inspector X' every two years. I have an idea for this, and I've just started work.

DJ: Can you remember a specific moment in performance when people laughed at your lines and you thought 'This is me'?

RB: With the willy-nilly gag, for example, and several others. It's often not a gag, but it's the way you translate a line that you feel in the original probably wasn't funny. 'Your least attractive feature is your wit, your mouth's quite nice until you open it'. That always got an enormous laugh; there the wit and the humour are very, very English, and it is nothing to do with the French, which is a more elegant paradox, '*Que vous seriez charmant si vous saviez vous taire*' – not a joke here, but rather an elegant put-down. Mine is definitely a gag and I remember a critic singled it out as being a good couplet.

DJ: I had the same sort of experience, not with jokes, but with *Blood Wedding* with Communicado at the Edinburgh Festival. In the scene where the two corpses are being brought back, Death describes them 'With teeth like fistfuls of frozen snow', and somebody in the audience went 'Oh' and I thought 'Those are my words'. At that point you have gone on to a different level *vis à vis* the text. You are suddenly aware that you are part of an equation somewhere. No matter whether you are working with Shakespeare into Italian or the great European writers into English, you're part of the negotiation.

RB: You *are* part of it, absolutely right. You can't pretend that some kind of accurate rendering conveys the play, because it's not the play any more; it's gone into English. You can't translate Racine into English verse and pretend it's Racine, because it's not. Neither can you translate, for example, Marivaux, into English prose and pretend it's Marivaux, because you're not as great a stylist as he was. Dryden says (to paraphrase) that a translator's job is to make the author appear as 'charming' as possible, while preserving what he calls the 'character' of the original. So, the basic point is don't deviate, don't say 'Bugger off!' if 'Bugger off!' is not required and not in keeping. By all means add and invent if you feel it is helpful and the kind of thing the playwright, if you can imagine him looking over your shoulder, would have been happy with. And might have done himself in rehearsal, if he were re-writing.

DJ: You've done versions of Goldoni, Corneille, Molière, dramatists well-known in this country. But you've also done *The Real Don Juan*, Zorrilla's play. It's certainly known to every Hispanist in the country, hugely known in Spain because of this curious procedure by which it is performed every year in Madrid. This year it ran, for example, for about four months to packed audiences. Because of that the play is a fixed play in Spain, you don't change it, it has pantomime status in that sense, you don't meddle with it. But this was a play that was unknown in this country at all.

RB: It was John Retallack who had the idea of doing it over here and it certainly paid off.

DJ: The point is that here the translator acted as a kind of cultural enabler. That strikes me as very important.

RB: *The Liar* was like that. *The Liar* hadn't been done for nearly two hundred and fifty years, and I really thought there, above all, that I was on to a winner. I think *Don Juan* is a good play – lyrical, romantic, tragic. But *The Liar* is a wonderful comedy, verging on a classic, and the discovery was a real coup because it was totally unknown. Nobody had ever seen or heard of it, apart from those who knew Corneille. I was wandering about in a bookshop looking for something to translate on spec, and the woman said to me 'Why not try *The Liar*, it's in verse, that's what you want to do, and no-one knows it'. I tried to find her afterwards, because in a way she actually changed my life. For all I know I'd still be in the City if it hadn't been for her.

DJ: But you had the confidence to look at *The Liar* and say 'This is a good play, this deserves to be translated'.

RB: I actually didn't read it, I took her on her word and just did it line by line. After a while, though, I could see that something good was happening.

DJ: In the relatively short time that you have been translating do you think that the figure of the translator has changed?

RB: I think it began with Tony Harrison. Maybe it was with his *Misanthrope* that the English really came out of their 'ivory tower' and started looking at foreign drama; that was probably about 20 years ago. Since then translators have become more and more important. For me Tony Harrison was the flagship of the modern movement of translating.

DJ: I think Tony Harrison was one of the first translators to translate in terms of theatre and not in terms of words.

RB: Exactly, and yet his words were all so brilliant. He became famous as a *translator* as well as a poet. Later on you have Robert David McDonald doing *The House Of Bernarda Alba*, with Glenda Jackson, and then people like me turn up a few years afterwards. Basically the English have realised that foreign drama exists, and if you ask me they've gone a bit too far. I'm pretty sure that quite a few plays that are classics in English would not be done in France, and that we're doing quite a lot of plays – French plays for example – that are not classics. I'd be very surprised if *The Way Of The World, The Country Wife* or even *The Alchemist* have been done all that much in France. We've developed something of an inferiority complex, I feel.

DJ: But translation can create classics. For example, Poe is much greater in

French than in English – at least that's what the French say.

RB: I think you're right. Dare I say that *The Liar* was said to be a better play than *Le menteur*, which in turn was an adaptation of an earlier piece. I think that's certainly possible... I mean in principle. It's interesting though, I think it is partly something to do with the French, that they have a way of making their authors into gods, so that theirs are instantly 'names to conjure with'. The Spanish don't do it nearly as much, but every French writer, whoever it is, immediately becomes some kind of major figure. The English seem to swallow it. We're apt to say: 'This is a Racine. It must be a work of genius'. Well – is it? Or is it always?

DJ: Can I take you on to the idea of translation and adaptation? I noticed in the Absolute Classics books of yours that they all had, apart from one, 'translated and adapted by...' The exception reads 'translated by...' – the Goldoni. Do you distinguish between translation and adaptation? Do you have clear ground rules for them?

RB: I think that speaks for itself in that the others are all translations of verse, whereas the Goldoni is prose. By 'adapted' what I am saying is that you can't translate verse. There is a distinction between translation and adaptation in that translation immediately has some connotation of being more faithful to something that we've already agreed probably doesn't exist anyway, so that kind of fidelity is a nonsense in a way. But there is a feeling that you might in some cases be misleading people if you say 'translated'.

DJ: *The Sisterhood*, your version of *Les femmes savantes*, is very clearly an adaptation rather than a translation.

RB: It's a very good example of a play that was screaming out for a particular treatment, in the same way that Zanetto was screaming out to be a Yorkshireman or a Lancastrian. It seemed to demand modernisation, complete with structuralism and post-structuralism and feminism – it was simply a wonderful opportunity, and as I went along I suddenly thought 'God this is really working'. But sometimes when I throw in the word 'adapted' it's just a kind of 'health warning': 'This product now contains lines that are not those of Molière, that are not those of Corneille'.

DJ: Sometimes, no matter how scrupulously honest we are in programme notes, and in using words like 'adaptation' (I know in the Platform Papers you talk about transformation, which seems to me to be a very reasonable word as well), there are always people who will come along and say 'But it's not like that in the original', without any serious thought for the problem of the reception of the play. I don't suppose we'll ever get away from that.

RB: Several times I've been rapped over the knuckles for taking liberties with people. It happened with Beaumarchais funnily enough, with *Figaro*: 'Who does he think he is, taking liberties with a great play and a great playwright?' I don't happen to think Beaumarchais's plays *are* great – or anything *like* great.

DJ: Let me go back to this idea of 'transformation'.

RB: I think I probably mean it almost as a pun on 'translation'. It's meant to illustrate what happens when you translate, and the fact that there is probably no such thing as a translation as we usually understand it. No translation is in fact a 'translation', in that sense; it's something else. Hence also, my use of 'translated and adapted'.

DJ: We're hard up for vocabulary, aren't we?

RB: 'Render' is a good word. And 'version'; 'A new version by...' is very good, because it doesn't make any pretence to be anything other than a loose rendering of a play.

DJ: How do you feel about somebody in an audience who says 'I paid my £10 to see this play and I thought I was going to see Corneille, but it was Ranjit Bolt that I saw?' Do you feel that that person has a legitimate complaint?

RB: Yes, I think they probably do.

DJ: Does it worry you?

RB: No, because for every one of those there'll be another one who enjoyed it. No, it doesn't worry me. I've heard people behind me in theatres say '*Ce n'est pas Molière*', and then walking out. There are obviously going to be people like that. The fact is that change, either excision or emendation (or, to a lesser extent, addition), is inevitable. If you have a long rhetorical speech, for example, the chances are that a modern audience are not going to enjoy it in the same way that a French audience did three hundred years ago when they probably loved rhetoric. We don't actually like rhetoric very much and we'd probably cut such speeches, for example in the early Shakespeare plays, as being too long-winded. You have to cut and sometimes you cut a forty-line speech by ten lines because it's too much.

DJ: One of the problems with Corneille and Racine is that the vocabulary is so limited in many ways, although it's also very intense. You are constantly being forced into finding alternatives.

RB: Yes, because you don't want to say 'honour' again or 'glory' again, or bang on about them again, for that matter.

DJ: And 'honour' and 'glory' are very difficult words to deal with.

RB: Absolutely.

DJ: It is interesting that you say you're aware of the horizon of expectations of your audience in English. That's always where you have to keep your eye when you're translating a play for the stage, isn't it?

RB: But to some extent, in the process itself, you're guessing, and then looking in previews to actually see. For example, in *The Illusion*, I made a real gaff. There's a great scene where it suddenly turns brilliantly into a tragedy... but it's actually people acting out a tragedy. It's a marvellous theatrical *trompe l'oeil*. The problem was that before the author pulls the gag there is this lengthy tragic scene – exacerbated by the fact that I was using the longer text as well. I just panicked because I could see the audience were really starting to shuffle about and cough, and do all the things audiences do when they're not interested any more. And I, like a real idiot, not knowing the ground rules, called the actors without consulting the director. 'We've got to cut this', I told them, and I made a complete dog's breakfast of the whole thing. Instead of cutting sixty lines we only cut thirty because the actors were furious. The director said to me 'If you'd only played it the right way you'd have had all sixty lines cut because I'd have handled this'. So what might have been a really good theatrical coup became only so-so. The audience was still impressed, but it could have been far more powerful.

DJ: You get the same thing in Spanish, the same love of rhetoric. In Golden Age Spanish theatre actors specialised in certain roles. They did cameo performances, like sax solos at a jazz concert. 'There's so and so, I've seen him doing this, he's going to go through his paces now'. So the playwright gives him a couple of pages of beautifully crafted script and the actor goes through his or her paces. And actors had followings, which they don't in our theatres, unless they're soap stars. How do you recreate that? At that moment your audience has taken time out, if you like, from the play saying 'Let's enjoy the rhetoric, let's enjoy this particular solo performance'. We can't do that.

RB: We don't do that. That's quite right. I think the English just aren't as attuned to rhetoric anyway. It's more of a Latin thing which Latin people like far more than we do, with certain notable exceptions, like Churchill.

DJ: And as you say the French theatre is more inclined to be rhetorical?

RB: Yes, you're certainly aware of that, and you start to make cuts yourself and you get bolder. You start to say 'This has been said, I'm not going to say this again' and you might even cut ten lines without asking the director.

DJ: Are there cases where you would be worried by transposing a play too *completely* from one culture into another, so that your audience loses track of the original?

RB: I don't know... I think that your *Bohemian Lights* was an example of a successful adaptation/transformation/transposition. It was very like *The Sisterhood*. It was screaming out to be done like that and it worked very well. It almost became your play – in a sense it is now your play. You found a period that people knew a lot about and for which there is also a good tradition in theatre, so it worked.

DJ: There are many great plays that are, in fact, adaptations. Is there a case where the translator can consider himself a creative writer working out of an original and developing something new from that?

RB: When I say 'I wrote well today', I'm always pleased I used the word 'wrote' instead of 'translated', but by and large I tend to get very coy and say 'I'm not a writer, I'm a translator'.

DJ: You said something in the Platform Papers about a translator as a writer with nothing of his or her own to say.

RB: I think in a way that's true. A good translator has ability, of course, but you're not anybody in my book until you have created from a to z yourself – not necessarily totally yourself, you may borrow a germ of an idea and there may be an adaptive dimension, but by and large you shouldn't be borrowing but inventing. Until I have done that I won't consider myself to be a writer I'm afraid.

DJ: You're describing a tension at the heart of what the translator does.

RB: Because he or she is doing a writing job, but isn't a writer. If I could write a really good novel I'd die a happy man. As it is I enjoy what I do. I think I contribute.

DJ: Do you find translation to be a viable means of making a living?

RB: I started *The Liar* safe in the knowledge that I had a job to go to every day. Now I'm a free-lance I always operate like a mole, carefully paying down my mortgage, first of all establishing economic stability. The next step is to have enough money to be able to say 'I can just stop translating now for a year or so' (if I can ever do that well) 'and maybe work on those novels'. Knowing me I'd probably keep translating because I'd be afraid of losing work. I'd write in my spare time, the same way I started translating in my spare time – and for the same reason: economics.

DJ: When you start translating a new play are you not also assailed with doubts that you can do it or that the play itself is viable?

RB: No, I tend to be quite brash about it, I tend to plunge in and hope it goes well. Perhaps I am too hard on us translators There are translations that are among the greatest works of the writers who did them, like Pope's *Homer*. It is a noble trade.

TRANSLATING THE SPIRIT OF THE PLAY

JOHN CLIFFORD

John Clifford, a Hispanist by training, lectures in drama in Queen Margaret College, Edinburgh. He has written over thirty-five original plays, including the acclaimed *Losing Venice*, about the Spanish poet Quevedo (Traverse, 1985), *Ines de Castro* (Traverse, 1989) and *Light In The Village* (Edinburgh Festival, 1992). His *Visões de Febre*, a play about the Portuguese writer Florbela Espanca opened in Lisbon in 1994 as part of the city's European Capital of Culture celebrations, and an opera based on *Ines de Castro* will be premiered at the 1996 Edinburgh Festival. John Clifford has also played a crucial role in establishing the Spanish Golden Age (he has completed a doctorate on Calderón) on the English-speaking stage. He has translated and adapted a number of plays by Calderón (including *The Surgeon Of His Honour, The House With Two Doors,* and *Schism In England* (this latter play for the National), Tirso de Molina's *Condenado por desconfiado* (performed as *Heavenbent, Hellbound* by The Actor's Touring Company), Cervantes's *Retablo de las maravillas* (performed as *Magic Theatre* by Winged Horse) and Lorca's *The House Of Bernarda Alba*. He is currently adapting Liliane Atlan's *Opéra pour Térézin* from the French.

Lorca once said that it would be impossible to translate one of his plays. Because even if you managed (by some miracle) to get the words right, you'd never translate the spirit behind the words. For it's the spirit of the words that is the most important part. And that, he argued, remains far beyond the translator's reach. To be sure, translating can be a frustrating business. It's certainly easy enough to get depressed. Perhaps especially when you're translating. All too easy to feel that really all you're doing as a translator is damaging the text: and that somehow the best you can hope for is some kind of damage limitation. That the best you can hope to achieve as you translate a text is to minimise the damage you do to it. To be sure, humility is useful; but it's usefulness has its limits.

I'd prefer to take Lorca's dictum in a more positive sense. It is helpful in that it reminds us of the complexity of our task; and useful, too, if it inspires us to aim high in our attempts to fulfil it. It is particularly useful, perhaps, when we are thinking about translating drama. For here, more than any other medium, we are not just translating words. Words in a dramatic text are not an end in themselves;

they are a kind of scaffolding on which the actor constructs his or her performance. And what counts are not just the words themselves, but the gaps between the words. The feeling behind the words. What is left unsaid matters as much as what is said: and as translators we have to be sensitive to both. And if we do our job properly, we can open out such amazing new perspectives to our audience. I cannot be the only one whose inner life has been immeasurably enriched by good translation. And I know, too, that my own creative life has been enhanced and enriched by the job of translating. My own inner creative history is all to often a tiresome record of uncertainties, doubts, fears, botched opportunities. It is immensely refreshing, now and then, to leave all those anxieties behind and try to enter the mind of a writer like Lorca or Calderón – writers in total command of their art and craft. And then try to follow, and faithfully mirror, the creative workings of that mind. Even when I fail, as I frequently do, my life has been enriched by the attempt. And so, I hope, has been the life of the audience.

I cannot offer any enlightening theories as to how to achieve this, since I never seem to have the time, or the patience, to read theories. And I cannot claim that the way I set about it is especially exemplary or instructive either. There must be thousands of translators whose work is more accurate, more honest, and more faithful than mine. All I want to try to do is describe a process. If I'm wrong, hopefully there'll be somebody out there to put me right. Like every other process, it all happens in stages. Stage one is obvious, trite, and often not a little tedious. It involves acquiring dictionaries, mostly; it involves reading footnotes. Working one's way through all those uninviting bits in small type at the bottom of or the back of texts. The bits that I generally, to my immense loss, don't bother reading. And then working one's way inch by inch, word by word, through the text to make sure you understand exactly what it means. And then without regard to elegance, without regard to speakability, without regard to anything but the dogged attempt to get at the literal meaning of the text, writing the results down. The results can be illuminating. They can be depressing. When I open up Calderón's *La vida es sueño* (*Life Is A Dream*), for instance, I read the first line:

Rosaura: Oh violent hippogriff...

...and I want to slam the book shut and run away from the task before I have scarcely begun it. (It is worth noting in passing that the play in question is an astonishing, wonderful piece of work, rich in emotion, intellect, and spiritual reach, and that the British theatre impoverishes itself immeasurably in its contemptible reluctance to stage it). Because a crucial part of getting it accepted into the repertory is the creation of a loving, accurate, skillful and stageable translation. Because an immensely important part of getting it accepted is to get the beginning right. Because the beginning – even if somehow (and God knows how) we negotiate the hippogriff – is such an astonishing virtuosic feat that it must reduce even the brashest of translators to a state of gibbering knock-kneed terror. The main problem, of course, with the hippogriff, and the wonderfully playful and beautifully ordered stream of imagery that follows it, is that it all belongs to a tradition of theatrical rhetoric that has disappeared. We are like tourists wondering bemusedly around the skeleton of some astonishing palace, getting lost in a maze of corridors, peering vaguely into rooms and trying, crudely and clumsily, to re-create their function, beauty and purpose. Full of admiration, perhaps, or a little tedium; but at a fundamental level failing to connect.

Scripts from a more recent past, such as Lorca's *The House Of Bernarda Alba*, entrap us in less obvious minefields. But minefields they certainly are. The first line of the play goes:

I already have the double tolling of those bells placed between my temples!

What's happening is that we're hitting the gap Lorca pointed out to us – the gap between the meaning of words and their spirit. Eventually, with the aid of immense persistence and a good few dictionaries, any fool can reach the meaning of the words; but conveying their spirit is another matter altogether. I would contend that to succeed, and particularly succeed in the theatre, you need to at least have an inkling of what is involved in writing for the theatre yourself. That is only partially a matter of technique; more importantly, it's a matter of 'feel'. The only way I know to create a good piece of theatre is to begin with the germ of a story. A situation that fires the imagination: something that moves, excites and intrigues me. That feels as if it could turn into a good story. Then I need to find out the characters that the story requires; clear a space for them in my imagination, give them room and time to grow. Get to know them, identify with them, feel with them, see the world through their eyes. The more successfully I can become one with my characters, the better, the more theatrically satisfying, the story will become. I'll get to be freed from the confines of my limited imagination, and the characters will instruct me as to how the story develops. I feel what they feel in the unfolding situation; I hear what they say, I write it down. So the best plays don't come from me, don't come from the writer: they come from the characters.

There is an obvious dilemma at the beginning of this process: you don't know who the characters are until they speak. And until you get to know them, you don't know what they're going to say. It's a vicious circle that can take months to break. But the joy, sometimes the main joy, of translating, is that someone else has done the groundwork for you. And that is another of the advantages of the painstaking process with the footnotes and the dictionaries; they enable you, as the translator, to get to know the characters. So becoming, say, Bernarda Alba, is so much easier: because someone else has made the journey before you. Someone has cleared the path through the jungle. And when that someone else is a Federico García Lorca, following in his footsteps is a real joy.

But the task of translating remains the basic creative task; to feel with the characters, become the characters. And listen to what they have to say. That is the foundation of a good translation. There remains, of course, the final stage, of going back to the original and painstakingly checking it line by line – to make sure that the characters haven't run away with themselves (as they often do) and given you lines, and feelings that in the original simply do not exist. But that is to anticipate ourselves. There are all kinds of traps and minefields on the way. Let's return to *The House Of Bernarda Alba* for a moment and see if we can disarm any of them. There's a wonderful scene in the second act of the play in which La Poncia, the housekeeper, is describing how the reapers hired a prostitute to have sex with in the olive grove. She describes the young man who hired her:

> *El que la contrataba era un muchacho de ojos verdes, apretado como una gavilla de trigo.*

The language seems very simple here, and it's perfectly obvious what La Poncia means. The boy had green eyes and was as thin as a wheatsheaf. That translated the words, certainly. But does it translate the spirit behind the words? In his lecture on 'The poetic image in Góngora', Lorca mentioned that an incredibly rich source of poetic imagery for him is the way people in Andalusia actually used to speak. According to him, they would spontaneously use poetic images in everyday speech. for instance, he says, 'they'll call a deep slow flowing watercourse an "ox of water" to communicate its volume, its cussedness, and its strength'; and elsewhere he spoke of the profound impression the speech of the people made on him:

> I'm far more interested in the people who inhabit a landscape than in the landscape itself. I can sit and look at a mountain for about half an hour; but then I'll want to talk to a woodcutter or a shepherd who actually lives there. I'll happily talk to them for hours. These conversations stay in the memory; so when I write, what comes out is the authentic way people actually speak. In my head I've got a huge archive of memories of conversations I had with such people when I was a child. It is my poetic memory, and I rely on it.

On the title page Lorca tells us of his intention, stating that 'The poet gives notice that he intends these three acts to be a photographic documentary'. After finishing the play, he boasted proudly to a friend that 'I've had to cut a lot of things in this tragedy. I cut out a lot of facile songs and little rhymes. I want the work to have a severe simplicity'.

All this should alert us to the fact that when Lorca uses images in this play, he's not using them in a slack, or conventionally 'poetic' way; he's using them as very precise methods of description. He's also basing them on very precise moments of observation. So when one of his characters describes a young man as 'slim as a wheatsheaf', this should conjure up a very precise, and very immediate impression in our mind. The problem is that the words conjure up for an urban British audience, a very different set of images. Nowadays wheat gets stacked up in rectangles, or big fat cylinders: the image no longer corresponds in any way with our experience. The kind of wheatsheaf that Lorca had in mind only occurs on the packets of sliced bread, when the manufacturer wishes to delude us into thinking that the denatured product inside is healthy and 'natural'. The feeling behind La Poncia's words is that the young man was very slim and very sexy. Does 'slim as a wheatsheaf' really convey that? I suspect not. What happens to be a correct translation of the words deforms the spirit behind the words. Of course, the further we go back in time, the more these problems become insolubly acute. It's useful, at this point, to take our courage in both hands and return to *La vida es sueño* (remember: this is the preliminary literal version, a starting off point).

Rosaura: Violent hippogriff
Who runs in a pair with the wind
Where, lightening flash without flame,
Bird without coloured feathers, fish without scales,
And brute without natural instinct
Where in the confused labyrinth
Of those naked crags
Are you running, bolting, and throwing yourself headlong?
Stay in this mountain
And let the beasts here have you as their Phaethon!

It's worth remembering at this point that all that has somehow to be turned into comprehensible, speakable, elegant, funny verse that bears at least a distant relationship to the original:

Rosaura: Hipogrifo violento
Que corriste parejas con el viento
Donde, rayo sin llama,
pájaro sin matiz, pez sin escama

y bruto sin instinto
natural, al confuso laberinto
de esas desnudas peñas,
te desbocas, te arrastras, y despeñas?
Quédate en este monte
donde tengan los brutos su Faetonte...

Assuming the magnitude of the task doesn't send you gibbering witless back to something simpler (like deciphering the Rosetta stone) and that you persist in this insane task (remembering there's another three thousand lines to go), perhaps it's helpful to try and put this into its context.

First impressions are again misleading. The speech is constructed with a degree of formal rhetoric that strikes us as extraordinary. We're simply not used to it. It wouldn't strike its first audience as that extraordinary at all – partly because a sizable section would have suffered, or perhaps enjoyed, an education founded on rhetorical principles. Whether educated or not, the regular audience would have come to expect speeches of such elegance from Calderón – they were a hallmark of his style, and one that he himself parodies later on in this play. So the extraordinary formality that we sense, from our historical perspective, the stiffness, the courtliness, would not be perceived as such by its first audience. It would be enjoyed, it would be savoured; but it would also be expected. And the setting of the story is anything but courtly. We're on a wild mountainside – something conveyed not by the scenery (there wouldn't be any) but by the language, and the angry gestures of the actress (*'esas peñas'*, *'este monte'*). She wouldn't even make a formal entrance at all – she would tumble on stage, she might even spectacularly fall. Then she's picking herself up to hurl imprecations at her disappearing horse. What's more, she's a woman dressed as a man. Our response to this is formed by pantomime: it conjures up the most respectable form of a safe, undemanding entertainment. But to its audience, it represented the breaking of a taboo.

The theatre's numerous opponents in seventeenth-century Spain positively foamed at the mouth when it came to considering the role of women dressed as men. This was seen as a total affront to decency. For one thing, the men in the audience could see the actress's legs (one of the sexiest passages in Cervantes is the description of a girl's foot), and anything that drew attention to anyone's sexuality was immensely suspect. For another, the figure of the woman on stage, freed of the voluminous garments (and stifling conventions) that imprisoned her sex, profoundly challenged the repressive sexual mores of the time. A figure like Rosaura, moving freely, taking control of her own destiny spoke to everyone in the theatre – including the sizable contingent of women – of the enticing and dangerous possibilities of freedom. Somehow, when we translate this play, we have to find a form of words that can help lead the actress – on a different stage, in a completely different theatrical setting – towards the expression of all this. And the only tool at our disposal is English. Our own language, apparently. But do we really understand it?

One of my first professional jobs in theatre was to translate *Romeo And Juliet* for the TAG theatre company. Based in the Glasgow Citizens, their remit was to perform to schools in deprived areas of the city. My task was to translate and adapt the play for a cast of seven to perform in under two hours to an audience of adolescents who would most likely know nothing about theatre, nothing about Shakespeare, and not be kindly disposed towards either. This involved going through the verse, rooting out difficult words, replacing them with intelligible ones which hopefully represented the verse's sound and scansion. And since they were unintelligible without a dictionary, I mostly had to rewrite the jokes in prose.

The first thing to do was read the play. I was shocked to discover how little I knew it; and how little I understood it. We assume, in a slack kind of way, that this is all part of our heritage, that it's all safe and familiar. The more I read the play, the more it seemed an undiscovered country. I came across this passage in act two, scene one:

Mercurio: Now he will sit under a medlar tree
And wish his mistress were that kind of fruit
As maids call medlars when they laugh alone.
O, Romeo, that she were, O that she were
An open arse and thou a poppering pear!

...and on first reading it, found it made no sense at all. Footnotes reluctantly, and rather prissily, slowly began to explain. The 'medlar' is a kind of fruit, to 'meddle' can also mean to have sex with, the medlar was thought to look like a vagina, or 'open arse', a 'country term' for medlar (as the editor delicately puts it), 'Poperinghe' was a Flemish town known for its delicious pears... To begin with I was astonished at the sexual frankness and explicitness of the jokes; and then delighted and moved and excited by the richness of the language. What's so exhilarating about this kind of use of language is that its meaning grows the more you think about it. One door opens, and then another, and another... there's a richness to it that makes our present language seem desperately thin and impoverished. 'Medlar' itself is a word that has died. Who's ever seen one? Like birds, like butterflies, like so many kinds of flowers, the medlar has disappeared from our landscape. A similar kind of impoverishment, of denuding, is happening to the landscape of our minds. Our language has been so long plundered by politicians, salesmen, advertising agents, by liars and crooks and thieves of every kind, that it is it has been bled dry. Distorted beyond repair: robbed of meaning. George Orwell wrote in 'Politics of the English Language', in 1946:

A man may take to drink because he feels himself a failure, and then fail all the more completely because he drinks. It is rather the same thing that is happening to the English language. It becomes ugly and inaccurate because our thoughts are foolish, but the slovenliness of our language makes it easier for us to have foolish thoughts.

This is a deliberate process. A politician doesn't want a language that opens up new and different levels of meaning; he and his sound bite engineer want a language that simply elicits the appropriate response. And as a result, words are drying out like so many endangered species. 'Care' for instance, is now almost empty of meaning after so many soulless corporations have told us they 'care' for the environment they are systematically destroying. We think of 'care in the community' – that grotesque euphemism for callous cost-cutting indifference – we stumble across a homeless drunk and the word dies a little death. What's more frightening about this process is that it happens little by little; words disappear, and we don't even notice that they've gone. It's another advantage of being engaged in the process of translating from another language – in that it teaches you something about what is happening to your own. It was working on *La Celestina* that alerted me to the death of our language. *La Celestina* is an amazing work – written in the 1490s, it's one of the first works that portrays the world not as it should be, but as it is. The book is full of the excitement from the discovery that it's possible to write like this, possible to communicate directly to people about their own experience – and possible to do it in the vernacular! And so the language, this wonderful young, crude, energetic Castilian – is overflowing with energy and vitality.

It makes our English feel so tired and old. I can remember frequently despairing of the impossibility of translating it. It was like returning to Britain after a visit to the Far East – to societies overflowing with energy and strength. How weak and tired we seem. How drained of vitality. How much our language has suffered the draining away of richness and meaning. At moments like this I long to wrote in Sanskrit. In Latin. In Gaelic or in Ancient Greek. In any language that hasn't been befouled by centuries of governing. By the mass media. By the desecrations of politicians and salesmen. But perhaps I don't have to go so far; perhaps there is a language on my doorstep that is still rich and vigorous, not corrupted through becoming the language of oppression or the jargon of the quick sale. A language which still has a power and an expressive capacity that has hardly been touched or exploited; the language of spoken Scots. Such a language remains close to me; but perhaps I can console myself with the thought that even the process of trying to coin an English that is rich, emotionally charged, elegant, intellectually accurate, is in itself a necessary act of resistance.

NICK DEAR: TRANSLATION AS CONSERVATIVE WRITING

IN CONVERSATION WITH DAVID JOHNSTON

Nick Dear's plays include *Zenobia*, *The Art Of Success* and *Pure Science* (all performed at the RSC), and *In The Ruins* (performed at the Bristol Old Vic). He has adapted Ostrovsky's *A Family Affair* for Cheek By Jowl, Tirso de Molina's *The Last Days Of Don Juan* for the RSC, and Molière's *Le bourgeois gentilhomme* for the Royal National Theatre. He collaborated with Peter Brook on the research for *Qui est là?* (Bouffes du Nord), and his screenplays include Jane Austen's *Persuasion* (for the BBC). He has also written extensively for radio.

DJ: First of all could you tell me what made you start work as a translator for the theatre?

ND: Declan Donnellan asked me. It had never occurred to me that this was something that I might do. I was working in Manchester as writer-in-residence at the Royal Exchange when I got a call saying they had a play which wasn't working in rehearsal, and would I attempt a new version with a month to do it in. This was *A Family Affair*, otherwise known as *The Bankrupt*, and I found I could do it very fast. I had a literal version to work from and I was excited by the subject matter. This was a story which in its original version had been a *cause célèbre*, because it had been about corruption in the Moscow business community, though that side of the story did not particularly have any resonance because we take that very much for granted now. But what did seem to me to have resonance in the story – this was at the end of '87 – was this young, very upwardly mobile couple, who struck me as being a great parallel with all the stuff about yuppies in the eighties. I thought, 'Great, I can do something with this that will make a historical play have resonance'.

It's perhaps worth saying at this point that I'm only ever interested in doing adaptations which are *revisions* of things. Not that they have to be relevant, in today's very functional sense, but I'm not interested in any academic or classical way. I'm intrigued by things that do immediately seem to strike a chord with me, so that if I were writing my own play about this subject, then this would be a good idea, a good way of looking at the subject. That's what I thought about *A Family Affair*, and I had great fun with it. But I could not say for a moment that it was translating, because I'm not really a translator, I'm an adaptor. Though I have translated one play from French.

DJ: So you speak French?

ND: I can speak and read some French, and can translate with a dictionary, but that still doesn't make me a translator.

DJ: How did you work from Spanish?

ND: With *The Last Days Of Don Juan* – *El burlador de Sevilla* – the RSC commissioned a literal translation. So I had the literal translation and the original Spanish – I always have a copy of the play in the original language in front of me, even if I have a very good literal translation, because you can see things like length of speeches, length of lines, exactly where the stage directions come and so on, which may be slightly different in a literal translation. Even though I don't actually speak Spanish, knowing French or Latin, which I did at school, I can work out Spanish on a page with a dictionary.

DJ: What about the quirks of speech, the very fine points of style and so on, does it worry you that perhaps you can't get inside those, that you might miss them, or do you have some type of process in which you are constantly consulting your literal translator?

ND: No, I don't consult literal translators at all, because I don't think the process of creating a new version of a classic play for the stage is about fine points of style at all. I think that's part of a much more serious and very respectable tradition of translation which is pure and which is generally done by poets. I think that there are very good reasons why somebody might, for instance, translate a Spanish Golden Age play, for its language qualities and try to find the fine points of style and translate them poetically and aptly, but that doesn't really have any status in my view of what my role is.

DJ: You once said that you 'translate for your own purposes'. How did you choose the three plays that you adapted?

ND: Firstly, they've all been commissioned, they've all been brought to me. Clearly, they have to have some point of contact with modern life, but not necessarily with my life, because I don't really write about my life. That usually emerges in some form or another, but it is never my starting point. But my own purpose, in the sense that I meant in your quotation, is as part of an exploration of what dramatic form is. One of the reasons why I was intrigued by and attracted to *A Family Affair*, for example, was that it is a four-act drawing-room comedy, four acts, two box sets, two rooms, eight people. If I'd been sitting down to try and write a new play of my own, I would never have dreamed of trying to do that, certainly not seven or eight years ago, although it's rather come back into vogue. As a writer, I grew up in the seventies tradition of the picaresque or epic, whatever you choose to call it, where there is really no set form. There was a great drive in those days to take plays out of domestic situations into the public world, some which may have been misguided, but that was certainly where my opinions were formed as a young writer and it was very intriguing for me to say 'Can I make this work – a comedy in a room?'

Similarly with *Don Juan*, what intrigued me about the form was that it was one of the first instances in literature of the anti-hero. I know of few others that look so crucially at how you can have a central character who is basically a bastard. I have since had the experience of trying to rewrite it as a movie, a Hollywood movie, and I ran into enormous trouble because they couldn't grasp the idea of a central character who is basically bad.

DJ: I can imagine that. When you are working with form and you are trying to make form work on the English-speaking stage, have you had to introduce structural cuts etc., the type of thing that we traditionally think of as 'adaptation'?

ND: In some ways what I have tended to do is take the original play and treat it as if it were a first draft of my own, which I then rework, re-shape and do with whatever I want to. Not so much cut characters, that is quite rare, but I certainly wouldn't baulk at giving a speech to a different character from the one it was intended for. In some of the ones I've done I've been more faithful than in others. In Molière, I thought the form was absolutely pure and perfect, and I felt no desire at all to tinker with it. In *Don Juan*, on the other hand, while I more or less faithfully adapted Tirso in the first half, the second half is almost entirely my own.

DJ: Do you see yourself then as a writer working out, developing, from other people's plays?

ND: I'm very dubious as to what this current position of 'adaptor' is in our literary culture. Throughout history writers have taken other plays and made their own plays out of them. We're in something of a cleft stick at the moment here because, while not really being clear about what an adaptation is or the status it might have, we also want to give credit to adaptors, who are of a much higher status in this country than, say, elsewhere in Europe, Elsewhere in Europe a dramaturg would have done what I did with *A Family Affair*, and not even get a credit. It's a dramaturg's job; no credit, no royalties. In Britain, we ask original playwrights to take on classic pieces. What status that gives such people, I'm not sure. We are clearly not classic translators or academic translators... I can't really think of anybody whose main drive would be to faithfully, authentically, translate the fine points of language.

DJ: How sympathetic – or not – would you be if we were in the foyer of *Don Juan*, the play had just finished and somebody said 'I came along to see Tirso, and that was not Tirso'?

ND: When it was first done at The Swan in Stratford, we used to get Americans coming along and saying 'I came along to see Shakespeare, this ain't Shakespeare'. I

ation to justify anything to an audience. I think that the phrase
.dapted by' or 'translated and adapted by' is for most people these
er that they're going to get a version of something, not necessarily
nal. And anyway, who is to say exactly what the original is? When
who I worked for at the National, commissioned Molière he felt that
a transla.. .ad a shelf life of about ten years and then the language starts to go out
of date. I think that's a very interesting notion because one can pick up many
Penguin Classics playscripts, most of which are translations dating from the fifties,
and they look absolutely ghastly. And these are the main things that are available to
directors and to theatre companies. It's because they look so ghastly, although many
of them are done by perfectly decent writers, that they feel 'we must get a new
translation of this because this looks out of date'. Now, the same thing doesn't
apply to original plays written in the fifties; pick up something written by John
Arden, for example, and it still looks very fresh and very vibrant. There is
something about translations which, unless it's Schiller doing Shakespeare, loses
credibility very quickly. Trying to answer your question, it's perfectly justifiable,
but the theatre's a show, not an academic exercise, and it doesn't bother me at all.
All I would say is 'Hard luck'. But I'm not going to lose any sleep over it.

DJ: So to borrow Gogol's metaphor, Nick Dear won't be a window through
which to gaze at the work in pristine isolation, but will actually be part and parcel
of that work as it is staged in this production.

ND: If it was a very commonplace response, then I think we would need to be
worried by it, but it is a minority response. Much more important to me is that a
lot of people, through the activities of myself and similar adaptors, are coming
along to see these old plays, and having a good time in the theatre. Only a few
years ago Spanish Golden Age was not represented in the British theatre, and it's
due to the work of people like myself that suddenly we've become increasingly
aware – though I'm not sure that theatre management shares this awareness – that
there are still vast reservoirs of dramatic literature out there that we've never even
touched. I think that there are lots of people who come to those kind of shows as
an alternative to the really very narrow repertoire of British plays. When you see
the kind of repertoire that other countries tend to put on, you realise that we need
to be stretching out and finding work that hasn't been done here before. A lot of
people have got enjoyment from that and have had their horizons stretched a little
bit as to what exists in world drama. I think that is much more important.

DJ: Do you think there can be a danger that one adapts too much to one's own
purposes, losing in that way something of the essential 'foreignness' of a play?
English theatre tends to anglicize foreign theatre very much. By bringing things too
close to home, one doesn't get the sense of the sort of 'journey towards otherness'
that both theatre and translation/adaptation are about.

ND: That's very possibly true. The last time I did one of these adaptations was six years ago, and I see it as part of my development as a writer. It was fascinating to see how these particular plays were constructed, and how they and their characters worked. I certainly feel that I learnt a lot from it, but I've also come to the conclusion that the popularity both with audiences and with theatre managements of adapted classic plays was doing a disservice to the development of original play writing in this country. This is partly the reason why I have stopped doing it. I feel that we've over-encouraged it, partly because it's easy, or easier, to sell. For some time, certainly abroad, I was making more money from adaptations than from my original plays. Adaptations were being produced all over the place and original plays weren't. I think it's slightly cosy that adaptation has become almost as applauded as original play writing – it's much easier than original play writing, vastly easier than dreaming up your own story and making it work on the stage. It takes two or three months, rather than two or three years. I had a big argument, in public, a couple of years ago with Jean-Claude Carrière, when I was working with Peter Brook's company for a while. Jean-Claude is a fine writer and a fine adaptor. He's also a great screen writer. He takes the view that there is absolutely no difference in quality between an adapted play and an original play. He also takes the view that all plays are effectively an adaptation of something. Now, I profoundly disagree with this, I don't think all plays are an adaption of something; he would say a newspaper story, or an old play, or a piece of history. I think that you can certainly argue that most of Shakespeare is an adaption of something, and you can also argue that most of Jonson isn't. I would argue, for example, that _The Cherry Orchard_ is not an adaptation of anything at all, but a piece of very pure and original dramatic poetry and imagination. And I think that _Waiting For Godot_ is another example; it's not an adaptation of anything.

DJ: I think _Waiting For Godot_ may well be an adaptation, in its own way, of a series of musical hall sketches, but that's a different point. Is there anything in your work as an adaptor which has contributed to your growth as a writer?

ND: Yes, though it would be very hard to pin down exactly what. A big question for me is 'how has the theatre managed to survive for two and a half, three thousand years, when compared to other forms like the novel, which is effectively one hundred and fifty years old, or movies or the symphony? Opera was only invented around the seventeenth century. In order for theatre to survive in any way, irrespective of financial arguments about subsidies and so on, it has to continue to reinvent itself and has done so throughout history. One way of finding the new form is to attempt to better understand the old ones. Every writer, I think, grows up within a national culture, a racial culture, which does things in certain ways. Talking about the Englishness of adaptation, there is a very specific English writing culture, which is very, very different from say, Italian writing culture, or

German writing culture. They do have national characteristics and I think you're probably quite right – an English adaptor will impose some of those characteristics on a foreign work. I think that, if to stretch the form of one's own cultural possibilities doesn't sound too anal, it's fantastically useful to try and properly understand things which are foreign to that.

DJ: To adapt a play, you have to understand the play inside out, don't you? Does adapting plays develop one's critical faculties of actually looking at the machinery of drama?

ND: Yes, I expect so. I certainly feel that I've never understood the way in which a play works better than when I've had to adapt it, not even when I direct one. I think that it would be a very good exercise for directors to actually attempt the job. Line by laborious line, you see exactly what is happening in a play. Rarely do you have the luxury really, in any field, to spend that amount of time of it.

DJ: Presumably when you are writing your own play, if you're too obsessively aware of the nuts and bolts of its machinery, your play is going to be stillborn in a way that when you are adapting, it's not. Is adaptation a good schooling in that sense for the incipient writer? Because it's certainly true that many translators/adaptors come to write their own plays, many of them immensely successfully.

ND: Yes, I think that's true. There was a rather misguided liberality in the way literature was taught in the sixties and seventies. I began writing in my mid-twenties, in the late seventies, and I was of the view that form was totally unimportant and that one could do anything, that it wasn't really necessary to understand the nuts and bolts. Why would I want to write a play in four acts, when I could write it in thirty-eight scenes? But part of my writing career has been to reclaim an understanding of what forms were and are. Theatre is very limited, there are only certain things you can do on stage. It isn't a complete 'free for all'. You can make a play of thirty minutes, or you can make a play of nine hours, but within that you can have one person on the stage, or you can have more than one person on the stage, or no people on the stage. You can't go in to close-up, like you can with a film camera. There are only certain things you can do and they are very much defined by formal conventions which change as time moves on. For me, learning about adaptation was about learning about forms that would not otherwise have occurred to me. Whether I ever use them or not personally is quite a separate thing.

DJ: We're talking about form as an agent of energy, a way of channelling the energy of the play towards an audience. What about the particular problems of formal conventions in the play which are socially rather than dramatically based – for example, the issue of the honour code which is central to *Don Juan*... how did you approach that?

ND: I was very aware that no matter how much I read – and I do research quite hard in these things – no matter how much I read in the short period that I had to do this work there was no way I was going to understand, either emotionally or intellectually, what the concept of honour meant to a Spanish nobleman in1620. I think that a British academic who has spent ten or twenty years on the subject would have a better understanding than me, but still would not have a perfect understanding. I've been to Seville, and you only have to see the way young men walk round Seville, or the young women for that matter, to see that there is a difference in self-awareness, not necessarily better or worse and very hard to define, that is radically different from the English sense. So there was this thing called honour, which was important to the story, but I was quite clear that there was no way I was going to be able to understand it... in a sense I'm just paying lip service to it.

DJ: Were you worried about this being something your audience could relate to and cope with?

ND: Not particularly. I was concerned to couch it in terms such that they would be able to understand it in the same way I did. I wasn't concerned to try and educate them to understand it in a true way; I was really only concerned that they would understand it as far as was necessary for the story of the play. That's a central difference between a theatrical adaptation and an academic reading.

It's very hard to think of an adaptation in recent years of anything which has tried to do more than that. Most people have been concerned, quite rightly I think, to make the play work for their domestic audience, not to try and input any fantastically original ideas, which is where the main difference with writing a new play comes in. With a new play, what one is trying to do is to put something into the market place as it were, put something into a common atmosphere of discussion. Adapting a classic play really isn't about that, not for me anyway. It's much more about trying to do something which hits the mood of the times, rather than taking you into a mood which hasn't yet been thought of. In other words, it's basically conservative, it's a conservative writing activity. It's very unlikely that it will push an audience's perception beyond the status quo, which ideally is what a new play is centrally concerned to do... bringing something which is unknown into our field of vision. Adaptation isn't about stretching our field of vision in a way which is profound. That's the crucial difference.

DJ: You don't think it is possible to locate a classic play which can radicalise, revolutionise, an audience's perceptions?

ND: About theatrical form, perhaps. About their own lives, very unlikely, and I can't think of an example.

DJ: What about modern plays in that case?

ND: I've no experience of that and I can't comment on it. I think that is much more a task for a formal translator. If my play is being translated into German, I don't want to go along and see somebody's changed the entire second act. It's the last thing I want. It's not a job I would ever take on. I think it is something which you need a much more conventional translator for, and quite rightly. I don't really think there is a true comparison between the two things.

DJ: So you would draw a distinction between somebody who is bringing classic plays into the country and someone bringing more contemporary plays?

ND: Yes, I think the contemporary translator has a duty to be pretty faithful to the original text.

DJ: How do you feel if, for example, you've gone along to see Lorca's *The House Of Bernarda Alba*, and suddenly find it's transferred to the Highlands of Scotland? Does that worry you?

ND: Not in principle, no.

DJ: You judge it entirely on its own merits as a production?

ND: Well, I think there is a sub-distinction to be drawn here between something which has been performed many, many times, and a first performance. If you are talking about the first performance of a work by a contemporary Spanish writer given in this country then it would be horrifying and you would think 'What a stupid notion, why have they done this?' Directors are always prey to stupid ideas; it's part of the job of being a director to think up stupid ways to do things. And on occasion you get something which is so bizarre it works. In principle I see nothing wrong with that, but I would feel very differently were it the first translation of a contemporary play. Going back to the example, of *Bernarda Alba*, I think it's actually a tribute to Lorca if that's done. It obviously sounds naff, as you intended it to, but the fact that Lorca has enough power as an author to be presented many times in many different ways and the play itself is good enough to stand up to a rendering which is not necessarily couched contemporaneously in Spain in the thirties is a tribute to the author. Probably a crap production, but...

DJ: Why do you no longer do adaptations?

ND: Because I felt that it was too easy a life, and although for three or four years it was very stimulating, I felt that in the end it was stultifying my development as a playwright, and that I should be forcing myself either to find clear new ideas I wanted to express for myself, or interesting and original ways in which to express them. And I felt 'this is a nice life, you get paid quite well'. It is not easy to do the work well but it's still much easier than writing an original play.

DJ: Do you think translators take their work too seriously?

ND: I think critics take them too seriously and I think that theatre managements take them slightly more seriously than they should, because I think again that it creates an easy life for theatres. It's easier for theatres than commissioning and producing original plays. There are some very talented people doing this work but most of them are not playwrights and I think there is a distinction between a good adaptor and the original playwright.

DJ: To some extent the number of translations which sprang up at a certain time, early seventies, late sixties, was partly in answer to the dearth of new writing. If the English theatre was in crisis, engaging in dialogues with the dead at that time, as Stafford-Clark said, this was a way of broadening a repertoire when there was very little new writing about.

ND: I don't disagree with that but I think there is something to add. I got into the field later, in the eighties, and I think that two things happened. Firstly, back in the seventies, beginning with *Nicholas Nickleby*, there was a huge fad, which still persists, for the adaptation for the stage of the nineteenth-century novel, very few of which are successful – artistically successful – as plays. What those things were doing, and continue to do, is feed a large audience desire for story, for event and for narrative, rather than for situation. Vast numbers of plays were written, and still get written, which are pure situation. I think there was a great hunger resulting in the success of those early nineteenth-century adaptations for 'Give me a great story'. That seems to have moved on slightly into the adaptation of classic plays. Very often that's a response to the audience's desire for 'Give me a good story', which most of these plays do. I think that the lesson which ought to be drawn from that, and very largely isn't, is that we ought to be writing new plays which give us some great stories about things which are pertinent to us.

The second thing I'd say is that I think that the rise of the translator/ adaptor and the 'new version', which came into prominence in the mid to late eighties, and is directly linked to the Thatcher years and their effect on our culture, is a conservative impulse in the theatre. I think that it's directly linked to the theatres finding that they no longer had subsidy. They had to operate in the market place, they had to sell tickets where they hadn't had to sell before. I think that there are many bad things about Thatcherism, and some good things. I think that theatres being forced to realise that they have to sell tickets is not necessarily a bad thing at all, but I think the quick response to that has been all too often 'Let's do a new adaptation of something' rather than finding an original work which is going to sell tickets. I don't think it's the same as an academic work of translation. It's about selling tickets for a show. It's a market place.

DJ: Do you see any merits in academic works of translation?

ND: Absolutely. I read them. To have a book on the shelf which is a translation by an academic of a play that I might never have come across before is absolutely valuable. It's just not the same thing as putting on theatre and selling tickets.

DJ: There are, of course, instances of academic translators killing authors stone-dead. Lorca was a case to point.

ND: I think there is a place for academic translations and for the modern adaptation of a play. We're talking to different audiences and my judgment, certainly as far as my own work goes, is that if you want to progress you're going to have to call a halt somewhere – and go back to the considerably harder work of trying to write a new play.

ROUND TABLE ON TRANSLATION

The round table took place at the Gate Theatre, in London, on the opening night of Gil Vicente's *Boat Plays*, in December 1994. The panel of critics and translators, chaired by the Gate's Literary Manager, Gaynor MacFarlane, sat on that part of the stage which represented Purgatory, while the audience crewed the Boat to Hell. The spatial dimensions of the Gate Theatre didn't lend themselves to any other arrangement. But the symbolism was still telling.

Gaynor MacFarlane: Welcome to the Gate Theatre. If you think we look silly down here, bear in mind that you're in Hell already. I'd like to introduce you to a distinguished and diverse panel, all with an interest in translation:

Laurence Boswell, Artistic Director of the Gate Theatre.

Kenneth McLeish, translator/writer extraordinaire.

Claire Armistead, theatre critic for the *Guardian*.

David Johnston, award-winning translator of many Spanish and Portuguese plays, including a number for the Gate. He is Professor of Hispanic Studies at Queen's University, Belfast.

Joseph Farrell, Senior Lecturer in Italian at Strathclyde University, Glasgow, and translator of *His Lordship's Fancy* for the Gate.

Meredith Oakes, a former writer in residence of the Gate, currently a writer, as well as the translator of a number of plays for the Gate.

Giles Croft, Literary Manager of the Royal National Theatre.

I'd like to begin by asking David why he translated the Boat Plays, how he would characterise his translation and what relation do the plays have to his own sense as a writer?

DAVID JOHNSTON: Well simply, I only ever work on commissioned plays and the Gate asked me to do the *Boat Plays*. That's not a statement of principle, but I simply don't have time to write translations on spec and hawk them round. Besides, I've developed a particular association with the Gate, which I regard as very valuable to me. Time, as usual, was pressing, so I read the plays first of all in the literal version (I do speak and can translate from Portuguese) and found them incomprehensible. I have to say that changed my mind about the wisdom of working from literal versions, at least with plays whose fundamental conception is poetic – that, I am sure, is a point that people will bring up afterwards. It was like working from a series of clues to crossword puzzles, or trying to recreate a Van Gogh when you're colour-blind. The plays are pre-modern drama, developed from church pageant plays, processional, ritualistic. When I read them in Portuguese, I was captivated by them, captivated by the curious modernity of how Gil Vicente writes, how he creates Spitting Image-type characters, latex characters with a whirlpool of action at the heart of each one. My job was to turn that into a dramatic action which would simply hold the play up in a way beyond its theological interest; the theological interest is very important as well, not in terms of a very recondite interest in our place in the scheme of things, but in the not-so-simple confrontation of good and evil. There was also the fact that the first play had been written and performed for a dying monarch, presumably as a form of consolation, but also as a warning about the materialism and greed growing in Portugal in the wake of the Discoveries. So, in order to give the Gate's audience a sense of the times and to give a context for the play's profound moral substance, I wrote an introduction to the plays, which I called an 'Introit', and invented an author called Gil Vicente, who would, chorus-like, bring the audience back to the context in which the play could work and be accepted in its own terms. The plays and their circumstances are inseparable, and I don't think they would work without their introit and linking elements. I'm trying to answer the third part of your question here. At times there is only a very thin line between one's own writing and translating. But all writing, like thinking and remembering, is a form of translation in a way... you're translating a character into words, translating an experience, a sensation, an idea. In this case, my words were a translation – or a verbal correlative, if you like – of the circumstances that shaped the play's genesis and meaning.

GAYNOR MCFARLANE: Following on, as you predicted, with this relationship between the translator and the literal translator, does that make the translator someone who is 'just adapting'? What is the relationship between the translation and the original language of the text. Have people here worked from a literal? Laurence, is that a different process?

LAURENCE BOSWELL: I come at translation from a different angle because I'm a director. In discussions like this about the act of translating or recreating a play for this country, there is a confrontation between the sacredness of the author, which I find myself in conflict with because as a director I see the sacredness of authors as a kind of a myth, and the desire to see plays function to their full potential on stage. In the theatre I pick plays and stories which I think mean something for the 'now'; my debate is not about academic history, my debate is with the audience, the world in which I live, the performers who come together around a story to create a piece of drama, and that gives me a specific objective. When I'm looking at a text, as a

lot of authors do as well, I pillage history to write the story which is imp
me to write now. Of course, I have great respect for the original a¹
primarily from the language base, but rather from the choreography of the
characters, the relationship base, because from that base the choice of words
becomes more precise and accurate. Language is the very surface of a play; as a
simple metaphor, it's a kind of wrapping. Faced with a blank sheet of paper, the
first time I tried to create a script, I found I could give a character almost any word
which would make a kind of sense of the relationship they were in and would kind
of relate to the original language. That's what David meant about translating not
just words, but also character, voice, experience. And I thought I couldn't be that
imprecise, so I then learnt the whole story and got in touch with the characters,
with the rhythm. The physical rhythm of theatre for me is like a dance, a three
dimensional structure which happens in time. Then when you go back to the
specific moment, the choice of words goes from infinity to two or three, because
that character couldn't use that word at that moment. That is how I come at it, like
someone who is making a wheel, as it were, trying to look at the hub of the play.
To answer your question, I am sure you lose something working from a literal
translation but not necessarily as much without a knowledge of the physicality of
the play, of its existence in time.

KENNETH MCLEISH: There *is* a question of rhythm at the heart of the whole
thing. I have just finished working on *Miss Julie*; translating the play proved very
easy because the rhythm of English speech mirrored that of the Swedish where I
wanted it to. That wasn't a problem, but then I had to translate Strindberg's 3,000
word preface, which is a piece of lateish nineteenth-century academic Swedish
written by a madman, and I couldn't do it for the simple reason that I couldn't find
a rhythm for it; I'm not used to writing academic prose. To read off a page which
was not to be acted was very strange, the form of the sentence was very strange,
and stirred into that constantly were his own asides. The only way I could cope
with it at the end was to write a literal of my own and work from that, so that I
could check each point not just against the Swedish but also against a hybrid thing
which was as close to the Swedish as I could get. Occasionally, a word, phrase or
expression would leap out at me from my literal and it would lead me into what I
thought the sentence/paragraph meant. In it I began to find what I believed was
Strindberg's tone of voice, and once I found that it was totally easy to write a form
of speech; Strindberg stands up and speaks a three thousand word monologue. I
wonder if people working from literal translations don't have the same experience.
Literals only serve a purpose if you depart from them, and the way you depart from
them is to find the original voice in it, whether it is the character's original voice as
you see it, or the author's original voice, and work from that. You have to work
from what you are experiencing, not just from the original author's experience. But

there's something else which is at the other end of the spectrum; here we are talking about plays which are distant from the original copyright, not about translating the work of living authors. because then life gets very complicated.

MEREDITH OAKES: Sometimes it's much easier to deal with a living author than with the estate, because the estate is whoever thinks they knew the writer best and probably they are the people who know that writer least. They have ideas about what you should do, which may not relate to what the author may have wanted.

However, I'd like to diverge utterly and say that Laurence is speaking like a director through and through. It is quite right that the director should be interested in finding the energy and inventing the wheel. I come from the other side. I am a curious person; when I translate something I want to know everything about the mentality that created that thing and I want to convey as much of that as I can in my own language. That is speaking as a translator, and speaking as a writer I know that I can create a wheel, as long as we follow the rules of theatrical energy we will always create wheels and they will always be just wheels. The whole struggle between the writer and the director is that the writer is trying to create something else which moves along, but which can be something different from a wheel this time round.

JOSEPH FARRELL: When Laurence was talking about the 'sacredness' of the author, what really worries me is that under phrases like that very often the question that is really being asked is 'What can the audience cope with?' If we give them something which is genuinely foreign and unfamiliar, and which is genuinely unchallenged, will the rather 'dubious' minds of these people be able to cope with it, or should we, in some way, water it down, sweeten the pill, so that nothing 'excessive' will be asked of them? Basically, if I'm going to see a writer from another age or a different language I want to get, as far as is possible, in contact with them. I was once asked to do a literal translation and I refused; it wasn't just arrogance, there were other considerations as well. I really don't know precisely what a literal translation might mean, because at each point you must be making an interpretation; you've got to be deciding obscure points, thinking this is possibly what it means, or this is the meaning that fits into the overall context of the play, or what do we know about the overall ideas of this man and what do we pick up from the language itself?

This is one of the other things that separates writer and translator. In this case the director, Laurence, says that the language is only the surface, and I'm sure he's right and there is no serious dispute about it, but that is precisely the level the translator is working with. The other matters which are going on in the play, which are going to concern other people, are part of the overall collaborative process of theatre, but it is the language that the translator/interpreter is dealing with. It is his/her responsibility to try and get as close as possible to what is being said in the original play; to provide a product which isn't too closely married into the expectations of the audience, but rather something that will challenge those expectations.

LAURENCE BOSWELL: Can I just respond to that? If ever I thought I was taking a play and making it easy for the audience to digest, I'd want to leave the theatre in disgrace. For example, David's translation of *Bohemian Lights*, that I was involved in, confronts this issue in a very interesting way. This is a play written in early twentieth-century Spain, set in Madrid. I felt that there was a direct political passion in Valle-Inclán; he was passionately annoyed and passionately angry at a lot of things that were happening in his society. He was interested in a lot of other things, but a direct engagement with the world he lived in was one rich theme of that text, and that leaves you with a problem. We felt that, not to make it easy for our audience but to make it alive for them, the political struggles that Valle-Inclán was discussing in Madrid in the twenties required to be transformed. Simply, we weren't involved in that struggle. I think we created what David called a 'working metaphor' for Valle-Inclán's original and we tried to put the conflict into a context that was alive and was contemporary and had a bite. I think we were serving the author not by a slavish accuracy to what he had written but to the spirit of a living writer engaged in a struggle, and we tried to find a correlative for what is alive to us now.

DAVID JOHNSTON: Translators are interrogators. You interrogate the world, the cultural-specific references, you interrogate them all at the level of how the text works, how it will function as theatre. As Joe has said, we can't escape from the basic battle with words, but neither can we escape from the battle with culturally-specific references. *Bohemian Lights* aroused a certain amount of controversy in both the British and the Spanish press. However, the Spaniards seemed to accept the necessity of our type of adaptation because they knew, as I, not just as translator/close-reader but as a Hispanist, also knew, that Valle-Inclán's theatre had been hermetically sealed and labelled 'virtually unperformable'. I was determined to break that seal. Joe also talks about the 'collaborative' nature of theatre, and I would add the collaborative and *ephemeral* nature of theatre. We did a certain show which may never happen again, but we did it for this space, for this audience, and we worked on it in that way. We looked at the cultural-specific references, we looked at the words and we were able to transpose them *en bloc* into a different context in which they were all re-energised with exactly the same force, I think, as in the original.

KENNETH MCLEISH: This is what's uppermost in your mind too in comedy. I've found that when you do comedy, you have to think first and foremost of your own audience, the audience the show is for. If they don't laugh, then it's not a comedy. I think that balance is harder to work than any other type of translation I've ever done. I have worked on Feydeau quite a lot, for example, and audiences of

Feydeau farces have to be licensed to laugh. The performance has to make them laugh very early on, and after that it flows; if it doesn't happen, the show just dies. The translator is the first person to deconstruct the text, as it were, before the director or the actors or the technicians, so, basically, what the translator has to do is look for laughs – for Feydeau, for his audience, and to see what way these laughs will register with a modern audience. The temptation is always to go a step further and to stick in your own laughs, in which case you might as well write your own play and be done with it. But I feel we are all being a little over-cautious in what we are saying. The more outrageous and tendentious I am in my work, the more people like it. It's not the further I get from the original – that's a different thing entirely. I think the tendentious best reflects what is actually there in the original. It's a question of instinct as much as anything else. You never really know whether it's 'right' or not.

For example, someone recently asked me to do a Molière and at first I said no I couldn't do it, because ten people have done it better. It took quite a long time to evolve a style which had the poise of the Molière language, which is created by rhyming alexandrines, but which at the same time dispelled the feeling you sometimes get when you see a rhymed Molière. Quite often you are listening so hard for the rhyme that you don't notice what the rest of the line says. I devised a style, after listening to quite a lot of Ella Fitzgerald which was full of rhyme that didn't all come at the end of the line, and the lines weren't always twelve syllables long, but as long as they needed to be; essentially it was free verse with a lot of rhyme thrown into it. The jury is still out because the audience won't be seeing this for another twelve weeks or so, and I shall be very interested to see what the audiences and critics think of this because now that I have done it I think 'Is it Molière?' I'm still not sure. I have to say also that occasionally I re-read my old translations of this or that old play against the original and the original always wins. You can never actually get it 100% right, precisely because translation *is* an ephemeral art.

GAYNOR MACFARLANE: The whole question of how best to re-create style is fascinating. Meredith, for example, translated the new *Minosa* for the Gate. It was an eighteenth-century play, and Meredith achieved an eighteenth-century style of English. Was that essentially what you were trying to do?

MEREDITH OAKES: Yes, although that was a particular choice that I wouldn't have made every time. But I wanted to do it in that play because it was full of ideas, social and philosophical ideas, that sprung bodily from their period and yet were very fresh for their period. Presented in modern English, they would have looked far more familiar than they actually should look. So, rather like David's *Boat Plays*, I wanted to show where the play had come from. So I read lots of Sheridan – it was a good excuse. And of course, you never do get it right, and my eighteenth-century English is as ephemeral an exercise in translation as any other. I think the only translation that really might last is the one that is written close to the time when the play is written. Once you get a couple of centuries away then probably whatever you do is only going to be of limited short use and then someone else is going to have to do it. That raises the question, how many translations can the world bear?

JOSEPH FARRELL: The other thing that really intrigues me about what's being said here is how much you're allowed to change the play to bring it back to what you think the original really was. I've a lot of experience of dealing with Dario Fo, and have seen Dario Fo performed in Hollywood. It really is strange to read them on the page, even in Italian, and not to understand what exactly caused that laughter in performance. On the page they are extremely dull and, as a matter of fact, I do think the most successful of Dario Fo's plays staged here are the ones where the translator has taken quite a lot of liberties. I do want to hold on to that distinction, but in Dario Fo it very often seems necessary to blurb his plays in some way. I remember going through this procedure in *Mistero Buffo*, with Robbie Coltrane. Morag Fullerton was directing it and we were initially intending to use the introductory pieces which Fo does. He supposedly extemporises, though in reality he does the same thing every night. It was essential that there be some sort of introduction because this is the explanation of the context of the play, this medieval material. The introductions are also used to update and point out parallels – Fo is extremely didactic. We decided that the only way to reproduce that was to keep, by and large, what he had done in the text, the supposedly medieval material which made up the individual sketches but then to completely rewrite the introductory lead into it. So we wrote in all kinds of jokes which had nothing whatsoever to do with Dario Fo. So, on occasions, re-writing *is* absolutely necessary because if you give something which is as close to a literal translation as is feasible, in fact you still end up with something which is lifeless, and which is much more treacherous fundamentally towards the original play and the original playwright.

KENNETH McLEISH: You have to be very careful about these incursions though. In the centre of each of his comedies Aristophanes, for instance, has a passage in which the chorus, as it were, steps out of stage-action and addresses the audience directly about some aspect of a theme in politics; usually about how bad the present day is and how good the other days were. I have worked on all of Aristophanes with a lot of companies and there is a strong temptation for modern actors to step out and say 'My God, things were better in Mrs. Thatcher's time', and the audience laughs dutifully. In fact, in one production, in *Wealth*, I saw one of the cast come on (as the goddess Poverty) looking like Mrs. Thatcher, droning with angels and trumpets, and it got a huge laugh. It was a wonderful set piece, but it had nothing to do with Aristophanes; it was a musical number to do with a modern performance. You have to be immensely careful about this sort of thing. I thought the *Mistero Buffo* worked perfectly well because Robbie Coltrane could appear to be improvising a lot of his material.

GILES CROFT: It seems to me that one of the other important things is that there are many authors whose work doesn't really translate. I think the one thing that distances Molière and his characters from us is the cultural form from which they come; it doesn't really make much sense to us. Goldoni is another example of where the humour in the play and a lot of what goes on in the production is not about the play itself but is about the tradition of business and all those sorts of things that can never be brought to the translation. I think very often what one has to do is to find alternatives or equivalences that can either come through the version or the production. I think one of the things that translators often do is to find a sort of linguistic equivalence to make up for what must have been a great visual gag – like Molière's gag about the toilet bowl. Something the translation has to do is to accept these linguistically dead moments and find some other way of delivering them – I think a lot of translations fall down because they don't manage that.

KENNETH MCLEISH: I like to be around the rehearsals, particularly in comedy as much as possible, simply because that's the time people come up against these problems. Quite often what you find is a collaborative solution, and the translator, in that case, is there *in loco* Vicar of God on Earth – for he/she holds the balance between the original writer and the new production.

LAURENCE BOSWELL: I think there is something else about literals which somebody really should defend. There are two rules for me. Firstly, literals are necessary because there are certain lines in the play in which you want a combination of their voice and the original. The hard reality is that very often the best or most appropriate theatre-people don't speak the original language and there is no other solution to this. So as a pragmatic response I would happily defend many instances where working on a text as a literal translation, then handing it over to a writer, has produced many wonderful pieces of dramatic literature; by the same token, the translation, as an traditional academic might understand it, can produce complete nonsense. It sort of goes both ways. But, of course, the best way to work with a literal translation is for the author to be in touch with the translator and to ask questions.

DAVID JOHNSTON: When I talked about literal translations at the start I certainly wasn't trying to make a case that the translation of plays should take place in the dusty studies of Academe. I agree that there is always a measure of intertextuality between the voice of the translator and the voice of the original author; voice is inevitable in any writing that commands attention. But we need to be very clear what we are calling these things. If, for example, you are putting on a play which is by David Hare, and is based on an original by Brecht, then we need to find a way of telling the audience exactly what they are going to see. Actually, not find a way. Just be more explicit about it. People are paying money to see Brecht, and that strikes me as being an issue which both critics and translators should be taking up at the moment. I talk about translating *and* adapting; as a translator I do my own first version from the original language – which is what the 'traditional academic' in me considers the *act* of translation. At that point the *process* of adaptation begins and I try and see how I can make it work as theatre or how I can adapt it to a particular director, a particular time or a particular space.

GAYNOR MACFARLANE: How does the attitude towards translation in this country compare with Europe?

GILES CROFT: I was in Madrid a couple of years ago participating in a conference. It was one of those jamboree things where people like me have to give papers, but living authors are invited along and their plays are translated into Spanish and then performed by a drama school as a way of introducing new writers and new plays into the Spanish repertoire. It was a very interesting event. As part of it, I was having a conversation with the organisers who were asking me how the National selected and paid for translations. I explained that if the play is out of copyright the translator's share increased. Some people make quite a lot of money, and they were absolutely staggered and couldn't believe that we took translation so seriously; they thought it was just something that people did. So the notion about the culture of translation is not accurate; a lot of translators abroad are just sort of 'jobbing translators' and they are very good at it. In Hungary, for example, where they do so many translations, people are better at it than we are, but their whole culture is not about producing great translations; it's just that they do translation; they exist and it is how they enrich their culture.

MEREDITH OAKES: But surely a translator gets paid more than a theatre translator?

JOSEPH FARRELL: I think there's something worth taking up here. My belief is that translation is being taken seriously here, in this country, very late in the day. Even if we leave the theatre and go into a bookshop in Rome or Paris, then you have the immediate sense that you are in a multicultural centre, in a way that you won't have if you go into any bookshop in Britain. I'd love to give the impression that the commercial and intellectual poverty surrounding translation, until comparatively recently at least, is to do with the insularity of the English, but it is not. There are historical reasons for this which are to do with the historical past of Britain, and also with how America and other countries use the English language. We simply already have access to a wide variety of writing. Frankly, I'm surprised about what Giles was saying about his conversation in Madrid, and I wonder how typical or representative it was. I know quite a lot of people who interpret and translate in Europe, and simply because of the volume of work that is done you find a greater variety and quality in other countries than you might get here. But, I've also always found that they do take the position of the translator very seriously, so much so that this notion of there being a literal translation which would be worked on by some superstar writer is one which you would find very difficult to explain to people within most other countries who assume they are going to be commissioning someone who has a knowledge of the other language but who can also write competently enough in his own language for the work to be published. In fact, this can go too far, because the cult of translation has been the death of the Italian theatre; it's virtually impossible to find *original* writers in Italian, apart from Dario Fo. If you go to Milan or Rome you discover that very often the theatres there are putting on plays that are identical to those that are on in London. No fresh work is now being produced by Italian writers, certainly not in any reasonably sized theatre.

GILES CROFT: My point wasn't that they don't do a lot of translation, but rather that the notion of having a discussion about the art of translating in many of these places would be a peculiar one because it is such a current part of their culture. It's a common and unremarkable practice.

DAVID JOHNSTON: That's not entirely true. Europe has been having the conversation that we are having at the moment since the fifteenth century, and in the academic world translation theory has tended to be led from Europe. But I'd like to ask Claire if she feels that critics coming to a show which is a version or adaptation are prepared to pay attention to the dynamics implicit in that fact?

CLAIRE ARMISTEAD: I think it is implicit in a conversation like this. What the critic sees is the product on the evening, a given work which is the director's views imposed upon the translation, views imposed upon the writer's view. You have spoken a lot about Molière, for example, and a lot of critics actually have read Molière in the original. So what we see is how successful it is as a piece of theatre. Let me give you an example; in the recent De Filippo at the National – the *Napoli Millionaire* – I was taken to task because I didn't like the approximation – linguistic and cultural – established in the production between the context of the original and Liverpool/Merseyside. It was quite interesting because I got a very stiff letter from the National saying I clearly wanted Spaghetti Italian and that I didn't understand the original, when I actually do know Italy and I don't think that the folksy Merseyside idiom is right for Naples. I thought the use of Merseyside related to a particular television culture which I thought confused what De Filippo is essentially about. Our view of Liverpool certainly isn't comparable with the Italian perspective of Naples. But it was interesting that the assumption was that I didn't know what I was talking about. I am not saying that I knew better than that production, but that was how it struck me on that particular night.

KENNETH McLEISH: The further back in time you go to the original culture the more problems there are, not only for all interpreters but for all translators, and right down to the director. They not only have to come to terms with an ancient or alien culture, but all the centuries in between and their interpretations of that culture. Over the last twenty years or so I have found that our attitude to Ancient Greece has changed, very largely because of the way people are now correctly interpreting Greek tragedy and its view on society. However, critics do quite often read these things in translation, and quite often old fashioned translations which basically have the wrong world view. It sounds slightly arrogant to suggest that the translator has an educational role, but in a way you are not only presenting your author but your society as well. If it is a radical view that you are presenting then you get the blame, not the original author.

CLAIRE ARMISTEAD: You are talking about language as the surface and language surely isn't the surface; language is an inextricable part of the whole.

LAURENCE BOSWELL: I think Joe's point about the dreary, dull script and the residue left when you remove the genius of Dario Fo exactly illustrates the place of language. Theatre isn't language; language is an important part of it, but words are only half of it; they're neither the beginning or the end.

CLAIRE ARMISTEAD: But words are what is left, the imprint of what those writers have left. You have to find a way of re-animating those words.

LAURENCE BOSWELL: Our only source isn't the word; we have a whole living theatrical tradition of performance style.

MEREDITH OAKES: Written words are about as useful as written musical notation. But there is still the crucial difference between one performance and another, a difference that can be like day and night.

DAVID JOHNSTON: Words are a form of codifying the drama that's implicit in the script. Somebody was talking about deconstructing in order to translate; that's basically what I mean when I refer to interrogating the script. In Valle-Inclán, for example, the stage-directions are all prose poems, which give insight into all sorts of dramatic movement in the words themselves. With other writers I have translated, like Lope de Vega or Lorca, what they have clearly written are starting points for theatre and the words themselves are arrows pointing in certain ways, very often in mutually contradictory ways and you have to make resolutions, clear decisions. But the words themselves are the master key to the theatre which will take place as a result of that linguistic interrogation or deconstruction..

JOSEPH FARRELL: The other thing that intrigues me is that I have just discovered that the National Theatre is obviously more assiduous than I'd realised.

When I saw the production of the play *Napoli Millionaire* there were a couple of things I'd like to say. First of all the adaptation was done by Peter Tinniswood, who is a Liverpool writer. Of course, he didn't do the translation, but worked from some sort of literal, and you had to search around the programme before you came to any sort of reference to the poor sod who had actually worked away at this and done the translation. It was actually mentioned if you had a magnifying glass and were prepared to look at something written upside down in a corner.

In connection with what Claire was saying, I thought the Liverpool dimension was a way of getting over a variety of difficulties. De Filippo's plays have a strong sense of place, which is Naples, and although not exclusively, in that play he does use a lot of Neapolitan dialect. I have just translated a novel written by a Sicilian writer who uses a lot of Sicilian dialect, and I tried very hard to think of ways to convey the sense that this wasn't written in standard Italian. How do you convey that in English? Well, there would be an obvious way for me, which is to use Scots. I didn't do it, though, because it creates a whole variety of different obstacles for people in London or Chicago. It would have been clearer leaving it in the Neapolitan or Sicilian than putting it into Scots. But I thought in that particular play they had avoided the risk of over-adaptation from switching the thing from Naples to Liverpool. They left it in the Neapolitan setting and used turns of phrase and accents which were those of a regional city, so it wasn't standard English but it was an English which was intelligible. It also made concessions to the original, to a Neapolitan setting, and that seemed to me to be almost the ideal compromise, one which I would like to follow on a number of occasions. I'm not sure if the Italian view of Naples is quite as unequivocal as I thought you were implying, in that Naples occupies a very dubious place in the Italian horizon. I don't know if Liverpool is quite the same thing in any British notion, but personally I do think it is the ideal way of dealing with a work from a specific province. It's still a compromise, but a good one.

GAYNOR MACFARLANE: On the point of compromise I would like to invite some questions from *The Boat to Hell*. Are there any?

MICHAEL IMMISON: Talking about *Napoli Millionaire*, it is interesting that the text that Peter Tineswood did was sold by me to an American publisher who found that there was very little that he had to change in the working of the dialogue. As Joe very rightly said, most of the Liverpudlian characteristics of the play came from the accents the actors adopted. They didn't need to make it very different for America. The Valle-Inclán *Bohemian Lights* raises the most important issue for translators, which is the issue of transparency. The ideal translation is a glass window through which you look at the original and I think that what you were criticised for, David, was that here was a Spanish author who had been neglected throughout theatrical history and was now being introduced, and people wanted to know what this guy was like. What was his characteristic as a dramatist? Clearly, as it was for Claire with Naples and Liverpool, your Irish setting of it put a barrier in the way. The Peter Tinniswood production put a barrier between her and that production, you put a barrier between the audience and that play through which they couldn't see. All they could see was your surface, which was very exciting and dramatic, but they kept thinking 'Is this really what it's all about?' Recently I had to go and see

Jeremy Sams's *Magic Flute* at the ENO. It is a very contemporary translation, and he uses words which are absolutely of the nineteenth and twentieth centuries, but in his dialogue you can see through them and see exactly why he is using those words, what the original intention was. At one point an actor came forward and started chatting to the audience asking if they came here often etc. You were immediately conscious that someone had introduced an element that was to try and cheer the audience up, but it was clearly not related to the original and it was a barrier between you and the original.

DAVID JOHNSTON: Of course. I take your point. The only thing I would say is that Valle-Inclán is a very special case, and that the translator must always bear in mind that in such cases, he or she can also sink an unknown author by preparing a disastrous version. Moreover, my version didn't *appropriate* Valle's original on a permanent basis. Anyone else can do their own version in their own way, and that's fine – as long as it works on stage.

GORDON FIELD: I am the secretary of the Translators' Association. Can I just make a plea to those who think that you need to commission a so-called literary translation and then adapt it, not to do that but to come to the Translators' Association where we actually have translators who know both the original culture and the original language extremely well, and they also know British audiences. There are people around who can do both jobs.

LAURENCE BOSWELL: Doing translation is like anything else in what is essentially an entrepreneurial business. Your members' scripts will always be welcome at most theatres... meanwhile, they should be maximising their contacts, as the people on the panel here this evening have done at one time.

UNIDENTIFIED SPEAKER: Going back to the earlier questions, it's clear there is a consensus on the panel that in fact the translation has to be a compromise somewhere between self-indulgence and taking risks; I was wondering if in fact translation wasn't something that we had lost the art of somewhere between the nineteen-twenties and the thirties in this country. Now, in the last ten years, we have been rediscovering how important translation is, especially for the theatre.

GAYNOR MACFARLANE: Have we lost the art of translation? Is it an 'art'?

DAVID JOHNSTON: The Cuban writer, who's now taken out British citizenship, Guillermo Cabrera Infante said 'Writers rush in where translators fear to tread'. I think that good translation, like good language, needs to have qualitative leaps of expression. In fact, there's no such thing as a clear pane of glass, nor is there language, even language which is the result of translation, which is so pure that it is transparent. And if there were, what a tedious thing it would be. Translating the instructions for making a video work clearly isn't an art form – although sometimes even these, when they're too literal from the Japanese or Korean, can make for a frustrating unintelligibility. Translating for the stage involves creating a literary language. Yeats once defined creativity as the point where passion and precision are one. In the case of the translator, precision must come from being totally familiar with the language. If you don't have that precision then the passion can't be dazzling, but we must not call it an accurate passion because it is not necessarily Molière or Lope.

EIVOR MARTINUS: That lack of accuracy sometimes worries me when it is arbitrary. For example, Miss Julie, which is not Miss Julie, because in the nineteenth-century in Sweden you addressed an unmarried woman in three ways, depending on her class. She should not be simply Miss Julie, and Ken McLeish should know that. It's Lady Julie. It has been mistranslated because of people's ignorance for the past fifty years.

KENNETH MCLEISH: That's very true. What has happened is that the title Miss Julie has become part of our national consciousness. If you put up a play bill saying Mademoiselle or Lady Julie people would wonder what it was.

EIVOR MARTINUS: Let me give one example of why I find working from literal translations dangerous. In Sweden I was directing Pinter, and of course Pinter is very difficult to translate because he uses the English language like a magician. All the language he uses has great undertones for us in England; we know what he is getting at because it has reference to Jewish and EastEnd culture. I was working on a translation by a Swede whose knowledge of English I assumed to be good but I couldn't understand why the actors couldn't feel the vibrations that an English actor would feel if he picked up a Pinter text. I found that it wasn't a very good translation because he hadn't understood the undertones of Pinter and he hadn't translated those into Swedish. Therefore he didn't have the intimate knowledge of the source language that is really necessary to try and translate into his own language. It must be dangerous if somebody makes a literal translation and doesn't spend the time choosing the right word to convey the meaning of the original. It then gives a very dangerous platform for the director to work from, because he is bound to start losing something.

DAVID JOHNSTON: A translator gives a play a different existence. Rather than being simply 'right' and 'wrong' versions, I think we should judge by what happens in a particular space for a particular audience. If I can go back to Valle-Inclán again, perhaps out of wounded pride, let me say that I think our production of Bohemian Lights will lead to future and very different sorts of Valle productions. One of the beauties of theatre – one of its central paradoxes, in spite of the museum mentality we still find in some areas – is that theatre goes on; the production doesn't.